MW00628908

CIRCULATING JIM CROW

MODERNIST LATITUDES

MODERNIST LATITUDES

Jessica Berman and Paul Saint-Amour, Editors

Modernist Latitudes aims to capture the energy and ferment of modernist studies by continuing to open up the range of forms, locations, temporalities, and theoretical approaches encompassed by the field. The series celebrates the growing latitude ("scope for freedom of action or thought") that this broadening affords scholars of modernism, whether they are investigating little-known works or revisiting canonical ones. Modernist Latitudes will pay particular attention to the texts and contexts of those latitudes (Africa, Latin America, Australia, Asia, southern Europe, and even the rural United States) that have long been misrecognized as ancillary to the canonical modernisms of the global North.

Barry McCrea, *In the Company of Strangers: Family and Narrative in Dickens, Conan Doyle, Joyce, and Proust*, 2011

Jessica Berman, *Modernist Commitments: Ethics, Politics, and Transnational Modernism*, 2011

Jennifer Scappettone, *Killing the Moonlight: Modernism in Venice*, 2014

Nico Israel, *Spirals: The Whirled Image in Twentieth-Century Literature and Art*, 2015

Carrie Noland, *Voices of Negritude in Modernist Print: Aesthetic Subjectivity, Diaspora, and the Lyric Regime*, 2015

Susan Stanford Friedman, *Planetary Modernisms: Provocations on Modernity Across Time*, 2015

Steven S. Lee, *The Ethnic Avant-Garde: Minority Cultures and World Revolution*, 2015

Thomas S. Davis, *The Extinct Scene: Late Modernism and Everyday Life*, 2016

Carrie J. Preston, *Learning to Kneel: Noh, Modernism, and Journeys in Teaching*, 2016

Gayle Rogers, *Incomparable Empires: Modernism and the Translation of Spanish and American Literature*, 2016

Donal Harris, *On Company Time: American Modernism in the Big Magazines*, 2016

Celia Marshik, *At the Mercy of Their Clothes: Modernism, the Middlebrow, and British Garment Culture*, 2016

Christopher Reed, *Bachelor Japanists: Japanese Aesthetics and Western Masculinities*, 2016

Eric Hayot and Rebecca L. Walkowitz, eds., *A New Vocabulary for Global Modernism*, 2016

Eric Bulson, *Little Magazine, World Form*, 2016

Aarthi Vadde, *Chimeras of Form: Modernist Internationalism Beyond Europe, 1914–2014*, 2016

Ben Conisbee Baer, *Indigenous Vanguards: Education, National Liberation, and the Limits of Modernism*, 2019

Claire Seiler, *Midcentury Suspension: Literature and Feeling in the Wake of World War II*, 2020

Jill Richards, *The Fury Archives: Female Citizenship, Human Rights, and the International Avant-Gardes*, 2020

Daniel Ryan Morse, *Radio Empire: The BBC's Eastern Service and the Emergence of the Global Anglophone Novel*, 2020

Hannah Freed-Thall, *Modernism at the Beach: Queer Ecologies and the Coastal Commons*, 2023

Circulating Jim Crow

THE *SATURDAY EVENING POST*
AND THE WAR AGAINST BLACK MODERNITY

Adam McKible

Columbia University Press
New York

Columbia University Press
Publishers Since 1893
New York   Chichester, West Sussex
cup.columbia.edu
Copyright © 2024 Columbia University Press
All rights reserved

Library of Congress Cataloging-in-Publication Data
Names: McKible, Adam, author.
Title: Circulating Jim Crow : the Saturday Evening Post and the war against black
modernity / Adam McKible.
Description: New York : Columbia University Press, 2024. | Series: Modernist latitudes |
Includes bibliographical references and index.
Identifiers: LCCN 2023032863 (print) | LCCN 2023032864 (ebook) | ISBN 9780231212649
(hardback) | ISBN 9780231212656 (trade paperback) | ISBN 9780231559492 (ebook)
Subjects: LCSH: Lorimer, George Horace, 1869–1937. | Saturday evening post—History. |
American periodicals—History—20th century. | African Americans—Legal status, laws, etc. |
Racism—United States. | African Americans in popular culture. | American literature—African
American authors—History and criticism. | Harlem Renaissance. | United States—Social life
and customs—20th century.
Classification: LCC PN4900.S3 M35 2024 (print) | LCC PN4900.S3 (ebook) |
DDC 051—dc23/eng/20230804
LC record available at https://lccn.loc.gov/2023032863
LC ebook record available at https://lccn.loc.gov/2023032864

Cover design: Elliott S. Cairns
Cover image: ClassicStock / Alamy Stock Photo

For Elijah and Oscar, my best work

Either the United Sates will destroy ignorance
or ignorance will destroy the United States.

—NIAGARA MOVEMENT, "AN ADDRESS TO THE COUNTRY"

CONTENTS

x

CONTENTS

Chapter Six
The End of the Lorimer Era   182

Epilogue   227

NOTES   231

BIBLIOGRAPHY   253

INDEX   267

ACKNOWLEDGMENTS

It also takes a village to make a book—not to mention money and time. To that effect, my first note of gratitude is to the Office for the Advancement of Research at John Jay College. Thanks to Anthony Carpi, Dan Stageman, Susy Mendes, Amrish Sugrim-Singh, Tahir Fazal, Kuralay Zharmagambetova, and Cherryanne Ward for all their help along the way. Thanks also to the Research Foundation of the City University of New York for many PSC-CUNY Research Awards and to my CUNY colleagues who approved those awards. I am also deeply grateful to the National Endowment for the Humanities for its Award for Faculty at Hispanic-Serving Institutions and to the NEH staff for all their prompt and courteous assistance and the reviewers who approved my proposal. I thank all of them for giving me the space to finish this book.

Thanks to the many libraries and librarians who helped suss out details large and small. On January 6, 2021, just one hour before the attack on the U.S. Capitol began in earnest, I sent a request to Bruce Kirby at the Library of Congress for information on archival material necessary to chapter 5. Bruce responded to my email while the attack was ongoing, and in the following days, while DC was under lockdown, he located, scanned, and emailed material that I could not have accessed otherwise. Thank you, Bruce. I am also grateful to the staff at the Hargrett Rare Book & Manuscript Library at the University of Georgia in Athens, Maureen Richards at the Lloyd Sealy Library of John Jay College, Jennifer Berzin at the University of Tennessee at Chattanooga, Kyle Hovious at the University of Tennessee, Tiffany Miller at Syracuse University, Anne Causey at the University of Virginia, Hannah Hertzler at Vassar, and the Local History and Genealogy Department of the Chattanooga Public Library. Thanks also to Max D. Brener at Mizpah Congregation and Sam Hall at chattanoogahistory.com for information on Blanche Goodman Eisendrath. On this note, I must also give a very big thanks to Dora Silva Santana, my colleague at John Jay. After I explained my project to a group of fellow aspirants at a grant-writing workshop, Dora asked, "But where are the women?" This now *so* obvious question led me back to my notes and allowed me to see Blanche Goodman's significance in the *Saturday Evening Post*—and this realization led to my much better understanding of how *Post* readers consumed and shared much of the material discussed in this book. Thank you, Dora!

Indeed, I could not have asked for better colleagues than the vibrant community of John Jay College. Thanks to Marny Tabb, Allison Pease, Jay Gates, and Jean Mills, the hardy souls who chaired the English Department while my project was underway; to Alicia Kelly and Dianne Rodgers for making sure all the *i*'s were dotted correctly; and to all my fellow instructors in the department. Your dedication to our students and our profession is inspiring and sustaining. Thanks especially to Andy Majeske for a friendship that has lasted many years and spans too many miles and to President Karol V. Mason for her shared love of Professor J. Lee Greene, who shaped both of our intellectual lives for the better. I also want to remember Jon-Christian Suggs, who graced so many of us with his humor, intelligence, and zeal.

The first real glimmer of this book happened in 2007, when I taught a course at the CUNY Graduate Center called Race, Ethnicity, and Pseudoscience in Modern American Literature. Without really understanding the size of the task, I required each student to give a presentation on one year of the *Saturday Evening Post*. This assignment was surprisingly generative and became the soul of the course. But pity the poor students, all of whom had to do their research on microfilm—sometimes for the years when a single *Post* issue could exceed two hundred pages. I am especially grateful to Joost Burgers, Philip Kadish, and my uncannily younger self, Jesse Schwartz, for being great students and even better friends. I also want to remember

Diana Colbert, a genuinely wonderful person who was taken from us far too soon.

For more than twenty years, my other family has been the Modernist Studies Association, and I fear leaving out names here because I cherish this entire community. The MSA has sustained my intellectual life since its inaugural New Modernisms conference in 1999. Initial thanks go to Ann Ardis and Bill Maxwell, first for their friendship but also especially for supporting my project repeatedly until the NEH finally said "uncle." Thanks also to Jessica Berman and Paul K. Saint-Amour for inviting me to contribute to the series Modernist Latitudes; their work on this series and for the MSA benefits so many of us. To Suzanne Churchill, whom I first met at the conference in 1999, I can never be thankful enough; I am proud to have worked with her on so many projects, and I am grateful for her reflected glory. I have made many friends at MSA—people whose love of provocative ideas, great talk, good food, and strong cocktails make me eager to see them every year. Here's my shout out to Patrick Collier, Tim Newcomb, Kathleen Pfeiffer, Matt Huculak, David Chinitz, Pamela Caughie, Gayle Rogers, Mark Morrisson, Clifford Wulfman, Darryl Dickson-Carr, Jean Scheper, Jeff Druin, Debra Rae Cohen, Jonathan Goldman, Mark Whalan, Daniel Worden, Venetria Patton, Stephen Ross, Cat Keyser, Benjy Kahan, Cherene Sherrard-Johnson, James Smethurst, Barbara Green, Michael Coyle, Lief Sorenson, Michael Soto, Lena Hill, Houston Baker, Brooks Hefner, Michael Bibby, Andrew Thacker, Mae Henderson, Sean Latham, Agnieszka Tuszynska, and Amanda Golden. For their reliable incorrigibility, I am always happy to be in the company of Len Diepeveen and Gary and Kim Holcomb. And then there is Welchie's lesser half, David Earle, who has been the source of many memorable adventures—periodical, intellectual, and gustatory. Cheers, my friend! I also want to remember Robert Scholes, who first led me to periodical studies when I took his seminar at the School of Theory and Criticism in 1995, and Mark Wollaeger, whose "Jameson's Orgasmatron" was a thing of terrible beauty at the Revolting Modernism roundtable in 2015.

I am profoundly grateful to Mark Noonan for inviting me to join him at the City of Print institute in 2015 and for introducing me to Kelley Kreitz, who is a joy to work with. Thanks also to Jim Casey, Sarah Salter, Vincent DiGirolamo, Karen Roggenkamp, Jean Lee Cole, Ayendy Bonifacio, Joey

Kim, Noreen O'Connor, Kathleen Hulser, Ed Timke, Shawn Anthony Christian, and all the 2015 and 2020 faculty and fellows. We met in person in 2015 and online in 2020, and both experiences enriched my work in ways large and small. Thank you, Mark, for your organizational skill and your tireless efforts—and for your friendship.

To Bob Jackson and Keith Clark: I am looking forward to our future endeavors on our book *Jim Crow Modernism*. It is my good fortune to be working with you. Thank you, Ana Maria Jimenez-Moreno, for your kindness and your interest in this project.

Many thanks to Philip Leventhal and Monique Laban at Columbia University Press for making this book a reality. And thank you, Annie Barva, for being such an excellent copy editor.

Sections of *Circulating Jim Crow* have appeared previously. Elements of the introduction and chapter 4 were first published in the special issue "War and Periodicals," edited by James Berkey and Mark Noonan, in *American Periodicals* 26, no. 2 (2016); thanks to Jean Lee Cole for her excellent editorial suggestions as I revised the piece. Parts of chapters 3 and 4 appear in the special issue "Investigating Big Magazines," edited by Anne Reynès-Delobel, Benoît Tadié, and Cécile Cottenet, in *Journal of Modern Periodical Studies* 11, no. 1 (2020); Anne, Cécile, and Frank Conesa also organized the "Big Magazines" conference in 2018, which allowed me to revel in the charms of Aix-en-Provence, a city I long to see again. An earlier version of chapter 5 was published in *African American Literature in Transition, 1920–1930*, edited by Miriam Thaggert and Rachel Farebrother (Cambridge: Cambridge University Press, 2022); I thank both, but Rachel in particular for her excellent editorial suggestions. I am delighted to have facilitated Rachel and Miriam's initial connection at MSA.

Finally, thanks to all my Hudson Valley friends and my family. I cannot possibly name all the Beaconites who have sustained me over the years, so please forgive me—but here are shoutouts to Stephen Clair for lunch and music, Alex Humphreys for beer and poker, Terry Nelson for letting me read his manuscript, the Happy Valley crew, and the Beacon Dems. Love, love, love to Josh, Miyuki, Nico, Isaac, Sue, Dan, Donna, Sam, Amanda, and all my family. Oscar and Elijah, I am lucky to be your father. And Julie, thank you for being my cynical girl.

INTRODUCTION

George Horace Lorimer's declining health and death were big news in late October 1937. A titan of the publishing world, a patron of multiple cultural and charitable institutions, and a very rich and influential man, Lorimer had only recently retired as editor of the *Saturday Evening Post* and chairman of the behemoth Curtis Corporation. Newspapers in every state announced his illness, breathed a sigh of relief when he seemed to rally, and then sadly carried his obituary after his death on October 22, often on the front page. Admiration for Lorimer's life and accomplishments was nearly universal, and the dispensation of his estate was also widely reported. According to the *New York Times*, Lorimer bequeathed land, art, and antiques to the public, and he left considerable wealth to his immediate family and a few of his closest employees. But Lorimer's will also included this provision: "To each and every white person in my employ at the time of my decease . . . I give and bequeath the sum of $500 in cash absolutely."[1] In what was essentially his final piece of published writing, Lorimer underscored the open secret that went virtually unmentioned in the hundreds of obituaries that followed his demise: that he was a lifelong anti-Black racist who wanted to make certain that no African American would get any of his money. Writing for the Black newspaper the *Chicago Defender* in November 1937, Lucius C. Harper denounced Lorimer as "An Enemy . . . the Fascist of literature, so far as our Race was concerned." Harper accurately faulted Lorimer for publishing fiction that portrays African Americans as "nitwits and verb crackers," and he bemoaned the fact that "white America laughed while black America protested to deaf ears." He concluded with this emphatic condemnation: "We have no cause to regret Lorimer's passing. He died as he lived, with hatred in his heart. His will epitomizes him. After making individual bequests to relatives, he dipped his pen and wrote: 'To each and every WHITE person in my employ. . . .' The tragedy of it is that for over thirty years such a man as this dominated American culture and the literature it fed on. If we were to write an epitaph, it would read: 'Who they have injured, they also hate.'"[2]

By imagining Lorimer dipping his fountain pen into an inkwell with the intent to issue a final insult, Harper underscored the conscious steps Lorimer took to write his nakedly racist final instructions. And by noting that Lorimer's white readers shared a laugh at the expense of their fellow citizens, Harper also indicated that the *Post* was central in shaping personal, domestic, and communal experiences in Jim Crow America. The *New York Times*, like pretty much every other news outlet in the nation, had nothing to say about the animus enshrined in Lorimer's will, even though it directly quoted his hateful instructions. Decades of subsequent scholarship have been similarly silent.

By the time George Horace Lorimer retired at the end of 1936, he had made the *Saturday Evening Post* the most widely read magazine in the United States. As F. Scott Fitzgerald wrote in 1925, "Everybody sees the *Post*"; in 1929, Robert S. Lynd and Helen Merrell Lynd reported in their study of middle America that the magazine was delivered to one in every six homes in "Middletown"; and in his autobiography of 1936, the radical bohemian writer Joseph Freeman described the magazine as "the new American Bible." In his foundational study *Magazines in the United States* (1949), James Playstead Wood emphasized the *Post*'s ubiquity and its domination of American print culture: "For years it was virtually without a competitor as the largest weekly and, if such could be said to have existed at all, the most typical of American magazines. . . . It was seen and read everywhere. People came to know it as they knew their own names. Its influence was pervasive and immeasurable, spreading simultaneously in many directions. . . . The *Post* became both a powerful and continuing social force and almost a sign and symbol of the country itself."[3]

Week after week, year after year for almost four decades, Lorimer produced a reliably consistent product that could be found in every state in the union and in the farthest reaches of the globe. The magazine was central to American power and national identity. Every week as many as one in ten Americans read the *Post*, and the other nine were almost certainly affected—for both good and ill—by Lorimer's profound influence on culture and politics.

The consistency of the *Saturday Evening Post* as a reliable commodity is matched by a certain uniformity in earlier critical assessments of Lorimer's tenure as editor. These appraisals tended to emphasize a shared set of key points: Lorimer's absolute control over his magazine and his prowess as both an editor and a businessman; his advocacy for both "common sense" and the possibility of self-made success in America, a belief he exemplified especially through the publication of business fiction; his firmly held belief that his magazine was actively creating an American identity; and after World War I the fact that the *Saturday Evening Post* became a central player in the racist xenophobia that culminated in the passage of the Immigration Act of 1924, a law designed to ban immigrants from southern and eastern Europe. In 1928, Leon Whipple described the *Post* as a "Niagara of print" read by "everybody—high-brow, low-brow, and mezzanine; the hard-boiled business man and the soft-boiled leisure woman; the intelligenzia [*sic*], often as a secret vice"—and called it "a quintuple enterprise": "(1) a giant money-making business; (2) a miracle of technical publishing; (3) a purveyor of entertainment in fiction and amusing articles by which it gathers perhaps the largest part of its great audience; (4) a supersalesman of things through advertising and so a main cog in our modern machine of mass-distribution; (5) an engine for propaganda in favor of American nationalism and the present economic system." According to Whipple, Lorimer's magazine not only reflected American life but also was, in fact, a machine that produced national identity and experience—American life, American psychology, and American bodies: "It creates us. What the SatEvePost is we are." Because of Lorimer's extraordinary control over every aspect of the magazine's production, Whipple called him "the dictator" of arguably "the most powerful force ever exerted on the American people in print."[4]

Two years later, Benjamin Stolberg echoed many of the same points, noting that Lorimer "profoundly believes that the editor should be the dictator of his publication" and that the *Post* is "nothing but the character of George Horace Lorimer." More pointedly critical than Whipple (who also threw a few punches at Lorimer), however, Stolberg castigated the *Post* editor for his nativist hostility: "He wants all aliens finger-printed, all foreign ideas suspiciously registered, a high tariff not merely on goods but also on culture." Lorimer's ideas, wrote Stolberg, are "muscular with ruthless prejudice." Although Stolberg was (inaccurately) skeptical about Lorimer's ultimate place in American history because of what he saw as the magazine's tendency toward homogeneity and predictable mediocrity, he nonetheless credited Lorimer as "the Henry Ford of the periodical world . . . one of the great arbiters of public opinion and the greatest merchant in letters."[5] In its front-page obituary on October 23, 1937, the *New York Times* highlighted similar points; Lorimer edited the "magazine which has probably had more influence upon the cultural life of America than any other. [He was] an ardent apostle of the virtues of Big Business and the middle class, [and he] built its circulation to phenomenal heights and its profits to an equally phenomenal level." The *Times* recorded that in addition to nurturing the talents of many successful authors, Lorimer shaped America by opposing child labor, unregulated monopolies, and Franklin D. Roosevelt's New Deal as well as by fighting against the immigration of "unassimilable aliens."[6] Subsequent histories of Lorimer's editorship of the *Saturday Evening Post* tend to highlight the same set of ideas—namely, Lorimer's acumen and tight control, his abiding interest in business, and his aggressive promotion of an American sensibility that became increasingly hostile to immigrants from anywhere but northwestern Europe.

This widely shared critical consensus about the salient points of Lorimer's *Post* is incontrovertibly true, but, of course, much more detail can be added about the magazine's contents, general philosophy, innovations in technology and distribution, and centrality to the evolution of American mass culture in the early twentieth century. And there is one element of *Post* that has ever received only cursory treatment: Lorimer's lifelong fondness for and regular publication of racist, anti-Black fiction written almost exclusively by white authors specializing in "humorous" dialect fiction. From his earliest days with the magazine—even before he assumed the editor's chair—until his retirement, Lorimer published white-authored

Black dialect fiction on a near monthly and sometimes weekly basis. Starting his career at the *Saturday Evening Post* in the wake of the *Plessy v. Ferguson* decision in 1896 and rising to prominence as the nadir of Black experience cratered and Jim Crow rose and spread across the United States, Lorimer used humor to normalize twentieth-century American white supremacy and to make the dehumanization of African Americans seem like nothing more than common sense and just good fun.

Lorimer's successful normalization of anti-Black racism can be gauged by the scant notice paid to this aspect of his work. Buried deep in Whipple's essay, when he criticized the *Post*'s "Machiavellian paternalism," he faulted "the *Post*'s slant on our race problem: its pseudo-real, but farcical, tales of Negro life perpetuate old concepts, but it does nothing to probe racial discrimination or set forth the economic or cultural roots and changes. Its Negro is funny, not tragic."[7] Stolberg, who relished the opportunity to trash the *Post* as the purveyor of more "second-rate literature than any other periodical," dedicated just a single sentence to one *Post* author's "caricatures of the Negro[, which] are obtuse and offensive travesties of the American race problem."[8] Other studies of the *Post* follow the same pattern. No mention is made of Black dialect fiction in either Wood's *Magazines in the United States* or in the forty-five pages dedicated exclusively to the *Post* in Frank Luther Mott's five-volume *History of American Magazines* (1957).[9] Wood's elision of Lorimer's long practice of publishing anti-Black fiction is even more pronounced in his book *The Curtis Magazines*, published in 1971 and devoted exclusively to the periodicals produced by the Curtis Corporation, where the closest he comes to recognizing the existence of such material is his anodyne mention of one of the magazine's most consistent purveyors of Black dialect, Octavus Roy Cohen, whose "humor became a *Post* feature."[10] John Tebbel, author of the standard Lorimer biography, pauses just long enough to call Cohen's fiction "hilarious"; he also claims Hugh Wiley, another white writer, churned out dialect stories that were "hilariously funny to his audience."[11] Subsequent scholarship on the *Saturday Evening Post* remains similarly silent on this topic. Jan Cohn, whose book *Creating America: George Horace Lorimer and the* Saturday Evening Post (1989) remains the definitive volume on the magazine and its editor, briefly excoriates Cohen's "grossly racist comedies,"[12] but she otherwise ignores this topic altogether. Helen Damon-Moore's monograph on the *Post* from 1994 and its sister publication, the *Ladies' Home Journal*, is entirely silent on the subject.[13] It is time to shine a light on this ignored element of Lorimer's editorial practice and to argue that it was essential to the magazine's history, and that is what this book does.

Lorimer's lifelong practice of publishing stereotypical dialect fiction constitutes a significant context for the creative and critical energies of contemporary Black writers and activists, whose work directly and indirectly engages with and challenges the racist material the *Post* sold for a nickel a week. Lorimer edited the magazine from 1899 to 1936, and these years fit snugly within—and are nearly coterminous with—the New Negro era, which Henry Louis Gates Jr. and Gene Andrew Jarrett identify as extending from 1892 to 1938. While Lorimer and other cultural producers (writers, filmmakers, advertisers, composers, etc.) promulgated a sustained and static version of "the Old Negro [as] a trope that depicted the African diaspora as an inferior race" in which "Negro uncles, mammies, and chillun' dressed, talked, behaved, and thought in ways that lacked the kind of sophistication and refinement generally attributed to Anglo America," African Americans were constructing various iterations of a "New Negro" who would serve "generations of black intellectuals as a sign of plenitude, regeneration, or a truly reconstructed *presence*."[14] At the same time that ideas about the New Negro were being developed and contested within Black America (for example, debates surrounding the efficacy of Booker T. Washington's efforts, the militancy of the New Negro manhood movement, the aesthetic politics of Alain Locke, etc.), Lorimer was perpetuating the caricatures and stereotypes that insistently denied any possibility of agency for, self-awareness of, political empowerment of, or communal support for Black Americans. The Harlem Renaissance, which can be dated roughly between the return of Black doughboys from service in France during World War I in 1919 and the Harlem race riot in 1935, can be understood as an important period within the longer New Negro era, and it coincided with the *Post*'s era of explosive growth and sociopolitical dominance.[15] By considering how Lorimer's magazine responded to the rise of African American modernity, we might better understand how New Negro and Harlem Renaissance writers encountered and contested America's print culture in the first decades of the twentieth century.

REGISTER AND RECONTAIN

From the beginning of Lorimer's editorship, the *Saturday Evening Post*'s Black dialect fiction was almost mind-numbingly formulaic. When read one after another, these stories seem to more closely resemble fungible commodities than individually formed pieces of writing. Of course, aesthetic formulae are one of the hallmarks of a great deal of commercial fiction, but such predictability seems even more noticeable in the *Post*'s dialect fiction because the same motifs, themes, and flat characters recurred repeatedly and without variation over many years. In addition to its emphasis on grammatically and typographically distorted language, some of the more notable conventions of dialect fiction include Black characters who are naive, childish, petty, and intellectually undeveloped; prone to thievery, chicanery, dishonesty, and deception; and characterized by vanity, an excessive interest in sartorial splendor, and hyperconsciousness about their social status in the Black community. They are also lazy, sleep all the time, and oftentimes physically grotesque; they eat excessively; and their names are often absurd and emphasize some sort of fleshiness, gluttony, or excessive pride. Good fortune comes to them by sheer accident, without intention; bad luck results from schemes gone awry; and characters are all too commonly hoist with their own petard.[16] Gambling, in particular shooting craps, is an astoundingly regular activity. "Good" Black characters are naturally servile; white people are beneficently paternalistic; and nobody—but nobody— "understands" African Americans as well as white southern men (especially those from families that once owned slaves). These stereotypical details are repeated endlessly in the *Post*, but one aspect of the American experience is always omitted or played down: the array of coercive practices, legal restrictions, and terrorism undergirding white supremacy in the United States. In Lorimer's *Post*, the vast machinery and pervasive violence of segregation is rarely addressed, and the Jim Crow regime is presented as an organic phenomenon rather than as a consciously developed social structure predicated on inequality, dehumanization, and theft.

In the *Saturday Evening Post*, in other words, dialect fiction constituted a static, reactionary genre, and Blackness represented a form of commodified knowledge that was reproduced endlessly and with few variations. But some things did change over the decades of Lorimer's editorship, for while the formal elements of dialect fiction remained fairly constant, shifts in American and African American historical experience often found their way into these stories. The magazine thus illustrated such phenomena as the fading away of the Old South; Black migration from rural to urban areas and from south to north; the rise of new technologies such as the automobile, the airplane, and the motion picture; and African Americans' military service overseas. Such combinations of sustained formal consistency and changing historical developments, I argue, *registered* and *recontained* social change—by which I mean that dialect fiction in the *Saturday Evening Post* chronicled new historical developments (what we might call "modernity") but then folded those developments back into older, stereotypical forms of knowledge and racially stratified social norms and practices. Black characters moved through history in the *Post*, but they were forever squeezed back into a predictable, debased representational schematic.

To put it simply, Lorimer wielded his influence as editor of America's most widely read magazine to thwart Black modernity. In *Paradoxy of Modernism* (2006), Robert Scholes describes "the disorder that was modernity" as being characterized by "increasing industrialization and urbanization, the growing power of materialistic capitalism which generated labor unrest, the rise of new media of communications, and the struggle of women for equality and independence."[17] Scholes refers to the "disorder" of modernity because the dizzying array of social, political, aesthetic, and technological changes that began gathering steam in the 1880s and then roared into the twentieth century was simultaneously exhilarating and terrifying. The *Post* could be almost schizophrenic in its approach to modernity, at once longing nostalgically for a purportedly unproblematic, premodern past while also encouraging increased modernization through its support of American business and industry. As Scholes and Clifford Wulfman note in *Modernism in the Magazines: An Introduction* (2010), mass magazines such as the *Post* were integral to modernity, which arose, "we should remember, before the first motion pictures appeared, before radio communication was possible, and long before television was invented and deployed—which is to say that it happened in a world of communications dominated by print, though later developments extended and modified it."[18] All of modernity's characteristics identified by Scholes also apply to African American modernity, but in addition to changes in gender norms, technology, transportation, urbanization, and so on, we must also consider the consequences of migration and the struggle for racial justice and equality. The legal slavery of the American past did not provide African Americans much opportunity for nostalgia, but modernization offered a chance at expanded rights and a new sense of agency. Darryl Dickson-Carr writes,

> American modernity signaled the United States' transformation from a largely agrarian economy into a thoroughly industrialized one, with urban centers in all regions attracting workers seeking higher wages, better working conditions, and a new subjectivity defined by liberalism, democracy, and urbanity, rather than servility. That new subject, at least in the Fourteenth Amendment's vision, would be treated equally before the law, despite any heritage as chattel or indentured servant. The modern subject could make himself anew. . . . Put simply: Jim Crow be damned, African Americans would enjoy full, unfettered citizenship, challenge their invisibility in American social and political life, and become not merely part of the American cultural mainstream, but also its avant-garde, opening the way to democracy's unfulfilled promises.[19]

Jeanette Eileen Jones makes a similar observation about the connection between modernity and greater freedom for African Americans, adding the idea that the New Negro movement was intrinsically modern: "They began making themselves over as modern men and women invested in the ever-changing world for Negroes. They understood that their very lives and experiences were touched by the forces of modernity—industrialization, migration, urbanization, and expanding capitalism—and responded accordingly. As modernization unfolded, New Negroes began asserting a new political and social consciousness that rejected Jim Crow–style legislation and efforts to curtail their economic independence and freedom of movement."[20] The struggle for citizenship rights and for human dignity is intrinsic to Black modernity. As I show throughout *Circulating Jim Crow: The* Saturday Evening Post *and the War Against Black Modernity,* Lorimer published fiction that delegitimized African Americans' efforts and denied their full humanity.

Harris Dickson's story "A Borgia of the Air" (May 1, 1926) provides a useful example of how the *Post* worked to register and recontain Black modernity. Beginning in 1907, Dickson regularly contributed dialect fiction and reportage about the South to the *Post*, most notably stories about the Black character Ole Reliable (I have more to say about Dickson in chapter 1). "A Borgia of the Air" begins in Country Isom's shack, where he and Town Isom are having breakfast. Suddenly, the cabin begins to shudder and fill with sound; while the uninitiated city dweller ducks for cover, his more experienced rural counterpart calmly eats his meal and tells Town not to worry. The noise is from a low-flying airplane; the fields near the cabin are being sprayed by a crop duster, which was a relatively new technology in 1926. Once Town regains his composure, Country explains the "sineytific" processes at work, and the pair engage in a minstrel discourse on the latest agricultural advances. Dickson's narrative voice (written in standard English) eventually assumes control, and blackface buffoonery is displaced by straightforward reportage on efforts to eradicate the boll weevil. As Dickson draws to a close, however, he reminds his readers of the racist ideology that frames his discussion: "Now the theoretical bugologist is about to step aside and let businessmen carry on. We'll see what we see. If these Borgias of the air accomplish nothing more, they bring joy to Country Isom, who dozes in the shade while a white feller runs his job."[21] Dickson's sketch of verbal pratfalls, laziness, and subpar intelligence is but one instance of the scores upon scores of dialect stories that Lorimer ran during his almost four decades as editor of the *Post*, and until the final years of his tenure little changed in the magazine's representations of African Americans during that period. No matter what developed in national or racial experience, the *Post* always crammed those dynamics back into the straitjacket of caricature. Dickson, like the other white writers discussed in this book, registered examples of Black modernity, accomplishments, ingenuity, and creativity but then recontained those facts within the inhuman confines of derogatory stereotypes and formulaic characterizations.

The spell-check software on my computer insists that *recontain* is an unsanctioned neologism, so a bit of explanation is in order. The Jim Crow regime was not simply a "natural" extension of the antebellum slave system; it was a conscious, programmatic, and extensive cultural and political effort to roll back the gains of Reconstruction and reinstate de facto Black enslavement and white domination. Through all sorts of legal trickery, including but not limited to disenfranchisement, through historical revisionism and cultural derogation, and through steadily increasing forms of segregation and violence, white Americans *took back* the rights and property of the formerly enslaved, who had been making great strides during Reconstruction. This "Redemption" of the South was a "white supremacist rollback to Reconstruction" that "essentially imposed a system of neo-enslavement on . . . the recently freed African Americans and their children," writes Gates.[22] Jim Crow, in other words, can be understood as a revanchist effort to reclaim the lost territory—geographic, material, symbolic, and spiritual—of the white racial hierarchy that was rooted in the American slave system and that dominated the complicitly racist North as much as the explicitly brutal South. Reinstatement, revisionism, Reconstruction, Redemption, revanchism—these are the phenomena I hope to conjure up through the *re-* in *recontain* because the *Saturday Evening Post* was part of the larger effort to take the nation back to the conditions of antebellum slavery. White-authored Black dialect fiction in the *Post* was an important part of Lorimer's effort to maintain white domination and, as the loathsome current phrase would put it, to "make America great again."[23] Lorimer's *Post*, "that Rockwellian slice of pure Americana,"[24] enjoys a widespread reputation as a purveyor of nostalgia for a simpler time—but it was, in fact, always nostalgia with teeth. As Jan Cohn notes, *Post* readers "found comfort in a weekly reconstitution of [a] vanished world." But comforting nostalgia was not the point for Lorimer, who "intended to recall the values of [the] traditional world in order to change the present situation."[25] When it came to the "present situation" of African Americans, Lorimer used his enormous influence to recontain them in the backward-looking straits of dialect fiction. In *Stony the Road: Reconstruction, White Supremacy, and the Rise of Jim Crow* (2019), Gates asks, "How, then, does a society attempt to transform a freedwoman or a freedman *back* into a slave?"[26] My book, by focusing on Lorimer's *Post*, offers an extended answer to Gates's question. The *Saturday Evening Post* was weaponized against Black modernity, methodically registering new developments and achievements always and only to deny full Black humanity and assert white supremacy. Further, as I argue especially in chapter 2, Lorimer's practice afforded white Americans opportunities not only to consume racial caricatures but also to share, embody, and perform those caricatures for one another in a variety of domestic and communal gatherings.

During the Harlem Renaissance, Lorimer's *Post* and its dialect writers were regular topics of concern for Black authors and activists. In *Circulating Jim Crow*, I focus primarily on Lorimer and his favored authors, but always with an eye to how Renaissance writers challenged the programmatic dehumanization embodied in the *Post*'s representations of Black life. For now, four examples will serve as indications of how the *Post* functioned as an important contextual element of the Harlem Renaissance. In 1924, Walter White complained in a letter, "I have told several publishers . . . that the reason colored people do not buy books is because publishers have not brought out the right sort, i.e. they have published caricatures of the Negro like the stories of Octavus Roy Cohen, Hugh Wiley, and Irvin Cobb, or base libels on the Negro like the vicious novels of Thomas Dixon."[27] Cohen, Wiley, and Cobb's stories were regular features of the *Post*, and each author is the subject of his own chapter here. Dixon placed only one essay with the magazine, "Booker T. Washington and the Negro" in 1905 (see chapter 1), but this enormously influential contribution was reprinted in newspapers throughout the United States and gave intellectual credence to rising Jim Crow. In a letter in 1932, Zora Neale Hurston echoed Walter White and added another name to the list, Roark Bradford, whom I discuss in chapter 6: "It makes me furious when some ham like Cohen or Roark Bradford gets off a nothing else but and calls it a high spot of Negro humor and imagery."[28] Five years later, the anthropologist Melville J. Herskovits defended Hurston's collection *Mules and Men* in the journal *Folklore* and drove his points home by contrasting Hurston's work with Lorimer's magazine: "One does not have to be a profound student of Negro life to understand that the stories of Octavus Roy Cohen are a travesty and a caricature on Negro life; and that while some persons of the type the writer portrays may exist somewhere, they are found far more often in the pages of the *Saturday Evening Post*, where these stories usually appear, than in the Negro communities of the United States."[29] Finally, in 1941 Langston Hughes wrote a statement after the *Post* editor Wesley Winans Stout (who succeeded Lorimer in 1937) reprinted a prejudicial handbill containing Hughes's poem "Goodbye Christ." Hughes characterized the *Post* as "a magazine whose columns, like the doors of many of our churches, has been until recently entirely closed to Negroes, and whose chief contribution in the past to a better understanding of Negro life in America has been the Octavious [*sic*] Roy Cohen stories with which most colored people have been utterly disgusted."[30] In each of these examples, Cohen was held up as the most egregious white author of Black dialect fiction, but he was also always a synecdoche for the *Post* as a whole. Lorimer's steady publication of Black stereotypes was a recurrent matter of concern throughout the literature of the Harlem Renaissance.[31]

ANTI-BLACK RACISM AND ANTI-IMMIGRANT XENOPHOBIA

Lorimer's anti-Black racism was of a piece with his broader white-supremacist xenophobia, and his animus against African Americans almost certainly preceded his more well-known attacks against non-Nordic, non-Anglo-Saxon immigrants from southern and eastern Europe, not to mention his predilection for orientalism. Virtually all contemporary journalism and subsequent scholarship comment on Lorimer's nearly hysterical anti-immigrant stance, which took root during World War I and the Russian Revolution and quickly metastasized in the 1920s. His vehemence is remarkable in part because Lorimer was originally quite sympathetic to newly arrived Americans. Years before he fell under the sway of eugenicists and pseudoscientists such as Madison Grant and Lothrop Stoddard (the latter became a regular *Post* author in the 1920s), Lorimer was staunchly pro-immigrant and even condemned the same biases he would later endorse. In an editorial on February 6, 1904, "The Flood of Immigration," for example, he praised immigration as "one of the great factors in upbuilding America," and he scorned "talk of shutting the gates against the immigrant on the ground that nowadays our immigration has enormously increased and is of a most undesirable kind." In fact, he claimed, the people who characterized the new arrivals as undesirable were "conspicuous examples of that type of supercilious, ignorant man of education which is such a deplorable feature of our public life today." Yet the same editorial page that included this clear example of Lorimer's earlier acceptance of Europeans of any ethnicity or nationality (*only* European immigration is implied in the piece) also offered "Another White Man's Burden," which relied on the anti-Black trope of "Congo savagery" to argue for the U.S. annexation of "the Black and Mahogany Republics" of Santo Domingo; this second editorial helps demonstrate that Lorimer's anti-Black racism preceded his later ethnic white nationalism by decades.[32]

Lorimer continued his support of mass migration from Europe with editorials, articles, and fiction until 1916, the same year Madison Grant published *The Passing of the Great Race*, which categorized white people on a sliding scale from superior Nordics to middling Alpines to lower-order Mediterraneans. According to Grant, Nordics were responsible for almost every advance in human civilization and were the only people worthy of admission to the United States. In January 1916, Lorimer—perhaps before he even read *The Passing of the Great Race*—printed an editorial that marked a shift in his thinking. In "The Asylum Business," after first asserting that "a big majority" of Americans agreed that "Chinese and Japanese should be excluded—or very much restricted," he argued that European immigration should also be limited by mandating a literacy test to new arrivals. Lorimer seemed to claim an economic basis for this changing position but also indicated his blossoming ethnic white nationalism by asserting, "We have always excluded those whose presence we judged likely to be injurious to us."[33]

By 1918, the *Post* was fully mobilized to fight for severe immigration restrictions based entirely on the purported racial superiority of northern and western Europeans. Articles with titles such as "The Overflowing Melting Pot: Why the Americanization of America Must Begin," "Our Imported Troubles and Troublemakers," and "America for Americans" began to appear frequently, and Lorimer became increasingly convinced that "lower-order" white people were innately dangerous. He left all subtlety aside in editorials such as "Scum of the Melting Pot," which railed against "the unassimilated foreigner" and "the scoundrel in Europe who fancied a trip to our shores" and which characterized native-born Americans who tolerated unchecked immigration as "fatuous fools—the nut-sundae Socialists from the ranks of the self-styled 'intellectuals' and well-to-do lemon-pop Bolsheviki uplifters" who supported and coddled foreigners. The editorial warned these "scum" that "Americanism is coming to a boiling point."[34]

Lorimer further drove the point home—that "inferior" Europeans are innately prone to crime and revolution—by running William Roscoe Thayer's article "Despotism by the Dregs" on the recto page of the spread that had "Scum of the Melting Pot" on the opposite verso, thus visually and thematically expanding on his own editorial. In Thayer's denunciation of the Bolsheviks, we see how the already-formed logic of American anti-Black racism shaped newer theories of racial difference:

During the period of reconstruction after our Civil War shortsighted politicians practiced the Bolshevik method when they handed over the control of some of our Southern States to the negroes—persons, that is, who had absolutely no training in government and who had recently been actual slaves. . . . And that episode stands out now as one of the most disgraceful in our history. Years later a well-known abolitionist, a friend of mine, was talking the matter over with a sensible old darky who said: "Dose yere politicians up No'th tried to put ign'rance on top of 'telligence; but it wouldn't stay dar." It would be well if every Bolshevik in Russia, and those who think like him in all parts of the world, would adopt and ponder the old darky's wise words.[35]

In this passage, Thayer applied the preexisting, ruthless logic of the U.S. Black–white racial hierarchy to a more recent object of racial animus: purportedly subpar and inherently ungovernable Russians. We also see in "Despotism by the Dregs" a brief example of how a white *Post* writer registered positive developments in African American modernity—that is, voting rights and self-governance—but then recontained and rolled back such advances symbolically through the incorporation of dialect. Under Lorimer's direction, the *Post* waged a strident and ultimately successful campaign to close U.S. borders to almost all immigrants. He championed the "scientific" racism of Grant and Stoddard, and, as Cohn notes, passage of the Immigration Act in 1924 was attributed directly to the *Post*, including the work of Kenneth Roberts, who got his start at the magazine by writing anti-immigrant articles for "the Boss."[36] Although many journalists and scholars have touched on this aspect of Lorimer's xenophobia—which was consequential in shaping U.S. demography for decades—a full-length treatment of this topic has yet to be published. There is a similar critical gap concerning the reams of oriental detective fiction published in the *Post* during Lorimer's tenure. Beginning in 1920, Hugh Wiley developed a side hustle to his Black dialect Wildcat stories (see chapter 4) by writing stories set in San Francisco's Chinatown. Earl Der Biggers contributed six serialized Charlie Chan novels to the *Post* between 1925 and 1932. When Der Biggers died in 1933, the *Post* recruited John P. Marquand to fill the gap,[37] and Marquand provided the magazine with three serialized Mr. Moto novels in 1935 and 1936 and another two after Lorimer retired. In fact, Lorimer nurtured a plethora of white authors who produced ethnic and dialect fiction of all sorts, and a great deal of scholarly work remains to be done on this key element of a magazine that promoted itself as "an American Institution." The present study offers a sustained examination of just one aspect of Lorimer's broader efforts at promoting white supremacy.

THE *POST* AND THE FIELD OF AMERICAN PERIODICALS

An exhaustive review of how other American magazines represented African Americans is beyond the scope of this project, but a brief comparison of some of the *Post*'s main competitors only underscores why Lucius Harper would single out Lorimer specifically as an anti-Black "Fascist of literature." To get some sense of how the *Post* fits in the larger universe of American magazines, I looked at a year's run of a handful of magazines published in 1909, 1925, and 1936. I chose 1909 because this is when, according to the Curtis Publishing Company, the *Post* assumed its "permanent character."[38] The year 1925 is widely considered a benchmark of the Harlem Renaissance. Alain Locke published both the *Survey Graphic* special issue "Harlem: Mecca of the New Negro" and *The New Negro* anthology in 1925, and it is also when the *Messenger* began serialization of Edward Christopher William's novel *The Letters of Davy Carr* (later retitled *When Washington Was in Vogue*); all these texts figure prominently in this book. Lorimer's final year as editor was 1936, which thus is an appropriate third data point. For my comparison, I analyzed the *Post*'s sister publication the *Ladies' Home Journal* as well as several general-interest weeklies and monthlies. The most pertinent are the weekly *Collier's* and the monthly *Cosmopolitan*, both of which offered a mix of fiction, nonfiction, and journalism, and the *Literary Digest*, a weekly roundup of the news that covered the arts and had a poetry column but did not publish fiction. All four mass-market magazines enjoyed relatively large national circulation figures comparable to the *Post*, and they were being published in the three years of my "soil sample." What my cursory review revealed with some clarity is that Lorimer's appetite for racist caricature far exceeded that of the stewards of similar periodicals.

All the magazines in my brief comparison contained occasional minor African American characters, usually domestic or manual laborers, and most of them also sometimes incorporated unproblematized racial slurs and other forms of casual racism. In 1909, *Collier's*, *Cosmopolitan*, the

Literary Digest, and the *Ladies' Home Journal* included at least some brief racist jokes, usually as space fillers or as components of regular humor columns. *Collier's* was for this year relatively sympathetic toward African Americans; it editorialized against lynching, offered praise for Black cavalrymen, and featured no white-authored Black dialect fiction (although it also serialized Wallace Irwin's "humorous" Asian dialect novel *Letters of a Japanese Schoolboy*). The *Literary Digest* in 1909 was even more supportive of African American rights and dignity. The magazine came out forcefully against lynching, the color line, and judicial and legal injustice, and it offered *almost* no racist jokes. *Cosmopolitan* had a small handful of such jokes in 1909, and it also ran two white-authored Black dialect stories accompanied by caricatured illustrations. The two Curtis publications, the *Post* and the *Ladies' Home Journal,* are markedly different from these competitors. In the *Journal,* the year 1909 began with the editorial "A Crime Against American Children," which took aim at "the inane and vulgar 'comic' supplement of the Sunday newspaper." Among the offending items castigated by the editorial were "a forlorn mule, badly drawn, and a repulsive negro boy, with the customary horrible ear-to-ear grin, which is the stock in trade of this kind of illustrative work, with huge, distorted feet, and eyes of the usual circle-and-dot pattern which is as conventional and as funny as were the hour-glass and wings on ancient tombstones."[39] Despite this strong language, the *Journal* published dialect jokes in almost every issue, and it regularly featured advertisements for Cream of Wheat, Knox Gelatin, Black Horn Chamois, and Gold Dust Powder, all of which used Black stereotypes to sell their products. For much of its history, the *Saturday Evening Post* also advertised these products, but this was not the case in 1909—an omission that appears to be anomalous rather than indicative of any change in editorial or advertising practice. However, in 1909 the *Post* did offer more brief jokes and full-length fiction than the other four magazines combined. In that year, Lorimer reliably published racist squibs in two regular columns, "Who's Who—and Why" and "Sense and Nonsense," as well as six dialect stories by Harris Dickson and one by Blanche Goodman (discussed in chapters 1 and 2). In other words, in 1909 the *Post* was more predictably anti-Black than its competitors, the possible exception being its sister publication, the *Ladies' Home Journal,* although most of the latter's caricatures were confined to its advertisements rather than also included in its editorial content.

In 1925, Black stereotypes in the *Ladies' Home Journal* were limited to a much smaller number of ads, primarily for Cream of Wheat. *Collier's* published two story-length pieces of dialect fiction by Courtney Riley Cooper as well as the story "Elfie" by Elsie Singmaster (a future *Post* author). The subtitle for Singmaster's contribution described it as "a story of pathos and beauty that the reader will long remember—the story of a Negro girl with the greatest voice in the world," and the story's sympathetic treatment of Black experience is matched by an antiracist, antilynching essay by Julius Rosenwald published in *Collier's* a month earlier. Similar in tone, the *Literary Digest* in 1925 also ran an editorial against extralegal racial violence and a lengthy appreciation of the African American singer Roland Hayes, a poem by Countee Cullen, and the essay "The Negro as an Artist," which applauded "the negro literary renaissance."[40] There is almost no mention of African Americans in *Cosmopolitan*, although in 1925 it did run two stories by a former *Post* author, Irvin S. Cobb, and a serious poem, "The Negro Cowboy," by William Rose Benét, which is written in dialect. Once again, the difference between these other periodicals and the *Post* could not be clearer. In 1925, Lorimer provided his readers with eleven Black dialect stories by Octavus Roy Cohen, three by Hugh Wiley, and one by Harris Dickson. This year's *Post* also contained a lengthy article by Marian Spitzer lauding minstrelsy and "The World's Largest Negro City" by Chester T. Crowell, a plagiarized version of Locke's *Survey Graphic* issue, which I address in chapter 6. Anti-Black caricatures can also be found in numerous advertisements and assorted briefer items. In other words, during a critical period of Black modernity and intensifying creativity, the *Post* served as a leader in delegitimizing African American achievement, citizenship, and humanity.

Lorimer moderated his magazine's tone slightly in his final years as editor, but the *Post* was still a reliable source for racist material when he retired in 1936, and it remained the most consistent purveyor of such items among the other magazines I surveyed. By 1936, the *Ladies' Home Journal* ran Cream of Wheat and Aunt Jemima ads, but otherwise African Americans in any form were almost entirely absent (an absence that in itself was part of the Jim Crowing of America). *Collier's* published three dialect stories, two of which were written by Roark Bradford (an occasional *Post* contributor), and *Cosmopolitan* ran just one Aunt Jemima ad for the entire year. In 1936, the *Literary Review* ran a positive review of Arna Bontemps's novel *Black*

Thunder, an objective report on the Scottsboro Boys case, a few other minor items, and a nostalgic poem called "Black Mammy" reprinted from *Catholic World* magazine. By contrast, in Lorimer's final year as editor the *Post* ran two dialect stories by Cohen, including one set in Harlem, and two stories by T. S. Stribling. The magazine also offered three prominent articles about the boxer Joe Louis and the Olympics star Jesse Owens. In sum, from the beginning of his career until its conclusion, George Horace Lorimer made his wildly popular magazine a reliable source of anti-Black racism that was consumed on a weekly basis by millions of Americans. Lorimer did not invent white supremacy, but he was certainly keen to help it along.

My admittedly inconclusive and largely anecdotal comparison of the *Post* with a handful of other magazines gestures toward an obvious point, but one that should be made: Lorimer and his magazine did not exist in a vacuum but were (extremely powerful) elements in the much larger universe of American print culture. As Sean Latham and Robert Scholes note in their seminal essay "The Rise of Periodical Studies" (2006), "Anyone who studies periodicals soon discovers that they are frequently in dialogue with one another" and that they "create and occupy typically complex and often unstable positions in sometimes collaborative and sometimes competitive cultural networks."[41] In the robust field of periodical studies, myriad theoretical approaches are available for conceptualizing magazines as elements within these networks. Pierre Bourdieu's formulation of human society in terms of a "field" continues to exert enormous influence over the study of magazines and print culture more generally. According to Bourdieu, "The literary or artistic field is a *field of forces*, but it is also a *field of struggles*." Elaborating on Bourdieu's ideas about cultural and power contestations within a field, Kinohi Nishikawa explains that "popular cultural forms" can be read as "dynamic strategies of representation" and that "Bourdieu's field attends not only to the individual work in its material specificity but to everything external to the work that determines its symbolic value."[42] In this sense, the *Post* operated within and often dominated a field of racial representation that was also inhabited by the emergent forces of the Harlem Renaissance, which contested Lorimer's efforts to register and recontain Black modernity within the static confines of dialect and stereotype. Eurie Dahn has more recently figured periodical culture in terms of "networks," a theoretical approach that encourages us to consider the "dialogic relationships between periodical components, between periodicals, between periodicals and literary texts, and between periodicals and readers." Dahn reads periodicals within an ever-multiplying series of intratextual and inter-textual networks and argues that any element of this cultural field can be understood as "a node within a sprawling network comprised of [other] nodes." Her suggestion that these "overlapping networks can only be mapped partially" certainly applies to the *Saturday Evening Post*,[43] a behe-moth of American print culture—and of sociopolitical life more broadly—whose influence reverberated across national and global networks in ways that can probably never be charted in their entirety. In fact, one might argue that the perpetually inconclusive findings of scholars who attend to mass-circulation magazines are an unavoidable occupational hazard for anyone who tries to make sense of a magazine such as the *Post*, with its hundreds of writers, thousands of individual contributions, hundreds of thousands of pages, and millions of readers. Using Dahn's model, we can imagine Lorimer functioning as a node in overlapping networks such as magazine publishing, Jim Crow segregation, Harlem Renaissance contestation, and so on.

Richard Ohmann offers a market-focused method to the study of mass-circulation magazines that perhaps applies most directly to my approach to the *Saturday Evening Post* because his focus on those magazines' prac-tice of creating consumers (rather than merely attracting readers) resonates with how the *Post* conceived of itself. The Curtis Publishing Company was imbricated in monopoly capitalism, a mode of production characterized by the "giant, vertically integrated corporation," which not only produces and distributes goods but also consciously and programmatically cultivates a massive pool of buyers, shaping more-or-less unpredictable individuals into reliable, reproducible consumers. As a corporate entity, the *Post* simulta-neously generated consumers of its own product (the magazine itself) and delivered those consumers to other corporations—directly through adver-tising but also indirectly through the editorial content that created mass-market Americans. Ohmann writes of large-circulation magazines as "a cultural industry of quite new dimensions which was not just a matter of size. [Mass magazines] reached a wider and *different* audience. . . . In other words, they [the magazine publishers] were no longer dealers in their phys-ical product and became dealers in groups of *consumers*. What they came to sell, like radio and television later on, was *us*—or more precisely, our attention. This appears to be a development of world-historical importance:

the invention of the mind industry or, more commonly, mass culture."
Ohmann's focus on monopoly capitalism does not obviate or contradict
frameworks such as Bourdieu's field or Dahn's networks, but it reminds us
that the *Post*, as a key player in the rise of American mass culture, was
always, as Ohmann points out, "inseparable from the circulation of commodities."[44] Cohn notes that Cyrus H. K. Curtis had always intended his
magazines "as vehicles for advertisers, and as the marketing sophistication
of the Curtis Company increased, the relationship between consumer and
advertiser was promoted as an economic nexus *created* by the *Post*."[45]
According to James Playstead Wood, the Curtis Advertising Department
proudly announced that it "manufactured customers," and in a speech about
the *Ladies' Home Journal* Curtis explained to a gathering of advertisers that
editors worked under the "illusion" that their goal is to benefit readers—
but "the real reason, the publisher's reason, is to give you people [who] want
and buy."[46] As a corporate manufacturer, Lorimer used his magazine—
including but certainly not limited to the white-authored Black dialect fiction studied here—as a machine that churned out the millions of consumers whom other manufacturers increasingly required as the mass culture
of monopoly capitalism arose and flourished.

WHAT THIS BOOK IS NOT—AND IS

Jan Cohn's *Creating America: George Horace Lorimer and the* Saturday Evening Post is foundational to understanding the *Post*, and she offers a
wealth of information to anyone interested in American print culture in
the early twentieth century. Because the magazine provides so many different paths for analysis, Cohn starts her introduction by outlining "what
[her] book is not,"[47] and a similar delimitation of my study is also in order.
Like Cohn's book, mine is not a study of Lorimer's life, although I occasionally make use of biographical material to support some assertions. As
previously noted, Lorimer had absolute control over the *Post*, and his philosophy, tastes, politics, and personality can be found everywhere in his own
early fiction, his editorials, and the material he chose to publish. Per Cohn,
"Against the deep personal imprint he left on the *Post*, most other personal
information becomes, with time, insignificant."[48] We can gauge Lorimer's
thoughts and intentions with a fair degree of accuracy by examining his
writing and editorial choices. Also like *Creating America*, my book does not

provide an extensive treatment of the magazine's history, which was integral to the development of American print culture and to the cultivation of mass marketing and mass audiences.[49] And *Circulating Jim Crow* is not—again I echo Cohn—a record of the magazine's "rise and fall,"[50] nor do I examine the *Post* after Lorimer's retirement, including the magazine's initial collapse and the subsequent efforts to revive it. The chronological focus of this book is Lorimer's editorship from 1899 through 1936; the history of the *Saturday Evening Post* began in 1821 (or 1728, according to the magazine's fabricated origin story linking it to Benjamin Franklin) and continued into the twenty-first century as a print publication out of Indianapolis and an online magazine.

Finally—and here I add to Cohn's list of caveats—*Circulating Jim Crow* is not an analysis of the broad and complex field of American dialect writing. As Gavin Jones demonstrates in *Strange Talk: The Politics of Dialect Literature in Gilded Age America* (1999), dialect fiction and poetry enjoyed widespread popularity. It portrayed orthographically a multiplicity of races, ethnicities, classes, and nationalities, and it was not necessarily a simple means of domination: "Dialect writing was not always a proof of hegemonic command. It could also register an anxious, constantly collapsing attempt to control the fragmentation and change that characterize any national tongue. And dialect could encode the possibility of resistance, not just by undermining the integrity of a dominant standard, but by recording the subversive voices in which alternative versions of reality were engendered."[51] Certainly, the *Post*'s efforts to register and recontain African Americans were fueled by anxieties over Black modernity specifically and by demographic, cultural, and political changes more broadly. And as I discuss at various points in the following chapters, resistance to and subversion of white supremacy can be found both within the white-authored material I examine and in African American responses to the *Post*. However, apart from the work of Paul Laurence Dunbar (chapter 1), perhaps Julia Peterkin, and *maybe* William Faulkner (chapter 6), the Black dialect found in Lorimer's magazine was uniformly "a popular means of encoding racist beliefs in black intellectual inferiority,"[52] and I do not delve into its linguistic complexity at any length. For the overwhelming majority of authors treated in this book, dialect writing at best signaled paternalistic condescension; at worst, it was a straightforward vehicle of sneering hatred and was deployed, as we see in Thayer's "Despotism by the Dregs," in the larger effort to promulgate Black subservience and inequality.

During the years of Lorimer's editorship, Black authors debated whether African American writers could successfully incorporate dialect into their work without falling prey to the traps of racial dehumanization endemic to the sort of material published in the *Post*. James Weldon Johnson (1871–1938), whose life overlapped almost entirely with Lorimer's (1867–1936), was generally doubtful about the possibilities of African American–authored Black dialect, and his skepticism is paradigmatic of the ambivalent status of dialect writing before, during, and after the Harlem Renaissance. In his preface to the first edition of *The Book of American Negro Poetry* in 1922, Johnson outlined the human and artistic limitations of dialect, claiming that it "is at present a medium that is not capable of giving expression to the varied conditions of Negro life in America, and much less is it capable of giving the fullest interpretation of Negro character and psychology. This is no indictment against the dialect as dialect, but against the mould of convention in which Negro dialect in the United States has been set."[53] Johnson objected to dialect writing because its dominant tendency was, as Miriam Thaggert suggests, to transmit "a stagnant picture of the black American, creating an anachronistic, rigid effect."[54] In his revised edition of *The Book of American Negro Poetry*, published in 1931, Johnson recognized the merit of younger poets such as Langston Hughes and Sterling Brown, whose dialect poetry successfully exploits "the common, racy, living, authentic speech of the Negro," but he also maintained his assertion that dialect is insufficient to expressing the fullness of Black experience: "The limitation is due to conventions that have been fixed[;] . . . Negro dialect poetry had its origin in the minstrel traditions, and a persisting pattern was set. When the individual writer attempted to step away from that pattern, the fixed conventions allowed him only to slip over into a slough of sentimentality. These conventions were not broken for the simple reason that the individual writers wrote chiefly to entertain an outside [i.e., white] audience, and in concord with its stereotyped ideas about the Negro."[55] Johnson's prefaces are indications of a much larger debate about dialect that engaged a broad spectrum of Black writers during the New Negro era, but, again, this debate is beyond the purview of my study.

The chapters of this book are arranged in rough chronological order, although there is overlap in the years covered in chapters 2 through 5, which address four white *Post* writers whose careers directly preceded or coincided with the Harlem Renaissance era. Chapters 1 and 6 chart the initial coalescence and the later fraying of Lorimer's publication of material that consistently registered and recontained Black modernity within the confines of dialect fiction. Chapter 1 sketches out Lorimer's first two decades as editor and illustrates how his magazine became an increasingly firm advocate for Jim Crow ideology. After a brief biographical sketch of Lorimer's ascent to the editor's chair, the chapter begins by considering the magazine's early embrace of Booker T. Washington and Paul Laurence Dunbar. Although Lorimer never published anything by Washington, he did run a fair amount of material that praised the Tuskegean as an exemplary self-made man, and the magazine bolstered Washington's status as the leader of Black America. Dunbar enjoyed more attention in the *Post* than Washington, all of it positive, and he placed dozens of dialect poems and stories with the magazine between 1899 and his death in 1906. Dunbar was the only African American author of Black dialect fiction Lorimer ever published, and he was the only author (until 1929) who used the conventions of dialect writing to reveal rather than deny Black complexity and humanity. However, as segregation and racial disenfranchisement intensified, the magazine became increasingly skeptical of even Washington's accommodationist politics. Beginning in 1904, Lorimer ran material by writers such as Joel Chandler Harris, Rebecca Harding Davis, and Thomas Dixon Jr. that argued against the possibility of full Black citizenship and in favor of social and political inequality and innate racial inferiority. In 1907, Lorimer began publishing Harris Dickson, a municipal judge from Vicksburg, Mississippi, who made no effort to conceal his racism. After first contributing essays that were blatantly hostile to African Americans, Dickson developed his long-running series about "Ole Reliable," a buffoonish Black character whose appearance announced the solidification of Lorimer's preference for fiction that registered and recontained African Americans within the narrow confines of dialect writing.

In chapter 2, I focus on Blanche Goodman, a minor literary figure who gained some local prominence in Chattanooga's cultural circles and has the distinction of being the most published white female author of Black dialect fiction in the *Post*. Between 1908 and 1925, Lorimer published nineteen monologues written by Goodman, which are spoken by a mammy figure named Viney Harris who embodies the stereotypical, faithful family retainer found everywhere in the fiction, illustrations, and imagery of the *Post*. Goodman aspired to being a professional writer, took note of the magazine's regular publication of Black dialect, and accordingly produced saleable material that Lorimer would accept and print. Through Goodman's example, we get some sense of how the *Post* was read by both typical, casual readers and more attentive aspirants to the title of "*Saturday Evening Post* author," a moniker that followed Goodman throughout her life from almost the moment she published her first Viney piece. In addition to demonstrating Lorimer's appetite for Black dialect, Goodman also reveals how *Post* stories were often read aloud in both small, domestic settings and larger, public events. Further, the recitation of Viney monologues, which were performed at gatherings across the country for many years, reveals how Black dialect fiction in the *Post* was one aspect of the much larger culture of amateur blackface minstrelsy that saturated U.S. culture in the first half of the twentieth century. We are generally familiar with the impact of minstrelsy on the development of American theater and film, and as Michael North shows in *The Dialect of Modernism* (1994), we can trace the influence of dialect writing on the development of literary modernism.[56] Goodman's contributions to the *Post* expose another area of consequence—namely, that amateur minstrelsy was a regular feature of the domestic and public spaces of Jim Crow culture. Americans were not merely passive consumers of minstrelsy; they were also participants in communal productions of racist caricature and demeaning stereotypes. Performed by fraternal, civic, and religious organizations at charitable events, amateur blackface minstrel shows were widely advertised and drew reliably large crowds. On a smaller scale, groups of women would gather in average American homes and recite dialect material during cultured luncheons, and an industry developed to meet the enormous demand for written material, props, costumes, and makeup. Goodman's monologues— and the *Post*'s dialogue-heavy dialect stories more generally—supplied the magazine's readers with a steady flow of material they could use at the water cooler, in their homes, and at public events. I conclude chapter 2 by examining F. Scott Fitzgerald's early contributions to the *Post*, which displayed a similar investment in domestic minstrelsy, and I discuss African Americans' responses to the prevalence of in-home minstrel performances, looking in particular at the fiction of Charles W. Chesnutt and Ann Petry.

Chapters 3 through 5 are in many ways the heart of this book because they examine the three *Post* regulars usually cited during the Harlem Renaissance as the most notorious perpetrators of stereotypical Black dialect fiction; I was initially drawn to this project when I started to realize just how often Cohen, Cobb, and Wiley appear in the Harlem Renaissance literature I study and teach. Irvin S. Cobb is the focus of chapter 3, and his contributions to the *Post* exemplify the magazine's approach to rising Black modernity during the Renaissance. Shortly after Cobb began writing for the *Post* in 1909, he and Lorimer became close friends, and Cobb achieved a reputation as one of the magazine's most beloved authors. A seasoned newspaperman and professional southernist, Cobb wrote about a variety of subjects and contributed highly anticipated dispatches from Europe during World War I. He also developed a pair of recurring characters, Judge William Priest and Jefferson Exodus Poindexter, a former Confederate officer and his faithful retainer, who embody Lorimer's sentimentality for the purported gentility and organicism of the antebellum slavocracy. Unlike *Post* authors such as Dickson, who rarely concealed his disdain for African Americans or his tolerance for racial violence, Cobb distanced himself from such violence while also endorsing the tenets of white supremacy. He was a kinder, gentler sort of racist. In 1918, Lorimer sent Cobb on a second tour of the European front, and he directed his friend to investigate the African American soldiers serving in combat overseas. Cobb's article, "Young Black Joe," drew national attention to the now-famed Harlem Hellfighters, and it was widely praised and cited by the press, including African American newspapers. Despite the problematic material Cobb published in the *Post* and elsewhere, he became—for a while at least—a welcome participant in interracial organizations supporting the war effort. Much to Lorimer's dismay, Cobb was lured away to *Cosmopolitan* magazine, but before Cobb left, he submitted his first novel, *J. Poindexter, Colored*, for serialization in the *Post*, and it ran in the summer of 1922. Cobb's novel explores topics that would become central concerns during the Harlem Renaissance, including the Great Migration, the advent of Harlem as a new Black urban community, the coming of the postwar New Negro, and the rise of Marcus Garvey. The book also incorporates scenes of the nascent Black film industry, which would be a focus of Cohen's writing a few years later. In addition, in chapter 3 I examine Lorimer's excisions from Cobb's novel; how the editor pared down *J. Poindexter, Colored* for publication reveals much about

Lorimer's parameters for representing Black modernity in his magazine. When Alain Locke wrote about the Old Negro in 1925, he was critiquing work like Cobb's, which denied the violence of white supremacy and waxed nostalgic over obsequious Black servility.

In chapter 4, I examine Hugh Wiley's popular caricature of the Black doughboy, a recurring character named Vitus "Wildcat" Marsden, and I argue that Edward Christopher Williams's Harlem Renaissance novel *When Washington Was in Vogue* can be read as an engagement with and refutation of Wiley's "humorous" take on Black service, heroism, and humanity. Wiley was another of Lorimer's close friends, and his views were even more aligned with the editor's than were Cobb's. Wiley's Wildcat stories ran in the *Post* from 1919 through 1934, thus throughout the Harlem Renaissance, and his character was a regular feature of the broader media landscape, including African American journalism and literature. In fact, I initially became interested in white-authored Black dialect fiction in the *Post* after reading this line from Williams's novel: "Of course, most of those present read Octavus Roy Cohen and Hugh Wiley out of the human race altogether." When I first encountered this sentiment, I had never heard of Wiley or Cohen, but I was fascinated by Williams's "of course," which indicates a consensus among African American intellectuals who were, as Williams puts it, paying attention to "the recent revival of interest in the Negro as a subject for writers of fiction."[57] Recognizing Wiley's ubiquity during the Harlem Renaissance deepens our contextual understanding of the era and reveals African Americans' efforts as literate consumers and producers of the printed word in a culture dominated by the endless commercial reproduction of predictable racial stereotype.

Octavus Roy Cohen, the subject of chapter 5, was—as this introduction has already intimated—the best-known *Post* author of Black dialect fiction and, among African Americans, the most disdained. Even more than Cobb and Wiley, Cohen's name is found everywhere in the literature and journalism of the era, particularly because of his (in)famous creation, a Black dandy named Florian Slappey. For most of his career, Cohen set his stories in and around Birmingham's "Darktown," which he populated with recurring characters, organizations, and businesses. Cohen came to the magazine with some experience in the film industry, and in 1924, six years after his first *Post* story, he began chronicling the misadventures of an all-Black film company called Midnight Motion Pictures. Cohen drew on his familiarity with making movies to register realistic details about the writing, financing, filming, and distribution of movies, while always, of course, demeaning and mocking his Black character's motivations and abilities. In 1926, Cohen sent his fictional film crew to Europe, and in chapter 5 I concentrate on this set of stories to discuss the global reach of U.S. segregationist culture. I counterpose Cohen's fiction with analyses by W. E. B. Du Bois, Locke, Hughes, and other Harlem Renaissance figures, who recognized the threat that Cohen's "humor" posed and who challenged the international reach of Jim Crow culture.

Finally, chapter 6 examines the last years of Lorimer's editorship, when his long-established practice of publishing material that registered and recontained African Americans began to loosen. The first glimmer of this change came just weeks after the release of the *Survey Graphic* special issue on Harlem, when Lorimer published "The World's Largest Negro City," a plagiarized condensation of Locke's collection. In 1925, this article by the journalist Chester T. Crowell stood alone at the *Post* in its appreciation of the Black modernity represented by Harlem because the magazine's approach to African Americans was absolutely dominated by the caricatures created by Cohen, Wiley, Cobb, and others like them. But beginning in 1929, the *Post* started publishing authors who tested the narrow limits of Lorimer's standard practices and expectations. Roark Bradford, Julia Peterkin, and "Colonel" Charles Givens placed Black dialect stories in the magazine, but with notable differences in tone and narrative structure. Their fiction is a far cry from the hateful writing of earlier *Post* contributors such as Dickson, offering more space for rounded Black characters than one finds in the caricatures produced by Cohen and others. Although these stories are not free from stereotypes and the condescension of white supremacy, they do allow for Black complexity and interiority in ways not seen in the *Post* since Dunbar's death. Perhaps most *Post* subscribers did not pay close attention to these subtle shifts, but at least one astute reader took note. In 1930, William Faulkner began a concerted effort to publish in the *Post*, and he ultimately succeeded, placing a total of twenty-one stories before and after Lorimer's retirement. In chapter 6, I discuss three of his contributions, "Red Leaves," "A Mountain Victory," and "A Bear Hunt," and explore how Faulkner's stories both critique and reify the white-supremacist assumptions nurtured by Lorimer during his editorial career. The chapter concludes with a look at the *Post*'s coverage of two Black athletes the magazine could not ignore or deny, Joe Louis and Jesse Owens. Unsurprisingly, these very famous African Americans were written about by white authors, and their successes were attributed, as much as possible, to their white trainers and handlers. Throughout his career, Lorimer would present African Americans only as objects to commodify, not as subjects with agency.

RESEARCHING A "NIAGARA OF PRINT": METHOD AND ACCESS

Leon Whipple was not hyperbolizing when he described the *Post* as a "Niagara of print," and the sheer volume of words and pages published during Lorimer's long career is nothing short of daunting for researchers. In 1919, the Curtis Publishing Company produced *One Issue*, a bound, promotional monograph version of the March 22 issue that was distributed to "Authorized Agents" of the magazine. In its original form, the eleven-by-fourteen-inch magazine number—with all its advertisements and illustrations—was 166 pages long, including the cover. In book form, with just a handful of the original illustrations and no ads at all, *One Issue* comes to 382 pages—the equivalent of a full-length novel. Between the issue of March 18, 1899, when Lorimer assumed editorial control of the magazine, and the issue of December 26, 1936, he oversaw the publication (with varying degrees of control) of approximately 1,864 numbers of the magazine. In the earliest years, the *Post* was just 16 pages; by the 1920s, depending on the health of the U.S. economy, the magazine could be between 150 and 200 pages long (sometimes even more). In other words, studying Lorimer's output is something akin to working with a thousand novels, which is no small feat for any scholar. A few words about method and access are therefore in order.

When I first started researching the *Saturday Evening Post* in 2007, the best and really only way to study the run of the magazine was on microfilm. However, because of the rise of digital technologies, microfilm and other analogue forms of storage were already falling into disuse. Complete collections of film were scattered and sometimes incomplete, and microfilm readers/printers—cranky tools in the best of times—were often outdated or in disrepair. Fortunately, Vassar College has maintained its microfilm collection and machinery, and during my 2013–2014 sabbatical year I spent countless hours in a fluorescent-lit basement room of the Thompson Library, scrolling through every reel of the *Post* from Curtis's initial purchase of the magazine in 1897 through Lorimer's final issue in 1936.[58]

Anyone who has worked extensively with microfilm can attest to the physical exhaustion and eye strain that develop after several hours staring at dim images as they roll up the screen, and I often felt torn between finding as much pertinent material as I could and getting through all the reels of film before my sabbatical (and eyesight) came to an end. Although I found copious material to work with—I examine only a fraction of it in this book—I was constantly pestered by the feeling that I *must* be missing any number of items worth considering.

But digital technology continues to improve, and ever more resources are becoming available and more accessible. HathiTrust, an extraordinary repository of digitized, searchable texts, came online in 2008, and, like other similar sites such as Google Books, the Internet Archive, and the Gutenberg Project, it provides digital access to material in the public domain. Hathi has much of the *Post* through 1926 (when copyright laws kicked in), so it is useful but incomplete. Also, although this site has a strong search engine, individual pages can load slowly; to view the *Post* in its entirety, I found it expedient to look first at the microfilm and then use Hathi to search for specific terms and phrases. To some extent, the ability to run digital searches assuaged the nagging feeling that I was missing important information—and I certainly did find online many items that I had unwittingly scrolled past in the basement of the Vassar library. An even more exciting development occurred ten years after the appearance of the Hathi site. In October 2018, the current owners of the *Post* (the nonprofit Saturday Evening Post Society, under the leadership of the publisher Joan Ser-Vaas) began providing digital access to all issues of the magazine going back to 1821. For a modest subscription, readers and scholars can easily flip through and search every page of every issue. In its current iteration as both a digital platform and a printed periodical, the *Post* is frequently a vehicle for uncomplicated nostalgia, and it rarely—if ever—recognizes its decades of complicity in promulgating racist ideologies and advocating for white-supremacist policies and culture. Nonetheless, I am entirely grateful for the introduction of this important digital resource and hope the online *Saturday Evening Post* will spawn many more studies in the years to come.

If the Jim Crow regime was a race war waged against African Americans to support white supremacy, then George Horace Lorimer held a high position in its propaganda ministry, and the *Saturday Evening Post* was one of its most influential house organs. This metaphor may feel like a stretch, but recall that in Lucius C. Harper's response to the publication of Lorimer's whites-only will, he described the editor as "An Enemy . . . the Fascist of literature, so far as our Race was concerned." As this book shows, Harper articulated an animosity toward Lorimer that cropped up regularly during the Harlem Renaissance because the *Post* was an important element of that era's print culture and a sustaining force for anti-Black racism. With the subtitle of this book, especially *"the War Against Black Modernity,"* I want to underscore Lorimer's intentionally hostile actions against his fellow citizens; as Harper asserted, Lorimer consciously took up his pen to undermine African Americans' achievements and aspirations. In *Notes of a Native Son* (1955), James Baldwin writes, "In the context of the Negro problem neither whites nor blacks, for excellent reasons of their own, have the faintest desire to look back; but I think that the past is all that makes the present coherent, and further, that the past will remain horrible for exactly as long as we refuse to assess it honestly."[59] I doubt this book can make the past any less horrible because the inequality the magazine normalized and the violence it covered with a smirk were very real and claimed so many victims. But what this book can do, I hope, is honor some of the ways Black authors of the period fought back against the inimical machinery of commodified racial caricature, an industry that was embodied by George Horace Lorimer's editing of the *Saturday Evening Post.*

A NOTE ON PERMISSIONS AND NOSTALGIA

There are no images from the *Saturday Evening Post* in this book, and there really should be. As I noted earlier, the current publishers of the *Post* are invested in the profitably of the magazine's nostalgic image. Although today's *Post* often takes on difficult issues from the past, including various aspects of the Jim Crow era, it rarely, if ever, acknowledges the magazine's long history of promulgating racist ideologies and xenophobic legislation or its complicity in propping up the American segregationist regime. When I sought permission to include images from the *Post,* I was forthright in explaining that this book would shine an unflattering light on Lorimer and his magazine, and so my request was flatly rejected. This denial was almost certainly a consequence of the Saturday Evening Post Society's desire to protect and maintain the magazine's aura—past and present—as a "Rockwellian slice of pure Americana," as David Earle succinctly puts it.

But as recent events reveal yet again, nostalgia is not neutral. In 2023, the cozily unethical and possibly illegal relationship between the conservative billionaire Harlan Crow and the insurrection-curious Supreme Court justice Clarence Thomas came to light. The revelations that developed as journalists investigated the potential criminality of these two powerful men included reports of Crow's collection of Nazi memorabilia, his garden of twentieth-century dictator statues, and a room with a startling trio of paintings: "something done by George W. Bush next to a Norman Rockwell next to one by Hitler." With this decorative triptych, Crow appears implicitly to recognize a link between political violence and the yearning for a mythically simpler and more homogenous past. The association between Rockwell-inspired nostalgia and ultraconservativism is further underscored by the painting the billionaire commissioned of himself, Thomas, and a few chums gathered in the Adirondacks beneath a kitschy statue of a Native American, in which the cigar-smoking justice holds forth to the other men. The painting was produced by Sharif Tarabay, who lists Rockwell as one of his most important influences; many of the images on the artist's website could easily serve as covers for the *Saturday Evening Post*.[60]

This political tidbit may be ruefully amusing on its own because Thomas and his secret benefactor were caught with their khaki pants down, but it is also a pointed reminder of the deep connections between nostalgia and ongoing efforts to curtail the freedom of American citizens. In his concurring opinion to the *Dobbs* decision in 2022, which took away American citizens' rights to abortion specifically and to bodily autonomy more generally, Thomas also suggests that the Supreme Court "should reconsider all of this Court's substantive due process precedents, including *Griswold, Lawrence,* and *Obergerfell*"—that is, the rights to contraception, consensual sexual activity, and same-sex marriage.[61] It is not hard to imagine Thomas outlining his plans to take away such rights and more as he lectures to Crow and company in Tarabay's Rockwellian phantasia—and it is also not too difficult to imagine that painting on the cover of today's *Saturday Evening Post*.

Perhaps the current owners of the *Post* will someday come to a full reckoning of the magazine's past, warts and all, but that time is apparently not yet here.

Chapter One

GEORGE HORACE LORIMER
AND RISING JIM CROW

George Horace Lorimer, who made the *Saturday Evening Post* one of the most widely read and influential magazines in U.S. history, was a lifelong white supremacist who always enjoyed a good chuckle at the expense of the victims of Jim Crow. From the earliest days of his nearly four-decade editorship, Lorimer published a steady stream of material reinforcing an ideology of African American inferiority that would cease only when he retired from the magazine in 1936 and died shortly thereafter. In the popular imagination, the *Post* is probably best remembered for its cheery, often nostalgic Norman Rockwell covers portraying American culture as quaint, wholesome, and idyllic, but between those covers—while Lorimer was editor, at least—lurked a more troubling reality. A lifelong advocate for white superiority and racial purity, Lorimer filled his magazine with material that deployed paternalistic condescension and demeaning humor against African Americans.

In the earliest years of Lorimer's editorship, however, the *Post* demonstrated a noticeable, if minimal, openness to African American self-determination and self-expression, and Lorimer invested his magazine's racial "tolerance" especially in two figures, Booker T. Washington and Paul Laurence Dunbar. In terms of self-expression, Dunbar was one of only a small handful of Black writers printed in the *Post*, and he was by far its most often published Black author. In Dunbar's contributions, we find the most sustained, albeit subtle, challenges to the assumptions of white-supremacist ideology that otherwise informed the *Post*. Washington's presence in the magazine was quite different. Although nothing with his byline ever appeared in its pages, Washington was held up regularly as an exemplary self-made man, and his accommodationist politics made him an acceptable Black leader who posed little threat to the established racial order. In conjunction with the rising ascendancy of Jim Crow ideology across the United States, however, Washington's reputation began to tarnish, and in the *Post* he was steadily transformed from an optimistic symbol of racial progress into the embodiment of intractable Black inferiority, and he was ultimately held up to readers as the greatest example of why segregation was necessary. By tracing Washington's representational arc during the first ten years of Lorimer's tenure, we can see how the magazine reflected the national movement toward increasing levels of segregation and racist hostility at the turn of the twentieth century. Focusing on Washington's trajectory, we also witness how Lorimer's early, tepid willingness to entertain multiple and sometimes contradictory representations of African Americans finally hardened into his career-long practice of registering and recontaining Black modernity through the regular publication of "humorous" black dialect fiction.

"LORIMER IS THE *POST* AND THE *POST* IS LORIMER"

My claims about Lorimer's control over the *Post*'s treatment of African Americans are based on repeated characterizations by both his contemporaries and subsequent scholars that he was the magazine's "dictator," an idea I address after a quick biographical sketch. Lorimer was born in Louisville in 1867. His father, George Claude Lorimer, was a Scottish immigrant who became a famous Baptist preacher. George Horace grew up in Chicago and Boston, and in 1888 he enrolled at Yale. Just before he would begin his sophomore year, Lorimer had a chance encounter with the meatpacker P. D. Armour, who was in his father's congregation. Armour convinced Lorimer to leave college and work for him in Chicago, where Lorimer started in the mail room and rose steadily until he became a well-paid department head. One key to his success was his ardent opposition to organized labor, a sentiment he would harbor throughout his life. Lorimer married Alma

Ennis in 1892 and left Armour in 1896. After an unsuccessful attempt at starting his own business, Lorimer and Alma moved to New England, where he worked as a newspaper reporter in Boston and attended Colby College in Maine for a year to study English and history.

In 1897, Lorimer learned that Cyrus H. K. Curtis, the immensely successful publisher of the *Ladies' Home Journal,* had recently purchased the moribund and nearly defunct *Saturday Evening Post,* a magazine that had existed in some form since 1821. (To burnish his new acquisition's history, Curtis made the false claim that the *Post* descended from Benjamin Franklin's *Pennsylvania Gazette,* a misrepresentation that was enshrined as fact once Franklin's bust became a permanent feature of the magazine's editorial page.) Lorimer immediately contacted Curtis and was soon hired as the magazine's literary editor. In 1897, the *Post* had a tiny circulation and little advertising revenue, and it was not financially viable, but Curtis was determined to create another powerhouse of American print culture. After some initial but unsuccessful efforts to find the right editor for his new acquisition, Curtis recognized Lorimer's drive and potential and promoted the thirty-one-year-old in March 1899; Lorimer's name first appeared on the masthead as editor on June 10, 1899.[1]

Once Lorimer took charge, he made the magazine in his image; as Jan Cohn notes, Lorimer always had "a remarkably clear sense of his audience and purpose," and "nothing—not a story or a piece of filler—appeared in the pages of the *Post* that he had not read or approved." As a general rule, one might assume a certain amount of distance between editors and the content they publish, but this was almost never the case for Lorimer's *Post,* which was most often a fairly direct reflection of his thoughts and attitudes. "Lorimer had some very definite ideas about the subjects he wanted the *Post* to address and about how those subjects should be presented. . . . Before too long, Lorimer would have a staff of writers intimately associated with the *Post* who became its collective voice."[2] John Tebbel puts it succinctly when he writes, "Lorimer is the *Post* and the *Post* is Lorimer."[3] If ever there was an editor who "wrote" through others' hands, that editor was George Horace Lorimer. Although control over the *Saturday Evening Post* was absolute from Lorimer's earliest days as editor, it took about a decade for him to shape the magazine to his satisfaction. According to the Curtis pamphlet *A Short History of the* Saturday Evening Post (1936), Lorimer's magazine "may be said to have roughed out its permanent character for the first time about 1909. Before that it had been another magazine."[4] Indeed, there was more give-and-take before 1909, more room for difference and disagreement. According to Cohn, "In the early years, the *Post* had taken on debate, used its pages for forums, fought to bring new values into play and prominence."[5]

Like the magazine's evolution as a whole, its approach toward African Americans began as a heterogeneous collection of voices and positions before hardening into the consistently anti-Black practice that would characterize the *Post* for the bulk of Lorimer's tenure. As Black modernity developed, the *Post* rose to meet it with an unshakable ideology of African American inferiority and servility. In this way, Lorimer, who liked to think of himself as an average American, both mirrored and helped to create the legal and cultural segregation of the post–*Plessy v. Ferguson* era. Indeed, Lorimer's editorship began at a crucial historical juncture: when the United States became an imperial power by claiming the necessity of the White Man's Burden; when Senator Albert Beveridge—Lorimer's close friend and a regular contributor to the *Post*—was advocating for Anglo-Saxon superiority; and when the American press more generally was capitulating to and endorsing the seeming inevitability and historical universality of domestic and global white supremacy. In his seminal analysis *The Strange Career of Jim Crow* (1957), C. Vann Woodward writes, "At the dawn of the new century the wave of Southern racism came as a swell upon a mounting tide of national sentiment and was a very much a part of that sentiment."[6] Lorimer's magazine, as Leon Whipple indicated with the title of his essay "SatEve-Post: Mirror of These States" in 1926, was a near perfect reflection of the moods and tendencies of the vast middle of American life, politics, and culture. But Lorimer did more than merely reflect the racism of his times; he helped produce and promulgate it. As Woodward demonstrates throughout *Strange Career*, Jim Crow expanded nationally through the conscious efforts of powerful figures such as Lorimer, who naturalized anti-Black racism and made inequity seem natural.

From the start, the *Post* editor printed a steady stream of white-authored dialect fiction and poetry that romanticized the antebellum South, fetishized faithful "servants" and their indulgent masters, and used humor to demean the intelligence and character of African Americans. The most prominent examples of this type of writing in the pages of the *Post* include the Uncle Remus poems and Civil War fiction of Joel Chandler Harris as well as the dialect poetry of Frank L. Stanton, both of whom were already well established when their work appeared in the magazine. This material is uniformly nostalgic for the phantasmagorical glories of the Old South and resonates with ideological narratives of the Lost Cause and Redemption.

In contrast to the overwhelming preponderance of white writers in his pages, Lorimer printed almost no African American authors during his editorship, and virtually all the Black writers he did publish can be found in the issues produced during his first ten years as editor. Well before the advent of the Harlem Renaissance, Lorimer consolidated a stereotypical approach to African Americans that would persist in the magazine without much variation for decades. Early on, Lorimer supported Booker T. Washington's efforts to pursue uplift through acquiescence to the "separate but equal" practices of Jim Crow America, and he published a small number of Black writers who by and large also endorsed Washington, although they also sometimes challenged the *Post*'s readers to consider the effects of white racism. The most significant of these African American contributors was Paul Laurence Dunbar. Over a few short years, however, as Jim Crow deepened and spread, as its advocates became increasingly vocal, and as Black leaders such as W. E. B. Du Bois became more resistant to white supremacy, Lorimer appears to have largely soured on all efforts for racial justice, and his magazine became a vehicle for inequality and an advocate for disempowerment and disenfranchisement. By 1909, he had firmly embraced a policy of publishing deeply racist material that castigated all Black leadership and portrayed African Americans as inferior in every sense.

This chapter sketches out Lorimer's first two decades as editor and illustrates how he evolved into an intransigent spokesman for white supremacy and the permanent subordination and humiliation of African Americans. The chapter moves through three pairs of authors, beginning with an examination of Washington's status and Dunbar's muted interventions. Next, works by two white authors, Joel Chandler Harris and Rebecca Harding Davis, exemplify both the height and the limits of Washington's reputation. The chapter concludes with Thomas Dixon Jr. and Harris Dickson, two professional racists whose *Post* contributions marked the end of Washington's acceptability and the beginning of the magazine's unalloyed disdain of African Americans. In the August 1897 issue of the *Atlantic Monthly*, W. E. B. Du Bois described his dawning awareness of the cruel realities of Jim Crow

America when he was still a child: "The 'shades of the prison-house' closed round about us all: walls strait and stubborn to the whitest, but relentlessly narrow, tall, and unscalable to sons of night who must plod darkly against the stone, or steadily, half hopelessly watch the streak of blue above."[7] If Lorimer wrote with others' hands, he also just as surely used the hands of his writers to build the walls that hemmed in Du Bois and millions of other American citizens.

BOOKER T. WASHINGTON AND THE LIMITS OF ACCEPTABILITY

In Lorimer's early years at the *Post*, Booker T. Washington and Paul Laurence Dunbar served as the magazine's two exemplary African Americans. An important difference between the two is that Dunbar wrote *for* the magazine, whereas Washington was instead written *about* and for a few years served symbolically as the principal figure of acceptable Black behavior in the *Post*. Lorimer favored Washington because he appeared to pose little threat to the racial order and because he embodied Lorimer's ideal of the self-made man. Although not a particularly vocal supporter of the Tuskegean, Lorimer allowed for a small but steady stream of items that burnished Washington's image and supported his stature as the principal race leader of Black America. As segregationist practices and ideology continued to rise at the turn of the century, however, the *Post* became a reliable medium for racial hostility, and Washington's reputation devolved from a hero whom African Americans should emulate into a conniving Trojan Horse of racial equality whom white people should fear and shun. Washington's evolving status in the *Post* mirrors the magazine's intensifying endorsement of Jim Crow ideology and its steady march toward its predictable patterns of anti-Black representation.

One of the earliest mentions of Washington is in "Men and Women of the Hour," a recurrent feature that provided commentary and photographs of people in the news. The specific item " 'Uncle Booker' and His People" (February 24, 1900) began by praising the "latest photographs of Booker T. Washington" because the images "reveal more plainly than ever the characteristics which have endeared Mr. Washington to the men and women of his race." Surprisingly, however, the feature did not include a photo of Washington. Instead, the brief item painted an unmistakable word picture of Washington as simultaneously laudable and unthreateningly comic.

Characterized as an effective educator who had endeared himself to his fellow African Americans, Washington was "Uncle Booker" to his people—a great leader but also the faithful servant to white people.[8] Calling Washington "uncle" resonated with the images of Black servility that began to appear with increasing frequency in the *Post*, perhaps most notably in the Cream of Wheat ads that started running regularly in 1899.

Washington's star rose farther in the *Post* after the publication of his autobiography, *Up from Slavery*, in 1901. In another regular feature, "Literary Folk—Their Ways and Their Work," contributing author Lindsay Swift's review "A Remarkable Autobiography" favorably compared Washington's book with Franklin's *Autobiography*, which was high praise from the magazine that inaccurately claimed Franklin as its founder. Repeatedly emphasizing Washington's humility and praising his "easy and natural humor," Swift placed *Up from Slavery* "on the same shelf where stand the few, the very few, great revelations of human experience," and he declared, "Such a book, like its famous predecessor, should be a necessary and strengthening part of the moral armor of every American child." A year later, in the *Post* article "The Leader of His Race" Dunbar similarly highlighted the "childlike simplicity of [Washington's] nature, and the utter lack of self-consciousness in his manner."[9] Early in Lorimer's tenure, before the magazine assumed its stability as an organ of white supremacy, Booker T. Washington was an acceptable Black leader in the *Post*—and to white America in general—because he did not threaten the post-Reconstruction racial hierarchy.

The tiny handful of Black writers Lorimer published in his first years as editor generally supported Washington's accommodationism, but they were also able to interject at least some sense of African American humanity in their writing and to challenge white racism, approaches that were otherwise largely absent in the magazine. For example, the issue for January 20, 1900, included Charles W. Chesnutt's book review of Washington's *The Future of the American Negro* (1899). The review began by characterizing Washington as "the prophet of the practical" but then dryly noted that Washington, being "a diplomatist as well as a philosopher[,] . . . does not dwell unduly upon race prejudice, which is the most obvious and to some minds the most serious feature of the negro problem."[10] With this small jab, Chesnutt reminded white *Post* readers that their own racism was no small part of the so-called negro problem. Five years later, Lorimer published

William H. Holtzclaw's "The Black Man's Burden: A Battle with Ignorance and Poverty, and How One Negro Won it" (April 22, 1905). Holtzclaw was the founder of a "little Tuskegee," the Utica Normal and Industrial Institute for the Training of Colored Young Men and Women in Mississippi.[11] As one might expect in the *Post*, Holtzclaw's memoir extolled the virtues of hard work and persistence valued by both Lorimer and Washington but did little to directly challenge the inequities of Jim Crow. Nonetheless, Holtzclaw portrayed loving Black families headed by thrifty, conscientious parents who were determined to educate and impart strong moral values to their children, and he reminded *Post* readers that the hardships he experienced could be attributed to the social injustices of the sharecropping system, the political failure of Reconstruction, and the extralegal violence of the "Kuklux Klan [sic]"—reminders of white racism that readers would otherwise rarely encounter in the *Post*.[12] Like Chesnutt, Holtzclaw ultimately supported Washington's accommodationism, which appealed to Lorimer's paternalistic racism, but he also gave muted voice to the idea that white supremacy posed an existential threat to African Americans and that white people were responsible for that threat. Again, however, these small notes of resistance were barely perceptible in the increasing white supremacy of the *Post*, and the contributions by Chesnutt and Holtzclaw were miniscule in number relative to all the publications in the magazine as a whole.

More significantly, with respect to Washington's symbolism during Lorimer's early years as editor, the magazine seemed to give tacit approval to the White House dinner President Theodore Roosevelt hosted for Washington on October 16, 1901. As Deborah Davis notes, after news of the meal got out, "all hell broke loose" in the U.S. press, particularly in the South, where "indignant Southerners couldn't stop talking about TR's great affront to their sensibilities."[13] The *Memphis Scimitar* exemplifies the unapologetic white-supremacist hysteria that ensued: "The most damnable outrage which has ever been perpetuated by any citizen of the United States was committed yesterday by the President when he invited a nigger to dine with him at the White House."[14] Before long, a scurrilous poem entitled "Niggers in the White House (Six Months Hence, Probably)" circulated widely in southern newspapers. The poem, which first ran in the *Sedalia (Missouri) Scimitar*, imagines the White House overrun by African Americans, one of whom marries Roosevelt's daughter, and it ends with this ominous prediction:

But everything is settled,
Roosevelt is dead;
Niggers in the White House
Out of Teddy's head.[15]

According to Clarence Lusane, the Washington–Roosevelt meal unleashed "a racist backlash that shut down black access to the White House for decades to follow."[16]

Although other national magazines offered more overt support for Roosevelt's decision to host Washington,[17] the *Post*'s initial, subdued response to the dinner seems almost enlightened by comparison to the racist fulminations found in the southern press. Three items appeared in the issue of December 14, 1901, that perhaps offered a tacit challenge to the rabid sentiments of other publications. The first, an editorial most likely written within a week or so of the dinner, praised Roosevelt's challenge to entrenched political interests and concluded, "The country, the decent end of the country, the part of the country that wants to see a clean, honest administration of its affairs by able, honest men, is with Mr. Roosevelt. . . . It is a pleasure to know you better, Mr. President."[18] Considered on its own, this editorial would not seem to be a reproof to the backlash against Washington's invitation to the White House, but the same issue of the *Post* also contained a recurring, highly adulatory advertisement for *Up from Slavery* as well as Paul Laurence Dunbar's substantial essay "Negro Society in Washington," which provided a detailed and laudatory portrait of the District of Columbia's Talented Tenth.[19] In a subsequent editorial, "The Record of a Notable Year," Lorimer included the information, without comment, that "Booker T. Washington dined with the President."[20] Unlike many other periodicals, perhaps especially southern newspapers, the *Post* did not denounce the president for sharing a meal with a Black man.

PAUL LAURENCE DUNBAR
AND THE LIMITS OF BLACK EXPRESSION

Mentions of Booker T. Washington in the *Post* were sparse but generally positive during the first years of Lorimer's editorship, but the arc of his treatment serves as a barometer for the magazine's steadily increasing embrace of "Jim Crow's caustic ascendency."[21] By 1905, Washington's position as a laudable self-made man would erode into a far more sinister symbol of absolute racial difference and inferiority, which I discuss in more detail later in this chapter. Paul Laurence Dunbar, the *only* African American author Lorimer ever published with any regularity or frequency, occupied a different position in the magazine. Like Washington, Dunbar did not directly challenge Lorimer's sense of white superiority, but like Chesnutt and Holtzclaw—and to a much greater and more sustained degree than any other Black writer in the *Post*—Dunbar was also able to contest the practice of Black dehumanization found everywhere else in the magazine. The publication of Dunbar's essay "Negro Society in Washington" in the immediate aftermath of the Washington–Roosevelt dinner can be read as a sign of Lorimer's continued, if lukewarm, support for Washington's nonthreatening accommodationism. Considered as a whole, Dunbar's contributions to the *Post* offered the only serious challenge to the Jim Crow logic being solidified in the pages of a magazine that was steadily becoming a dominant force in U.S. print culture.

"Negro Society in Washington" epitomizes Dunbar's manipulation of audience expectations in the *Post*, where he had been appearing regularly since 1898. By 1901, white America had produced and consumed decades—if not centuries—of caricatures portraying African Americans as indolent and pleasure seeking, and these forms of representation were only intensifying in the post-Reconstruction and Redemption era. Writing about Booker T. Washington's uphill struggle against popular white supremacy, Robert Norrell notes that "newspapers and popular magazines . . . reinforced pessimism about the Negro Problem with illustrations and humor that demeaned black character. *Harpers Weekly*, the *Atlantic Monthly*, and *Century* ran short stories, poetry, and cartoons that depicted Blacks speaking outlandishly, acting crudely, and looking grotesque . . . and regularly described them as savage, uncouth, bestial-looking, dishonest, and idle. . . . Popular culture in the 1890s reinforced the antiblack propaganda. . . . Coon imagery was everywhere."[22]

In the early days of his editorship, Lorimer more frequently ran material emphasizing Black servility and comic inferiority rather than images of dangerous brutality (although the stereotype of the Black brute could certainly be found in the pages of the magazine, and this trope did play an important role when the *Post* turned away from Washington). Dunbar set mass-manufactured "humorous" stereotypes on their head by beginning

"Negro Society in Washington" with the suggestion that most white people thought of African Americans not as comic fodder but as overly staid and thoughtful: "It seems to be the commonly accepted belief . . . that the colored people of this country [have] since emancipation . . . gone around being busy and looking serious." But, he informed his readers, "any one who believes that all of our time is taken up with dealing with knotty problems, or forever bearing around heavy missions, is doomed to disappointment." As a regular contributor to the *Post*, Dunbar must have been well aware that the predominant representation of African Americans was in terms of humor and condescension and that the magazine's readers were not often—if ever—presented with examples of Black seriousness or intellection. Dunbar instead drew readers' attention to a thriving African American middle class, and he maneuvered them to see through the more sympathetic lens of a shared sense of class identity rather than through the distorting lens of stereotype. But Dunbar also placated white readers' fear of social equality by informing them that Black society in DC "is satisfied with its own condition, and . . . is not asking for social intercourse with whites," thereby assuring these readers that they would not need to host their own interracial dinners anytime soon. Treading a delicate line between accommodation and self-assertion, Dunbar claimed that African Americans could "no longer be laughed at or caricatured under the name 'Colored Sassiety'" because the "term is still funny, but has now lost its pertinence."[23]

Dunbar recognized and to a certain extent embraced or allowed for the conventions of dialect and minstrelsy that dominated American culture, but he did so to compel recognition of Black achievement and refinement as well as the inherent falsity of caricature. Most of "Negro Society in Washington" described Black social pleasures rarely seen by "uninitiated" white people, whose imaginations were shaped by "the comic papers and cartoonists." Dunbar also gently reminded these readers, whom he implicitly recognized as fellow middle-class Americans, that the white working classes, just like their Black counterparts, enjoyed the less refined pleasures of "butchers' picnics and Red Men's dances." In other words, the same socioeconomic divisions and behaviors found in American society as a whole could also be found in Black Washington, and Dunbar urged readers of the *Post*, "View us at any time, but make sure you view the right sort."[24] This assertion relied on class-based snobbery, certainly, but Dunbar also emphasized the heterogeneity of African American life that was rarely presented in the *Saturday Evening Post*. "Negro Society in Washington," coming directly in the wake of the Roosevelt–Washington dinner and its fallout in the press, was arguably one of Lorimer's more enlightened publishing choices in his four decades as editor.

Lorimer was in fact very fond of Dunbar's work, which was occasionally subversive in the pages of the *Post* while also often capitulating to Lorimer's appetite for demeaning caricatures. Dunbar was already a widely recognized author when he came to the magazine, and between 1898 and 1906 Lorimer published more than forty pieces of his fiction, poetry, and journalism. Dunbar was clearly one of Lorimer's favored and most frequently published authors during his first years as editor. A brief, unsigned entry entitled "Paul Dunbar's Gifted Wife" underscored Lorimer's high estimation by praising Alice Nelson Dunbar for her work and naming her husband "the foremost writer of his race." Likewise, Dunbar's appreciation for Lorimer was also unmistakable; many of the short stories he published in the *Post* were collected into *In Old Plantation Days* (1903), which is dedicated "To GEORGE HORACE LORIMER Out of whose suggestion these stories were born, and by whose kindness they first saw light."[25] Dunbar's dedication highlights an idea that informs my book as a whole—namely, that Lorimer actively cultivated authors who could provide him with the Black dialect fiction that he would publish throughout his career. Many years after Dunbar's death, Lorimer defended himself against charges of racism from W. E. B. Du Bois by pointing toward his earlier publication of Dunbar—essentially claiming he had a Black friend and therefore could not possibly be racist.[26]

As Lillian S. Robinson and Greg Robinson document in "Paul Laurence Dunbar: A Credit to His Race?" (2007), Dunbar's complicity with or subversion of the production of racial stereotype is an ongoing and unsettled critical debate.[27] According to Peter Revell, for example, the fiction Dunbar provided to Lorimer represents the writer's "most nearly total concession to the stereotyping and obligatory distortion of reality that the [Negro dialect story] imposed. . . . These stories are essentially light fiction written to provide undemanding entertainment for a white audience."[28] Revell's characterization of Dunbar's *Post* stories as complicit with anti-Black racism is incontrovertible, and it resonates with the suggestion in Dunbar's dedication that he was providing the material Lorimer expected, but

Dunbar was also virtually the only author in the magazine—Black or white—to construct African American characters with anything even approaching full humanity. Gene Andrew Jarrett and Thomas Lewis Morgan's introduction to *The Complete Stories of Paul Laurence Dunbar* (1998) offers a more accurate estimation of Dunbar's short fiction, and their insights are applicable to Dunbar's contributions to the *Post*. His short stories, they write, are "where his most serious political interventions occur. . . . In general, Dunbar complicates the simplistic caricatures of African Americans at the turn of the century, revealing the nuances of racial identity and reflecting the elaborate and provocative structure of America's racial landscape."[29] Dunbar's work in the *Post* reveals that he simultaneously fed Lorimer's appetite for plantation nostalgia while also challenging the editor's stereotypical and generic expectations. Whether Lorimer and his primarily white audience actually perceived Dunbar's subversion or not remains an open question,[30] but Dunbar's assertion of Black humanity can be read plainly in the pages of the magazine. His sotto voce challenge of white-supremacist literary conventions and ideological expectations can be found throughout his poetry and prose in the magazine. The short story "Mr. Groby's Slippery Gift" and two poems, "When Sam'l Sings" and "Two Little Boots," exemplify his quiet subversion.

"Mr. Groby's Slippery Gift" (June 24, 1899) typifies Dunbar's manipulation of plantation narrative nostalgia. On one hand, the story offers typical generic tropes such as the kindhearted master and the lazy Black man, but it also concludes by portraying family love and mutual support among its African American characters—and this is a distinct difference from the usual fare of African American venality that white authors in the *Post* would produce for decades. In "Mr. Groby's Slippery Gift," two brothers, Jim and Joe, are enslaved to Stuart Mordaunt. Whereas Jim is notable for his religious fervor and strong work ethic, "a lazier, more unreliable scamp than Joe could not have been found within a radius of fifty miles." In other words, Dunbar's character Jim conforms to the generic conventions of the faithful servant, while Joe comports with images of lazy shiftlessness. Mordaunt, the generically compassionate master, is contrasted with the unsympathetic overseer, Mr. Groby, who suggests that the recalcitrant Joe can be managed properly by starving him into submission and compliance. Mordaunt is repelled by this suggestion, and he resents Groby's stereotypical characterization of the "good" brother Jim as not having "sense enough to be corrupted as long as he gets his feed."[31] In other words, the master's rejection of the overseer's plainly stated racism underscores Mordaunt's more palatable beneficence and paternalism. In this *Saturday Evening Post* story, Jim, Joe, and Mordaunt serve collectively as a synecdoche for the organically harmonious Old South fetishized regularly by Lorimer's white authors.

Because of his kindness and his unwillingness to punish slaves, Mordaunt wishes aloud that the unreliable Joe would run away, and the financially unstable Groby jumps at this chance to buy a slave of his own. Mordaunt, the enlightened patriarch, prides himself on never selling his slaves, but he does agree to give Joe to Groby free of charge. When Joe learns of this transaction, he begs piteously to remain with Mordaunt and runs away when his pleas are denied. Joe's escape appears to have immediate, deleterious effects on his brother; before long, the once trustworthy Jim is repeatedly caught stealing food until, finally, Mordaunt has him tied up and whipped. But after the first blows land on Jim's back, Joe emerges "from nowhere" and demands to be whipped instead. "I was comin' to gi' myse'f up anyhow. He done it all to keep me from sta'vin; but I's done hidin' now. I'll be dat Groby's slave ravver dan let [Jim] tek my blows." Jim responds to his brother "in disgust[,] . . .'you's done come hyeah an' sp'iled evaht'ing; you nevah did know yo' place.'"[32] Jim steals food so his brother will not starve, and Joe would rather be whipped and returned to the intolerable Groby than see his brother suffer. Through these actions and statements, Dunbar illustrates the impossible cruelty of slavery; the brothers must choose among physical well-being, freedom, and love—and they choose love. Dunbar also turns the idea of knowing one's "place" on its head by implying that Jim's obligation is loyalty to his family, not subservience to his master. These acts of Black love, family feeling, and self-sacrifice were otherwise absent in the *Post* for almost forty years—not just in the 1890s but throughout Lorimer's tenure. Dunbar's ability within this context to establish the humanity of his characters is therefore notable. "Mr. Groby's Slippery Gift" concludes happily with the reunion of the two brothers, with Joe's return to Mordaunt's plantation, and with the master demonstrating greater concern for his Black slaves than for his white overseer. Over the years, as Lorimer's *Post* settled more and more into its formulaic treatment of flat Black characters devoid of full emotional complexity, the white master would continue most often to be represented as a benevolent patriarch. But the idea that African

American characters would be motivated by mutual affection rather than by self-interest, pettiness, or a doglike faithfulness to their masters would rarely, if ever, find a space in the pages of the magazine after Dunbar's early death.

The poetry Dunbar published in the *Post* embodies a similar strategy of capitulation and resistance, and, like "Mr. Groby's Slippery Gift," his poems limn the tension between the dehumanizing cruelty of slavery and the resilient humanity of the enslaved. Although many of Dunbar's poems do little to dispel racial stereotyping, some of them do challenge the flattened representations of African Americans' emotional and intellectual life that otherwise dominated the magazine's history. For example, in Lorimer's first year as editor, he published Dunbar's "When Sam'l Sings," a dialect poem that reminds readers of the effort and love it took to keep Black families together under slavery. The speaker, a fellow slave on the same plantation, notes that Sam'l is singing joyfully despite their hard work in the fields and that the reason for his happiness is " 'ca'se he been to see his wife," who lives on another plantation, twenty miles away. When Sam'l leaves, he dresses

> hisse'f in all he had,
> Tuk a cane an' went a-strollin'
> Lookin' mighty pleased and glad.[33]

In these lines, Dunbar recycles the stereotypical image of the foppish, self-important Black dandy, but the implication is, instead, that Sam'l is trying his best to make himself as presentable for his wife as the impoverishment of slavery will allow; his attire underscores his love and is not evidence of excessive self-regard or childish egomania. Sam'l is always happy when he returns because even though walking such a distance "allus ain' de nices," he must seek permission from his master to see his own wife, and he does not always "git de chanst to go." Dunbar thus implies that slave families were never secure and always prone to the vagaries of their masters, who could sell a relative or spouse whenever the mood or need arose (as we see in "Mr. Groby's Slippery Gift"). Having expounded on the reason for Sam'l's temporary happiness, the speaker confesses his temporary jealousy because he shares the same plight; like Sam'l', his own wife is enslaved on a distant plantation, and he can see her only when their master grants him permission for a brief visit:

48

But I know dis comin' Sad'day
Dey'll be brighter days in life;
An' I'll be ez glad ez Sam'l
W'en I go to see my wife.[34]

The poignancy of this final stanza is unmistakable. The speaker is annoyed by Sam'l's exuberance, but his ill feelings are motivated by his own sense of loss and separation. The speaker is in fact happy for Sam'l—and miserable about their shared condition of powerlessness. Dunbar's indictment of slavery is evident in "When Sam'l Sings," but he couched his condemnation in the only form Lorimer was willing to accept: the language and images of minstrelsy. The effectiveness of Dunbar's gentle but pointed subversion of generic expectation can be further gauged by the fact that "When Sam'l Sings" was promptly reprinted in numerous newspapers across the country after appearing in the *Post*.

Dunbar's insistence on the humanity of his subjects despite the demeaning formulae of caricature is further exemplified by "Two Little Boots," which Lorimer published two years after "When Sam'l Sings." The poem begins with a mother contemplating her son's worn-out baby shoes, and she recalls how playful he was as he "tromped de livelong day, / Laffin' in his happy way." The mother thinks about how proud her growing son was as he explored the world and tested its limits with his "many, baby stride." The last two stanzas of this lyric, six-stanza poem take a turn, however, when the mother thinks that the boots "don' seem so gay . . . Since yo' ownah went erway."[35] At this point, the reader might infer that this mother is thinking about a child who has grown and left his home—or, worse, a slave child who has been sold away from his mother. But the final stanza reveals instead that the child has died, and his boots are all the grieving mother now has. The reader cannot help but grieve with her over this tragic loss. In the *Post*, Dunbar's poem frames an illustration of a Black mammy figure that projects certain stereotypical elements of this stock character, but the illustration is also filled with details that create the portrait of an individual with interiority; her face is drawn with sympathy rather than scorn, and the items on her dresser point toward a rich emotional life. Dunbar's collection *Lyrics of Love and Laughter*, published in 1903, deploys similar paratextual clues. "Two Little Boots" is the first poem in the collection, and the frontispiece is a photograph of a young Black child that invites interpretation as the dead son of the poem's grieving mother.

With only a few exceptions, Dunbar's work, which Lorimer published in his first decade as editor, represents the most complex and sympathetic depictions of African Americans ever published in the *Post*. Jay Martin and Gossie H. Hudson characterize Dunbar as "the first black writer to counterbalance American race prejudice with receptivity to the strengths of the black community";[36] works such as "Mr. Groby's Slippery Gift," "When Sam'l Sings," and "Little Two Boots"—when considered within Lorimer's long tenure at the *Post*—certainly bear out this judgment. As Gavin Jones notes in *Strange Talk*, "Dunbar was a wily manipulator of literary conventions, a subtle overturner of racial stereotypes, and a sensitive recorder of the multiple facets of black consciousness at the turn of the twentieth century."[37] All of this was no small feat in the pages of a magazine that was increasingly unsympathetic toward African Americans as Jim Crow continued its steady rise.

Dunbar and Washington occupied a similarly impossible position in the *Post*, but whereas Dunbar was given some space for his own voice, Washington was always only the object of others' writing. He was a voiceless but still potent symbol of acceptable Black behavior and politics. When Washington shared a stage with former president Grover Cleveland in December 1902, Lorimer used the event to extol the virtues of the self-made man. Notably, however, Lorimer named neither Cleveland nor Washington in his editorial:

Probably no stranger sight was offered in this country last year than a meeting held in Philadelphia on behalf of a training school for colored working-people. An ex-President of the United States presided, and the chief speaker was a negro, born a homeless, nameless chattel, but who ranks now among the foremost genuine orators of the country. The significance of the incident was not in the school, nor in the white man, nor in the black, it was in the chance which this country offers to the individual, the possibility in it for a black slave to push his way up and up.[38]

It is worth recalling that Lorimer's contemporaries considered the famous editor both an accurate reflection of American ideology as well as a driver of politics and culture. Beginning in 1902—after the Roosevelt–Washington dinner and the spur it gave to even more vehement white supremacy—Lorimer's approach to African Americans made a decided shift away from support of Black uplift and toward regular assertions of permanent servility and inferiority. The *Saturday Evening Post* was part and parcel of the hardening of American apartheid in the early twentieth century, and the first *Post* cover to feature African Americans highlighted Lorimer's embrace of Jim Crow. Rather than depicting the uplift embodied by Washington's life story, *Cotton Pickers* by the illustrator Emlen McConnell (August 29, 1903) celebrated the bended back of an elderly man whose hair is nearly as white as the cotton bolls he picks—thus suggesting a "natural" link between servitude and Blackness.

"THE BLACKS WILL HAVE TO POSSESS THEIR *SOULS* IN PATIENCE": JOEL CHANDLER HARRIS, REBECCA HARDING DAVIS, AND THE ACCEPTABLE LIMITS OF BLACK LEADERSHIP

The tipping point for Washington's reputational slide from admirable race leader into an exemplar of permanent racial inferiority happened in the *Post* in 1904 and 1905, when Lorimer printed relatively laudatory contributions from Joel Chandler Harris and Rebecca Harding Davis but then followed those publications with Thomas Dixon Jr.'s vicious attack "Booker T. Washington and the Negro." Like other *Post* authors of the era, both Harris and Davis praised Washington's leadership but only because he did little, in their minds, to challenge the existing racial order. What also emerged during this pivotal moment was a growing sense of concern over the advent of a more strident Black politics, and this wariness seemed to be responding perhaps especially to Du Bois's publication of *The Souls of Black Folk* in 1903. Like Washington, Du Bois was never afforded his own voice in the *Post*, but the perceived threat he presented to white power could be felt nevertheless. Harris and Davis gave full-throated endorsements of Washington as a symbol of a tolerable Black leadership premised on the advocacy of patience, humility, and subservience. In their *Post* contributions, they held up Washington as a welcome reiteration of the faithful family servant—as the leader who knows his place and encourages other African Americans to know theirs. This section of the chapter examines a three-part series by Harris titled "The Negro Problem" and two pieces by Davis, "Has the Free Negro

Failed? What Forty Years of Independence Have Brought Him" and "Half a Dozen Silhouettes."

In the early weeks of 1904, Lorimer ran a series on the "Negro problem" by Harris, who was a regular *Post* contributor of poetry, prose, and fiction from 1899 through 1907. By 1904, Harris enjoyed preeminence as a white writer of Black dialect that dominated American magazines.[39] His Uncle Remus stories "initiated a literary boom of sentimental old black characters set vaguely between slavery and freedom," and he managed to create characters that had "downright dignity" in comparison to the characters of subsequent white writers of such material.[40] Like Dunbar, Harris provided *Post* readers with greater levels of Black complexity than could be found elsewhere in the magazine's history—despite the incontrovertible fact that his Uncle Remus character was nonetheless "the Redemption archetype of the contented black man."[41] Taken as a whole, Harris's three essays on the "Negro problem" sided with Booker T. Washington's accommodationism and gradualism while implicitly attacking Du Bois's challenge to the racial status quo. Harris did both by romanticizing the antebellum South, justifying racist violence while claiming an enlightened benevolence, and blaming the North for ignorant meddling. In other words, Harris used Washington's form of uplift as a rhetorical tool for keeping African Americans in the kind of "place" ironized by Dunbar in "Mr. Groby's Slippery Gift."

Lorimer highlighted the significance of Harris's tripart series by making the inaugural essay the lead item for the January 2, 1904, issue. In "The Negro as the South Sees Him," Harris set the stage for his subsequent defense of Washington's leadership by idealizing the slaveholding South and waxing nostalgic over kindly antebellum masters and their faithful retainers. He began by appropriating an abolitionist text and characterizing it as a justification for slavery—the kind of rhetorical doublespeak that has since become foundational to authoritarian movements. In the twenty-first century, conservatives trot out Martin Luther King Jr.'s "I Have a Dream" speech whenever they want to erode civil rights and legal protections; Harris modeled this sort of logic at the beginning of the twentieth century by claiming that Harriet Beecher Stowe's *Uncle Tom's Cabin* constituted a defense of slavery because her "genius" was the ability to capture the "tender and romantic situation" of the master–slave relationship. It is impossible, he claimed, "for any unprejudiced person to read Mrs. Stowe's book and fail to see in it a defense of American slavery as she found it in Kentucky." According to Harris, "the real moral" of the novel is the nobility of slavery when it was practiced "under the best and happiest conditions," a system that produced the "oldest and most venerable of the negroes . . . the old time darky." The bulk of the essay comprises anecdotes of "the confidential family servant," "the dusky mammy," and their loyal service to kindly masters. Harris concluded with a paean to a system that "was far more beautiful and inspiring than any of the relations that we have between employers and employed in this day and time."[42] This sort of nostalgia for a fictionally harmonious Old South sealed Harris's reputation as "the historian most responsible for promoting the image of the plantation pastorale,"[43] and it helped fuel rising Jim Crow by asserting the purported benevolence of the American racial hierarchy. Harris extended his fetishization of faithful "servants" to Booker T. Washington in the next two essays in the series to pursue an argument intended to naturalize the continuation and expansion of segregation. In Harris's hands, "Old South nostalgia" served as "the funhouse mirror of New South progress."[44]

In the second essay, "The Negro of To-Day: His Prospects and Discouragements" (January 30, 1904), Harris defended Washington's vaunted status by blaming the "negro problem" on northern agitation and dysfunctional Black leadership. Harris began by relating the story of a northern friend who became discouraged about African Americans' future prospects after he "had been made the astonished victim of the insolence of a negro porter of a sleeping-car." Harris reminded his friend—and *Post* readers—that every race has its share of undesirable characters and that this subset "of irresponsibles . . . is made to stand for the race in the comic papers, where the 'coon' plays a leading part." Like Dunbar in "Negro Society in Washington," Harris suggested that it would be more accurate to judge any race or institution by its "best representatives" and "best products,"[45] a line of reasoning that set up his essay to advocate for Booker T. First, however, Harris argued that hostility against African Americans occurred only when northerners interfered in southern affairs:

> There can be no doubt that since the day of emancipation the negro has experienced the seamy side of justice; but who has been responsible all along for this state of things? There can be but one answer to this question: whatever form or system of injustice he has been made the victim of has been almost

entirely due to the unwise and unnecessary crusade inaugurated in his behalf by the politicians of the North, who neither knew nor cared for the situation at the South. Indeed, there was a time when negro outrages at the South were deemed so essential to the welfare of these politicians that when real ones failed to occur their newspaper organs made a business of inventing them.[46]

Harris claimed that violence and injustice against African Americans in the South were the direct consequences of northern political agitation and press coverage and not at all the fault of the southerners who were actively practicing and promulgating an entire system of oppression. (I am not for a moment, however, suggesting northern innocence of racial oppression.) This historian of the plantation pastorale then rewrote the past whole cloth by denying that the South had ever *really* wanted to maintain slavery and that any such suggestion was the malevolent invention of northerners: "There was an assiduous effort made to convince the negro that the Southern people were his worst enemies, bent on subjecting him to some form of permanent servitude."[47] Needless to say, Harris's claims are patently false. The white South had seceded from the Union, fought a civil war, suffered hundreds of thousands of casualties and a devastated economy all to keep African Americans in "permanent servitude," and from the moment federal troops withdrew, the same region made extraordinary efforts to reimpose both de jure and de facto forms of slavery. But for Harris—and, through tacit editorial endorsement, for Lorimer—northern interference was the real cause of America's race problems. Neither Harris nor the *Post* originated this argument, of course, but by virtue of their prominence they were significant contributors to making such thinking "common sense" in the United States. According to Harris, northerners made matters even worse by granting political power and the franchise to former slaves, an "experiment [that] was the beginning of all the troubles and difficulties that the negro has been made the victim of."[48] Without writing it directly, Harris suggested that northern interference had done nothing but make Black people uppity and that African Americans were too childlike to know their own minds and to decide their own courses of action. One measure of the tenacity of this idea can be found in the *Post* decades later. In 1932, Lorimer published William Faulkner's story "A Mountain Victory" (see chapter 6), which characterizes African Americans as "an oppressed race burdened with freedom."[49] For Joel Chandler Harris, the "discouragements" of too much freedom and too many rights could be remedied only through Washingtonian gradualism and accommodation. "[The negro] is beginning to perceive that a negro's surest road to the respect and confidence of the white man is along the old route of individual industry and thrift and general usefulness to the community."[50] In Harris's hands, and on Lorimer's pages, Washington was an updated version of the faithful family retainer who was willing to work hard without upsetting the status quo.

But Harris did not conclude his second essay by merely extolling Washington's exemplary virtues and leadership. He also sought to legitimize extralegal violence and delegitimize less accommodating African American leadership by raising the trope of Black bestiality. He warned, "There have been among the negroes manifestations of brutality unparalleled, so far as I know, since the dawn of civilization, and the reprisals that have been made are but the natural result of the horror that must fill the bosoms of the best men who are brought sharply face to face with such cruelty and bestiality." Harris barely veiled his advocacy of lynching, and rather than criticizing the white supremacists who engaged in murderous terrorism, he blamed Black leadership, especially "the negro preachers who have a taste for politics." Because such leaders did not acquiesce to the demands of white supremacy, they had "a very bad effect on public opinion" and were therefore the actual cause or their own problems. Nonetheless, Harris was "hopeful" for the future because "representative negroes" such as Washington "have discovered the main source of trouble among Blacks," which is not the entire system of institutionalized and socialized white racism but rather a need to start living "morally and decently [and] to look sharply after the comings and goings of their children." Without irony, Harris concluded this second essay in his series by asking, "Having once seen the evil, is it too much to hope they [African Americans] will finally provide a remedy for the immorality that now exists?"[51] No remedy for the immorality of lynching was ever suggested.

In this second essay, "The Negro of To-Day," Harris implied that the evils of racism did not stem from the actions of the white South but rather from northern agitators and their gullible Black dupes. Perhaps the most astounding aspect of this essay is not what Harris wrote but the response it elicited from Booker T. Washington. In a letter to Lorimer dated February 9, 1904, Washington wrote: "Enclosed I send you a copy of a letter which I have written to Joel Chandler Harris. It has been a long time since any article has been written on the race question which has attracted so much favorable attention from the colored people as this one has. I think you will be surprised to find what a wide reading your paper has among the members of my race."[52] Having no voice in the pages of the *Post* itself, Washington gave his personal approval to both Lorimer and Harris for contrasting his form of loyalty and leadership with more vocal methods of agitation for Black rights. Implicit in both Harris's essay and Washington's letter is a critique of Du Bois, whose *Souls of Black Folk*—with its direct challenge to both Washington and to the idea that white supremacy is not responsible for African American suffering—was published in 1903, one year before Harris published his series. The push against Du Bois became more apparent in his third essay.

In his final installment, "The Negro Problem: Can the South Solve It— and How?" (February 27, 1904), Harris once again denied any claims of white accountability and argued that African Americans alone were responsible for improving their condition; in fact, he claimed, they were already being afforded every opportunity by their benevolent white neighbors. Harris began by dispelling various definitions of "the negro problem." First, tacitly endorsing Washington's emphasis on the value of hard work and amassing property, Harris rejected the idea of Black "idleness and unthrift" by noting African American financial successes. Next, he repudiated the claim that white southerners were opposed to Black education, claiming that they were "contributing more money for educational purposes than the North" and were, in fact, "anxious for the enlightenment of the negro." Finally, Harris questioned the suggestion that Black and white people could not peaceably share the same space because they had already been "side by side" with each other for three centuries; white people, therefore, already "know all the characteristic peculiarities of the negro."[53]

Having dispensed with questions of work ethic, education, and proximity, Harris turned to the issue of social equality, which was inflamed "when the President dined Booker Washington." Speaking of the Reconstruction era, Harris noted, "Some of the negroes made melancholy exhibitions of their folly and ignorance by thrusting themselves into places where they were not wanted," but—echoing the blame he placed on northerners in his second essay—he suggested "their conduct could be traced to the teachings of their political instructors," implying once again that all of the problems in the South were the consequence of outside interference. Ultimately, the white fear of equality was merely a "bugaboo" because "no person, no matter what his condition or color, is likely to thrust himself where his presence will be resented, or where his company will give the slightest offense." For Harris, there was, finally, no "negro problem" at all—or, at least, not any sort of a problem that entails white responsibility. Drawing on the "pace and example . . . set by the president of Tuskegee Institute," Harris concluded his series by excusing the South from making any efforts whatsoever in addressing the problems created by either slavery or hegemonic racial oppression: "There is certainly a problem for the negroes to solve— the problem of moral, social, and industrial development; but this is a problem with which all individuals and all races have had to contend at one time or another, and there is no solution save hard work and right living."[54]

Harris, in other words, offered a full-throated endorsement of Washington's accommodationism, and he saw in the Tuskegean a convenient vehicle for promoting white hegemony and for arguing against northern interference as the South pursued the expansion of Jim Crow. Harris's support of Washington also inhered a dismissal of the more insistent politics of leaders such as Du Bois. Famously, *Souls of Black Folk* challenged Washington's surrender of African American civil rights, voting rights, and access to higher education, and Du Bois insisted that white America bore responsibility for creating a more just nation. Implicitly opposing Du Bois, Harris extolled African Americans who patiently followed Washington's example and who expected or demanded no immediate relief from racial inequality. Making an unmistakable allusion to the title of Du Bois's book, Harris counseled, "The blacks will have to possess their *souls* in patience, for the evolution of a race requires time." No similar evolution of white souls was anticipated or deemed necessary.[55]

For the next few years, Lorimer ran material that more or less followed Harris's lead by directly promoting Washington's agenda while also tacitly challenging Du Bois, who served as a rarely mentioned but nonetheless perceivable threat to the racial status quo in the magazine. Rebecca Harding Davis, a regular *Post* author between 1902 and 1906, exemplified this approach in two of her contributions, "Has the Free Negro Failed? What Forty Years of Independence Have Brought Him" (July 2, 1904) and "Half a Dozen Silhouettes" (August 12, 1905). Taken together, these essays offered a paternalistic endorsement of Washingtonian gradualism for a people

Davis characterized alternately as innately childlike and hopelessly brut-ish. Basing her cogitations on annual journeys through the South, Davis began her essay "Has the Free Negro Failed?" (an obvious rhetorical ques-tion that was answered in the affirmative) by describing the "coal-Black negroes" she saw through her train coach window as animal-like, aimless, and lazy—"these idle millions of negroes in the Gulf States." Taking aim at the unnamed Du Bois while openly praising Washington, Davis echoed Joel Chandler Harris by faulting

> the negro leaders [who] hold that there are two things essential, first of all, for the uplifting of the race: education and the right of suffrage. But surely, when a man has sunk to the level of the brute, his first chance in manhood lies in the quickened desire in him not to be a brute, to work, to make a home for himself, his wife and children, and to live in it honestly and decently. Booker Washington, by the simple, rational method of providing self-respecting work for them, is lifting thousands of his race out of brutality to manhood.[56]

Black brutality was ever present for Davis, and she drove this point home incessantly. After describing a few African Americans who demonstrated Washington's qualities of humility, thrift, and industry, she turned seam-lessly in "Has the Free Negro Failed?" from paternalism to its ever-present counterpart, naked racial violence, by noting approvingly that two Black men were recently lynched, "both for good cause." Education was not needed for such a debased people, she asserted, and the right to vote was even more unnecessary. To back up her argument against Black suffrage, Davis made the extraordinary claim that women would rather be disenfran-chised if that meant keeping Black men from the ballot box: "And as for the right of suffrage—For more than a century it has been justly denied to more than thirty millions of white educated Americans, who have well served their country and their God without it. The majority of them have wisely decided that they do not want it. We women, at least, need not wring our hands in despair at the legislation which keeps Toby away from the polls a year or two longer."[57]

Ultimately, Davis echoed Washington and Harris and rejected the legal, political, and educational remedies to racial inequality advocated by Du Bois, arguing for purported benefits of continued white paternalism: "This childish folk need to be taught first the lessons of life, which we teach to children: not to read or to vote but to stand on their feet, to use their hands, to help themselves." Davis fashioned her concluding paragraph as a final dig at Du Bois, especially his emphasis on the arts and education: "Here is a great work which, it seems to me, is waiting for the young negro men and women who have had college training: surely a more wholesome, higher task in life than the pouring out of morbid essays or poems in which they bewail the injustice of Fate in giving them colored skins."[58] Again, and like Harris, Davis castigated Du Bois as a false leader without mentioning him directly.

A year later, most likely on the heels of her next foray south, Davis provided *Post* readers with "Half a Dozen Silhouettes," written portraits of African Americans that she insisted were merely "photographs" of "negroes" that make "no argument" about her subjects. "The only value in such pictures is, of course, their absolute truth. The negroes that I give you are actual men and women." These silhouettes shuttle between sketches of "good" African Americans, on the one hand, who follow Washington's example, and, on the other, more troubling figures who either offer derisive examples of what Du Bois called the "Talented Tenth" or provide evidence of the necessity of extralegal violence because of supposedly innate Black brutality. Davis began "Silhouettes" by briefly describing a man who embodied Washingtonian humility and then moved to a caricature of a Talented Tenth achiever—"Pearl, a chambermaid in a hotel in Atlantic City . . . a Canadian, a tall yellow quadroon" with eyes that "are glassy and absolutely without meaning. You see such eyes in fish sometimes." Davis was haughtily amused by Pearl's sense of agency but clearly disturbed by her "shrill, insolent voice, in which are neither the softness nor the accent of the Southern negro." Pearl exemplified Du Boisian cultural striving, and the pride she took in her accomplishments provided fodder for Davis's derision: "My name's Miss Cornelia Pearl Heminway. You might have seen it in the papers. I have wrote poems and a novel[;] . . . my perfession is writing for the colored folks' papers. I am pretty smart at drawin', too. Some of my pictures has been in the Afro-American Miscellany. The way I make money at Atlantic City, though, is by givin' cakewalks." Pearl had even invented two new dances that appeared in a New York vaudeville theater. All of Pearl's work had a purpose: she wanted to shield her nine-year-old daughter from the racism she herself had experienced. Davis claimed to be surprised by Pearl's observations about American racism: "It was curious that this woman, removed by three generations from slavery, and treated from birth as an equal by the white race, was the only one who seemed to feel any antipathy toward them [white people]."[59] Davis's unstated implications are devastatingly clear: first, there was no racial injustice in the United States; second, northern African Americans lacked gratitude for their purported freedom; and third, slavery produced better Black people than unfettered freedom ever could. Davis drove this last point home by following her sketch of Pearl with that of a Black minister who pleased the author with his obsequiousness and his Washingtonian drive to acquire property.

Davis's last two sketches in "Silhouettes" limn the continuum of white racial fantasy between the always faithful, desexualized Black mammy and her ever-present counterpart, the hypersexualized Black male rapist who preys on white women. Davis's final sketch is of Winny, "a skillful cook of the old Virginia type" descended from "Congo stock," whose service earned her the tender care of her employers in her old age. Davis preceded this stereotypical fantasy with her portrait of the brutish Kreeshy, "a large Black negro" she saw while passing through Florida, "who was squatted on the track, eating a fried fish. . . . His lips lay like slabs of fat on the heavier layers of fat that made up his face and jowl[;] . . . he turned over into the mud and squatted there, still tearing and gorging." As Davis watched this crude display of animalism, the white stationmaster's wife appeared with a baby in her arms; Kreeshy watched her wolfishly with "his sore, red eyes" and followed the woman toward the house as Davis's train pulled away. Traveling through the same town a year later, Davis inquired about the woman, who, she learned, was raped and murdered, a crime that led inevitably to a lynching. "D'ye see them three trees across the road?," she was asked. "Two niggers was hung on them trees with no talk of trial. The third got off—the worst of the gang."[60] This third was, of course, Kreeshy, who now wandered the swamp, thus serving as a constant reminder of the need for repressive violence in Jim Crow America. In Davis and Harris's *Post* contributions of 1904 and 1905, then, we see both the highest esteem and the obvious limitations of Washington's emblematic value in Lorimer's magazine as an avatar of racial change in America. Haunted by the more militant challenge to the status quo posed by the always unnamed Du Bois, these two representative *Post* authors demonstrated how Washington was held up as a way to keep African Americans in their "place."

DIXON, DICKSON, AND THE
"PERMANENT CHARACTER" OF THE *POST*

Just one week after Kreeshy's appearance in the *Post*, Washington's status as a generally acceptable Black leader came to a definitive end when Lorimer published Thomas Dixon Jr.'s venomous screed "Booker T. Washington and the Negro" (August 19, 1905). The appearance of this essay marked a decided shift because even Washington's polite challenge to the racial status quo was discredited by Dixon, and the possibility of Black humanity, equity, or equality would henceforth be only a source of humor and derision in the magazine. As the title of Dixon's essay suggests, he anchored his broad attack on all African Americans by focusing on Washington, whose efforts at uplift, Dixon claimed, were actually designed to lead the nation toward interracial sexuality and racial warfare. Ultimately, Dixon argued for an American racial cleansing by promoting the mass deportation of all Black people to Liberia.

Dixon was already a well-known preacher, public speaker, and novelist by the time his essay ran in the *Post*. His debut novel, *The Leopard's Spots* (1902), offered up all the nostalgia and fear that supported segregationist ideology. As Michele Gillespie and Randall Hall describe it, "Steeped in nineteenth-century southern romantic fiction, Dixon's novel idealized the plantation, promulgated the myth of the happy slave, gave white women some measure of moral authority for safeguarding the hearth, and insisted on the dominance of white patriarchy."[61] Samuel Roberts adds that Dixon's portrait of the Old South also asserted "the innate brutishness of Blacks, their natural inferiority, and the constant danger they presented to American civilization."[62] According to the *Baltimore Afro-American* in August 1903, *The Leopard's Spots* "has done more to disparage the cause of the black man in the minds of the American people than everything else that has ever been written."[63] Dixon's fame and notoriety only increased with his publication of *The Clansman* in 1905, the novel that would later serve as the basis of D. W. Griffith's film *Birth of a Nation* (1915). By the end of 1905, Dixon had adapted both of his novels into successful stage plays, and he was in many ways the face and voice of acceptable anti-Black racism across the United Sates. His appearance in the *Post* amounted to the magazine's definitive statement of support for white supremacy and its discrediting of all Black leadership, including Washington's. Lorimer emphasized his endorsement of Dixon by making "Booker T. Washington and the Negro" the lead story. The issue in which it appeared featured what was only the second image of an African American on the cover—this time a female servant created by Emlen McConnell, a regular *Post* illustrator who specialized in drawing African Americans for the magazine and had previously produced the *Cotton Pickers* cover.

Dixon opened his essay with paternalistic condescension before ultimately baring his fangs and reveling in naked threats of violence and murder against African Americans in order to deny them any entitlement to rights or security. He initially portrayed Washington in familiar *Post* terms as an exemplary self-made man, playing to Lorimer's well-known preference for stories about hard work and achievement before arguing that these qualities were merely pretexts for Black villainy. Claiming "the warmest admiration" for Washington, Dixon described his life in the familiar terms of a *Post* "romance" of self-improvement: "The story of a little ragged, barefooted piccaninny who lifted his eyes from a cabin in the hills of Virginia, saw a vision and followed it, until at last he presides over the richest and most powerful institution of learning in the South, and sits down with crowned heads and Presidents, has no parallel even in the Tales of the Arabian nights." However, Dixon continued, Washington's exemplary life, his plans, and efforts toward uplift "will not solve the Negro problem" but will only exacerbate racial tensions and make life more dangerous for African Americans. "As a friend of the Negro race I claim that he should have the opportunity for the highest, noblest, and freest development of his full, rounded manhood," but—Dixon quickly added—"he can never have it." Permanent Black inferiority, he stated, must be accepted by all, including such misguided white people as the "opportunists, politicians, weak-minded optimists . . . female men . . . the pot-house politician, the ostrich man, the pooh-pooh man, and the benevolent old maid."[64] Leaning heavily on social Darwinism throughout his essay,[65] Dixon proclaimed himself a truth teller who was merely pointing out the inevitable results of racial conflict—namely, the ascendancy of white Americans at the expense of African Americans.

Dixon's argument for mass expulsion began by denying the feasibility of ever educating African Americans, which stabbed at the heart of Washington's efforts at Tuskegee: "No amount of education of any kind, industrial, classical, or religious, can make a Negro a white man or bridge the chasm of the centuries which separate him from the white man in the evolution of human civilization." Frederick Douglass, "the greatest Negro that has ever lived according to Mr. Booker T. Washington," served as Dixon's example of innate inferiority because Douglass's only accomplishment was a life spent "in bombastic vituperation of the men whose genius created the American Republic[,] . . . and [he] at last achieved the climax of Negro sainthood by marrying a white woman."[66] Unsurprisingly, Dixon used the example of Douglass's marriage to warn that the ultimate goals of all Black leaders, from Washington to Du Bois and everyone in between, were "assimilation" and "amalgamation"—in other words, interracial sex and miscegenation.

Booker T. Washington, therefore, was no longer the solution to the problem of race in America, as many previous *Post* writers claimed; he was instead an imminent threat to white hegemony and racial purity because of his seeming acceptability, and his agenda would inexorably lead to racial violence: "He is storing dynamite beneath the pathway of our children—the end at least can only be in bloodshed." Washington's nefarious scheme, according to Dixon, was to train African Americans to "be masters of men . . . and in every shape and form destroy the last vestige of dependence on the white man for anything." For Dixon, the only reason for Black people to live in North America was to serve the labor demands of the white South. If they could no longer be used in this capacity, or if they educated themselves out of their "dependence," then they were living in the United States on borrowed time because "if there is one thing a Southern white man cannot endure it is an educated Negro." "And then," he warned, "the real tragedy will begin" because white people would not tolerate competition with Black people on an equal educational or economic basis. "Competition is war—the most fierce and brutal in all its forms." And what would the white man do "when he is put to the test? He will do exactly what his white neighbor in the North does when the Negro threatens his bread—kill him!" With this blunt warning, Dixon openly articulated the previous, barely concealed endorsement of extralegal violence and racial terror in the contributions of previous *Post* authors such as Harris and Davis. The only way out of a racial apocalypse, wrote Dixon, was "to colonize the whole Negro race." Rather than spending any more on educating African Americans domestically, money should be used to establish a branch of Tuskegee in Liberia, which would ultimately "solve our race problem within twenty-five years" through the expulsion of all Black people from not only the United

States but all of North America. This scheme, Dixon concluded, would be the merciful, benevolent action of a superior race to the people it has wronged: "We owe this to the Negro. At present we are deceiving him and allowing him to deceive himself. He hopes and dreams of amalgamation, forgetting that self-preservation is the first law of Nature. Our present attitude of hypocrisy is inhuman toward a weaker race brought to our shores by the sins of our fathers. We owe him a square deal, and we will never give it to him on this Continent."[67]

"Booker T. Washington and the Negro" ended as it began, with a feigned sympathy toward African Americans that barely hid, or even tried to hide, the animosity beneath. In a scorching pamphlet, *As to the Leopard's Spots: Open Letter to Thomas Dixon, Jr.* (1905), Kelly Miller responded to the professional racist's *Post* essay by characterizing Dixon as "the chief priest of those who worship at the shrine of race hatred and wrath." Miller demolished Dixon nearly line by line, pointing out, for example, that Dixon's "doctrine of hate" actually promoted racial amalgamation by driving "persons of lighter hue" across the color line and that Liberian colonization was the "climax of absurdity" simply from a logistical standpoint. (A mathematician and Howard University professor of sociology, Miller took particular delight in crunching these numbers.) Miller's analysis, which—like Dixon's essay—was circulated and reported on by many newspapers, concluded by pointing to the blood on Dixon's hands, who presided "at every cross road lynching of a helpless victim; wherever the midnight murderer rides with rope and torch, in quest of the blood of his black brother, you ride by his side." Ultimately, however, Miller argued that the greatest victim of Dixon's hatred was not African Americans but the white people who absorbed his message because "race hatred is the most malignant poison that can afflict the mind. . . . You are a greater enemy to your own race than you are to mine."[68]

To be accurate, Lorimer did also publish a trenchant retort to Dixon's essay a few months later: "The African Riddle: Another Side of Mr. Dixon's Negro Question" by Albert Bushnell Hart (October 28, 1905). Hart, who taught history at Harvard and was one of Du Bois's professors, treated Dixon's essay as representative of the array of white-supremacist arguments emanating especially from the South and dismantled their many hypocrisies and inconsistencies, focusing, for example, on white fears of interracial sexuality and the contradictory handling of the results of such unions:

"The same writer will tell you that the mulattos are feebler, more vicious and more unhealthy than the pure negroes, and in the same breath that all the negro leaders are mulattos. If Booker Washington founds a great school, or Du Bois writes a great book, they are told that their white blood is responsible for such achievements; if they offer to ride in the same car with a white man, they are bidden to betake themselves to the Jim Crow car." The greatest inconsistency of American racism, Hart wrote, was the claim that people of African descent are, at one and the same time, hopelessly inferior to white people and incapable of competing with them but that they also require extraordinary means of legal and extralegal repression.[69] Hart dispensed with all of Dixon's points, including the latter's suggestion of mass deportation under threat of violence, but Lorimer's estimation of Hart's argument can be gauged through paratext. Whereas Dixon's essay enjoyed prominence as the lead story of the August 19, 1905, issue, Hart's response was buried farther in the magazine, and arguments like his that contradicted white supremacy were never—ever—published again during Lorimer's editorship. In addition, rather than suggesting the propriety and success embodied by Washington, who functioned now as the magazine's discredited avatar for Black America, the illustration Lorimer chose for Hart's article naturalized African slavery. McConnell's illustration features two naked slaves, presumably in Africa, being transported in a canoe, which had the force of normalizing ideological constructions of Black servility and thus providing a visual retort to Hart's argument.

After the publication of Dixon's essay, Washington was almost never mentioned again in the *Post*, and any serious consideration of race relations in America was permanently supplanted in the magazine by "humorous" material that emphasized Black inferiority and chuckled about lynching. *Up from Slavery*, which had once been extolled as a shelf mate of Franklin's *Autobiography*, was now little more than fodder for a vacuum cleaner advertisement proclaiming the arrival of a "new servant in the house" (figure 1.1).

Ultimately, contributions by writers sympathetic toward African Americans, such as Albert Bushnell Hart and Paul Laurence Dunbar, were very few in number during the first decade of Lorimer's editorship, and they were dwarfed by the far greater number of white-authored editorials, essays, fiction, and poetry devoted to the caricaturing, belittlement, and demonization of African Americans. Whatever room there was in Lorimer's

FIGURE 1.1. New York Vacuum Cleaner Company, "New Servant in the House," advertisement in "The Housekeepers' Directory," *Good Housekeeping* 49, no. 6 (December 1909): n.p. This ad also ran in the *Saturday Evening Post*, November 6, 1909, 62.

mind for something like a debate about Black–white race relations in the United States and about African American humanity more generally appears to have been largely decided by 1905 and decisively settled by 1907, when he started publishing Harris Dickson, a municipal court judge from Vicksburg, Mississippi, who turned to a writing career after a few years practicing at the bar.[70] Lorimer obviously valued Dickson's contributions, publishing almost eighty pieces by the southern author over the years. The bulk of Dickson's work appeared in the magazine with greatest regularity between 1907 and 1916, and the tropes and contours of his fiction would become defining features of the white-authored dialect fiction in the *Post* for the remainder of Lorimer's career. While Thomas Dixon Jr.'s single essay on Washington announced the permanent shift in Lorimer's handling of African Americans in the *Post*, Dickson's numerous appearances in the magazine constituted the first significant instantiation of that solidifying approach. With the appearance of Dickson's Black dialect fiction, Lorimer's expectations for future material hardened into the endlessly repeated practice of registering and recontaining Black modernity within the narrow parameters of caricature, stereotype, and formulaic predictability.

Dickson published a number of nonfiction articles before turning to short stories, and these initial essays establish his racial animosity with painful clarity. "The Way of the Reformer" (January 12, 1907), his first contribution to the *Post*, set the tone for his career by establishing an unconcealed disdain for African Americans that matched Dixon's and had none of the gentleness (however feigned) of previous white authors such as Harris and Davis or of subsequent white writers of Black dialect such as Octavus Roy Cohen and Hugh Wiley. Beginning with the observation that northern standards could not be applied to southern culture, "The Way of the Reformer" provided a history of Vicksburg as a longtime gambling town on the Mississippi River. After several columns of more or less genial treatment of the city's white gamblers and murderers as "jolly good fellows, after all," Dickson singled out Black men as posing the greatest danger to the citizenry: "The overshadowing menace to all Southern towns is the negro vagrant[, who is] the prolific parent of every crime—the exceptional crime in almost every instance." The undefined "exceptional crime" was, of course, the sexual assault of white women. The Black vagrant was all the more dangerous because "he 'takes up' with a woman who cooks for white people" and is therefore an ever-present malevolence lurking in white homes and on the peripheries of white consciousness. The best way to control the Black male population, according to Dickson, was by using the criminal justice system to impose coerced, unpaid labor. When a yellow-fever epidemic hit Vicksburg in 1905, the city judge (most likely Dickson) ordered the mass arrest of Black men to extract free labor. "The joke was on the negroes and they appreciated it. In less than an hour two hundred of them were at work."[71] Throughout his writings, Dickson jested regularly about how the justice system could be used to extract cheap or free labor from Black men.

Dickson elaborated further on the purported criminality and general inferiority of African Americans in his next *Post* article, "Please Y'Onner: The Testimony and Facts in Certain Cote-House Scrapes" (February 16, 1907), which characterized Black people as childish, lawless, untrustworthy, and undeserving of legal treatment under the law. Dickson claimed that whereas white people are generally reliable witnesses in court, African Americans lack the inborn capacity for accuracy or truth telling. "Every Southerner knows that an average servant cannot bear a message from her mistress at the front door to a huckster at the front gate without mangling it beyond recognition. . . . In matters of this kind there is an amiable irresponsibility about the negro servants which is as unconquerable and impregnable as Gibraltar." According to Dickson—a municipal judge, remember—Black Americans are perpetually given to perjury and unreliable testimony, and "this is so well understood in the South that many intelligent men sitting as jurors would refuse to convict a white man of a capital offense, and sentence him to be hanged, on uncorroborated negro testimony." But the presumption of innocence need not be extended similarly to Black defendants because although "intelligent" white jurors might be equally skeptical about uncorroborated testimony, "sheer necessity" demanded a lower bar of proof; "otherwise the law could rarely be enforced." The lower value of Black life in Dickson's mind could not be clearer, and the rest of "Please Y'Onner" does nothing to dispel this point. Echoing the sentiments in "Booker T. Washington and the Negro," Dickson attributed Black amorality and lawlessness to a difference in racial heritage. Whereas the "white man of Anglo-Saxon origin" is the inheritor of a two-thousand-year legal heritage, "the negro has no such tradition, no such history of the past and no such history for the future. As a race he never erected a government, never erected a code of laws or enforced a rule of morals."[72]

In his third *Post* essay, Dickson reflected the magazine's increasing embrace of anti-Black racism as well as the expansion of Jim Crow in the United States more generally. Despite the states' rights argument against northern interference in the South that began his first *Post* contribution, Dickson called for a Dixie-inspired, nationwide approach to "the negro problem" in "The Vardaman Idea: How the Governor of Mississippi Would Solve the Race Question" (April 27, 1907). Dickson's essay provided a hearty endorsement of the rabid segregationist Governor James K. Vardaman's "idea": the disenfranchisement of the entire African American population through the repeal of the Fifteenth Amendment and a modification to the Fourteenth. According to Vardaman, quoted by Dickson, "The negro should never have been trusted with the ballot. He is different from the white man. He is congenitally unqualified to exercise the most responsible duty of citizenship. He is physically, mentally, morally, racially and eternally the white man's inferior. There is nothing in his individual character, nothing in his achievements of the past nor his promise for the future which entitles him to stand side by side with the white man at the ballot box." Dickson praised Vardaman for articulating something that "a vast number of patriotic citizens" think. "The only difference is Vardaman *says* it." Thus, for Dickson, the proper solution to the race problem was to assign African Americans "a permanent position of inferiority." Again echoing Dixon, he wrote that direct competition between Black and white people could only lead to violence, and if African Americans were not shielded from such competition, they "must die. It is Nature's law."[73] Dickson's complete denunciation of any racial equality whatsoever entailed a final rejection in the *Saturday Evening Post* of the gradualism and the accommodationist politics symbolized by the now entirely discredited Booker T. Washington.

Drawing on shoddy history and racial pseudoscience, Dickson, continuing to reinforce the arguments advanced by Dixon, eliminated any possibility of full humanity for Black people, and he made no effort to conceal his complete hatred of them. Working up to a high dudgeon in his advocacy for the virulently racist Vardaman, Dickson claimed Africans "executed nothing in any wise more intellectual than the accomplishments of a gorilla. . . . Left alone in his jungle, he had progressed backward and became a feeder upon human flesh, a polygamist, without religion, family ties or morals. He was the inventor and promulgator of slavery, the patentee and proprietor of cannibalism—these being the twin institutions which he had contributed to human progress." To make matters even more dire in Dickson's eyes, Black people in America came primarily from the West Coast of Africa, and "all historians and explorers agree in assigning to them the lowest position in the scale of Equatorial Africa." These ancestors "are naked cannibals, selling their own flesh and blood when they do not eat it," which "is precisely what the Afro-American voter would be had he been left to his own devices." Given any sort of freedom or chance at equal treatment, African Americans would immediately "revert" to their "natural state" because "twenty thousand years of jungle habit cannot be eradicated in a day." Ultimately, the "Vardaman Idea" that Dickson praised entailed the complete eradication of civil and political rights for African Americans, and it was based on the premise of white genetic and cultural superiority—an idea characterized as the same sort of benevolence claimed by Dixon: "There has never been a Governor in the South who has striven more earnestly to protect negroes." Denying African Americans the vote "is not so much for the protection of the white man against the encroachment of the Black man as it is to protect the Black man against inevitable destruction by the white man."[74] The "idea" for Vardaman, Dixon, Dickson, and Lorimer was Black disenfranchisement, permanent subjugation, economic exploitation—or death.

Dickson's initial publications in the *Post* are significant for two reasons. First, their appearance signaled the end of what was in reality a paltry "debate" over Black rights and Black humanity in the magazine during Lorimer's first decade as editor. Just as important, Lorimer's apparently keen appreciation of Dickson's take on African Americans led in just a few years to a long-running series of "Ole Reliable" short stories, which appeared in the *Post* until 1916 (and were then taken up by *Cosmopolitan* for a few more stories). "Ole Reliable" is the ironic nickname for the former slave Zack Foster, who personifies many of Dickson's fantasies about African American inadequacy. Although Dickson, as an author, is largely forgettable (and has been almost entirely ignored by literary critics and historians), he was "known the world over as the creator of 'Ole Reliable'" in his day.[75] His fiction is significant here because it solidifies the basic contours of the Black dialect fiction that Lorimer would publish consistently for the remaining years of his editorship. Other white writers, including Irvin S. Cobb, Blanche Goodman, L. B. Yates, and Harry Snowden Stabler, also contributed similar stories to the *Post* during the earlier years of Lorimer's editorship, but Dickson dominated the genre in the decade leading up to the Harlem Renaissance. In 1917, the *Hartford Daily Courant* noted that Dickson's "stories of 'Ole Reliable' have not only delighted millions of readers, but have given the Northerner a distinctly new impression of the darkey [*sic*]."[76] Years later, in 1931, the journalist Strickland Gillilan described Dickson as "the man who wrote those stories you never missed a chance to read—the 'Old Reliable' stories that were the father and mother of all the interesting stories you have read since pertaining to colored people."[77] The popularity of his fiction led Dickson in 1917 to write a stage play based on Ole Reliable, blithely titled *The Nigger in the Woodpile*, and a bit later he established the short-lived Harris Dickson Film Corporation and made a few two-reel comedy films.

Dickson's first story, "The Job Hunter" (January 8, 1910), is characteristic of his work, and it wastes no time in demonstrating Dickson's feelings toward African Americans. Within the first ten lines, "Ole Reliable" Zack Foster is animalized as "a little Black beetle suddenly uncovered beneath a chip" and "a rabbit that had been shot at and was watching to dodge the second barrel," and these descriptions are followed promptly by a discussion between Zack and his wife that establishes Ole Reliable as lazy, gluttonous, and prone to casual thievery. As the story unfolds, Zack accumulates money from various white people by promising to do work that he never remembers to finish, a character trait Dickson believed was a genetic "racial" inheritance, and he meets Colonel Spottiswoode, a former Confederate officer who feels perfectly entitled to demand domestic service from Zack the moment he lays eyes on the old man. Articulating a sentiment that would become a common trope in the *Post's* dialect stories, both Zack and Spottiswoode understand each other as only a southern master and his Black servant can: "Zack knew this kind of man, and this kind of man knew Zack. Neither of them asked a question."[78] Spottiswoode's gruff, peremptory treatment of Zack is never challenged or resented, which implies that the master–servant relationship is the natural one and that only a strong white hand can control the weaker Black mind. Subsequent *Post* authors, from Irvin S. Cobb in the 1910s and 1920s to William Faulkner in the 1930s, would make regular use of this trope.

With Dickson's arrival at the *Post*, Lorimer settled into his practice of cultivating authors who would provide him with a steady diet of Black dialect fiction that would dependably register and recontain African American modernity into the narrow and dehumanizing confines of plantation fiction and the conventions of caricature and minstrelsy. The idea that African Americans might be loving and mutually self-supporting, as Dunbar's work sometimes showed, was forever supplanted by portraits of African Americans as venal, selfish, and loyal only to their benevolent white overlords. The promise of uplift through Washington's example of the successful, self-made man gave way to constructions of Black leaders who were always suspect and the source of derision. In another short story, "That Mule, Old Bluffer" (February 13, 1909), Dickson gave his Black protagonist the name "Olympian Jove"—a moniker intended to mock the idea of African Americans' achievement:

> His head was long, like a flabby football, wrinkled and leather-colored, with shriveled features set at the far end. Prominent ears stood out from either side as wings from a dirigible balloon. Quizzical little black eyes glittered, and lent a saving grace of humor to his fascinating features. . . . Nobody could determine whether he had descended from the monkeys, or whether in the process of evolution he was headed that way. His quick, apelike movements added to the resemblance. He had outlived his usefulness, his brood of young deserted him, and the acres that he pretended to cultivate had dwindled steadily.[79]

By calling his character "Olympian Jove," Dickson satirized even the possibility of a plausible Black leader such as Booker T. Washington. Now, instead, Black leaders in the magazine—and all African Americans more generally—would be forever consigned to their inferior place on the Great Chain of Being[80] and never considered as fully human as white people.

As the first decades of the twentieth century unfolded, as Jim Crow hardened and spread, and as the New Negro movement was gaining strength and leading toward the era known as the Harlem Renaissance, George Horace Lorimer became fully committed to a fairly inflexible approach to the magazine's portrayal of African Americans. The brief, in-house history of the *Post* produced by the Curtis Publishing Company in 1936 claimed that the magazine's "permanent character" coalesced around 1909. This was certainly the case for the *Post's* treatment of African Americans, which was marginally more sympathetic in 1899 than it would be ten years later, when the magazine hardened into its characteristic anti-Black strategies of representation. There was nothing particularly new about using "humor" and stereotype in American print culture, but the *Post's* ever-expanding circulation and its increasingly dominant position made it one of the main purveyors of the barely polite racism that normalized segregation and naturalized racial hierarchy. In a few short years after Washington's disappearance and Dickson's arrival, phenomena leading to the Harlem Renaissance would arise, such as the Great Migration of African Americans out of the South and Black overseas military service during World War I. But the *Saturday Evening Post* had a set of practices in place that allowed Lorimer's audience simultaneously to read about these historic phenomena and to dismiss them as risible.

Chapter Two

LITERARY ASPIRATION
AND INTIMATE MINSTRELSY

Lorimer's editorial trajectory—from his tepid endorsement of Booker T. Washington and warmer embrace of Paul Laurence Dunbar, through his publication of Thomas Dixon Jr.'s racist screed, and finally to his hardened practice of registering and recontaining Black modernity in the Black dialect fiction of white writers such as Harris Dickson—did not, of course, happen in a vacuum. Lorimer assumed control of the *Saturday Evening Post* in the 1890s, "when race relations were at their worst, most violent level." As Stanley J. Lemons also notes, American print culture was already saturated with Black caricatures that "were spread and maintained in advertising cards, songs from Tin Pan Alley, phonograph records, children's books . . . cartoons, magazine ads, valentines, and post cards." As the violence against African Americans intensified with the deepening and expansion of Jim Crow, "the comic black man became the most common figure in America's new popular entertainment. . . . When he was being treated the worst, the Negro became the butt of the national joke, its principal comic character. In this way, popular culture's treatment of blacks reflected society's humiliation of them."[1] Because of the *Post*'s dominant position among periodicals, it functioned as both a reflection of the era's anti-Black racism and a powerful driver of racial dehumanization and legal segregation. The *Saturday Evening Post* helped normalize and naturalize the logic of Jim Crow through Lorimer's reliable publication of white-authored Black dialect fiction.

Demeaning stereotypes were not the domain of print culture alone; they were an everyday feature of physically embodied and personally experienced American life. "White" Americans—perhaps "white-aspiring Americans" is more accurate—not only encountered racial caricatures through print and other media but also inhabited and performed ideological fantasies of Blackness. Lemons's list of cards, songs, records, and so on indicates that this material was commercially manufactured and consumed and performed by Americans inside a variety of domestic and public spaces. As Rhae Lynn Barnes demonstrates, amateur minstrel performances, which are now a largely forgotten aspect of Jim Crow culture, were a primary form of entertainment and racialized indoctrination for many decades of the nineteenth and twentieth century. As well as the stereotypes promulgated by the forms of popular culture identified by Lemon, additional physical traces demonstrate the widespread nature of the commodification, circulation, consumption, and performance of Blackness, explains Barnes: "The print ephemera related to the performance of amateur blackface minstrel plays, like scripts and programs, can be found scattered across the United States. Together, these materials are evidence of a bottom-up intellectual and political history of race maintenance, the remnants of white supremacy's intellectual life and affective history after the Civil War that detailed who could be part of the American political body." In her careful study of amateur blackface minstrelsy, Barnes shows how this form of entertainment was constitutive of national life, and she argues that "*most* Americans were routinely performing or attending these shows."[2] There was an enormous and profitable market for minstrelsy in the United States, and, accordingly, Lorimer made the *Post* a reliable purveyor of the language, tropes, gags, and imagery of blackface. His magazine functioned as a source of the material Americans drew upon when performing Black dialect and Black caricature in the comfort of their homes and in the places they would gather.

Barnes writes, "Once you start to look for minstrelsy, you see it everywhere in American culture."[3] This ubiquity is true not only for the shows staged at all manner of public venues, including theaters, churches, schools, firehouses, and other public places, but also for in-home performances and recitations. Take, for example, the following social notice from the *Downs (Kansas) News and the Downs Times* on May 13, 1920:

> The Crescent club met with Mrs. Chas. Mann on Wednesday afternoon, May 5th. . . . The program by Mrs. D. B. Harrison, was one of the most entertaining programs given during the year. Mrs. Harrison brought out the pathetic superstitions and humorous characteristics of the Negro, giving first one of Viney's sketches, "A change of heart," after which "Darky" jokes were read by each member of the club. Mrs. Petit then played twelve southern melodies, the ladies guessing the title of each as played. . . . The club then listened to several southern songs as delightfully rendered by Misses Janice Mann and Freda Irey. At the concluding number of the program, Mrs. Harrison gave a musical reading, "The First Banjo." During the social hour we were served by the hostess to a dainty lunch.[4]

Mrs. Harrison, the hostess of this intimate gathering in a very small midwestern town, bookended her southern-themed party with two texts that must have been familiar enough to *News and Times* readers that their authorship required no mention. She concluded the event with Irwin Russell's much-anthologized dialect poem "De Fust Banjo," and for her opener she recited the monologue "A Change of Heart," which appeared in Blanche Goodman's booklet *The Viney Sketches* from 1919.[5] Although Mrs. Harrison almost certainly recited from this recent publication, monologues from *The Viney Sketches* had already been performed at similar gatherings around the United States for years because all of Goodman's material in the booklet had initially appeared in the *Saturday Evening Post*.

Blanche Goodman's role as a *Post* author is notable for at least two reasons. First, although Lorimer printed a considerable amount of material written by women during his editorship, the number of white female authors of Black dialect fiction in the magazine can almost be counted on one hand. In addition to Goodman, who was most successful at placing her dialect fiction in the magazine, Lorimer published one story by Mary Tracy Earle in 1901, one by Susan Teackle Moore in 1903, two by Sarah Johnson Cocke in 1917, three by Elsie Singmaster in the mid-1920s, and two by Marian Sims in 1934—and that's it. Male authors otherwise dominated the Black dialect genre in the *Post*. The number of female-authored stories in this vein is so small that I hesitate to make any broad claims about the gendered nature of this fiction beyond the observation that the female writers placed greater emphasis on the domestic sphere than did the male authors. Goodman published nineteen Viney monologues in the *Post* between 1908 and 1925, but this number is dwarfed by the publications of the white male authors Lorimer relied on for his regular doses of Black caricature. But Goodman is notable for a second, potentially more revealing reason—namely, that her life and work yield a great deal of information about how the *Post* was consumed and shared by readers and about how an aspiring author might write and sell fiction catering to Lorimer's literary predilection for racial stereotype. Blanche Goodman gives us a glimpse into how white Americans read the *Post*—both silently and aloud.

A surprising aspect of Goodman's biography is her evolution as a writer, thinker, and activist in the years after her time with the *Post*, and this evolution helps us understand the earlier, conscious decisions she must have made to write and sell her Viney monologues to Lorimer. None of the more prominent *Post* dialect writers I discuss in subsequent chapters ever moved away from the profitability of anti-Black "humor." Goodman was very different from these authors, and that difference may even explain why she disappeared from the pages of Lorimer's magazine. Indeed, by the 1930s, more than two decades after her first *Post* publication, Goodman represented much of what Lorimer had grown to hate in Franklin D. Roosevelt's New Deal America. A very public peace and labor activist, Goodman served on the boards of various left-leaning organizations and was a highly visible player in the cultural and political life of Chattanooga, Tennessee. In early 1936, coincidentally just weeks after Lorimer announced his retirement, the *Chattanooga News* devoted several column inches to Goodman, extolling her as a "liberal thinker and writer [and] example of feminine leadership."[6] Goodman's many forms of activism included her involvement in the Chattanooga Peace League, the Interracial Committee, the League for Industrial Democracy, and the Socialist Party. In her writing from this later period of her life (often in the form of letters to the editor), she challenged segregation, advocated for the environment, supported public expenditures for African Americans, and—in one of her last published pieces—offered a glowing appraisal of Benjamin Banneker, the eighteenth-century African American almanac writer. In today's parlance, the Blanche

Goodman of the 1930s was woke. The same, however, cannot be said about Goodman earlier in her life, when she both dreamed of becoming a professional writer and performed blackface amateur minstrelsy. At this point, she was a typical *Post* reader who considered publishing in the magazine as a sure marker of literary achievement—and she figured out how to make that happen.

This chapter focuses primarily on Blanche Goodman as an average white American and an exemplary *Post* author, one whose life and writing reveal the saturation of minstrelsy in the hearts and homes of her fellow citizens. Goodman's measured success at publishing in the *Post* reflects the national appetite for minstrelsy and reveals Lorimer's obvious predilection for Black dialect and caricature. I begin by examining her life in Chattanooga, where she both consumed and performed minstrelsy, and then I turn to a few of her Viney monologues to demonstrate how she formulated her fiction to appeal to the *Post*'s many readers and its singular editor. The chapter then follows Goodman's monologues from the pages of the magazine into the domestic and public spaces where this material was recited and performed. Taken together, Goodman's life and writing and the performance of her work help us better understand that Lorimer provided his audience with decades of formulaic, stereotypical, racist Black dialect writing because his readers craved new material to share with each other.

As I am suggesting, Goodman represents larger trends in the *Post* specifically and in the United States more generally. Numerous authors—as *Circulating Jim Crow* strives to demonstrate—also understood Lorimer's racial preferences and shaped their material accordingly. One such writer was the young F. Scott Fitzgerald. Without exception, all his early *Post* stories contain at least some element of racial caricature, and in a few stories minstrelsy is essential to plot development and romantic affect. The chapter concludes with a brief discussion of how two Black authors, Charles W. Chesnutt and Ann Petry, portrayed the ever-present but unacknowledged racial violence that is always implicit in the purportedly innocent pleasures of minstrelsy. In chapter 1, I charted out the hardening of Lorimer's editorial approach to representing African Americans as the inferior servitors of American modernity. In this chapter, I explore why—at least in part—Lorimer and his audience felt so connected to a sense of whiteness produced through the performance of phantasmatic Blackness.

BLANCHE GOODMAN:
AMATEUR MINSTREL, ASPIRING *POST* WRITER

Blanche Goodman was born in Chattanooga in 1878. Her father, Herman, a Hungarian immigrant, established a leather-finishing company and was a prominent member of the local Reformed synagogue, Mizpah Congregation. Her mother, the daughter of the congregation's first rabbi, was also very active in the synagogue and the Jewish community as a whole. Blanche was interested in performance and literature from an early age, and she started teaching at a high school in 1897, just one year after graduation. In 1910, she married Oscar Eisendrath, "a prominent cigar manufacturer of Chicago [who was] connected with one of the most aristocratic families of Chicago."[7] The young couple lived primarily in Chicago and Philadelphia for about twenty years before returning to Chattanooga permanently, at which point Blanche became deeply involved in her community. Oscar died in 1947, and Blanche appears to have led a quieter, less public life after that. She died in 1972 at the age of ninety-four and is buried in the Mizpah Cemetery. As it happens, her longtime family home on 710 East Fourth Street, which has since been demolished, was a block away from Chattanooga's Confederate Cemetery, a larger burial ground that abuts the Mizpah site. She may very well have been able to see the Confederate Cemetery from her window, and she sometimes incorporated this location into her writing.

Before the dominance of American print culture was hobbled by the digital era, local newspapers functioned as the social media of the day. Items such as the previously mentioned report on the Crescent Club gathering in Kansas in 1920 were standard fare for papers across the country, which reported on the smallest details of personal and family life, and this granular level of reporting about the affairs of local citizens allows us to chart Blanche Goodman's trajectory because she and her family were relatively prominent members of their community. According to the Chattanooga newspapers, Goodman appeared onstage at her synagogue from a very young age, and her social and working life as a teacher was reported on regularly. In 1904, when she was twenty-six, Goodman started to pursue her writing in earnest; she placed two poems in the local papers and one, "A Toast," in *Smart Set* magazine. Both "A Bachelor's Den" and "A Toast" are lyrics written in standard English and poetic diction, but "Johnny on the Weather" is a white dialect poem spoken by a young boy.[8]

In addition to being a felicitous year for the budding writer, 1904 was also significant for Blanche as a performer because she served as interlocutor—the master of ceremonies—in her synagogue's production of "Darktown Belles" at Chattanooga's Conservatory Hall. The *Chattanooga Daily Times* noted this amateur minstrel show in a recurring column, "Drawing-Room Chat," which reported on the social and domestic lives of Chattanooga residents. "Darktown Belles" was organized by Blanche's mother, "whose taste and skill arranged and managed it." Many of Blanche's friends and relatives participated, enjoying laughs at the "roll call[,] . . . a highly ludicrous feature" whose purpose was to ridicule "a string of negro names." The column gives Blanche copious praise for her "great" performance: "Her lines were scintillating, and she took the part excellently. Her climax was when she read the names of a number of leading gentlemen and said they had written notes asking, that on account of their modesty and social prominence, that their names not be mentioned. She was the recipient of many felicitations."[9] As I discuss further in a moment, Goodman's wink-and-nudge list of local, putatively modest "leading gentlemen" was a standard feature of blackface performance.

Goodman's participation in this amateur minstrel show exposes a great deal about the world she lived in and wrote from. As the laudatory "Drawing-Room Chat" item makes clear, young women putting on blackface and mocking African Americans were normal behavior and a standard form of entertainment. For example, "Darktown Belles" not only circulated widely in the United States as a popular song but was also the title of many amateur female minstrel groups and performances and used as a "humorous" reference to African American women more generally. There was nothing out of the ordinary in the young Blanche participating in such an event. In fact, at least ten other minstrel shows were staged in Chattanooga in 1904, most of them by professional traveling companies, including all-Black troupes, but there were also amateur benefit shows like Mizpah's for both a firehouse and the local cavalry troop as well as numerous other minstrel shows in surrounding municipalities. Amateur blackface performances such as "Darktown Belles" were an "unquestioned and ubiquitous part of everyday life" and "the amateur plays of choice for charity entertainment," states Barnes. "As a result, American towns revered amateur minstrelsy as a communal, participatory, and celebrated form of popular entertainment that increasingly became synonymous with Americanness."[10]

In Jim Crow America, a young Jewish schoolteacher blacking up for a benefit show was a typical feature of everyday life.

In addition to the unexceptional nature of Goodman's participation in "Darktown Belles," one more observation about the show's title is necessary. The name "Darktown" was regularly used in the literature and performances of the era as an appellation for Black urban districts.[11] Although this name as well as the similarly common "Blackville" were generally marked as humorous, they also point us toward the repression and violence undergirding the putative joke. Less than a month after the *Daily Times* sang praises for the Mizpah minstrel show, the same local paper also reported on, as its headline announced, the "'Darktown' Easter egg hunt." Although we cannot be certain that Goodman read this item, we might assume she did because her family and social circle appeared with such frequency in the papers that they must have been regular consumers of local media:

> The pickaninnies of Blue Goose Hollow and Tannery Flats . . . gathered in force on the brow of Cameron hill and celebrated the day with an egg hunt that baffles description in Anglo-Saxon; it could, perhaps, be described in the language of the Hottentot or Senegambian. There were black pickaninnies, "yaller" pickaninnies, kinky-headed pickaninnies, straight-haired pickaninnies and pickaninnies with no hair at all, and if a forest of monkeys or ourang-outangs had suddenly been transported from Africa and turned loose on the historic hill there could not possibly have been greater chattering or more fantastic monkey-shines performed. They simply took the hill by assault, and besides furnishing some amusement to the many visitors to Boynton park, caused the residents in the neighborhood much annoyance.[12]

The language in the first paragraph of this "news" item, with its repetition of the term *pickaninnies* and its riff on Africa and monkeys, was written to be humorous. But the real purpose of the article—like the ultimate purpose of minstrelsy itself—was to advocate for white supremacy, naturalize Black inferiority, and support racial segregation. The annoyance to the white neighbors around the park (the neighbors' race is unnamed, so we can assume they are white) leads to the article's real goal—to promote the Jim Crowing of another public space: "Along this line the question of whether Boynton park is going to be for white people or negroes—or

both—is one that should be settled at once." The rest of "'Darktown' Easter Egg Hunt" implicitly argued for racial segregation as a matter of "public safety," and—like the Mizpah's "Darktown Belles"—propped up white
hegemony by caricaturing African Americans. Boyton Park, by the way, is
about a mile and a half from the site of the Goodman family home. Even
closer to her house than the park is the Walnut Street Bridge, where two
Black men were lynched—Alfred Blount in 1893, while Blanche was in high
school, and Ed Johnson in 1906, just as her literary career was taking off.
Although I am not claiming a direct connection between Goodman's participation in the Mizpah minstrel show and these extralegal atrocities, it is
nonetheless hard to ignore the role that dehumanizing "humor" played in
sustaining the racist culture in Chattanooga that denigrated and murdered
its own citizens.

The appetite for minstrelsy in white America was enormous. First developed professionally in the Northeast in the nineteenth century, the amateur form of minstrelsy was promulgated initially by the Benevolent Order
of the Elks and other fraternal organizations; it proliferated nationally and
globally at a rapid pace, until even the U.S. federal government was involved
in its promotion. In tandem with the spread of such performances, a publishing industry arose that sold how-to guides, gag books, and other material for amateurs.[13] One of those distributors was so commercially successful that it required a new post office: "The Franklin, Ohio Post Office cites
Eldridge Entertainment House and the surge of mail-in order request forms
that they received for amateur play material as the reason the Franklin
branch post office was established in the first place. The opening of a federal post office to accommodate the unprecedented amount of mail shipped
to Franklin, Ohio, is strong evidence of how influential amateur black face
minstrelsy could be in a literal sense."[14] Eldridge was just one of many publishers and suppliers of printed material, costumes, stage equipment, cos-
metics, and so on used by amateur performers across the country. The *Saturday Evening Post*, which printed everything from brief "darky" gags to
an entire serialized novel written in Black dialect (see chapter 3), was a regular participant in this media ecology.

So was Blanche Goodman, who published her dialect material first in
the *Post* and then as a collection produced by the same outfit that required
its own post office. Harry C. Eldridge founded his company in 1906 (it still
exists today as Eldridge Publishing), which means the cast and crew of

Chattanooga's "Darktown Belles" in 1904 would have acquired their material from another supplier. One possible vendor is the Crest Trading Company, which advertised in the *Post* on December 16, 1905. The small ad, which asks, "Are You Interested in Amateur Theatricals?," featured a blackface figure, offered readers a free catalog of material for various entertainments, and emphasized in bold type that its material was well suited for "Charitable, Club, Lodge or Home Amusement."[15] It must be noted, however, that while minstrel imagery and racist gags in the *Post* can be found throughout Lorimer's tenure, advertisements for companies such as Crest were actually rather rare in the magazine's pages. Nonetheless, the description of Goodman's performance, particularly when she called out "the names of a number of leading gentlemen," indicates that she was most likely taking her cues from a how-to guide or gag book from a purveyor such as Crest. These texts were constructed to be interactive and "encouraged ownership [of the performance] by asking readers to insert personal anecdotes into plot lines and to use the names of local community leaders in punch lines."[16] In her role as interlocutor, Goodman may have literally taken a page from a how-to book when preparing for her leading role in blackface.

Considered together, the "Darktown Belles" of 1904 and the Crest Trading Company advertisement of 1905 allow me to draw two initial conclusions about Blanche Goodman and her world: blackface performance was "normal" and pervasive, and minstrelsy was not limited to the stage but was also an aspect of the domestic sphere. First, although I can find no direct evidence that Goodman blacked up for other amateur shows in Chattanooga or elsewhere, she was almost certainly in the audience for such events. Whether she went to any of the professional shows staged at local theaters by traveling troupes or to amateur events put on by other local, non-Jewish organizations, she probably attended at least some of the many minstrel performances staged by such Jewish organizations as Chattanooga's Young Zionists, Mizpah Sisterhood, and Jewish Community Center. While Goodman was writing for the *Post*, minstrelsy was a feature of her world, and there was nothing out of the ordinary about this state of affairs across most of Jim Crow America. Second, as the Crest advertisement demonstrates, minstrelsy was not simply viewed on the stage by passive spectators but was also a participatory "home amusement." Although "home amusement" might imply the silent, solitary reading of printed matter, it also suggests the home as a performance space, where friends and family—members of the Crescent Club, say, or readers of "Drawing-Room Chat"—might amuse each other by sharing jokes, making music, and reading to each other. With these two points in mind, we can understand the young Blanche Goodman as a consumer, producer, and performer of Black dialect, and it is this Blanche Goodman who figured out how to sell her material to George Horace Lorimer.

THE VINEY MONOLOGUES:
"I DON' WANT NO MO' RIGHTS DAN I HAS ALREADY"

In mid-1907, Goodman took significant concrete steps toward her goal of becoming a professional writer. Three years after her star turn in "Darktown Belles," she was elected secretary of the Tennessee Women's Press and Authors' Club, and shortly after that she resigned from her job as a teacher.[17] According to the *Chattanooga Star*, "Miss Goodman has been identified with the educational interests of the city for the past several years, during which time she has made an enviable record. It is understood that she will devote her time to literary work."[18] Goodman became noticeably productive in 1907, and by 1908 the *Chattanooga Daily Times* could report that she had placed her poetry and fiction with *Century, Smart Set,* and the *Delineator*.[19] At the end of the same year came even more exciting news, as reported in the society page, "Chattanooga Day by Day: Social and Personal": "The friends of Miss Blanche Goodman will be interested to know that she has a humorous negro dialect story in the Christmas number of the *Saturday Evening Post*, entitled 'Helping Rosabel, or Borrowed Plumes and a Blow to Pride.'"[20] Goodman's efforts were starting to bear fruit, and the publication of "Helping Rosabel" initiated a trend in her published work. When she was not selling fiction to the *Post*, she almost always wrote in standard English and on conventional themes. She made her leap from local papers and smaller-circulation magazines to the *Post*, American print culture's remunerative juggernaut, by submitting a Black dialect story to Lorimer's magazine, which, coincidentally, would officially reach a circulation of one million just a week after Goodman's first publication there. Goodman was a perspicacious reader of the *Post*, and she crafted her Viney monologues to appeal to Lorimer's predilection for dialect and caricature as well as to his magazine's unmistakable nostalgia for an unchallenged white patriarchy.

Goodman achieved qualified success at becoming a *Post* author. Almost without exception, Lorimer always placed Goodman's Viney monologues toward the back of the magazine (this is also true for Goodman's straight poetry, which she would publish in the *Post* later in her writing career), and only one of her nineteen dialect pieces merited its own dedicated illustrations. Although Lorimer published a fair amount of Goodman's writing overall, he seemed to regard her work primarily as filler for back pages devoted mostly to smaller, less expensive advertisements. This is certainly the case for Goodman's first *Post* story, "Helping Rosabel," which is located on the last page of the December 5, 1908, issue. Viney's monologue is sandwiched between advertisements for such items as a Catholic prayer book, a posthole augur, sausages, and a booklet of shoe extensions for "Lame People." On the inside back cover, dwarfing Goodman's contribution, is a full-page ad for Everwear Hosiery featuring a nearly half-page image of a black sock. Goodman's writing helped fill a page and, to a certain extent, to satisfy Lorimer's taste for dialect, but she never achieved the same stature as her male counterparts, whose work was *always* featured more prominently. Nevertheless, Goodman managed to publish her monologues from 1908 to 1925, and by virtue of her almost singular status as a white female author of Black dialect fiction in the *Post*, her protagonist, Viney, has more speaking lines than any other Black female character during Lorimer's entire editorship. Considered collectively and despite their lower status in the magazine, the Viney monologues exemplify almost perfectly Lorimer's editorial preference for dialect fiction that registered Black experiences of modernity and recontained them within the straitjacket of caricature and antebellum nostalgia.

Goodman's protagonist, Viney Harris, is the longtime family factotum of Colonel Slocum and his wife, Fanny, serving variously as their nursemaid, seamstress, washerwoman, and cook, and her monologues are usually set in Chattanooga. As Joel Chandler Harris rhapsodized more generally about family servants and dusky mammies in "The Negro as the South Sees Him" (see chapter 1), Viney represents the "oldest and most venerable of the negroes," "the old time darky."[21] Her monologues are usually framed by brief exchanges with a friend or neighbor, most often the elderly Uncle Peter, whom Goodman portrays as even more impossibly ignorant than Viney. Each story typically takes up some aspect of contemporary life and contrasts Viney's incomplete understanding of modernity with the seemingly instinctual wisdom of her folk knowledge—a knowledge that always naturalizes her servility and justifies the rigidity of the existing racial caste structure. Whereas Goodman's earliest *Post* monologues tend to impute moral laxity, innate criminality, and violent tendencies to African Americans, her later monologues focus more on social and political changes, often with an emphasis on changing gender norms.

Two monologues published at the beginning of Goodman's *Post* career establish Viney's racially determined inferiority as well as her fawning relationship to her white employers. These monologues implicitly argue that although Viney is generally trustworthy, she nonetheless requires white supervision—as do African Americans generally. In "Helping Rosabel," Viney explains that she lent one of Miss Fanny's dresses to Rosabel to help in Rosabel's romantic pursuit of a local preacher. As Viney tells the story, she reveals that she habitually uses the Slocum family's clothes and linens for her own purposes and lends them out freely to other members of the local Black community. In a previous transgression, "I let de folks over at de strawbe'y festibul have one of Mis' Fanny's baffinbug tidies for de table . . . I had to scorch it with a hot iron to cover up de place where a stain was made on it, an' den preten' to Mis' Fanny like I scorched it by ax'dent." After Fanny finds Rosabel wearing her dress, she demands the return of her family's clothing. While Viney's conclusion from these events is that "white folks got no business pokin' around where dey don't belong," a *Post* reader would infer from the story that African Americans, no matter how faithful, require surveillance and close management.[22] This assertion amplified Harris Dickson's warning in 1907 about Black domestics in "The Way of the Reformer" (see chapter 1), which warned against the "stealage" by female Black domestic workers, whose presence in white homes threatened the supposed impermeability of the color line.[23] In "Helping Rosabel," African American characters wearing white people's clothing served to remind *Post* readers that without vigilance the color line would be crossed more often than they realized.

Goodman made the need for white control over African Americans crystal clear in "Out on Bail" (March 4, 1911), her fourth *Post* monologue. Viney narrates the story of Katie Belle, who is in jail because she slashed her man with a razor, had a second razor at the ready for her beau's "yaller gal," and was excessively drunk when arrested. Despite her reputation for violence, Katie is also a renowned cook, and Colonel Slocum pays her bail so he can hire her. Although Katie at first demonstrates her skills in the kitchen, she cannot help but get drunk and go berserk at a large social event. Viney describes "Katie Belle in de middle o' de kitchen flo', whoopin' like a Injun, wid a razor in each han'. She had broke into de drinkables an' busted thoo her bail, an' what was lef' o' de wine wouldn't 'a' drownded a flea com'for'ble." Viney saves the day when she retrieves the Colonel's hidden brandy bottle—which she knows about because she also breaks into the Slocums' drinkables—and waves it in front of Katie, who robotically ends her rampage like a hypnotized cartoon character following an imagined, beckoning hand. "Down come dat coon's han's, de razors draps to do flo' an' she grabbed fo' dat bottle like greased lightnin'."[24] Katie's purportedly inevitable bad behavior (because she is Black) threatens to harm the Slocum family, and it happens because the Colonel ignores the white-supremacist tenet that African Americans are innately violent and require careful supervision. Or, as Thomas Dixon Jr. warned *Post* readers in 1905, the "real tragedy begins . . . when the Negro ceases to work under the direction of the Southern man."[25] And because Slocum ignores his wife's obvious hesitancy about hiring Katie in the first place, he also undermines the order of the domestic sphere. In her early monologues for the *Post*, then, Goodman reinforced the ideology of an impermeable color line predicated on Black inferiority as well as the necessity of white surveillance and control and the "separate but equal" spheres of gendered power and responsibility. In the Viney monologues, white men should be men, white women be women, and both should be mindful about how they maintain dominance over Black people in the racial hierarchy.

"Helping Rosabel" and "Out on Bail" naturalize racial hierarchy and the necessity of white paternalism. Goodman's third publication in the *Post*, "Educating Sally Ann" (April 9, 1910), continued these themes as well as Goodman's endorsement of patriarchal gender norms. "Educating Sally Ann" appears to have enjoyed a measure of national success as a performance piece. Nineteen years after the monologue's first appearance, for example, the *Wausau (Wisconsin) Daily Record-Herald* reported on a "meeting of the ladies' aid society of the First Methodist church," where students performed musical numbers and a puppet show, "and another comical feature of the program was a monologue 'Educating Sally Anne,' one of the famous Viney sketches in negro dialect, given by Mrs. J. G. Sanders."[26] The paper's reference to Viney's fame seems to indicate that despite being lost to subsequent literary history, Goodman's work circulated widely and was read aloud in all sorts of gatherings. "Educating Sally Ann" also exemplifies how white-authored Black dialect fiction in the *Post* registered modern Black experience only to recontain it within the straits of white supremacy. In this story and without referring either to Booker T. Washington or W. E. B. Du Bois, Goodman staged a contest between their competing ideas about African American education. As could be predicted, and despite Washington's diminished status in the *Post* by 1910, Sally Ann's studies are complete only once she sets aside her books and assumes a vocation by putting on an apron to cook for white people.

Sally Ann's earlier miseducation happened when a "Yankee woman" took her to a school in the North to "git aidgecated." Two years later, after her northern benefactor dies, Sally Ann returns to Chattanooga a changed person—and not for the better, according to Viney. Sally Ann now "talks prissy," has learned personal hygiene the "same as white folks," has the temerity to sit in a window reading books, and now wants to be called "Sarah." With this characterization, Goodman echoed the charges against northern interference in southern affairs by other *Post* contributors such as Joel Chandler Harris, Thomas Dixon Jr., and Harris Dickson. Before long, exigent family circumstances force Sally Ann to leave her books to work in Miss Fanny's kitchen, but the first dinner she prepares is a disaster, and she is promptly fired. At this point, Viney provides Sally Ann with the "real" education of the monologue: "You needn't wall yo' eyes roun' at me, fo' you is a niggah, an' you'se mighty nigh a white-livered one at dat. . . . All yo aidgecation . . . ain't learnt you no respec'. . . . You knows how to han'le a pen . . . but you can't bake a batch er biscuits. . . . You knows how to shine up yo' nails like white folks, but you can't beat up a plain cup cake. . . . You knows how to set up by de winder and show off to folks how you can read printin', but you ain't never done a week's washin'."[27]

Viney concludes her excoriation of Sally Ann with a gesture toward the work ethic of the self-made man that Lorimer championed in his magazine. But, of course, the implication here is that in America Sally Ann's—a Black woman's—bootstraps would lift her only up to Miss Fanny's service and no farther: "Ef you is got a mossel er sense left in you what ain't been aidgecated out of you, you's gwine drap yo' persnickety ways an' git down to business an' show what kin' er stuff you's made of."[28] Viney's lesson has its intended result. Sally Anne learns to accept her subservient position in the racial hierarchy by becoming a reliably good cook, and Goodman's *Post* readers had another example of the acceptable place for African Americans in Lorimer's Jim Crow America.

Sally Ann also learns to accept her limited options in the patriarchy. By the publication of this monologue in 1910, Lorimer and the *Post* were moving toward a greater acceptance of women's expanding rights in the United States, and he had become extremely conscious of women's powerful role as consumers of the many products advertised in his magazine. But when Blanche Goodman was contemplating becoming a professional writer just a few years earlier and was considering the *Post* a desirable goal, Lorimer and his publisher, Cyrus Curtis, envisioned the magazine primarily as a male version of its sister periodical, the *Ladies' Home Journal*. According to Jan Cohn, the *Post* of this era was characterized by "sour editorials repining over the lost virtues of grandmother's time. Like the occasional article on the subject, the rare *Post* editorial treated women as object and other."[29] Cohn cites "Why Women Go to Seed" (December 10, 1904) as an example, and we can see how this editorial, which took aim at financially secure white women, also applied to the Black, northern-educated Sally Ann, who initially eschews domestic service so she can keep her nails clean and read. "There is the problem," the editorial claimed, "of the emancipated woman. This name has often been absurdly applied to the woman who has, or is reputed to have, or fancies she has, a 'higher education'—whatever that may be." Idle women, warned the editorialist, are "either going to seed or plotting mischief."[30] In 1904, states Cohn, the "world of women in general, as far as the *Post* was concerned, was a world fallen sadly away from the nostalgic ideal of homemaker, wife, and mother."[31] By 1909, however, especially after Lorimer hired Adelaide Neall, who would quickly become "one of [his] trusted editorial lieutenants,"[32] the magazine began shifting its attitudes about—and marketing for—women. By contrast, Goodman served both in the rearguard of the gendered hierarchy and as a willing soldier in Lorimer's literary race war against African Americans.

These antimodern, antifreedom racial and gender sentiments can be found everywhere in Goodman's fiction. In "The Equalizing Bug" (April 8, 1911), for example, Viney attends a white women's club meeting, where race relations will be the topic of discussion. When the invited speaker has the audacity to identify white people as the cause of injustice, Viney rises with great indignation, declaring that Black people are happy staying in their place, that white people are innately benevolent and smarter, and that Black people will insist on equal rights in their own good time: "I knows good an' well when de time comes fo' us niggers to equalize ourselves we's a-gwine to do hit of our own free will, jes' de way you white folks has done wid yo'selves, an' we don't need no one to keep punchin' us in de back fo' to make us move faster[;] . . . you can say whatever you wants to 'bout us niggers ez long's hits in front of our backs. But when you commences pickin' on my white folks . . . dat's a dif'unt thing. . . . I'd lay down on de groun' an' let any of 'em walk on my ol' black neck ef dey tuck a notion to."[33]

Goodman continued her defense of the racialized patriarchy in "White Folks' Rights" (December 2, 1911), which also offers a challenge to the suffrage movement and concludes with Viney's assertion that women should "quit politics an' leave 'em to the men." According to Viney, white women should abandon their campaign for voting rights and remember that they already have the "right" to bear and raise children and to tend to their husbands. Black women have even more rights: "I don' want no mo' rights dan I has already. I has so many of 'em now dat sometimes I sets back an' wonders dat some of 'em don't spill off'n me 'cause dey am so crowded fo' room. I has de right to take in five washin's a week. I has de righ to pay de rent . . . I has de right to nuss [my husband] an' de chillen when dey am sick. Dem's de big rights I has, an' I don't know how many li'l rights I has."[34] Echoing the "sour" editorial "Why Women Go to Seed," Goodman's monologue endorsed restrictive gender norms and even more constraining racial roles. Her monologue also resonated with Rebecca Harding Davis's claim in 1904 (see chapter 1) that white women would rather be disenfranchised than allow Black men to have the vote.

Lorimer would continue printing Goodman's monologues sporadically until 1925, but his interest in this writer reached its pinnacle with the publication of "Checkmating Miss Fanny" on October 11, 1913. Previously, with "White Folks' Rights," Goodman's work had inched farther away from the back of the magazine. This monologue is decorated with unrelated but attractive illustrations and placed before the editorials page, which generally served as the dividing line between featured work and recurrent items such as "Who's Who—and Why" and "Sense and Nonsense" as well as continuations of long articles or stories and—most importantly—almost all the magazine's advertisements. "Checkmating Miss Fanny"—Goodman's greatest *Post* success—appears on page 8, warrants a continuation to a later page, and has three dedicated images. The artist assigned to the story, Henry Raleigh, was a prominent illustrator at the magazine; in the same year Raleigh created images for Goodman, he also drew for such notable *Post* authors as Will Irwin, Maximillian Foster, Charles E. Van Loan, Edna Ferber, and Will Payne—not to mention for a Judge Priest story by Irvin S. Cobb and two dialect stories by Harris Dickson.

"Checkmating Miss Fanny," akin to "White Folks' Rights" before it, mocks the women's rights movement. This monologue once again hinges on the idea that Viney is never quite intelligent enough to understand all the implications of the stories she recounts. In this instance, Colonel Slocum takes Viney's unintended advice about how to tame his wife, who has become active in the suffrage movement. Much to the Colonel's dismay, Miss Fanny "wan't doin' a thing but sashayin' roun' fum one meetin' to another." Exasperated by his wife's crusading, the Colonel patronizingly asks Viney when she will also start asking for greater rights, and Viney replies—with her unwitting wisdom—that she will do so as soon as her husband says she cannot. This comment sets the inevitable wheels of a *Post* dialect story in motion, and soon enough the Colonel becomes one of the most ardent and visible suffragists in Chattanooga. Miss Fanny is pleased at first, but as her husband continues to work by her side, friends and neighbors begin teasing her, and she starts longing for the ancien regime of separate gender spheres. Her increasing discomfort with the Colonel's behavior prompts him to perform even greater and more public acts for "the Cause," and "Checkmating Miss Fanny" comes to its climax when the Colonel says he is preparing to march in the all-women's suffrage parade being organized by his wife. Crumbling under this final piece of reverse psychology, Fanny demands her husband keep away from the march, and he agrees to her request—with this proviso: "'Leave votin' an' politics to me,' says de Cunnel, smilin' at huh lak a sweetheart. 'Be lak you used to be fo' dis suffidge business come up—a gyahden of flowers where I can come an' enjoy de loveliness an' sweetness, an' res' aftah a day of toil!'"[35] Miss Fanny, blushing like a teenager, acquiesces; peace and the old order are restored in the Slocum house. Once again, Goodman's monologue asserts the rectitude of patriarchal white supremacy. She sold Lorimer exactly the kind of story he liked to publish.

Henry Raleigh's accompanying illustrations to "Checkmating Miss Fanny" magnify the ideological implications of Goodman's monologue and

reflect a more general practice of image making in the *Post*. Two illustrations are at the top of the first page of this story. On the left, the elegantly
dressed and coifed Miss Fanny leisurely sits in a chair surrounded by books
as she gazes out a window, and she very much resembles one of the small
army of white women increasingly featured on *Post* covers once Lorimer
decided to attract more female readers. By contrast, from the top right side
of the page and dressed in her maid's apron, Viney stares with concern
across the columns of print toward her mistress, pausing only briefly from
her work, while her counterpart sits and thinks. Viney's role as an old-timey
servant is further emphasized by the third illustration on the page, which
features Viney and Uncle Peter sitting on the front steps of her quaint, ramshackle cabin. Peter's fringe of white hair is an unmistakable allusion to
the more famous Uncle Remus. Viney and Peter are perfect visual and textual examples of the Old Negro as defined by Alain Locke: "His has been a
stock figure perpetuated as an historical fiction partly in sentimentalism,
partly in deliberate reactionism."[36]

The juxtaposition of idealized images of white womanhood with
demeaning caricatures of African Americans was a regular feature of the
Saturday Evening Post. This stark contrast is especially evident when one
considers the covers of the magazine that contain Goodman's monologues.
The same issue offering the animalistic portrayal of Katie Belle, the berserk cook in "Out on Bail," whom Viney characterizes as "de blackes', fattes'
coon 'ooman,"[37] features a cover illustration of a young white woman happily sledding in winter. "Educating Sally Ann," which narrates the taming
of a young Black woman who wants a better life, can be found in an issue
whose cover is *Sweatered Girl Trying to Fly a Kite*, a title that only intensifies the distinction between the possibilities of white freedom and the
impermissibility of Black aspiration. The cover for "Checkmating Miss
Fanny" features a white woman staring confidently at the viewer, secure in
"incandescent beauty," according to the illustration's title. One of the notable exceptions to this juxtaposition between Goodman's demeaning word
portraits and Lorimer's promotion of white female beauty is the cover for
the Christmas issue of December 2, 1911, which contains the story "White
Folks' Rights," where Viney vociferously insists on her "right" to toil and
drudgery. The cover, illustrated by J. C. Leyendecker, one of the *Post*'s most
iconic artists, portrays an older Black servant, with the same fringe of white
hair as Uncle Peter, serving a suckling pig. Unlike the self-assured white

woman accompanying the "Checkmating Miss Fanny" issue, the Black servant in Leyendecker's image has downturned eyes, signifying his subservience and obeisance to the prevailing racial order. Leyendecker's cover is one of only a tiny handful that feature African Americans, and—as one would expect of Lorimer—all these covers represent African Americans as either domestic or manual laborers.

In October 1911, the *Chattanooga News* ran a long piece boasting that many "Chattanoogans can claim high rank in [the] literary world," and Goodman was included in this roundup of local authors. Her fame and popularity, the article suggested, developed as she increasingly understood what kind of material would be salable to the *Post*: "Gradually, her work assumed the form so acceptable to magazine readers, the picturing of the antebellum negro. Her dialect sketches have been widely published and recited."[38] With "Checkmating Miss Fanny" in 1913, Goodman created her most "acceptable" sketch for those readers and achieved her highest visibility in the magazine, but it is possible she was also starting to have some misgivings about the implications of her fiction. Five years after the monologue's publication, Goodman attended a Chattanooga suffrage meeting, where she announced a change of mind about women's rights: "Mrs. Eisendrath told of her conversion to suffrage in a very animated and interesting talk. She intends to write an antisuffrage story, purposely to convert the anti in the next story."[39] After the publication of "Checkmating Miss Fanny," Lorimer published Viney monologues addressing current topics such as food conservation during World War I, the internal workings of civic clubs, Prohibition, and Freudian psychology. It is unclear if Goodman ever wrote her suffrage/antisuffrage diptych, but it is perfectly clear that Lorimer never published such items. In fact, it is impossible to imagine Lorimer publishing anything that would present a Black character—male or female—successfully advocating for expanded rights for *anyone*. Goodman's acumen at determining what Lorimer would buy took her far enough to achieve some measure of national name recognition and a great deal of local fame in Chattanooga, but as the years wore on, her political inclinations diverged from her literary ambitions, and she began using her writing and organizing talents to challenge the world she grew up in—the same world Lorimer was trying to conserve in part through the dialect fiction that worked for decades to convince *Saturday Evening Post* readers that African Americans were best understood as "prototypical anti-modern anti-citizens."[40]

PERFORMING VINEY

Despite Goodman's ultimate evolution into someone consciously less racist than the twenty-six-year-old schoolteacher who happily applied blackface along with her friends and family at Mizpah Congregation, the "comic"
image of Black servility and inferiority she created through her Viney
monologues lived on. Whenever Goodman was discussed at any length in
Chattanooga newspapers, up to and including her obituaries, she was always
cited as a successful *Post* author. Although the white male authors I discuss in other chapters enjoyed far greater success—with a large number of
their racist fantasies being adapted for stage, screen, and radio—Goodman's
monologues were nonetheless read at large and small gatherings throughout the country. Evidence of the performative nature of Goodman's work
is literally written into remaining copies of her inexpensively produced
monograph *The Viney Sketches*. The eighty-two-page booklet, which features two barely legible images of what appear to be Black children on the
cover, is dedicated to Goodman's mother and was "*Reprinted by permission
from the Saturday Evening Post.*" The Library of Congress has a photodigi-
tized copy on its website, and in it the first monologue, "Book-Raisin'," contains markings made in advance of a public reading. I was also able to
obtain my own copy of the booklet, and it appears that someone named
Dorothy Clair was scheduled to read from "Helping Rosabel"—Goodman's
first *Post* publication—on a forthcoming Saturday (figure 2.1).

Goodman achieved a measurable level of success by consciously becoming a Black dialect writer for the *Post*. Because her monologues were written to be performed, they afforded her audience opportunities not only to
laugh along with the "humor" of white supremacy but also to perform intimate acts of racial love and theft. For example, at a Daughters of the
American Revolution gathering in Tampa in 1919, "Mrs. T. Roy Young, dis-
guised as an old negro mammy, came to see her 'white folks,' presenting
each of the honor [*sic*] guests with old-fashioned nosegays, and giving in
her inimitable style, a negro dialect reading" of a Goodman monologue.
In El Paso, Texas, another monologue was read to kindergarteners by one
of their mothers at a school event in 1923.[41] Barnes notes, "The performa-
tivity of this kind of reading (mimicking performance directions as it related
to personifying blackness) involved the body, voice, and mind, which committed these texts to sensory memory for many participants[,] making

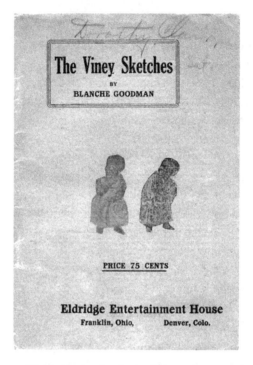

FIGURE 2.1. Front cover of Blanche Goodman's collection *The Viney Sketches* (Franklin, OH: Eldridge Entertainment House, 1919), inscribed with "Dorothy Clair, Sat[urday]."

them feel very personal."[42] Imagine for a moment the emotional cathexis to phantasmatic Blackness experienced by the kindergarten child whose mother performed a Viney monologue at the front of the class. This was the readership and audience Lorimer was consciously developing as his image of American life.

I want to insert a personal note here. As I researched the *Post* and read through a seemingly endless archive of predictable, interchangeable "humor" that repeats the same set of jokes, recycles a limited number of plot structures, and relies on the same two-dimensional characters, I often wondered why anyone would want to read this stuff again and again. Blanche Goodman as an aspiring *Post* writer and the success of her Viney monologues help me answer this question by considering the broad demand for minstrelsy that Lorimer both shared and satisfied. Wanting to perform for each other, *Post* readers kept returning to predictable dialect fiction

because they had an enormous thirst for *material*. Goodman's writing was
certainly read silently, but it was also read aloud—in the privacy of families, in the intimate gatherings of clubs, and at larger events such as recit-
als, school functions, and other public performances. Before, during, and
after Goodman's publications in the magazine and in addition to more
prominent, longer Black dialect fiction, Lorimer also incorporated brief,
incidental racist jokes into his magazine for years. Such items were certainly
meant for an immediate and perhaps silent chuckle, but they were also fodder for white Americans who wanted something to say at the office water
cooler or at genteel gatherings such as those at the Crescent Club of Downs,
Kansas, where "'Darky' jokes were read by each member of the club." These
club women might very well have found Goodman's monologue and their
jokes in the *Post*, or perhaps they gleaned their material from one of the
booklets produced by minstrel-paraphernalia suppliers such as Eldridge
and Crest. Or maybe they stored away something they saw at an amateur
or professional minstrel show. What Goodman shows us is that intimate
performances of white supremacy were a regular feature of the American
culture Lorimer strove to produce through his magazine. In the laudatory
Post article "Old-Time Minstrel Men" (September 29, 1900), the anonymous
author, an "Old-Timer," described the ecology of minstrelsy as a regularly
refreshing source of material for everyday white Americans: "Negro minstrelsy to-day has settled into a regular thing; people go to a show, enjoy it,
memorize the 'gags,' work them off with an unconscious and spontaneous
air on less fortunate friends, and then wait for the return of the show to lay
in a new supply."[43] Readers of the *Post*, including Blanche Goodman, needed
to wait only a few weeks at most for "new" gags because Lorimer made sure
to lay in a new supply on a reliable basis.

F. SCOTT FITZGERALD AND THE *POST* FORMULA

Neither Goodman's imbrication in the broadly shared American culture of
intimate minstrel performance nor her efforts to write marketable fiction
for the *Post* were unique to her. Countless authors tried to figure out how
to satisfy Lorimer's tastes and predilections. In *The Writer's Yearbook and
Market Guide* of 1930, for example, Thomas H. Uzzell attempted to define
"'the Saturday Evening Post' formula," and he began by noting, "To many
thousands of writers in this country literary success means selling a story

in *The Saturday Evening Post.*" Because of its circulation, fame, reputation, and generous payment policy, the magazine was the "most inviting target for the fiction writer."[44] In addition to Goodman, another aspiring author who targeted the *Post* at the beginning of his career was F. Scott Fitzgerald, who burst on the literary scene with the publication of his first novel, *This Side of Paradise*, in 1920 and then solidified his burgeoning literary reputation by becoming a *Post* author. Like Goodman, Fitzgerald also took note of Lorimer's penchant for anti-Black humor—as one simple set of numbers reveals. In 1920, Fitzgerald published six short stories each in both the *Post* and *Smart Set* magazine published by H. L. Mencken and George Jean Nathan. In those printed by Mencken and Nathan ("The Débutante," "Porcelain and Pink," "Benediction," "Mr. Icky," "The Smilers," and "May Day"), there are no examples of Black dialect, caricatures, or characters. By contrast, in the six stories Lorimer published in his magazine ("Head and Shoulders," "Myra Meets His Family," "The Camel's Back," "Bernice Bobs Her Hair," "The Ice Palace," and "The Offshore Pirate"), every story includes at least one Black character, some element of racial caricature, or some sort of minstrelsy. In some of Fitzgerald's first *Post* stories, Black characters or motifs are fleeting, but in others ideological constructions of Blackness are key to advancing plot or developing characters. And a few of these stories reveal that Fitzgerald, like Goodman, understood white America's deep emotional and psychological investment in domestic and public performances of embodied Blackness.

Two stories, "The Ice Palace" (May 22, 1920) and "The Offshore Pirate" (May 29, 1920), are most pertinent here. "The Ice Palace" romanticizes a small Georgia city as a "languid paradise of dreamy skies and firefly evenings and noisy street fairs," and its protagonist, Sally Carol Happer, takes her northern fiancé to the Confederate section of the local cemetery, where she moons over "the most beautiful thing in the world—the dead South." Strolling past the graves, Sally Carol recalls the stories of "strange courtliness and chivalry" she heard from "a Confederate soldier who lived next door, and a few old darkies." I can envision Blanche Goodman of Chattanooga taking her own northern-born fiancé, Oscar Eisendrath of Chicago, into her city's nearby Confederate cemetery and making a similar speech about the romance of the Lost Cause, although this is purely a figment of my imagination. And here is an even more speculative thought: one of the only sympathetic northern characters in "The Ice Palace" is Mr. Bellamy, who "was born in Kentucky" and has "iron-gray hair."[45] Because of Lorimer's stature as an American success story, his biography and appearance were well known. He was, in fact, a northerner who was born in Louisville, and photographs of him in the 1910s and 1920s show that his hair had started to gray. It is tempting to imagine Fitzgerald inserting this minor character as an offering to Lorimer, one of the most powerful and best-paying gatekeepers of national literary prominence.

Better evidence of Fitzgerald's careful attention to Lorimer's predilection for Black caricature—if still circumstantial—is found in "The Offshore Pirate," a story that also thematizes the type of domestic minstrel performance exemplified by Goodman's monologues. Two lines from Fitzgerald's story provide strong indication that while he was crafting "The Offshore Pirate," he was also reading another rising *Post* star—Hugh Wiley, who had published his first Black dialect story featuring the Wildcat in March 1919 (see chapter 4). According to Matthew Bruccoli, Fitzgerald wrote "The Offshore Pirate" "between November 1919 and February 1920."[46] In this story, the male love interest, Toby Moreland, who is masquerading as "Curtis Carlyle," tells the flapper protagonist, Ardita Farnam, "You're our Lady Luck. Guess we'll have to keep you as our mascot." By November 1919, "Lady Luck" was already established as a recurrent motif in Wiley's stories, as was the reference to Wildcat's pet goat, Lily, as his "mascot." In addition, Fitzgerald describes the story's Black characters as having an "unconquerable African craving for sleep,"[47] which is a distinct echo of the Wildcat's repeated scenes of sleeping and especially of his line "Africa ain't so bad. . . . Sleep mos' all de time."[48] As Jade Broughton Adams notes, Fitzgerald understood the profitability of the *Post* (and other national magazines), and he "set about establishing what they enjoyed in a story, by going through back issues and noting recurring themes and patterns."[49] Regular readers of the *Post*, especially those who looked forward to new material from its Black dialect writers, would have easily ascertained Fitzgerald's allusion to Wiley's fiction through the inclusion of references to "Lady Luck" and "mascot."

These details about "The Offshore Pirate" offer tantalizing, if not entirely conclusive, suggestions about Fitzgerald's preparation for submitting manuscripts to Lorimer's magazine. But there is no mistaking the private performance of white-imagined Blackness that comprises most of this early

Fitzgerald *Post* story. On its surface, "The Offshore Pirate" is sprinkled with the sort of racist characterizations found elsewhere in the *Post* ("pickaninnies," "darkies," and "wharf nigger" appear together on one page, for example),[50] and when the Black characters shoot dice, they again echo the many examples of craps games in Wiley's Wildcat fiction. More to the point, however, is Toby Moreland's private minstrel performance for Ardita Farnam, which constitutes nothing less than a "mode of seduction"[51] rooted in the racialized pleasures of blackface that—as Goodman's monologues reveal—could be found everywhere in the homes and hearts of white-supremacist America. The formulaic, taming-of-the-flapper plot in "The Offshore Pirate" is almost entirely predictable, and Toby's ruse and manipulation of Ardita resemble the sort of trickery common to stories by Wiley and Cohen (and to many humorous *Post* stories more generally). The story begins aboard a yacht, establishes Ardita as a "willful, self-centered debutante,"[52] and then moves quickly to the appearance of "Curtis Carlyle and his Six Black Buddies." This crew of ersatz pirates assumes control of the ship and sails to a tropical island, where Toby successfully woos Ardita before revealing his scheme and securing the love of his future bride.

Toby's ploy is predicated on the white intimacy produced through performances of Blackness. Fitzgerald establishes this character's white masculinity by first contrasting him with "a great hulking negro." Toby, by comparison, has blue eyes, looks like a Greek statue, and "was trimly built, trimly dressed, and graceful as an agile quarterback." After the Black "pirates" board the yacht, they arrange themselves before Toby, "a coal-black and burly darky at one end and a miniature mulatto of four feet nine at the other." In this formation, they conjure the image of a staged minstrel performance, with an endman on either side and Toby—like the young Blanche Goodman in "The Darktown Belles"—standing in the middle, serving as the interlocutor. With this unmistakable gesture toward minstrelsy, Toby's seduction of Ardita begins in earnest. As the story unfolds, every moment of increased intimacy between the two white lovers is facilitated through the presence of Blackness. For example, just before Toby relates his fictionalized origin story—he tells Ardita he grew up in a Black neighborhood and became a ragtime musician—she invites him to "lie to me by moonlight." As if by magic, one of the Black characters appears, turns on some mood lighting, and sets the table for them. As Toby finishes his falsified romantic biography, the Black Buddies start singing "a haunting melody." Ardita listens to them "in enchantment," and love becomes increasingly certain. "The Offshore Pirate" culminates formulaically with Ardita melting in Toby's arms, accompanied by "negroes' voices [floating] drowsily back, [mingling] in an air that she had heard them sing before."[53] Fitzgerald gives his story an exotic setting, but Toby's figurative act of blackface[54] is as familiar and homey to Ardita on a tropical island as it would have been in the American heartland—to, say, the women of the Crescent Club in Downs, Kansas.

Fitzgerald made a similar connection between white love and intimate performances of minstrelsy elsewhere in his early *Post* stories, two of which I will mention briefly. In "Myra Meets His Family" (March 20, 1920), a romantic hoax is advanced during an at-home, "informal neighborhood vaudeville," when the titular flapper heroine concludes her performance—an olio of popular dance and musical forms—by ending "in a burst of inspiration . . . in an Al Jolson position, on her knees with her arms stretched out to her audience in syncopated appeal."[55] Like Toby Moreland, Myra summons both love and blackface by embodying Jolson, one of America's best-known "negro delineators." Finally, during a country club cotilion in "The Camel's Back" (April 4, 1920), the story's young lovers get married through the auspices of Jumbo, an African American character who speaks in dialect and behaves according to the white fantasies fueled by the broad proliferation of minstrelsy in American homes, in social gatherings, and in popular and material culture more broadly.[56] In other words, F. Scott Fitzgerald, like Blanche Goodman before him, became a *Saturday Evening Post* author by providing Lorimer and his audience with new, racialized material they could read privately or perform for each other.

CHARLES W. CHESNUTT, ANN PETRY, AND MINSTRELSY'S LETHAL COUNTERPART

Black dialect fiction in the *Post* as well as the private and amateur performances of minstrelsy across the United States most often purported to be merely humorous. But the underlying violence of this white-supremacist ecology of imagined and embodied Blackness was never far below the surface of these "pleasures," as writing by African Americans throughout Lorimer's long tenure reveals. In the final pages of this chapter, I discuss two Black-authored responses to the prevalence of amateur blackface in

American hearts and homes: Charles W. Chesnutt's novel *The Marrow of Tradition* (1901) and Ann Petry's novel *The Narrows*. Petry's third novel was published in 1953 and is set in the late 1940s or early 1950s, so it was published well after Lorimer's editorship, but Petry provides a devastating depiction of the psychological and physiological harm done to African Americans by the widespread practice of amateur minstrelsy. *The Narrows* and the earlier *Marrow of Tradition* bookend Lorimer's career and indicate the harmful persistence of the broad cultural phenomenon that the *Saturday Evening Post* both participated in and fueled.

Charles W. Chesnutt deploys elements of minstrelsy in much of his fiction. For example, Julius McAdoo, the monologist in many of Chesnutt's conjure stories, can be read as a minstrel performer who manipulates and subverts the racialized expectations of his auditors, John and Annie, to exert his will. A similar dynamic can be found in "The Passing of Grandison," in which the titular protagonist stages an elaborate performance of subservience for his master with the intention of freeing all the members of his enslaved family. In *The Marrow of Tradition*, Chesnutt also thematizes white amateur minstrelsy and reveals the violence that accompanies the ideological pleasures of blackface. In this historical novel, which is based on the Wilmington Massacre of 1898, the white-supremacist leaders of "Wellington" host a group of northerners with the express purpose of gaining sympathy for "the Southern white man's views of the negro." Through careful staging and propaganda, the northern visitors become convinced that African Americans are "content with their position in life" and "could not be very much oppressed." The city's white hosts, to guarantee the success of their efforts, arrange a private performance: "In order to give the visitors, ere they left Wellington, a pleasing impression of Southern customs, and particularly of the joyous, happy-go-lucky disposition of the Southern darky and his entire contentment with existing conditions, it was decided by the hotel management to treat them, on the last night of their visit, to a little diversion, in the shape of a genuine negro cakewalk." The event is held on an upstairs floor of the hotel and is not open to the general public, but one uninvited white participant joins the entertainment—not as part of the audience but as a performer. Tom Delamere, one of the novel's most villainous characters, steals an African American character's clothing, puts on blackface, and wins the cakewalk. Completing his performance, Tom gives a speech "which sent the Northern visitors into spasms of delight at

the quaintness of the darky dialect and the darky wit." The northerners'
pleasure comes at a steep price. Sandy Campbell, the victim of Tom's theft,
is immediately ostracized by his church for his ostensible participation in
a the "sinful diversion called a cakewalk," and that is only the beginning of
his troubles. Later in the novel, Tom again blacks up and masquerades as
Sandy, this time for the purpose of robbing and murdering his own aunt.
Tom's ruse is ultimately discovered by his grandfather, who searches his
room and discovers a box of "burnt cork" from "a firm of manufacturers
of theatrical supplies in a Northern city"—no doubt the same type of supplier Blanche Goodman and her fellow citizens in Chattanooga used when
staging their minstrel shows.[57]

Unlike Goodman and Fitzgerald, Chesnutt makes the connection
between "humor" and violence perfectly clear. Tom's private blackface performance has immediate, fatal consequences for his own relative (and later
for his grandfather), and Sandy is nearly killed in a widely announced public lynching. But even though Sandy escapes becoming the victim of spectacular, extralegal violence, great damage has been done: "All over the
United States the Associated Press has flashed the report of another das-
tardly outrage by a burly black brute, all black brutes it seems are burly";
the pent-up white rage originally directed at Sandy eventually bursts out
in the race riot that consumes Wellington and results in mayhem, murder,
and a successful coup d'état by the city's white supremacists.[58] Much of this
violence flows directly from Tom's performance of amateur minstrelsy.

Like Chesnutt, Ann Petry connects physical violence and amateur minstrelsy, and she examines how this popular form of white-supremacist performance generated physical and psychological harm. In *The Narrows*, the
main character, Link Williams, goes to a show at Radio City Music Hall
with his love interest, a young white heiress who is having an extramarital
affair with Link. When the Rockettes leave the stage, they are "followed by a
pair of dancing colored comedians," and their appearance jars Link into a
memory from his childhood. When he was eight, his teacher, Eleanora
Dwight, "decided that his class would give a minstrel show, to raise money,
to help raise money for the Parent Teacher's Association."[59] Lynn Rhae
Barnes explains that by the 1930s various government entities—including
but not at all limited to the Department of Education—had become directly
involved in the production, promotion, and dissemination of amateur minstrel material. As we have seen through the example of Blanche Goodman,

minstrel shows were already a common form of fundraising early in the twentieth century. When Petry wrote her novel decades later, America was in the middle of the nation's "most expansive stage of amateur minstrelsy," which Barnes identifies as from 1920 through 1970, when minstrelsy was performed in homes, synagogues, firehouses, school auditoriums, and similar public venues across the United States.[60]

Miss Dwight already harbors a barely concealed racist animus toward Link, and she describes the minstrel show and Link's role in it with an intentional cruelty that traumatizes the young child. Link's white classmates "laughed until they almost cried. He was the butt of all the jokes, he was to say all of the yessuhs and the nosuhs, he was to explain what he was doing in the chicken house. Ain't nobody here, boss, but us chickens; he was to be caught stealing watermelons; he was to dance something that Miss Dwight called the buck and wing; he was to act sleepy and be late for everything. His name in the minstrel was Sambo." Miss Dwight instructs Link to act "like Al Jolson in Mammy" and jokes that she "won't have to use burnt cork" on the boy's face. The consequences of Miss Dwight's comments and actions are immediate. Link's schoolmates start calling him "Sambo," and "for the first time in his life he was ashamed of the color of his skin."[61] Although Link initially decides to fake an illness and sabotage the performance, he becomes actually sick. The minstrel show is canceled, but because of the humiliation he faced, Link stops attending school for a while. He has been traumatized by his teacher's attempt to force him into the straitjacket of minstrelsy. Through this interlude in her novel, Petry reveals the cruelty and damage inherent in the ostensible pleasures of amateur minstrelsy, and she connects the psychological harm Link experienced as a child with the cultural and physical violence that ultimately leads to his death. Miss Dwight almost disappears from the novel entirely, but in the book's final pages she surfaces just long enough to report being pushed down at night by an escaped Black convict. The local newspaper editor, hoping to distract the community from the white heiress's latest misdeeds, amplifies Miss Dwight's fear of Blackness (the ever-present obverse of minstrel pleasures), and this front-page news item becomes an instigating event that leads to Link's murder. He is kidnapped by the white woman's husband, who takes him inside the family mansion and executes him in a sitting room. With this in-home lynching, Petry provides a mirror image of the unacknowledged violence at the heart of white, domestic performances of embodied

Blackness. In *The Narrows*, minstrelsy ultimately entails "lynching, its most lethal counterpart," to borrow a phrase from Sonnet Retman.[62]

In chapter 1 of *The Great Gatsby*, before Fitzgerald's novel unravels the dysfunctionality of the Buchanan family, the author includes a scene that conveys at least a modicum of domestic tranquility: "Tom and Miss Baker sat at either end of the long couch and she read aloud to him from the 'Saturday Evening Post'—the words, murmurous and uninflected, running together in a soothing tone. . . . 'To be continued,' she said, tossing the magazine on the table, 'in our very next issue.'" Jordan reads to Tom from one of the many serialized novels Lorimer published in every issue, and her "murmurous and uninflected" words indicate that she is not reading something written in Black dialect. Fitzgerald, as it happens, saved the minstrel show in his third novel for the Queensborough Bridge, where Nick sees "three modish Negroes [and laughs] aloud as the yolks of their eyeballs rolled toward us in haughty rivalry."[63] But the scene in chapter 1 of *Gatsby* highlights something that is largely lost to us now in our bowling-alone, digital era—namely, that magazines like the *Post* operated in both print and oral culture. People read magazines silently, and they also read them to each other. Black dialect and amateur minstrelsy allowed white readers to inhabit Blackness and thereby to "craft a more solid and confident white identity."[64] Blanche Goodman and F. Scott Fitzgerald proved themselves astute readers of Lorimer's magazine, and they created their material for the *Post* accordingly. As Charles W. Chesnutt and Ann Petry reveal, that confident whiteness was always predicated on the trauma inflicted by white supremacy.

Chapter Three

IRVIN S. COBB:
MAKING THE NEW NEGRO OLD AGAIN

The March 1925 issue of the *Survey Graphic*, entitled "Harlem, Mecca of the New Negro," is widely recognized as a watershed moment of the Harlem Renaissance. In his introductory essay, "Enter the New Negro," Alain Locke proclaimed the waning of the Old Negro, including such stock figures as " 'aunties,' 'uncles' and 'mammies,' " arguing that in the past the African American's stereotypical "shadow, so to speak, has been more real to him than his personality."[1] The first visual representation of Locke's ideal New Negro was Winold Reiss's sensitive portrait of the singer Roland Hayes, which was featured both on the cover of this issue of *Survey Graphic* and again in the magazine's first pages (figure 3.1). According to Martha Jane Nadell, the illustration highlights Hayes's "complex identity" as an "epitome of changes wrought by the urbanization of the African American population, a typical and representative New Negro."[2] David Levering Lewis makes the inaccurate claim that the Hayes cover is mirrored by Reiss's portrait of Harold Jackman "at the back," but Jackman's image appears less than halfway through the magazine.[3] In fact, Hayes's New Negro image on the front of the *Survey Graphic* is inversely mirrored on the back cover by an advertisement for the collection *Black Cameos* by R. Emmet Kennedy, a white author who, according to the ad, "reproduces real, verbatim Negro dialect" and catches "the true spirit of the Negro as he is still to be found away from the sophistication of town life" (figure 3.2). The accompanying

FIGURE 3.1. Portrait of Roland Hayes by Winold Reiss, front cover of *Survey Graphic* 53, no.11 (March1, 1925).

illustration is the cameo of an older man with a fringe of hair reminiscent of Uncle Remus imagery, and he looks every bit the Old Negro. In the *Survey Graphic*, in other words, Locke's aspirational image of Black modernity, the New Negro, is shadowed by a commercial, mass-cultural reiteration of fungible caricature, the Old Negro.

Reiss's illustration has garnered its share of critical analysis, but the ad for *Black Cameos* appears to have received little attention. In 1925, however, Kennedy and his book attracted a fair amount of press. He engaged in a promotional tour for *Black Cameos*, and newspapers across the United States praised his book as "amusing and fascinating" for his "likable" portrayal of "barbarous African characteristics" and for his "little sketches

FIGURE 3.2. Advertisement for *Black Cameos* by R. Emmet Kennedy, back cover of *Survey Graphic* 53, no. 11 (March 1, 1925).

showing the childlike innocence and peculiar viewpoint of the uneducated Negro."[4] Most tellingly for the purposes of this chapter, the *Owensboro Messenger* in Kentucky reported the following in March 1925 (the same month and year as the publication of Locke's *Survey Graphic* "Harlem" issue): "When R. Emmet Kennedy, author of 'Black Cameos,' disclaimed the title of colonel at the Dutch Treat club luncheon at the Hotel Martinique yesterday, Irvin S. Cobb leaned over to me and said: 'He must be a Northerner.' But when Mr. Kennedy finished telling some of his negro stories—he specializes on the New Orleans negroes and their activities—Cobb admitted that he would qualify as a consul in Paducah—his [Cobb's] home town in Kentucky."[5] In this brief social note, a lesser-known white journalist drew

on the much broader national reputation of another white writer to validate
the authenticity of Kennedy's "negro stories." By the release of the *Survey
Graphic* issue and *Black Cameos* in 1925, that far more famous writer, Irvin S.
Cobb, had attained star status as a beloved author associated with the *Saturday Evening Post*, and his writing about Black life cast the very sort of shadows Locke castigated in both "Harlem, Mecca of the New Negro" and his
subsequent, expanded anthology *The New Negro: An Interpretation* (1925).[6]

Cobb enjoyed an elevated stature as a *Post* author that eclipsed by far
most of the authors discussed in chapters 1 and 2, especially as the twentieth century entered its second decade. Joel Chandler Harris and Paul
Laurence Dunbar were already well known and popular when Lorimer published their work, but both died early in the century. Harris Dickson preceded Cobb in the *Post* by just a couple of years and continued publishing
in the magazine well after his departure, but Dickson's star never rose as
high Cobb's. And even if Blanche Goodman's Viney monologues were
sometimes referred to as "famous," Goodman remained a minor figure in
the *Saturday Evening Post* and in American culture more generally. Cobb,
in contrast, was a renowned and beloved author, and, along with Octavus
Roy Cohen and Hugh Wiley, he became one of the *Post* contributors who
attracted regular scrutiny, occasional praise, and sharp criticism from African American writers associated with the Harlem Renaissance. Indeed,
Cobb played a pivotal role in the *Post*'s hardening into a pattern of registering and recontaining Black modernity through "humorous" Black dialect fiction in the years leading up to the Harlem Renaissance. One of
Lorimer's closest friends and most cherished writers, Cobb came to the *Post*
with all the predilections of a paternalistic racist firmly intact, and he was
able to feed his boss the steady diet of caricature Lorimer wanted to read
and publish. Before leaving the *Post*, Cobb initiated many of the tropes that
would dominate the magazine, including the Black veteran of overseas service in France, the newly migrated southerner in Harlem, the nascent
Black film industry, and the rise of untrustworthy Black leadership. Registering African American modernity in his widely popular fiction, Cobb
recontained all these experiences within the confines of dialect fiction, thus
asserting that only white people are entitled to the full benefits and protections of citizenship. When Locke wrote about Old and New Negroes in 1925,
he was responding to the anti-Black print ecology that Cobb and other white

Post authors had been developing since the earliest glimmers of the Harlem Renaissance.

Chapters 1 and 2 concentrated primarily on the first decade or so of Lorimer's editorship, when the New Negro movement was gaining steam, and the Harlem Renaissance had yet to begin. In those chapters, we see how and why Lorimer's approach to African Americans coalesced into the repeated pattern of registering and recontaining Black modernity. This chapter focuses on Irvin S. Cobb, who was for a time one of Lorimer's closest associates and whose writing was of great interest to both Black and white audiences during the early years of the Renaissance. In particular, I examine four of Cobb's contributions to the *Post*— "The Mob from Massac," "Young Black Joe," "The Ravelin' Wolf," and *J. Poindexter, Colored*—to establish the magazine's rhetorical posture toward the Black modernity of the Harlem Renaissance. Cobb's work, I argue, reinforced the palatability of white supremacy by denying its inherent violence, and it attempted to elevate and enshrine the figure of the Old Negro as a rearguard action against the rise of the New Negro; this effort at a nostalgic reclamation of supposed antebellum race relations made Cobb a representative *Saturday Evening Post* author of the first order.

"SOMEWHAT MORE ENLIGHTENED": COBB COMES TO THE *POST*

When Cobb published his first *Post* short story, "The Escape of Mr. Trimm," in 1909, he was already a well-known journalist but an untried fiction writer; by the 1920s, he had become so famous that his likeness was printed on cigar boxes as a celebrity endorsement.[7] One of the *Post's* most widely read and beloved contributors for more than a dozen years, Cobb left the magazine when William Randolph Hearst's *Cosmopolitan* made a "spectacular raid on the *Post* stable" in late 1922.[8] During his time working for Lorimer, Cobb contributed more than 170 pieces, providing the *Post* with fiction, reportage, and humorous sketches on any number of topics at a prodigious rate, and before he was lured away to a rival magazine, he had become a friend of his editor. "Whenever the Lorimer circle gathered in the old days, the globular figure of Cobb could be found, whether at Atlantic City, the [Grand] Canyon, Philadelphia or Palm Springs. . . . Cobb was frequently one of the celebrants at the parties Lorimer arranged in the earlier days of the *Post*."[9]

Despite his former popular renown, Cobb is now a mostly forgotten figure of literary history. Before his reputation began its steady decline in the late 1930s, however, he "enjoyed a level of fame in the early twentieth century that rivaled fellow-humorist Mark Twain's popularity in the nineteenth century, which led to public speaking engagements and lectures, radio guest spots, syndicated columns, and his involvement in the early development of the film industry."[10] Beginning as a reporter for his hometown Kentucky newspaper, the *Paducah Daily News*, he quickly became a very young managing editor as well as a correspondent for larger urban papers and then moved to New York City in 1904, where "he soon became the highest paid staff reporter" on Joseph Pulitzer's *New York Evening and Sunday World*.[11] Once Lorimer began publishing Cobb's work regularly, the writer's steady rise became meteoric, ultimately leading to film adaptations of his work by the actor Will Rogers and the director John Ford, recognition in newspapers and magazines across the United States, and even that cigar box endorsement. Before his death in 1944, Cobb had published sixty books and more than three hundred short stories;[12] he drew on his experiences as a war reporter and his skills as a raconteur to develop a robust presence on public-lecture circuits; and he was a known commodity on the stage, behind the camera, and on the screen.

From the start, Cobb always understood what Lorimer was looking for in a southern writer, and he shaped his career at the *Post* by satisfying its editor's predilections. When he was first hoping to place his work at the *Post*, he introduced himself in a letter on May 22, 1908, by emphasizing his family's history of military service for the Confederacy and by expounding on various southern speech conventions. With his typical wit, Cobb also invited Lorimer to an authentic southern meal: "Down home we have a lovely and succulent creature known as The Shote. I'd like to introduce you to him sometime in connection with country sausage and spare ribs."[13] Cobb, who was already establishing his reputation as a professional southerner in the North, understood Lorimer's appetite for Black stereotypes, and he knew how to feed it. The easy banter of Cobb's first letter to Lorimer characterizes much of their correspondence until Cobb's departure for the rival *Cosmopolitan*, and it is clear from their exchanges that he was adept at reading Lorimer and that he was willing to produce material that generally reflected his editor's tastes, prejudices, and worldview.

In his work for Lorimer, Cobb often included Black characters and Black caricature, but unlike other *Post* authors who specialized in dialect fiction, such as Blanche Goodman and Harris Dickson, he only occasionally made African Americans the central focus of his writing for the magazine. (This is not the case, however, for the "humorous" sketches he produced for newspapers or the "darky" stories he was fond of telling on the lecture circuit.) Cobb's fiction about southern life instead centers primarily on a white character, Judge William Priest. A paunchy, rumpled, "bourbon-swilling sage" and "slightly ridiculous" Confederate veteran, Priest keeps the peace in a picturesque version of Paducah that is imbued with nostalgia for the Lost Cause of a mythically glorious slavocracy, where the masters were kind and the "servants" were always grateful and happy to serve. Priest would become Cobb's "most popular and enduring character."[14]

In his Judge Priest stories and in his work more generally, Cobb never made secret his sense of racial superiority or his nostalgia for the antebellum South; indeed, these feelings are essential to his written work and his public persona. William Ellis notes, "Like many white southerners of his age and time, Cobb developed a paternalistic, even loving view of African Americans, but he never harbored any thoughts of full equality for them."[15] In his writing, Cobb regularly professed affection and a qualified admiration for African Americans but not full humanity, and he often advocated for white hegemony. According to Grace Elizabeth Hale, this form of "mostly imagined intimacy with blacks" facilitated the development of a white southern identity predicated on segregation, racial hierarchy, and willing Black servitude.[16] For an article published in 1924, for example, Cobb described a list of fictional characters he would want to invite to his home, and he concluded by placing Joel Chandler Harris's racialist fantasy Uncle Remus on his guest list: "As a Southerner I'd want Uncle Remus. Naturally we might not want him as a guest since we still draw the color line in some respects. But at least he could wait on the table. He'd give a real American tone to the proceedings by reason of the fact that he is an authentic, black-skinned American and so utterly different from the average popular conception today of what a real negro is."[17] Like the millions of white Americans whom Cobb assumed share "the average popular conception today," he attributed reality to a fictional character while simultaneously denying the humanity of actual people. In making this rhetorical move, which argued that "a real American tone" relies on the presence of Black subservience, Cobb illustrated Toni Morrison's assertion that "a real or fabricated Africanist presence was crucial to [white people's] sense of Americanness."[18]

Cobb's biographer, Wayne Chatterton, describes him as "somewhat more enlightened" than many contemporaneous white southerners,[19] and this relative enlightenment appears to have contributed toward a shift in Lorimer's approach to portraying African Americans. As I describe it in chapter 1, Lorimer's qualified endorsement of Booker T. Washington's accommodationism had shriveled away and was ultimately replaced by the open scorn—and sometimes naked bloodthirstiness—of writers such as Dickson and Dixon before Cobb came on the scene. Endorsements of segregation, extralegal violence, and the disenfranchisement of African Americans could be found often in the *Post*, and white terrorism was a regular source of humor. For example, in his unsigned recurring feature "The Senator's Secretary" on January 5, 1907, Samuel Blythe—one of Lorimer's closest associates—included a sketch told by John Sharp Williams, who was then serving as Speaker of the House of Representatives. Williams joked

about the lynching party who took out a negro, hanged him, burned him, shot him and otherwise killed him.

Just as they were dispersing an old negro came down the road. "Here!" shouted the leader, "what are you doing around here?"

"Nothin', boss; 'deed I ain't. I'm jess on my way."

"You didn't see anything?"

"'Deed, boss, I ain't seen a thing."

"Look at that," commended the leader sternly, pointing to the dead negro; "What do you think of that?"

"Foh th' land's sake, boss," said the old negro as he shuffled off, "I done think you let him off light."[20]

The acquiescence of the story's "old negro" gave the imprimatur for a permanent racial hierarchy; rationalizations of mob violence, brutal murder, and intimidation appeared with regularity in the magazine in the first decade of the twentieth century. However, during Cobb's rising ascendancy at the *Post*, open approval of racial violence and terrorism diminished noticeably. In 1905, Dixon asked rhetorically what would happen if African Americans started successfully competing with white Americans, and his answer leaves little room for interpretation: "He will do exactly what his white neighbor in the North does when the Negro threatens his bread—kill him!"[21] Cobb's "somewhat more enlightened" dialect writing demonstrated how humor, without explicit recourse to violence, could be used to promulgate white supremacy in the pages of the magazine.

In my discussion of Cobb, I am trying to tease out the evolution of a rhetorical stance but perhaps not much of a shift in actual politics. Cobb made very clear his disavowal of racial violence, as I will show, but it would be naive to argue that his humor in any way defanged the inherent violence of white supremacy. If anything, Cobb's comparatively gentle form of dehumanization was more dangerous because he helped soften the openly hostile racism of previous *Post* writers such as Dixon into a more broadly acceptable "common sense" that naturalized segregation and racial hierarchy. The racial violence behind Cobb's "enlightened" humor was not lost on his contemporaries. In its September 1909 issue, *Cosmopolitan* magazine offered a retelling of the lynching joke reproduced by Samuel Blythe in the *Post* in 1907 and concluded with an older Black man who says the victim "got off mighty light." The description of the violence in this "funny" sketch delights in its gruesomeness by describing the victim's flesh as "cut to ribbons with whips, his body all perforated with bullets, and, in the language of Irving [*sic*] Cobb, 'a pleasant time was being had by all.'"[22]

"I AM QUALIFIED TO MAKE A FIRST RATE KLANSMAN. WE DO NOT DIFFER IN OUR PRINCIPLE BUT ONLY IN OUR PLANS FOR APPLYING THEM."

Cobb promoted the mythology of an Old South characterized by benevolent masters and grateful servants living together harmoniously, where violence was an aberration rather than a structural necessity. He made a good living by demeaning African Americans while also denouncing the systems of brutalization that were always the yin to his humor's yang. In late 1922, for example, Cobb made a guest appearance as managing editor of his former newspaper, the *Paducah News-Democrat*, where he featured a front-page editorial disparaging the Klan, entitled "Praise God from Whom All Blessings Flow, for the Ku Klux Has Failed in Paducah!" In no uncertain terms, Cobb decried the organization as an affront to "law, order, and decency" and proclaimed, "It is a damnable outrage that it should now exist in this country." But while Cobb disagreed with the Klan's methods and the violent expressions of its intolerance, he did not challenge its central principle: "As a Southern man, the son and grandson of Southerners, I believe with all my heart in white supremacy. [However,] I do not believe in a campaign of terror and violence aimed against black men. If a negro disobeys the law or willfully disregards it the law itself is for his punishment. . . . Taking it by and large, I figure that in all broad essentials I am qualified to make a first rate Klansman. We do not differ in our principle but only in our plans for applying them."[23] In other words, Cobb disagreed with the Klan's methods and its threat to civil stability but not with its message or its goal of racial domination.

Additional evidence of Cobb's "somewhat more enlightened" position on race is found in his memoir, *Stickfuls (Myself to Date)* (1923), which was published just one year after his final contribution to the *Saturday Evening Post*. In it, Cobb recalls an experience while still a young editor in Kentucky when he reported on witnessing his first hanging. He treats what must have been a traumatic moment with both pathos and humor, and although one gets the sense that Cobb sympathizes with the man being executed, it is equally clear that he milks the scene for the laughs he derives through caricature. Cobb personally knew the condemned man, named George, because he "worked for my father. When I drove that ice wagon he rode on the back and handled the ice." Portrayed as being an ideal Black worker, George was "always polite and respectful in dealing with white people," but local African Americans called him "Devil" because of his violent ways. In other words, George embodied both the ideal, deferential servant and the dangerous Black brute. Cobb recalls George in the prison, "working himself up to the state of exaltation that sends so many of his race to the gallows shouting-happy." Warming to his theme, Cobb writes, "Plastered against the barred cell-doors beyond, like bats, hung ten or a dozen negroes, their eyeballs standing out from the shadowy background like so many pairs of shiny china marbles. In time to the cadences of Devil they crooned and groaned in a wholly sympathetic half-hysterical chorus." As this scene comes to its climax, Cobb himself had to participate in the hanging, first by reading the death warrant (because the sheriff was too sickened by the task to proceed) and then—more gruesomely—by holding George's legs off the ground as he died. As it happened, the rope was too long, the condemned man's legs touched the ground, and he was experiencing a tortured death; Cobb's intervention ended George's suffering. When it was time to officially report his experience, Cobb excluded most of these details and instead "wrote four columns of commonplace" that gave a dry record of the execution because he did not believe the paper's subscribers would appreciate his livelier account. Cobb concludes this scene in his autobiography by noting that he has "thought a thousand times since what an opportunity I missed then" to write a thrilling story, but he expresses no additional feelings for the suffering and death of a man who had worked alongside him just a few years earlier.[24] Cobb regretted the lost opportunity to publish a good story early in his career, and he uses his memoir to finally profit from George's execution. As this episode from *Stickfuls* demonstrates, Cobb occasionally disavowed anti-Black violence, but he was also adept at profiting from it, especially through humor.

Cobb's *Saturday Evening Post* story "The Mob from Massac" (February 10, 1912) exemplifies his disavowal of white terrorism and his concomitant endorsement of the ideological underpinnings of white supremacy. The story is sometimes held up as an example of Cobb's challenge to extralegal violence, and some scholars argue further that the story, as Richmond Adams claims, "reads as a condemnation of not simply the Klan, but also the Lost Cause, and ultimately, the means by which white America had come to understand itself in the generations following Appomattox."[25] Although it is true that Cobb's beloved Judge Priest singlehandedly faces down a lynch mob and talks them out of completing their murderous goal, "The Mob from Massac" as a whole does nothing to challenge one of the basic tenets of white supremacy, a tenet previously advocated in the *Post* by Dixon and Dickson and illustrated ominously by Rebecca Harding Davis through her character Kreeshy: the claim that Black men require the occasional application of extralegal violence because they constitute an ever-present threat to white women.

As the story unfolds, Cobb vacillates between predictable stereotyping and critical, "somewhat more enlightened" thinking about the structures and practices of race. The main plot of "The Mob from Massac" begins when an accused Black rapist of a white girl is brought to the Paducah jail. The suspect is "a little negro, skinny and slight and seemingly not over eighteen years old." With this detail, Cobb appears to question media portrayals of accused Black men as animalistic; a jailer comments, "The papers call 'em burly black brutes . . . and I never seen one of 'em yit that was more'n twenty year old or run over a hundred and thirty pound." Cobb's moment of ideological critique, however, is immediately undermined when he introduces an African American character who is described in stereotypical terms and as "a confirmed chicken thief." "The Mob from Massac" comes to a climax when Judge Priest, alone and armed with a pistol, steps in front of a lynch mob, draws a line in the sand with his umbrella, and promises to "kill the first man who puts his foot across that line!"[26]

Priest's demonstration of individual courage and his insistence on the rule of law win the day; the crowd dissipates, and the lynching of an innocent man is avoided. However, although the spectacle of murder has been averted in this one instance, the putative need for extralegal violence—that is, the seemingly inherent lawlessness and brutality of Black men—remains uncontested in the story and in Cobb's oeuvre more generally. As the story concludes, the judge receives a phone call announcing the capture of the guilty man, who is of course a Black man: "They got the nigger what done that devilmint. . . . He was a nigger named Moore." After his guilt is discovered, Moore tries to escape but is fatally shot. Before he dies, though, he confesses to the rape and clears "the nigger that's there in the jail."[27] With this dénouement, although Cobb demonstrates that mob law inevitably leads to injustice because the crowd from Massac would have killed an innocent man, he leaves intact the stereotypical image of the Black man as rapist. Cobb disagreed with the illegal terrorism of organizations such as the Klan, but he shared many of their cherished beliefs about white supremacy and racial hierarchies. In sum, violence is disavowed on the surface of Cobb's sometimes humorous story, but the segregationist insistence on repression, punitive "justice," and excessive social control of African Americans remains intact.

"TRUSTING IT MAY FILL THE BILL": THE PUBLICATION AND RECEPTION OF "YOUNG BLACK JOE"

Six years after "The Mob from Massac," Cobb published an article about Black soldiers or "doughboys" in the Great War, "Young Black Joe," which made him an even more famous *Post* author, and the success of that article propelled him to center an African American character and African American modernity in some of his more significant fiction. Cobb would produce Judge Priest stories for decades, but this endeavor was interrupted twice by World War I. Lorimer first sent Cobb to Europe in 1914, and Cobb's "war articles proved a sensation."[28] Three years later, when the United States entered the conflict, Lorimer sent Cobb over again, and this second visit resulted in the publication of one of his most influential articles, "Young Black Joe." After Cobb had already arrived in Europe, Lorimer decided on a new angle for reporting the war because he had become interested in the Black servicemen he saw shipping out for France. On April 23, 1918, Lorimer made a suggestion that would have significant consequences: "My dear Cobb: I think there ought to be a good article in [*sic*] our negro troops and stevedores abroad. They show up mighty well when they swing by over here." Cobb acted quickly on Lorimer's suggestion, and before long he sent a manuscript with a note saying, "Trusting it may fill the bill, here's the yarn about the darkies."[29] "Young Black Joe" (the title plays on Stephen Foster's nostalgic song for the antebellum South, "Old Black Joe") was published on August 24, 1918, and immediately garnered broad interest and public approval. Just one day after it was published, Lorimer wrote Cobb that "we are hearing a lot of nice things about Young Black Joe,"[30] and within the week Cobb's story was being reprinted, excerpted, and commented on by newspapers around the country. By 1918, Cobb's writing had already made him famous, but "Young Black Joe" also made this white grandson of a former Confederate officer a national authority on Black soldiers and on African Americans more broadly.

In a rhetorical move that would characterize many of Cobb's subsequent *Post* contributions, "Young Black Joe" professed a newfound respect for Black humanity while still clinging tenaciously to caricatures. The article began with an implied analogy between African Americans and animals and concluded by reinvigorating America's most hateful racial slur. Cobb started his story in the French countryside, fixing initially on an incongruously placed "North American mule" wearing a gas mask and contemplating its surroundings "with half-closed, indolent eyes. . . . He was just standing there, letting the hot sunshine seep into him through all his pores." Regular consumers of the *Post's* dialect fiction would have undoubtedly drawn a parallel between this outlandish-looking mule and the cartoonish "darkies" populating Lorimer's magazine, and Cobb drove the analogy home by claiming, "In our own land you somehow expect, when you find a mule engaged in industry, to find an American of African antecedents managing him. So the combination was in keeping with the popular conception." This mule and its driver served with "the Three Hundred and Somethingth of the American Expeditionary Force"—the 369th Infantry Regiment, which would become famous as the Harlem Hellfighters.[31]

Making his way toward the front, Cobb first came across a unit of drafted African Americans primarily from the South. Like the mule, these men were "lying at ease . . . in the bright, baking sunshine." Upon further observation, however, Cobb's preconceptions about Black laziness appeared to soften because while he "used to think that sitting down was the natural gait of the tidewater darky," he realized that these soldiers "bore themselves as smartly [and] were as snappy at the salute and as sharp set at the drill as any of their lighter-skinned fellow Americans in service anywhere." But Cobb immediately undercut this assertion by praising the army's "sane" decision to appoint white southern officers to the unit "because of a belief that they would understand the negro temperament," thus invoking a standard trope in the *Post*: that no one comprehended African Americans as well as their former enslavers. Speaking with putative authority and obvious condescension, one white officer from Tennessee joked, "We're going to have a mighty disappointed regiment on our hands in about two months from now, when these black boys find out that even in the middle of August watermelons don't grow in Northern France."[32] Cobb's "humor" here echoed the pernicious efforts of the U.S. Army to export southern racial mores to the French army, which was initially friendlier to African American troops than were their own commanders.[33]

Cobb was then taken to the Harlem Hellfighters stationed in the trenches at the front, and the following characterization of their bravery and comportment would be reprinted in periodicals across the United States:

I am of the opinion personally—and I make the assertion with all the better grace, I think, seeing that I am a Southerner with all of the Southerner's inherited prejudices touching on the race question—that as a result of what our black soldiers are going to do in this war, a word that has been uttered billions of times in our country, sometimes in derision, sometimes in hate, sometimes in all kindliness—but which I am sure never fell on black ears but it left behind a sting for the heart—is going to have a new meaning for all of us, South and North too, and that hereafter n-i-g-g-e-r will merely be another way of spelling the word American.

Cobb underscored these sentiments by portraying the heroism of Henry Johnson and Needham Roberts, whose actions in combat earned each of them "the War Cross and for each a special citation before the whole French Army, and in addition a gold palm, signifying extraordinary valor, across the red-and-green ribbon of Johnson's decoration. So it was shortly coming to pass that a negro, almost surely, would be the first private of the American Expeditionary Forces to get a golden palm along with his Croix de Guerre. It might be added, though the statement is quite superfluous in view of the attendant circumstances, that he earned it."[34]

Despite—or, more likely, because of—this description of Black Americans' valor, Cobb then immediately recontained his news of that bravery within the language and imagery of minstrelsy, describing "a stumpy little private, with a complexion like the bottom of a coal mine and a smile like the sudden lifting of a piano lid," who called out, "Henry Johnson, he did right well, didn't he? But say, boy, effen they'll jes gimme a razor an'a arm-load of bricks an' one half pint of bust-haid licker I kin go plum to Berlin." Cobb next described another soldier sharpening a bolo knife: "A United States soldier whose remote ancestors by preference fought hand to hand with their jungle enemies was qualifying to see Henry Johnson and go him one better." Pairing up Johnson and Roberts with these two unnamed Black soldiers, Cobb countered examples of African American heroism by recycling tropes of Black primitivism and savagery. Having also heard James Reese Europe's band—"the best regimental band in our Army"—Cobb summed up his time in the trenches as "two days of a superior variety of black-face vaudeville."[35] African American heroism, patriotic service, and artistic talent are, therefore, recontained in the "popular conceptions" of

Blackness that *Post* writers such as Cobb churned out for Lorimer, who circulated such material for a nickel an issue.

The public response to "Young Black Joe" was immediate, widespread, and overwhelmingly positive; within days and for months afterward, periodicals around the country were reporting on and reproducing Cobb's story. The *Charlotte News*, for example, announced a charity game between the Charlotte Red Sox and a team of Black soldiers stationed at Camp Greene: "The cause will probably appeal to the imagination of both white and colored people and a large attendance of both is expected at the game. Irvin S. Cobb in his great story in the current Saturday Evening Post, entitled 'Young Black Joe,' tells that the finest military band he has heard in Europe during the four years of the great war . . . was with an American regiment of negro soldiers. . . . Hence the point in providing instruments for the colored soldiers as soon as possible."[36] A few days later the *Louisville Courier-Journal* excitedly announced, "There is no man writing for the press to-day better qualified than Cobb to make such a report. He knows the negroes as only a Southerner 'raised' with them from boyhood and babyhood can know them. He knows both the Southern negro and the Northern negro."[37] Cobb's report from the front was so popular that "Young Black Joe" became a common term in the U.S. press for any Black doughboy.

African Americans also embraced "Young Black Joe" and in general did so with enthusiasm. W. E. B. Du Bois's journal *The Crisis* excerpted a section approvingly and without comment, and the *Nashville Globe* declared, "No higher praise has been accorded the valiant Negro troops in the great world war than by Irvin Cobb[, who] gives a stirring account of how finely both the Negro draft and volunteer regiments have rendered their patriotic service."[38] In *New York Age*, James Weldon Johnson offered a measured appraisal of the story, noting Cobb's lack of "meanness" and his "spirit of sympathy" for the Black soldiers while also critiquing his overreliance on "the worn out 'literary color' of Negro stories." But Johnson recognized that "between four and five million people will read Cobb's article," and these readers—like Cobb himself, Johnson implied—might come closer to recognizing African American humanity.[39] James Reese Europe and the 369th U.S. Infantry Jazz Band capitalized on the reputation of the story upon their return stateside. In a handbill promoting upcoming concerts in

New York in 1919, Lieutenant Noble Sissle was touted as "The Greatest Singer of his race . . . Acclaimed by Press and Public America's Own 'Young Black Joe,'" which was immediately followed by "'The best Military Band in Europe.' IRVING COBB [*sic*] in the Saturday Evening Post."[40] Even quicker to cash in on the name recognition of Cobb's story, the Pace & Handy Music Company advertised a "High Class Ballad" by Joe Simms and Charlie Warfield in *The Crisis* on December 1918, several months before the 369th marched up Fifth Avenue: "Our late march song, 'Young Black Joe,' inspired by the wonderful article by Irvin S. Cobb in the Saturday Evening Post."[41] As late as 1940, Langston Hughes used the name Cobb introduced in "America's Young Black Joe!," "a song coupling race pride with national pride."[42] Because of Cobb's warm welcome by African Americans, he became a principal speaker at meetings of the Circle for Negro War Relief, an interracial "organization designed to provide material support for black soldiers," whose "most active participants" were African American women.[43]

The runaway success of "Young Black Joe" appears to have prompted Cobb to focus more directly on African American characters, and he consequently moved Judge Priest's manservant, Jefferson Exodus Poindexter, from a supporting role to center stage. The ultimate product—and Cobb's final major contribution to the magazine—was the abridged, serialized novel *J. Poindexter, Colored*, which ran in four consecutive issues of the magazine in June and July 1922. George Doran published the unabridged monograph almost simultaneously, and despite Cobb's many years of writing fiction, *J. Poindexter, Colored* was his first novel. Told from the first-person perspective of Jeff Poindexter, the text recounts his adventures in New York City at the very cusp of the Harlem Renaissance. Lorimer had been lobbying Cobb to write such a novel for nearly a decade. In a letter dated July 9, 1913, five years before "Young Black Joe" was published, Cobb wrote Lorimer that he planned to "tackle . . . your Negro in New York notion."[44] He must have struggled with this assignment, however, because in 1915, Cobb complained jokingly in *Pearson's Magazine* about his inability to produce a viable Black protagonist: "The stories were never intended, at the start, to center about Judge Priest. The big character was to have been 'Jeff' the smart negro. But Judge Priest just naturally absorbed the spotlight and wouldn't be obscured. 'I just couldn't keep that lazy nigger on the job.'"[45] A year and a half later, on January 5, 1917, Cobb again wrote to Lorimer about the project, this time with the title in hand: "I'm aiming to get the decks cleared for the *J. Poindexter Colored* series."[46] But Cobb must have continued struggling because nothing more was written about a possible Poindexter book until after the success of "Young Black Joe."

GETTING POINDEXTER ON THE JOB: "THE RAVELIN' WOLF"

Before Cobb published his novel, he experimented with getting his African American character "on the job" by making Poindexter the protagonist of "The Ravelin' Wolf" (February 21, 1920). This short story serves as a bridge between Cobb's previous work, especially "Young Black Joe," and his first novel by capitalizing on his experiences with Black soldiers while also conforming with many of the tropes and tactics common to the *Post's* long history of dialect fiction. What is ultimately notable about this story, beyond Cobb's formal efforts to create fiction with a Black main character, is how it addresses the genesis of the Red Summer, when race riots—largely fomented by white Americans—raged in dozens of municipalities across the United States. The story's attention to extralegal violence links it back to "The Mob from Massac." Through "Young Black Joe" and "The Ravelin' Wolf," Cobb's focus on Black veterans and the racist, antidemocratic turmoil that ensued upon their return stateside brings his fiction and the *Post* toward some of the cultural phenomena intrinsic to the Harlem Renaissance.

"The Ravelin' Wolf" opens with the coming of the draft to Paducah, and in its opening paragraphs Cobb immediately recalls "Young Black Joe" by touching on the work of both labor and combat battalions and by echoing some of the sentiments about African Americans that framed his famous article. When the unwilling Poindexter appears before the draft board, an agent remarks, "You look to be as strong as a mule," a comment that resonates with the mule trope in "Young Black Joe." Jeff is spared from the draft because of his flat feet, however, and the doctor observes, "I don't understand it either. So far as I've been able to observe you've spent the greater part of life sitting down."[47] Like the mule analogy, Cobb recycled his claim about putative African American indolence from "Young Black Joe," in which he had claimed that "sitting down was the natural gait of the tidewater darky." Assertions of Black people's laziness were a common feature of the *Post* more generally; years earlier, for example, Rebecca Harding

Davis had complained in "Has the Free Negro Failed?" of "these idle millions of negroes" (see chapter 1).

"The Ravelin' Wolf" moves swiftly to the Armistice, when Poindexter is serving as part of the local African American reception committee for "the first returning squad of service men of color" (12). The Black veterans come back home and share their experiences overseas, especially their improved treatment in France, which lacked the legal barriers and cultural practices of American Jim Crow. Before long and because of this new information, race relations deteriorate in Paducah, and a "ferment of discontent began to stir under the surface of things; a sort of inarticulate rebellion against existing conditions, which presently manifested itself in small irritations at various points of contact with the white race" (12). Judge Priest is reticent to ask Poindexter about this changing mood because he adheres to a code of conduct, according to Cobb, that supposedly prevents white people from prying into the private lives of their Black subordinates and governs race relations in the South. Cobb alludes to this code throughout his oeuvre and expands upon it in *J. Poindexter, Colored*; tactful white ignorance of Black life and thought appears to be one of his most deeply held beliefs about maintaining the integrity of the color line.

In "The Ravelin' Wolf," Cobb begins his explanation of Black–white relations with an allusion to Booker T. Washington's endorsement of segregation in his Atlanta Exposition speech. Reworking Washington's separate-but-equal sentiment, Cobb writes that "there are two separate and distinct worlds—a black one and a white one—interrelated by necessities of civic coordination and in an economic sense measurably dependent one upon the other, and yet in many other aspects as far apart as the North Pole is from the South" (13). In this fantasized world of mutually respectful segregation, according to Cobb, African Americans are "nearly always better informed" about white people than white people are about them because African Americans must bear "observant witness to the moods and emotions of his or her employer" (13). White people, however, especially those graced with tact and good sense, refrain from knowing too much about their African American neighbors and employees; "a Southern-born white man, wise in his generation, seeks to look no further, for surface garrulity and surface exuberance do not deceive him, but serve only to make him realize all the more clearly that he is dealing with members of what is at heart the most secretive and sensitive of all the breeds of men" (13). For these reasons, Judge Priest hesitates asking Poindexter about the recent "under-current of discontent stirrin' amongst you people—and no logical reason fur it either, so far as I kin see" (66). Phrasing his question this way, Priest skirts the suggestion that Black people's unhappiness is rooted in the enhanced awareness of oppression made possible by Black soldiers' experiences overseas, where they were momentarily freer of virulent American racism and segregation. In the interest of maintaining the status quo ante of the prewar South (in this case, really, before *both* the Civil War and the Great War), and despite his professed desire to stay on his side of the color line, the judge presses Poindexter for answers, but Poindexter is equally reluctant to breach the codes of conduct and silence that govern Black–white relations: "For all his loyalty to his master, a certain race consciousness in him would have bade him keep his hands and tongues locked" (66). However—with the foreseeable logic of many a *Post* dialect story—Poindexter is involved in a romantic rivalry that prompts him to sacrifice racial solidarity in service to his own desires. Petty jealousy and self-interest almost always supersede principled loyalty to the Black community in Black dialect fiction in the *Post*, and Poindexter thus gives Priest the information he seeks.

Because Cobb adheres to generic expectations, the cause of racial disquiet in Paducah is *not* the return of African American veterans, whose new insights provide fresh perspectives on the centuries-long history of de jure and de facto slavery and dehumanization that benefited white people such as Cobb. The culprit is instead a recent interloper named Dr. J. Talbott Duvall, whose characteristics seem to imply that he is primarily a burlesque of W. E. B. Du Bois, with a soupçon of Marcus Garvey thrown in for good measure. Duvall's "speech dripped gorgeous ear-filling Latin words," and his "title, it seemed, was by virtue of a degree conferred upon him by a college—a white man's college—somewhere in the North" (13). A dapper dresser and a womanizer—which are also standard traits of the ne'er-do-well Black fop in this sort of fiction—Duval's "accent was that of a traveled cosmopolite superimposed upon the speech of a place away off somewhere called the West Indies" (13). After arriving in town, he establishes the Shining Star Colored Uplift and Progress League, which creates a "sensation" (13) in the Black community. Poindexter gives up Duvall's name to Priest only because the recent interloper has captured the attention of Poindexter's love interest, the "straw-colored" Ophelia Stubblefield, who is just one of the many women in town falling prey to Duvall's charm. Once the Judge helps Poindexter hatch a scheme, the plot moves predictably toward Duvall's public embarrassment as a putative Black leader who is, in fact, an embezzler and a bigamist who has been duping African Americans in cities throughout the South; Duvall beats a hasty and ignominious retreat after he is exposed, and, predictably, Poindexter thus successfully removes his romantic adversary from contention.

By constructing this plot, Cobb satisfied Lorimer's desire for formulaic dialect fiction that would reinforce white-supremacist notions about African American inferiority and childishness, and regular consumers of this type of material would have had a good sense of how the story would end as soon as Cobb established Duvall as Poindexter's rival. "The Ravelin' Wolf" also constitutes a *Saturday Evening Post* dialect story that registers and recontains a significant moment in African American modernity: the experience of African American military service overseas and the subsequent impact it had on Black and white communities when the soldiers returned to the States. The story's approach to Black soldiers differs from Cobb's mostly laudatory treatment in "Young Black Joe" because this author (and the *Post* as a whole) was now crafting fiction that would deny African Americans' valor in an effort to return race relations to a more firmly hierarchical, prewar footing. After his experiences abroad and at home, Cobb clearly understood the consequences of African Americans' service overseas, and he tried mightily to put the genie back in the bottle by attributing Black domestic resistance to Jim Crow inequity to the misdirected and self-serving leadership of impostors and "organizers" as well as to a gullible, infantilized Black population. But "The Ravelin' Wolf" also acknowledges that dangerous new knowledge had come back from France and had to be addressed in some fashion.

After Poindexter reveals Duvall's actions to Priest, but before he will explain exactly what the interloper is doing, he asks the Judge some pointed questions that underscore the real reasons for the current mood in Paducah. First, Poindexter asks, "Is it true dat over dere in some of dem Youropean countries black folks is jes' the same ez white folks, ef not more so?" (66). This question demonstrates that Black soldiers came home and spoke about their better treatment and reception abroad and that they were able to point with authority toward the arbitrary construction of the color line in the United States. Judge Priest answers Poindexter's question carefully and in the affirmative; the American segregation of African Americans is not practiced in Europe. Poindexter, however, being an idealized loyal servant who knows his place in the ordained *Saturday Evening Post* racial landscape, challenges the desirability of equal treatment: "I reckin' mebbe one main trouble over dere is, jedge, dat dem folks ain't been raised de way you an' me is" (66).

The soldiers returned with new ideas not only about race but also about class. Poindexter presses Priest further by asking about "all dem furrin countries—Russia an' Germany an' Bombay an' all [where] de po' people, w'ite or black or whatever color dey is, is fixin' to rise up in dere might an' tek de money an' de gover'mint an' de fine houses an' de cream of ever'thing away frum dem dat's had it all 'long?" (66). Once again, Judge Priest answers with care, this time laying the blame for domestic unrest on the defeated kaiser, who is apparently still pursuing the war by sowing dissent through subterfuge: "I'm prone to believe that when the Germans stopped fightin' us with guns they begun fightin' us with other weapons almost as dangersome to our peace of mind and future well bein'. Different parts of this country are in quite a swivet—agitators preachin' bad doctrine—some of 'em drawing pay from secret enemies across the sea. . . . But I was hopin' that mebbe our little corner of the world wouldn't be pestered. But now it looks ez ef we weren't goin' to escape our share of the trouble" (66). These sentiments perfectly reflect Lorimer's intensifying xenophobia; in 1920, his wartime distrust of German Americans was evolving into the postwar, anti-immigrant activism that drew him toward the pseudoscientific racism of Lothrop Stoddard and Madison Grant and propelled him toward his successful campaign to close the borders to immigrants from southern and eastern Europe.

Poindexter's response to the judge's analysis is to suggest organizing a mob to run Duvall and other such troublemakers out of town. "Ropes is powerful influential. An' de sight of tar an' feathers meks a mighty strong argument, too, Ise heard tell" (66). Through this sentiment, Cobb portrays the idealized Black servant who is more loyal to his master than to his fellow African Americans, one who does not challenge violence as a natural part of the Jim Crow racial hierarchy. But Judge Priest, who previously convinced the mob from Massac to obey the law, argues that Duvall has a lawful right to speak and organize, and he reminds Jeff (and his readers), "Mob law is even worse than no law at all" (66). Through a formulaic plot

that relies on stereotypical assumptions about African American simplicity and cupidity, "The Ravelin' Wolf" depicts a new Black consciousness
born of World War I as a mistaken turn that could be fixed with the aid
and guidance of intelligent, tactful white southerners, such as Judge Priest,
who "understand the negro temperament."[48]

RECONTAINING THE "NEW-ISSUED COLORED":
J. POINDEXTER, COLORED

"The Ravelin' Wolf" also allowed Cobb to create in Jeff Poindexter a Black
character who has the intelligence to find his own way in New York and
hatch a scheme that saves his hapless boss, all while remaining faithful to
his "master" and to the segregated racial hierarchy, and it is this character
who assumes the narrative voice in Cobb's novel *J. Poindexter, Colored*
(1922). Marking the growing importance of the Great Migration of African
Americans out of the South, Cobb tracks Poindexter's journey from Paducah
to New York City, where the small-town Poindexter transforms into a new
Black urbanite while clinging loyally to his subservient place in the social
order. The main plot of the story concerns Poindexter's efforts to save Dallas Pulliam, his new employer, from the clutches of northern hucksters, who
prey on Pulliam's youthful gullibility and come close to both bankrupting
and shaming him into an unwanted wedding with a gold digger. At the story's climax, Poindexter manipulates the Yankee scam artists by exploiting
their preconceptions about southerners and scares them away from their
erstwhile mark. In *J. Poindexter, Colored*, Cobb produced a text that highlights many of the hallmarks of modernity that would prove intrinsic to
the development of the Harlem Renaissance, all the while portraying
those phenomena within the familiar language and tropes of *Post*-friendly
minstrelsy.

Cobb's formulaic novel concerns Poindexter's ultimately successful
efforts to save his younger, gullible white employer from the clutches of
northern hucksters, who attempt to squeeze the southerner for all he's
worth. Although the main plot is entirely predictable, the novel merits attention here in at least three ways. First, it incorporates many of the tropes
and narrative devices common to much of the white-authored Black dialect fiction published in Lorimer's *Post*, and in this sense the novel

illustrates the machinations of commercial white supremacy more broadly in the early twentieth century. Second, because of its historical details, *J. Poindexter, Colored* addresses and to a certain extent anticipates a number of topics that would become primary concerns of the Harlem Renaissance, including the Great Migration, the advent of Harlem as a new Black urban community, the coming of the post–World War I New Negro, and the rise of Marcus Garvey. Cobb also portrays the nascent Black film industry and explores the idea of Black double-consciousness through the lens of white, paternalistic racism. In this sense, the novel can be read as an example of the "'Negro vogue' of the 1920s," which Shane Vogel identifies as the "growing white and corporate interest" in Black urban life and culture.[49] *J. Poindexter, Colored*, in other words, registers burgeoning Black modernity simply in order to recontain it within the commercial and ideological practices of Jim Crow America. Third, Lorimer's editorial decisions concerning the abridgment and serialization of Cobb's novel underscore his systematic approach to both producing and erasing specific ideas about African Americans.

The novel opens by naturalizing African American servility, a putative Black trait nurtured by the *Post* and cherished by its readers. Judge Priest has left Poindexter in charge of his house in Paducah while he is away visiting family, and before very long the ever-willing servant misses his white master. To Poindexter's relief, "a young white gentleman by the name of Mr. Dallas Pulliam" is about to visit New York City, and "he's made up his mind to take some likely black boy along with him." This "boy," of course, is at least ten years Pulliam's senior. Poindexter is eager to see New York, but he will leave the empty house only with Priest's permission and Pulliam's promise that "he ain't adopting me, he's just borrowing me."[50] Thinking of himself as an object to be exchanged and utilized by others, Poindexter is a near perfect example of what Saidiya V. Hartman describes as the post-bellum white demand for the "joyfully bent back" of the Black laborer, whose body is "no longer harnessed or governed by the whip" but is "instead tethered by the weight of conscience, duty, and obligation."[51]

Poindexter's train journey north allows Cobb to register the Great Migration, which accelerated after the return of Black soldiers from France and the subsequent terrorism of the Red Summer. Yet again reiterating Cobb's analogy between Black doughboys and mules found in "Young Black Joe" and "The Ravelin' Wolf," Poindexter notes that his scant knowledge of New York comes from the "few head of draft-boys which were there enduring of the early part of the war" (23). So far as Poindexter can tell, most African Americans who venture north are delighted at first because there are "no Jim Crow cars nor separate seats for colored at the moving-pictures nor nothing like that" (27). But—despite historical evidence to the contrary—Poindexter maintains that more African Americans are returning to the South than leaving it permanently. When the train crosses the Mason–Dixon Line, Pulliam insists that Poindexter join him in the now unsegregated Pullman car, which Poindexter does, but he is "lesser easy in my mind" and would feel better in his segregated place by returning to the Jim Crow car (27). With such sentiments, Poindexter continually embodies Cobb's ideal of the faithful Black servant and the concomitant claim that the happiest African Americans are the ones who comply with unequal racial stratification.

Cobb also uses Poindexter's train ride to address the advent of the New Negro, which he exemplifies through two contrasting Pullman porters named Harold and Gabe (Gabe is called "Roscoe" in the unabridged novel). These porters embody Cobb's ideas about how African Americans should and should not think and behave in a white racial hierarchy. Gabe, whose appearance suggests that he is a racially "pure" Old Negro, is "black as pots and powerful nappy-headed besides. . . . But he's smart; he knows what's service" (28). Like Poindexter, Gabe is attentive to white needs and expectations, and he has developed a remunerative method for getting tips that succeeds by reifying stereotypes of servility. Gabe's practices anticipate Poindexter's behavior in New York, where he will experience wider horizons and greater freedom but will never challenge his subservient relationship to white people and, despite being above the Mason–Dixon Line, will thrive in direct proportion to his adherence to Jim Crow social relations and expectations.

The other porter, Harold, exemplifies everything that is going wrong in modernizing America, according to Cobb, beginning with the character's name and appearance. Like Blanche Goodman's tentative New Negro character Sally Ann, who presumptuously changes her name to "Sarah" after spending time in the North (see chapter 2), Cobb's second porter appears to signal his modernity through his name. Poindexter says that "Harold" cannot possibly be his given name because "I knows just from looking at him that he's too old for such a fancy entitlement as that. 'Cause Harold is a new-issue name amongst us colored" (30). In addition, unlike Gabe, Harold is "yellow-complected" (30) and therefore bears evidence of race mixing, a phenomenon Dixon railed against in his essay "Booker T. Washington and the Negro" in 1905 and that Lorimer was growing increasingly hysterical about after World War I. Worse still, Harold becomes increasingly "uppidity" as the train continues north. In the segregated South, the porter says, "Thanky, *suh*," but in the North he says, "*I* thank you" (30). Cobb's implication here is that there is something wrong with an African American asserting personal pride and a sense of agency or—like Dr. J. Talbott Duvall in "The Ravelin' Wolf," whose "speech dripped gorgeous earfilling Latin words"—that speaking without a "darky" dialect is somehow dangerous and to be distrusted. To Poindexter, such behavior is unthinkable, and "about Pittsburgh he's got so brash that I keeps watching for some white man to rise up and knock that boy's mouth so far round from the middle of his face it'll look like his side entrance" (30–31). Poindexter's endorsement of white violence against "uppidity" African Americans resonates with Hale's observation that southerners used the "figure of the loyal ex-slave" as justification for "the often violent treatment of African Americans."[52] Poindexter warns Harold against such brazen self-assertion, but the porter does not accept the racial status quo: "He tells me he don't aim to let nobody run him over. He tells me he considers himself just as good as they is, if not better. He says he lives in a place called Jersey City where the colored race gets their bounden rights and if they don't get 'em they up and contends for 'em until they do" (31–32). But—predictably—Harold's racially conscious politics are undermined by his personal ethics because he is also portrayed as little more than a thief. Unlike Gabe, who makes his money by performing his subservience, Harold matches his New Negro insolence with what is portrayed as Old Negro petty thievery by stealing money from passengers' pockets while they sleep. Since at least the publication of Dixon's article "Booker T. Washington and the Negro," if not earlier, African American leaders' purportedly larcenous motivation and behavior were standard fare in Lorimer's *Post*, and Harold's combination of professed racial pride and demonstrable moral failure is an example of this trope.

Cobb continues to naturalize the idea of innate Black criminality when Poindexter begins his stay in Manhattan. Shortly after his arrival, he gets lost and bumbles his way to Harlem; his amazement at the variety and liveliness of urban Black life, including an African American police officer, anticipates a similar sense of wonder in Rudolph Fisher's short story "The City of Refuge" (1925), when Rudolph's protagonist emerges from the subway and thinks, "Done died an' woke up in Heaven."[53] And as in "The City of Refuge," the very first Black people Poindexter encounters in Harlem are swindlers who try to sell him a piece of worthless jewelry that supposedly belongs to "the Colored Arabian Prince" (78). Through this fictionalized prince, Cobb once again satirizes Black leadership as an empty show and ties it to criminality. And true to another standard *Post* formula, Poindexter ultimately outfoxes the swindlers and escapes with their money in his pockets; this turn of events (unsympathetic characters getting hoisted with their own petard) informs countless dialect stories in the *Post*, especially during the Harlem Renaissance.

To be fair, many of the novel's major characters, Black and white, are either con artists or dupes (which is a regular feature of much satirical fiction in the *Post* and of American humor generally in this era), and after Poindexter and the younger Pulliam arrive in New York, the plot centers on Poindexter's efforts to save his naive employer from white Yankee sharpers. Cobb bookends this main action with meditations on Black and white structures of knowledge in Jim Crow America, and he ascribes differing forms of consciousness to the exigencies and privileges of segregation. On the one hand, *J. Poindexter, Colored* attributes to white southerners, especially "gentlemen" descended from slaveholders, a special ability to understand Black consciousness. As Hale notes, this assertion comports with "standard plantation romance" claims that "southern whites know and love blacks better than [do] white northerners."[54] On the other hand, Cobb writes about Black interiority and perception in ways that resonate, perhaps surprisingly, with Du Bois's famous formulation of double-consciousness. Through Poindexter, Cobb articulates an idea of bifurcated perception produced by racial segregation, but in his telling of this formulation Black consciousness functions to anticipate white needs, accept Black servility, and make no claims to additional rights or agency. After overhearing the scheme to bilk Pulliam, Poindexter informs the reader, "There's a whole heap of white folks, mainly Northerners, which thinks that because us black folks talk loud and laughs a-plenty in public that we ain't got no secret feelings of our own. .... Which I reckon that is one of the most monstrous mistakes in natural history that ever was" (115). Instead, African Americans working for white people know "what they-all hopes and what they-all fears," while white people know very little in exchange (116). Toward the end of the novel, after Poindexter foils his employer's nemeses by manipulating their white northern expectations about white southern behavior, he tells Pulliam that segregation provides him (Poindexter) an advantageous way of seeing the world: "I's on the outside lookin' in, whilst you is on the inside lookin' out, ez you mout say; so mebbe I kin 'scover things w'ich you'd utterly overlook" (227–28).

Unlike Du Bois, in other words, Cobb appeared to conceive of Black consciousness shaped by segregation primarily as a useful tool for a willingly subservient race rather than as a form of alienation to be contested. Through dialect fiction, Cobb—and the *Post* more generally—created "a most intimate invasion whereby the dominant actually attempts to create the thoughts of the subordinate by providing it speech."[55] Despite this conception, Cobb apparently recognized the harm done by cultural producers such as himself who profited from the "humorous" derogation of African Americans. In a revealing passage in the novel, he highlights the damaging consequences of this second sight derived from racial oppression. Poindexter says:

> Yes sir, the run of colored folks is much more secretious than what the run of the white folks give 'em credit for. I reckon they has been made so. In times past they has met up with so many white folks which taken the view that everything black men and black women done in their lodges or their churches or amongst their own color was something to joke and poke fun at. Now, you take me. I is perfectly willing to laugh with the white folks and I can laugh to order for 'em, but I is not filled up with no deep yearnings to have 'em laughing at me and my private doings. 'Specially if it's strange white folks. (116–17)

"Strange white folks" laughing at Black life was, of course, the entire point of Lorimer's decades-long investment in cultivating white writers working in Black dialect, and this hateful "humor" was also Cobb's bread and butter. With this passage, Cobb seems to suggest that portraying one reasonably intelligent, sympathetic Black character constitutes an adequate corrective to and even justifies all the rest of his crude and formulaic stereotyping and racism. But as Michelle Alexander notes in *The New Jim Crow* (2010, rev. 2012), the American racial caste "system of control depends on black exceptionalism,"[56] and therefore Poindexter's singular intelligence only serves to underscore putative Black inferiority more generally. And as Hale demonstrates throughout *Making Whiteness* (1998), feigned sympathy toward African Americans was regularly mobilized in the service and furtherance of white supremacy. Poindexter's critique of the Black dialect genre might seem surprising, but despite such insights Cobb would continue producing this type of harmful—but profitable—material throughout his career.

We find further evidence of Lorimer's practices concerning African Americans in how he edited the magazine version of the novel. As Cobb prepared *J. Poindexter, Colored* for serialization, Lorimer suggested trimming it down to three installments. The author apparently resisted because *Poindexter* was ultimately published in four parts, but Lorimer did request serious revisions, and he cut chapters 9 through 12 entirely from the serialization.[57] Although these excised chapters do not contribute to the primary story of Poindexter's efforts to protect his employer, they arguably constitute the most noteworthy section of the book because they portray early African American contributions to the development of the motion-picture industry and because they offer an extended discussion of a figure meant to satirize Marcus Garvey. Cobb's focus on film is perhaps especially interesting because the movie-making industry (as opposed to attending the movies) receives scant attention in the literature of the Harlem Renaissance.

Pulliam's New York friends include two aspiring actresses, and Poindexter accompanies them to a movie studio uptown, where he voices a perceptive analysis of the makeup and performance of a white actor in blackface, who "must have studied the business of acting like colored folks from watching nigger minstrel shows[,] . . . which does not fill the bill when you is letting on to be a sure-enough black person; because for years past I ain't never seen scarsely no minstrel man which really deported himself as though he had colored feelings inside of him" (128–29). The studio boss overhears Poindexter muttering these sentiments and convinces him to play the role. In short order, Poindexter's successful performance prompts the executive to consider producing all-Black, two-reel comedies for distribution to the "three or four thousand [movie] houses being run by colored people and being played for colored people" (136). Poindexter approves of this plan and urges the executive to focus primarily on comedies, with an occasional sop tossed to more high-minded moviegoers:

> "An' ef, once't in awhile, you meks a kind of serious-lak pitcher, showin', mebbe, how the race is a-strivin' to get ahaid in the world, 'at ought to fetch these yere new-issue cullid folks w'ich . . . is seemin'ly become so plentiful up Nawth. But mainly I'd stick to the laffin' line ef I wuz you— niggers is one kind of folks in 'is country w'ich they ain't afeard to laff. An' whatever else you does . . . don't mess wid no race problem. We gits mouty tired, sometimes, of bein' treated like the way we of'en is. Tek my own case. . . . I ain't no problem, I's a pusson. I craves to be so reguarded. An' tha's the way I alluz is been reguarded by my own kind of w'ite folks down whar I comes frum."
> (138)

In *Scenes of Subjection* (1997), Hartman demonstrates how paradoxically but systematically the legal and cultural "recognition of humanity and individuality acted to tether, bind, and oppress" African Americans after Emancipation rather than guarantee greater freedom and protection under the law.[58] Poindexter's insistence that white southerners, not northerners, are best at recognizing him as a unique "pusson" illustrates Cobb's preferred form of consciousness for Black people in an era of rapidly changing modernity: rather than being "new-issue cullid," Poindexter embodies a form of self-mastery that functions, in Hartman's terms, as the "willing submission to the dictates of former masters, the market, and the inquisitor within."[59] In other words, Poindexter articulates the oft-made claims by *Post* authors such as Joel Chandler Harris that the "Negro problem" is a northern invention, Black people are content with Jim Crow, and there is no need to worry about race in the United States because benevolent southerners are already treating African Americans just fine. *J. Poindexter, Colored* registers Black resistance to Jim Crow through characters such as the porter Harold and through the protagonist's critique of blackface only to recontain that resistance by insisting that real African American humanity resides in the mind and body of the loyal servant.

In addition to editing out Cobb's portrait of nascent African American cinema, Lorimer also excised his satire of Marcus Garvey, who figures in the novel as "Gabriel, the Black Prophet of Abyssinia." Gabriel claims to come from Africa, not Jamaica, like Garvey, but his characterization is unmistakable: "He's a great big overbearing-looking man . . . just overflowing with noble large words" (146) who has come to New York with a mission: "[The] plan as he preaches it is that all us black folks everywhere must straight-away rise ourselves up and follow after him, which he will then lead us back to our original own country of Affika where he will cause all the white folks which has settled there to pull out and leave us in sole charge for to run our own government and be a free and independent people from thenceforth on forever" (148). To promote this scheme, Gabriel requires his followers to pay monthly dues so they can build a fleet of ships—a direct allusion to Garvey's ill-fated Black Star Line, which was in the news while Cobb was preparing his manuscript.[60]

Poindexter learns about the obviously fraudulent Gabriel through conversations at a Harlem social club, where he and a likeminded friend named "U.S.G. Petty, Colored" (140) mock ideas about African heritage and Black leadership. Through his characters' discussions about Gabriel, Cobb registers the rise of Pan-Africanism in the United States and then recontains this element of Black international modernity through reiterations of standard minstrel tropes that emphasize Black savagery and naturalize white dominance over nonwhite people globally. Poindexter states: "I ain't frum Affika, I is frum Paducah, Kintucky. . . . Mo'over, ef whut I heah's 'bout it is correc', Affika is full of alligators an' lions an' onreconciled Bengal tigers an' man-eatin' cannibals, w'ich I wouldn't be surprised but whut they all of 'em 'specially favors the dark meat. An' yere I is, a pernounced brunette!" (149–50). When one of Gabriel's followers proudly describes the first ship as having an African American captain, Petty echoes Poindexter's skepticism of Black capability and his allegiance to white supremacy by challenging the wisdom of trusting "a cullid cap'n" who would not know how to command a ship on the high seas: "I craves me a w'ite cap'n—yas, an' a w'ite crew, too" (155). Poindexter's friend (and temporary mouthpiece) extends his insistence on sailing on a white-run ship to an analogy of white global domination. While the Black Prophet Gabriel insists on self-determination and anticolonialism, Petty argues that white people are naturally dominant and cannot be stopped from building their empires: "Lis'sen: Once't you let w'ite folks git they feets rooted in the ground an' they stays fast, reguard-less of whut the former perprietors may think 'bout it. W'ite folks in gin'el is very funny that way. . . . Next to holdin' on to the land, runnin' the gov'mint is the most fav'rit' sport they follows after" (157–58).[61]

Lorimer abridged Cobb's novel, therefore, by removing chapters that most directly represent urban Black modernity and that consider compet-ing ideas about African American self-determination and self-expression. It is tempting and would be convenient to suggest Lorimer did so to dimin-ish the very small efforts Cobb made to humanize and deepen his Black characters, but I have no direct evidence for this. When the serialized novel picks up again after the deleted chapters, it returns its focus to the perils and needs of Jeff's white employer and draws inexorably toward Poindexter's cleverly handled manipulation of Pulliam's tormentors. Poindexter ultimately wards off the dangerous Yankees who are trying to dupe Pulliam when he plays on their stereotypical preconceptions about southerners.

Undoubtedly, the most clever and perceptive figure in Cobb's novel is not any of the white characters but rather Poindexter himself. His most val-ued form of intelligence, however, is that he knows to submit to and uphold the racial hierarchy and would never dream of challenging the Jim Crow regime. As the novel concludes, Pulliam asks how he can repay Poindex-ter, and his faithful servant replies, "Well suh . . . you mout start in to please me by eatin' a lil' something" (251). Pulliam jumps at the chance to reassert his position as a white master by ordering Poindexter to bring him lunch, and he dines with gusto while his servant stands behind his chair, an image Cobb would reprise in his invitation in 1924 to have Uncle Remus wait table for his fictional dinner guests. Nonetheless, Pulliam gratefully provides Poindexter with a considerable sum of money so he can stay in New York to continue working in the movie business. In turn, Pulliam's offer of finan-cial independence elicits voluntary assurances from Poindexter that his future success will never become a challenge to the racial order or to his faithful servility: "Tell the Jedghe 'at . . . ef he finds the home-place ain't run-nin' to suit him widout me on hand to he'p look after his comfort, w'y all he's got do is jest lemme know an' I'll ketch the next train fur home." He makes this promise because unlike "the new-issue cullid" who "furgits favors an' bre'ks pledges an sometime turns an' bites the hand w'ich has fed an' fondled 'em," he—echoing the "good" porter Gabe from the beginning of the novel—"is one shiny black nigger jest rearin' to prove the contrary-wise" (258–59). As Poindexter bids Pulliam farewell at the novel's close, he vows, "W'en I meets up wid one of my own kind of w'ite folks in these parts or w'en I goes back ag'in amongst my own folks down below the Line, I'll know my place and my station an' I'll respec' 'em both; an' I'll be jest the same plain reg'lar ole J. Poindexter, Cullid, w'ich you alluz has knowed" (268–69). Having created a Black protagonist who encounters many of the hallmark phenomena of African American modernity, Cobb registered historical change in order to recontain it all within the ideologically stifling and politically retrograde nostalgia of the loyal former slave who is smart enough to stay in his white-delineated place.

Lorimer welcomed Cobb's characterization of Blackness with open arms, as did the U.S. press more generally. Although a number of reviewers faulted *J. Poindexter, Colored* for being thin on plot and overly conventional, they also lauded as truthful the psychology of his Black protagonist and his understanding of race relations. In a review that was syndicated in a number of newspapers, George Wood praised Cobb for his "carefully thought out contribution to the discussion of that portentous affair, the Problem of the American Negro," by creating a character who demonstrates "the sterling worth of the unspoiled negro" in maintaining his "loyalty and steadfastness" to white people. Homing in on Poindexter's exchange with the porter named Harold, Wood wrote, "The whole thing brings out subtly and clearly the really superior self-respect and dignity of Jeff's own attitude toward both his own and the white race over that of the bumptious, mottled mulatto of the North. It is really the gist of the whole book; the possibility of mutual respect and affection between races, provided neither attempts to intrude upon the other."[62] Cobb succeeded, in other words, by reproducing the fantasy of the willing servant who knows how to keep in his Jim Crow place. As Cora Annette Harris wrote in the *Charlotte Observer,* "To those who know the real negro, this book will afford unlimited amusement and pleasure."[63]

Perhaps, however, Cobbs's efforts at recontainment were not fully complete. Eric Lott describes minstrelsy as acts of "love and theft," revealing the always inadequate nature of ideologically driven racial appropriation, and his observations shed light on the white anxieties about Black progress percolating just under the surface of Cobb's writing. According to Lott, "It was a cross-racial desire that coupled a nearly insupportable fascination and a self-protective derision with respect to black people and their cultural practices, and that made blackface minstrelsy less a sign of absolute white power and control than of panic, anxiety, terror, and pleasure."[64] Hale similarly argues, "Whites created the culture of segregation in large part to counter black success, to make a myth of absolute racial difference, to stop the rising" of a burgeoning Black middle class.[65] In "Young Black Joe," Cobb attempted to return Black doughboys to the tropes of antebellum minstrelsy, but his article nonetheless incorporated portraits of bravery, talent, and patriotism that challenged dominant caricatures. In "The Ravelin' Wolf," we see Black doughboys returning from France with a new consciousness about race relations. And in *J. Poindexter, Colored*, Cobb insisted on the authenticity of willing Black servility by putting on his own authorial blackface, but he also, to borrow from Alain Locke, provided his protagonist with "the larger and more democratic chance—in the Negro's case a deliberate flight not only from countryside to city, but from medieval America to modern."[66] After all, by the end of the novel Poindexter has left Paducah for Harlem, and once Pulliam departs, he exchanges a place behind his master's chair for a spot behind the movie camera.

Benjamin Brawley, a contemporaneous Black literary critic, took note of Poindexter's agency in both 1922 and 1929 and observed the potency of a New Negro consciousness that exceeded Cobb and Lorimer's intentions. In 1922, Brawley wrote, "J. Poindexter of Paducah . . . awakens our interest . . . and is so thoroughly equal to the wiles and pitfalls of New York."[67] In 1929, he further recognized Poindexter's historical significance, noting how Cobb caught on to the New Negro "attitude that for two decades has made for great restlessness on the part of many Negro people, and within the last few years, on the part of some young members of the race, the revolt has become vociferous." Concluding his thoughts about Cobb's novel with the same quotation he used in 1922, Brawley continued, "At the base of the new temper was the opinion voiced by J. Poindexter, Colored, 'I ain't no problem: I's a pusson.' "[68] However, despite this glimmer of recognition in Cobb's last significant contribution to the *Post*, Lorimer would continue to insist on the erasure of Black personhood in his magazine for many years to come, Cobb would continue his acts of theft across all available media platforms, and the ravages of Jim Crow would persist for decades.

From the start, Irvin S. Cobb always understood what George Horace Lorimer was looking for in a southern writer, and he shaped his career at the *Saturday Evening Post* by satisfying its editor's racist, paternalistic pre-dilections. With the publication of *J. Poindexter, Colored*, Cobb served up the perfect meal for his boss before departing for *Cosmopolitan*. Lorimer was no doubt crushed by losing his friend to a competing magazine, but he did not need to worry about his bottom line. By 1922, the *Post* editor had developed a reliable stable of white authors working in Black dialect fiction as well as a mass audience that relished the type of commercial fiction that trivialized and joked about the gross inequities of Jim Crow. A few years later, in 1925, when Alain Locke produced his groundbreaking *Survey Graphic* issue, the New Negro represented on the cover by Roland Hayes was still being shadowed by the Old Negro on the back cover advertising R. Emmet Kennedy's *Black Cameos*. As the following chapters demonstrate, Lorimer's *Post* would continue casting this shadow persistently through-out the Harlem Renaissance.

Chapter Four

HUGH WILEY,
EDWARD CHRISTOPHER WILLIAMS,
AND BLACK DOUGHBOYS

The publication of Irvin S. Cobb's article "Young Black Joe" in 1918 marked the beginning of a new object of interest for the *Saturday Evening Post*, the Black World War I veteran of overseas service. Just a few years later, as African Americans' efforts and creativity were coalescing into the distinct energies of the Harlem Renaissance, caricatures of the Black doughboy were becoming a regular feature of the *Post*. Cobb's article—albeit in its proscribed fashion—trumpeted Black bravery, but the disavowal of white violence and anti-Black oppression found regularly in the *Post* was soon being matched by efforts to deny the purposeful heroism of "the Three Hundred and Somethingth of the American Expeditionary Force" and all other Black servicemen.[1]

Almost two decades earlier, in his *Post* article "Negro Society in Washington" (1901), Paul Laurence Dunbar had proclaimed that the District of Columbia was where "the colored man's life has reached its highest development" and was, therefore, the natural destination of Black soldiers returning stateside from the Philippines.[2] In 1922, Captain Davy Carr, a fictionalized Black veteran who saw combat in France, settles into the same lively social world described by Dunbar in the *Post* all those years earlier. Davy Carr, who is the narrator and protagonist of Edward Christopher Williams's epistolary novel *When Washington Was in Vogue* (1925–1926), recently met a dispirited James Weldon Johnson on Capitol Hill, where "the Dyer Anti-Lynching Bill [is] being slowly strangled to death." Davy's violent metaphor amplifies an observation he makes earlier in the novel: "Those scheming birds in Congress are planning in cold blood to do it up. . . . I firmly believe the word was passed around some time ago, that the Republicans were to let the Democrats do it to death, while some of the former went through the motions of mourning. I met James Weldon Johnson as I left the Capitol, and he looked pale and worn, completely done up, in fact. He agrees the bill is done for."[3] Shortly after meeting Johnson and during the type of cultured DC gathering extolled by Dunbar, Captain Carr and his fellow attendees single out two well-known *Post* authors, Hugh Wiley and Octavus Roy Cohen, for particular disapprobation. Like most of the authors treated in my book, Wiley and Cohen are almost entirely forgotten today, but their fiction in the *Post* was wildly popular and essential to broad cultural efforts to delegitimize Black overseas service during and after World War I. Cohen, whom I examine in chapter 5, produced a much larger and broader body of fiction than Wiley, whose Black dialect stories center more exclusively on a fictional Black veteran. Davy Carr's pronounced aversion to Wiley marks the response of an African American soldier who fought for democracy abroad, only to return to the violence and inequality of Jim Crow at home.

Davy's comment about Wiley and Cohen occurs in a chapter that reports on one of the many social events he attends. He writes of "a rather stimulating conversation" focusing on "the recent revival of interest in the Negro as a subject for writers of fiction." The discussion touches on a number of novels written by white authors—"Stribling's *Birthright*, Shands's *White and Black*, and Clement Woods's *Nigger*" (176)—and these texts generate serious if "conflicting views" on white authorship of Black subject matter. Two *Post* authors, however, spark no debate but garner instant disdain. Davy claims: "*Of course*, most of those present read Octavus Roy Cohen and Hugh Wiley out of the human race altogether" (176, emphasis added). This chapter and the next take their cue from Davy's "of course."[4] Williams, the author of *When Washington Was in Vogue*, clearly assumed that his contemporary readers were familiar with Cohen and Wiley because of their status as well-known, frequently published authors of Black dialect fiction in the *Post*, and Williams also assumed his readers shared his character's disdain for their work and their hegemonic cultural position in Jim Crow America. No further explanation was required to understand why these *Post* authors mattered, how their work harmed Black America, and why their disappearance might be greeted with relief, if not outright joy.

As a commissioned officer and combat veteran, Davy abhors Wiley because of his fame as a purveyor of fiction that regularly demeaned Black military service in World War I. Indeed, while the American Expeditionary Forces fought and ostensibly won the War for Democracy in Europe, another campaign was being pursued in the United States against some of the same soldiers who honored their country and sacrificed their lives in France. Part of the latter battle was waged in the pages of the *Post*, and its target was the manhood, honor, and intelligence of the African American soldiers who served—sometimes with notable distinction and heroism—in the combat and labor units of the U.S. forces. Wiley's fiction, which follows the mishaps of a buffoonish African American soldier first during and then long after the Great War, played an essential role in the *Post*'s efforts at minimizing Black soldiers' abilities and their contributions to the war effort.

In response to the machinations of the *Post* and American culture more broadly to register and recontain the Black experience of the war and its aftermath, African American authors mounted a sustained challenge against the delegitimization of the Black doughboy during the Harlem Renaissance. In his introduction to Victor Daly's World War I novel *Not Only War* (1932, reissued in 2010), David A. Davis notes that even the briefest list of novels about Black soldiers authored by African Americans includes Jessie Redmon Fauset's *There Is Confusion* (1924), Walter White's *The Fire in the Flint* (1924), Claude McKay's *Home to Harlem* (1928), Nella Larsen's *Quicksand* (1928) and *Passing* (1929), Langston Hughes's *Not Without Laughter* (1930), and Zora Neale Hurston's *Jonah's Gourd Vine* (1934),[5] and this roster is by no means complete and does not account for the short stories, nonfiction, and poetry that also address the topic. One important example of African American literary efforts to challenge the Jim Crowing of Black servicemen is Edward Christopher Williams's serialized novel *The Letters of Davy Carr: A True Story of Colored Vanity Fair*, which ran in the *Messenger* magazine in 1925 and 1926. Republished under the title *When Washington Was in Vogue* in 2004, Williams's novel effectively counters Wiley and the *Post* by presenting Black veterans and African Americans more generally as the literate producers and consumers of the written word rather than merely the playthings of commercial American print and entertainment culture.[6]

When Washington Was in Vogue is set in the lively African American community around Howard University. Writing for the *Messenger* in 1923, Neval H. Thomas described the District of Columbia as a "paradise of paradoxes," boasting a "social life [that] is the most cultured in the country." It is populated by "forward-looking men and women who study the world movements from such able and progressive magazines as THE MESSENGER, the *Nation*, the *New Republic*, and the *Liberator*," and Black Washingtonians hear "messages from every thinking group in the world."[7] Edward Christopher Williams, the first professionally trained Black librarian in America and the head librarian at Howard University during the Harlem Renaissance, dramatized this same "beautiful little world of striving," as Thomas called it,[8] in his epistolary romance novel, thus vivifying the vibrant cultural and intellectual life celebrated by Thomas and earlier by Dunbar.[9] With Davy Carr's "of course" in mind, this chapter first examines how the depiction of the African American veteran functioned in the larger project of racist representation in the *Saturday Evening Post* and then suggests that *When Washington Was in Vogue* can be read as a critique and correction of such representations.

After World War I, beginning in 1919 and running through 1934, one of the most recognizable Black veterans in the American press was the fictional Vitus Marsden, nicknamed "the military Wildcat." Created by Wiley, the Wildcat and his misadventures were published in the *Post* with great regularity. Before Lorimer's retirement in 1936, Wiley had published more than thirty Wildcat stories in the *Post* as well as a smaller number in other magazines. He also reorganized his stories into five loosely constructed Wildcat novels.[10] Any recurring character in the *Post* was sure to become widely familiar in the United States, and this was certainly true for the Wildcat. In a real sense, the Wildcat was already in the works well before the publication of Wiley's first story because he drew upon the *Post*'s long history of stereotypical, derogatory Black dialect fiction, pulling together many familiar tropes and plot devices and thus recasting African Americans' heroism and military service as clownish and accidental. Vitus "Wildcat" Marsden exemplifies the *Post*'s strategy to register and recontain historical developments of Black experience in order to reify racialized discourse and bolster rigid social stratification.

Six years, twenty-three short stories, and three novels after the initial appearance of the Wildcat in the *Post* in 1919, the *Messenger* magazine, which was published in Harlem by A. Philip Randolph and Chandler Owen, began serializing Williams's *The Letters of Davy Carr: A True Story of Colored Vanity Fair*. The novel, which was published anonymously and ran in the *Messenger* from January 1925 through June 1926, can be understood as one component in the magazine's long-running advocacy for the rights and respect of Black soldiers. According to Chad Williams, during the run-up to U.S. participation in the war, the "federal government feared that individuals like Randolph and Owen were only the tip of a much larger iceberg of black antiwar sentiment." After the war, the *Messenger* regularly promoted the idea that Black veterans were especially appropriate for challenging the swelling racist violence that would explode during the Red Summer of 1919. For example, in September of that year Randolph and Owen published a cartoon depicting a Black veteran violently repelling the kind of lynch mob that the failed Dyer bill was intended to oppose (figure 4.1). They also began publishing the work of Second Lieutenant William N. Colson, a combat veteran who became a contributing editor; Colson's exposés of unfair treatment overseas and his advocacy for veterans back home earned him the attention of federal and state authorities, who considered him "a person of potential danger."[11] Captain Davy Carr, who is decidedly less militant than Colson or the "New Crowd Negro" depicted in the *Messenger* cartoon, comes to Washington to research and write a book on African American history. Poised, well educated, worldly, and, most importantly, a rounded, fully human character rather than a stereotype, Davy Carr is a necessary corrective to Wiley's flat, clownish image of Black veterans.

Of course, by the time Wiley began publishing his Wildcat stories, the *Post* had an established practice of portraying African Americans as bumblers, buffoons, and connivers. More importantly in the context of this chapter, Lorimer had already started the magazine's efforts to register and recontain the awakened consciousness of Black servicemen within previously existing structures of caricature, beginning even with the article "Young Black Joe." In that article, as discussed in chapter 3, Cobb praised the valor of Black soldiers, but he ultimately characterized them in stereotypical terms of indolence, animality, savagery, and minstrelsy. In January 1919, the same year that the exceedingly small-circulation magazine

THE "NEW CROWD NEGRO" MAKING AMERICA SAFE FOR HIMSELF

FIGURE 4.1. "The 'New Crowd Negro' Making America Safe for Himself," *Messenger*, September 1919. *Source*: Marxist Internet Archive, https://www.marxists.org/history/usa/pubs/messenger/1919-09 -v2n09-sep-Messenger.pdf.

the *Messenger* published its image of the radicalized New Crowd Negro, the *Post* ran an advertisement for Columbia Records promoting a recording of "You'll Find Old Dixieland in France." The ad's image of three caricatured Black soldiers manning a machine gun is accompanied by copy that proclaims, "Instead of picking melons off the vine, they're picking Germans off the Rhine."[12] These two images—of the militant New Negro on the offensive back home and of the caricatured soldiers in France—visualize the tension between racial self-respect, on the one hand, and cultural dehumanization, on the other, embodied in the tension between Williams's Davy Carr and Wiley's Wildcat.

"WHO IN THE HELL DO YOU THINK YOU BELONG TO?":
HUGH WILEY AND THE WILDCAT

Born in Ohio in 1884 and raised in Oregon, Hugh Wiley was drafted into
the army and "served as a captain in the 18th Engineers" in France.[13] According to John Tebbel in his biography of Lorimer, Wiley ultimately became
one of Lorimer's closest friends: "This lovable, improvident man had gone
to war in charge of a Negro labor battalion and come back to write the yarns
about Negro crapshooters which *Post* readers enjoyed. It was the only kind
of story he knew how to write, and he wrote it over and over with variations. The spontaneous crap-game chatter he reproduced was hilariously
funny to his audience."[14] Wiley was arguably best known for his Wildcat
fiction, but he also produced a considerable number of popular books, stories, and screenplays set in San Francisco's Chinatown; one of his recurring
characters, the detective James Lee Wong, would be played by Boris Karloff in several films.

As Tebbel accurately notes, Wiley wrote one story "over and over with
variations." Pick a story from 1919, 1925, or 1934, and you are likely to encounter the same elements every time. Almost every story will touch on the
Wildcat's excessive eating and sleeping; his diction will be mangled, and
his illiteracy emphasized; there will be at least one gambling scene—usually
but not always a craps game—accompanied by the gamblers' argot and the
winning and losing of large sums of money; and the Wildcat will usually
invoke "Lady Luck" at some point. Wiley also incorporated mockery of
African American social organizations. Black women, if they appear at all,
are almost always obese harridans and caricatures of the mammy figure.
Finally, and most salient for my argument here, Wiley emphasized that his
character served with the American Expeditionary Forces, a point he drove
home in almost every story by referring to the Wildcat's pet goat, Lily, a
mascot acquired in France—and a symbolic reminder, much like Cobb's
mules, of the stereotypical conflation of African Americans with beasts of
burden and other animals.

To give this chapter some coherence, I focus on the stories Wiley collected into his loosely constructed debut novel, *The Wildcat* (1920), which
comprises the first stories he published in the *Post*. As a whole, they develop
an arc that begins with a less threatening version of Harris Dickson's "negro

vagrant" and ends by portraying a faithful servant who has much in common with Cobb's Jeff Poindexter. Wiley's first *Post* contribution, "The Four-Leaved Wildcat" (March 8, 1919), begins in Memphis, where the improvident Marsden does just enough yard work to keep himself fed and in fancy shoes. Marsden is called up to the First Service Battalion, and after an unsuccessful attempt at dodging the draft, he reports for duty, is made a corporal, and is shipped to France. The "military Wildcat," as he now calls himself, is "pretty handy when there were any jobs of eating or sleeping to be done."[15] After he arrives in France, the Wildcat stumbles through a series of self-serving schemes and various acts of unintended heroism. While in charge of transporting mules, he gets lost in No Man's Land and blunders upon some equally hapless German soldiers, who promptly surrender. After delivering both mules and prisoners, the Wildcat goes AWOL, gets caught, and is about to be court-martialed. But the military brass learn of his exploits, and by the conclusion of "The Four-Leaved Wildcat," Marsden is awarded the U.S. Distinguished Service Cross and the French Croix de Guerre and is promoted to sergeant. Marsden's medals are almost certainly intended to echo and spoof the Croix de Guerre awarded to Henry Johnson and Needham Roberts for their valor; with this element of the story, Wiley recontained the Black heroism Cobb had registered a year earlier. Everything that befalls the Wildcat in Wiley's first story happens by chance, not by intention or choice, implying that African Americans' military valor in Europe was only ever aberrant or accidental. In 1918, Cobb had proclaimed in "Young Black Joe" that "hereafter n-i-g-g-er will be another way of spelling the word American." One year later, Wiley both literally and figuratively removed Cobb's dashes from the slur to deny the full humanity and citizenship of his protagonist.

In the subsequent stories shaped into Wiley's picaresque first novel, the Wildcat concocts a scheme to hire out Senegalese soldiers as laborers to French farmers and the U.S. Army; accidentally foils a U-boat attack; sojourns with "jazz bean"–eating cannibals in Africa; becomes a brief dance sensation back in France with the aid of those jazz beans; and settles the peace process by turning an overhead fan into a roulette wheel. With the war over, he returns to the States, where he is duped by Italian gamblers and a Black con man in Manhattan and then travels across country as a waiter on a train until he finally returns to Memphis. All of these events—the encounter with an unwanted draft, the performance of valor in the field, the exposure of African Americans to both Africans and internationalism, the development of jazz in Europe, and the economic plight and ensuing rootlessness of many returning servicemen after the war—are recast in the familiar tropes and language of the all too familiar *Saturday Evening Post* dialect story. Wiley continued churning out his Wildcat stories for years, sending his protagonist across the nation and the globe; Wildcat encounters modernity everywhere but remains forever in possession of an "infantile mentality"[16] and renders a putatively natural subservience to most white people.

Two additional characters exemplify Wiley's portrayal of Black military service. The first is Huntington Boone, whose name gets mangled into "Honey Tone" by the Wildcat. Boone calls himself "Special Representer of the Colored Heroes' Home Tie [sic] Band," and Wiley describes him as "a goggle-eyed mulatto product in linoleum puttees whose mission in life was to impose an uplifting influence on soldiers who could get along fine without it."[17] Boone gives the impression of being a true race man, but in reality he is a shirker and a sharp, a characterization that taps into the long-running practice of the *Saturday Evening Post* to portray almost all African American men as gamblers, layabouts, and schemers—especially if those men are in any way seen as leaders of the Black community. "Honey Tone was a creature whose motto was action and lots of it—as long as somebody else did the work."[18] In other words, through this character Wiley registered Black sociopolitical efforts to acquire greater agency and self-awareness but then recontained those efforts within the debased language and actions of minstrelsy.

Captain Jack, the main white character encountered by the Wildcat, may well be a fictionalization of Wiley himself.[19] Over the course of the stories, the Wildcat—almost naturally, it seems—becomes the captain's body servant; only later do we learn that the Wildcat worked for Jack in Memphis (this sloppy plotting indicates the slapdash nature of Wiley's rapidly produced fiction).[20] When the war is over and the Wildcat is discharged, he happens upon the captain aboard a transport ship, and they immediately enter into a master–servant relationship. Jack is disdainfully paternalistic and repeatedly threatens the Wildcat with violence, but Vitus Marsden is always willingly servile. When they first meet on the ship, the Wildcat immediately asks:

"Capn'n, suh—kin I take keer you on de way home?"
"If you don't," the Captain said, "if you don't, I aim to kill you whenever
I get time."
"Cap'n, yessuh."[21]

The Wildcat accepts without question this sort of verbal abuse from Jack
and just about any other white man who comes his way. A disagreement
later arises between Jack and his father-in-law, Senator Benton, over who is
rightfully the Wildcat's master. The Wildcat asks,

"Cap'n Jack. suh . . . when does us leave?"
The Senator turned to him quickly. "Who in the hell do you think you
belong to?" he said.
The Wildcat faced the place of decision. He hesitated only an instant.
"Judge, suh, I 'spect I'se Cap'n Jack's boy."
The Judge looked at him. "What do you mean expectin' round where gen-
tlemen are? I expect I'll kill you tonight."
"Judge, yessuh."
[Captain Jack says,] "Let's cut the cards for him."[22]

As this exchange demonstrates, the Wildcat is more than willing to be the
property of white southerners. One of the hallmarks of the *Post*'s dialect
fiction is the resuscitation of the romanticized master–slave relationship of
the antebellum South, as we have already seen, for example, in Viney's
obeisance to "my white folks" and Jeff Poindexter's self-regard as an object
to be borrowed. This element persists throughout Wiley's Wildcat fiction.

For twenty-five years, Wiley churned out depictions of African Americans as objects of humorous derision, and his stories exemplify generally
the predictable dialect fiction of America's predominant national magazine
and specifically that magazine's dismissive treatment of Black veterans. Following the success of his initial stories and first novel, Wiley sent his protagonist across the country and all over the globe. Before his final story, the
Wildcat encounters anarchists, Wobblies, and Hindu nationalists on a train
heading west as well as revolutionaries in Mexico, among many other col-
orful characters; he even serves as Lorimer's mouthpiece when in one of
the final Wildcat *Post* stories, the Wildcat denounces Roosevelt's New Deal.
Wiley also recognized his own kinship with other white *Post* writers of

Black dialect fiction. In one story, "The Pluvitor" (June 5, 1926), he nods to Paducah, which *Post* readers would recognize as Irvin S. Cobb's hometown. In another, he pays deference to Octavus Roy Cohen's notorious Black dandy: "Wust cleanin' I ever got in a cube ruckus come off a Bumminham boy name' Florian Slappey."[23] Wiley's inclusion of Slappey was notable enough that the *Charlotte News* was soon reporting breathlessly that "two writers use same character."[24]

Indeed, the Wildcat not only circulated widely in the pages of Lorimer's magazine but was a well-known and beloved figure in the United States almost from the start. Reviews of the first novel featuring him ran in newspapers everywhere and were overwhelmingly positive. The *Oklahoma City Times* pronounced "the four-leaf-wildcat . . . a joy forever. We may not know much, but we know what we like." In his nationally syndicated column "The Conning Tower," Franklin P. Adams advised, "Read Hugh Wiley's 'The Wildcat,' very comicall [*sic*], and the best negro talk ever I saw in print." Emphasizing the Wildcat's military service, the *Lincoln Journal Star* described Wiley as "one of the first platoon of American short story writers," and Alexander Woollcott praised "the Wildcat stories of the unquenchable Hugh Wiley" because they are "good and true."[25] Such reviews followed the publication of each of Wiley's novels, and the Wildcat—and sometimes his goat, Lily—were quoted with loving pleasure in the white press.

Vitus Marsden also caught the attention of the film industry. In January 1920, well before Doran published Wiley's first novel, the *Los Angeles Times* announced that "Bert Williams, famous negro comedian of Ziegfield Follies fame" was in negotiations with Wiley to bring Vitus Marsden to the screen, to make not slapstick but rather "comedies of character and situation."[26] These negotiations appear to have fizzled out. In 1922—when Davy Carr bemoans the fate of the Dyer bill and writes Wiley out of the human race and five years before *The Jazz Singer* was produced—Al Jolson came very close to performing as the Wildcat in his first movie. The same year, the *Salt Lake Tribune* reported that Jolson was going to drive from Chicago to the Southwest, where he would work on a "six-reel moving picture" featuring the Wildcat and produced by the First National film company. Plans for this movie were apparently well developed; exterior shots would be filmed primarily in Arizona, and Wiley's stories were to be adapted so that "the 'Fighting Wildcat'" would play a "principal part [in] a

Mexican revolution."[27] According to the *San Francisco Examiner*, "Jolson will use troops of the Tenth Cavalry to give the proper military atmosphere to the film recital of Vitus' experience in France."[28] These plans must have also fallen through, but in 1930 the Pathé film studio brought out the two-reel talkie *High Toned*, which stars the Black vaudeville duo Buck and Bubbles.

In other words, the Wildcat made Hugh Wiley a household name in Jim Crow America, especially in the two to three million homes receiving the *Saturday Evening Post* every week. In 1920, Wiley had predicted a very short shelf life for his character, stating, "Four more stories, I think, will finish the Wildcat. . . . I want to quit while the going is good. Stories of that sort will travel only so far, and then the public will begin to tire of them."[29] But as Peter Rollins and Harry Menig note, "The sheer volume of Wiley stories indicates that *Post* readers never tired" of reading about the Wildcat's misadventures.[30] On at least one occasion, Wiley's peripatetic character was invited by a California city's leaders to come for a visit. In a front-page story, *The Californian* of Salinas reported, "Last week, Wildcat, Lily and Lady Luck in one of the well-known Hugh Wiley stories in the Saturday Evening Post visited the Monterey Coast and when last heard from they were headed toward Salinas. Mayor Daugherty, through the Chamber of Commerce has extended to them, in a letter to Hugh Wiley an invitation to Salinas."[31]

Upon learning of the invitation, Wiley wrote back and promised to deliver the Wildcat "into your excellent country"—and he made good on that promise.[32] In "Pop" (November 7, 1925), a character leads the Wildcat to "dis town Salinas. Mighty good town. Folks is lib'ral. Dey makes lots of money in dis place, an' dey is broad-minded,"[33] and the Wildcat makes another brief stop there in a subsequent story, "The Pluvitor." Because of his fame, Wiley was enlisted by the Associated Oil Company in 1927 for a national advertising campaign to promote ethyl gasoline. Images of the Wildcat and Lily ran throughout the country (figure 4.2).

White America loved Hugh Wiley's humor. Upon the publication of *The Wildcat* in book form in 1920,[34] Irvin S. Cobb recognized a comrade in the production of racial stereotype. According to the *Winston-Salem Journal*, Cobb, "the author of more side-splitting fun than probably any American since Mark Twain[,] . . . finds a veritable addition to native American literature in Hugh Wiley's inimitable tales. . . . Mr. Cobb writes: 'Hugh Wiley

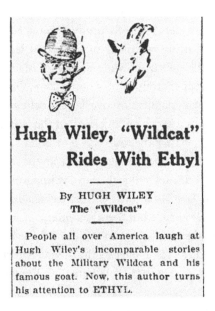

FIGURE 4.2. Associated Oil Company ad featuring Hugh Wiley and his characters, *Auburn (California) Journal-Republican*, April 21, 1927. Versions of this advertisement ran in hundreds of newspapers in at least nineteen states.

not only knows the modern Southern negro, but knows how to put him down in black and white. Most admirably he has done this in that book of his, 'The Wildcat,' every page of which abounds in racy humor.'" Not wanting readers to miss his pun, Cobb concluded by pointing out, "In this connection I used the word 'racy' advisedly."[35] Like Cobb, whose work disavowed anti-Black violence while undergirding the ideology and oppression of Jim Crow, Wiley's "humor" was never very far from that violence. Cobb described writing about Jeff Poindexter as keeping "that lazy nigger on the job." Similarly, Wiley conceived of himself as a white boss demanding fealty from his inferior. In a widely reprinted story in late 1921 featuring a photo of Wiley with fellow *Post* authors Samuel G. Blythe and Harry Leon Wilson and intended to highlight his status as a wit and humorist, "Golf Is the Curse of American Literature, Hugh Wiley Asserts; Has Given It Up, Except the African Brand," Wiley claimed, "My Wildcat has begun to act a little uppity here on the coast. . . . A short session in Louisiana and Tennessee will learn him how to act in the presence of 'white folks.'"[36] Wiley's creation might roam far and wide, see the world and all its many customs, but he would never stray too far from the discipline and subservience expected of him by readers of the *Saturday Evening Post.*

A particularly chilling reminder of the racial terrorism that always existed just below the surface of white-authored, Black dialect fiction can be found in a newspaper from Cobb's home state. On December 17, 1925, the same month as the publication of Alaine Locke's collection *The New Negro* and one month after the publication of the Wildcat story "Sick Per Cent" (November 21, 1925),[37] the *Knoxville Journal* ran an advertisement for the Fidelity Trust Co. that quotes extensively from the story, using its "amusing plans of Honeytone and Wildcat from the imagination of Hugh Wiley in Saturday Evening Post" to sell bonds: "'*Amortoizate de compound refunding collateral!*' utterly absurd but there *is a financial* sound to the words— and if the fact were known how many millions have been invested for no better reason!"[38] On the same page as this jovial advertisement, in which white readers were encouraged to celebrate their higher racial intelligence and firmer grasp of standard English, a *Journal* headline announced, "NEGRO LYNCHED FOR INSULTS—Riddled Body Is Answer to Remarks to White Woman" (figure 4.3). The victim, Grant Cole, was shot to death in Montgomery, Alabama, "near the spot where earlier in the evening he was alleged to have insulted and abused" an unnamed white woman.[39] Wiley's joke about sending his character back south because he "has begun to act a little uppity" was never very far in its intent from the terrorism that led to Cole's murder for refusing to run an errand for a white woman.

"IT IS HARD TO CONTROL HER IN LETTERS OR ANYWHERE ELSE": EDWARD CHRISTOPHER WILLIAMS'S *WHEN WASHINGTON WAS IN VOGUE*

No wonder, then, that Captain Davy Carr, a product of the Fort Des Moines Black officer training camp[40] and a battle-seasoned veteran, shares the disdain for Wiley expressed by "most of those present" at the literary discussion described at the beginning of this chapter. Illustrating Wiley's widespread notoriety in African American communities, Mary White Ovington, the chair of the NAACP Board of Directors in 1922 (and not unlikely a personal acquaintance of E. C. Williams), wrote in the *Afro-American* newspaper, "Probably the majority of my readers have already met 'The

FIGURE 4.3. "NEGRO LYNCHED FOR INSULTS—Riddled Body Is Answer to Remarks to White Woman," *Knoxville Journal*, December 17, 1925.

Wild Cat' in the pages of the Saturday Evening Post."[41] Davy and his Talented Tenth friends, even if they are more interested in magazines such as "the *Nation,* the *Dial,* the *Republic,* the *Atlantic,* and several other periodicals of the highest type" (32), as Williams wrote, cannot avoid the pervasive influence of the culturally omnipresent *Saturday Evening Post.* Williams's novel can thus be read as a sustained challenge to the dehumanization of Black veterans in the *Post* in general and in Wiley's fiction in particular.

In this sense, *When Washington Was in Vogue* represents the defense of Black doughboys found regularly in the pages of the *Messenger*.

Well educated and widely traveled even before the war, Davy Carr trained as an officer, saw action at the front, and returned home to resume his intellectual work; residing in Washington, DC, he is researching a book on Black history. Davy only occasionally mentions his participation in the war, but when he does, it always illustrates his resourcefulness, worldliness, and courage. Although he is painfully unaware of his own emotional life throughout much of the novel, he does not stumble through his experiences like the hapless Wildcat but instead calls upon his time both in France and in battle to understand more fully the world in which he lives.

Two scenes in particular not only demonstrate how Davy's experiences in France highlight his masculinity and humanity but also propel the book's romantic plot. Toward the beginning of the novel, while he is still oblivious of his dawning feelings toward Caroline Rhodes, the book's love interest, Davy shows her a scrapbook, his "big brown book," that chronicles "the epic of the great war" (89). Contained in these pages are keepsakes and photographs of a French woman named Mademoiselle Hortense de Figuieres, whom Caroline recognizes right away as something of a rival:

> Trust Caroline . . . not to miss a little thing. . . . After looking silently and without comment . . . at Hortense in Captain Carr's overseas cap and Sam Brown belt, and Hortense pinning a spring flower on Capt. Carr's manly bosom, and Hortense in that wonderful evening gown with the inscription, "A Davy, m'ami, de son Hortense," . . . Caroline said, in her blandest manner:
> "Teacher, what does 'son' mean in French?"
> "Hers or its," I answered . . .
> "From *his* Hortense," murmured Caroline to herself, as if in deep reflection. "Oh, you soldier boys, making the world safe for democracy!" Then she said quickly, "I supposed she's the one who writes you those fat letters with the French stamps?" . . .
> "She writes now and then," said I, "but I have several correspondents in France."
> (90)

As the passage demonstrates, this African American soldier, unlike Wiley's Wildcat, is romantically desirable, capable of equal and genuine friendships with men and women of any race or nation, and fluent and literate in both English and French.[42] Davy Carr does not merely respond or react to the flux of history; he grows and thrives. In stark contrast to the *Post*'s dialect writers, Williams registered both historical change *and* personal/racial development in his work.

Toward the end of *When Washington Was in Vogue*, a confrontation with the novel's villain, Morris Jeffreys, prods Davy and Caroline toward a final, happy kiss. Here again, Captain Carr's war experience comes into play. While the hesitant lovers and their friends are seated at a nightclub, Jeffreys bursts in, and Davy finds himself facing "the dull blue steel of a long army automatic." Addressing his war buddy Bob, Davy writes, "To you, who have looked down the barrel of one of those devilish things in time of war, I have no need to say that it was not a happy moment" (250). In a flash, Caroline gets between Davy and the gun—instantly proving her love for him as well as her pluck—and Davy swings into action:

> The menacing blue steel barrel now pointing straight at Caroline galvanized me into life, and grasping her by the shoulders, I swung her about, aware as I did so that if Jeffreys would only fire at that moment, he would have a point-blank target. What he would have done in another second I have no means of knowing, for as I braced myself to feel the tearing of a bullet through my vitals, something hit Jeffreys from the side like a catapult, and he went down with a crash, while the pistol fell far from him. My good friend Scott Green [another Black veteran] had executed a flank movement with the happiest results.
>
> (250–51)

Unlike the Wildcat's military feats, which are always accidental and never motivated by heroism, Davy, Caroline, and Lieutenant Scott Green act bravely, consciously, and selflessly to protect each other and face down danger. In Williams's novel, the Great War underscores Black humanity and courage and illustrates how and why African Americans were capable of and deserved first-class citizenship and equal respect under both custom and law—sentiments rarely if ever found in Lorimer's *Post*.

Wiley's Wildcat stories participate in a long tradition of Black dialect fiction in the *Saturday Evening Post*, and this fiction imprisons its African American characters within pre-Emancipation regimes of knowledge and

practice. Vitus Marsden might travel the world and witness history first-
hand, but he will never be more than a stereotypical minstrel figure imbricated in antebellum, antimodern nostalgia. Yet *When Washington Was in
Vogue* is also in its own way indebted to an earlier time. Williams crafted
Davy Carr's story as an epistolary novel, which is a centuries-old form, and
Davy's written voice is always carefully proper and decorous. In addition
to calling himself "an old campaigner" (88) because of his war experience,
he also refers to himself as both "medieval" (25) and "mid-Victorian" (30).
As Christina Moore notes in her study of the novel, "While [Williams's]
characters are modern citizens on the cutting edge of 1920s politics and culture, their voices and stories are narrated in a genre reminiscent of
eighteenth-century England."[43] But Williams, unlike *Post* writers such as
Wiley, used this older form to demonstrate that his Black characters, rather
than being frozen in time and subject to the vagaries of history and the hostile fantasies of racist American culture, have agency, self-possession, and
the ability to speak and write for themselves; the "old-fashioned" epistolary form serves to highlight the evolving, modern consciousness of the
novel's protagonist. In Williams's hands, African American service in
World War I becomes an opportunity to catch hold of the past, wrest agency
from it, and write genuine Black humanity onto the pages of the future.

In fact, it is the ability to write oneself *into* humanity (rather than out of
it, as Davy would like to do to Wiley) that ultimately animates Williams's
epistolary novel and propels us toward its happy conclusion. In the *Post*'s
dialect stories, African American characters are not three-dimensional
human beings but instead mere *things* being manipulated and mocked for
the amusement of a white readership.[44] These minstrel characters are, in
other words, the property of print culture, objects to be bought and sold
for five cents an issue, rather than subjects with intelligence and agency. In
stark contradistinction to the Black characters created by Wiley and other
Post writers of his ilk, Caroline's constant and intelligent attitudes about
and consumption of print media make her Davy's ideal romantic partner.
Davy puzzles over Caroline's transgressive behavior as a flapper, and he
unconsciously resists her because of her darker skin tone, but he falls in love
with her because of her literacy and her fluency in the world of books,
magazines, and writing. None of the other marriageable female characters
in Williams's novel is ever described in conjunction with print culture. The
beautiful Lillian Barton, for example, has a parlor in "an old man's house,

a rich man's house, made over, and redecorated on modern lines—some ultramodern. . . . Dark walls, with a few good paintings; heavy furniture in keeping with the size of the room; a wonderful rug; and a big fireplace with a real fire. Altogether it is the most attractive room I have been in . . . it seemed a perfect setting for Miss Barton" (38). However attractive Lillian and her room may be, there appears to be nothing worth reading in her parlor. She is not a suitable romantic partner for Davy because books and literature do not feature prominently enough in her life.

Not so for Caroline Rhodes. When Davy first arrives at her home, he notes that the family's "library-living room," as he calls it, has "walls lined with bookcases filled with good books" (6). Much later in the novel, just a few pages before Davy impulsively kisses Caroline, he gushes over the contents of the Rhodeses' library, and while doing so he makes a direct connection between print culture and the ownership of property:

> I figured casually that there were at least seven or eight hundred dollars' worth of books in sets . . . not to mention the hundreds of single volumes. The fact which struck me was that every set present represented the very best scholarship and was what one would call the standard or definite edition, and in the separate volumes I noted practically every one of the best English and American works of imaginative literature, both prose and verse, for the period between about 1890 and 1910. . . . No wonder Caroline, for all her occasional "jazzy" manners, has such an unusual speaking vocabulary. (205)

Davy's admiration for the financial and literary value of the Rhodeses' books takes on additional significance when one recalls that Williams was a working librarian with a keen understanding of book collecting and presentation.[45]

From the beginning of their acquaintance, Caroline understands Davy's penchant for the printed word. In the first half of the novel, when Caroline is trying to entice the romantically obtuse Davy, she highlights her attainments as a reader and writer. Shortly after becoming a roomer in the Rhodes house, Davy finds Caroline "attired in a most attractive negligee, curled up on my couch reading Flaubert's *Madame Bovary*" (28). A few pages later he discovers "my French dictionary open on the table . . . and several sheets of monogrammed paper scattered about, in the midst one of Caroline's

dainty little handkerchiefs, and pervading the whole room the very faintest trace of that wonderful perfume which I am beginning . . . to associate
with her personality" (35). Caroline, a grade-school instructor who attends
night classes at Howard University so that she can become a high school
teacher, does her homework in Davy's room, where "the arm of my chair . . .
seems to be her favorite post." One evening, she asks for Davy's help trans-
lating a French text; he writes, "While we looked on the book together, she
leaned against me, and put her arm over my shoulder. It was very sweet and
intimate" (51–52).

The difference between Caroline's agency within print culture and the
Wildcat's thinglike status in Wiley's fiction is clear, and, above all other con-
siderations, Caroline's polymorphous literacy marks her as the most suitable recipient of Davy Carr's affections. In an early letter to Bob, Davy
writes, "This is a dreadfully long letter, and, as I look it over, seems rather
full of Caroline, perhaps too much to be interesting to you. If you knew the
young lady herself, you would realize how hard it is to control her in letters
or anywhere else" (45). Caroline cannot be controlled in letters, and she will
not be registered and recontained by the ideology of caricature and stereotype. This is what makes Caroline desirable in a print culture otherwise
dominated by the manufactured fantasies of American white supremacy.
When Black veterans were demobilized and coming back home, W. E. B.
Du Bois famously wrote, "We *return fighting!*"[46] For Edward Christopher
Williams, one of the enemies in this fight was—"of course"—Hugh Wiley's
military Wildcat, and the stakes were nothing less than the narration of history and the full humanity of African Americans, especially those who
served their nation on the fields of France.

Significantly, 1922 is the same year that Davy Carr witnesses James Weldon Johnson's unsuccessful lobbying efforts for an antilynching bill, the
same year as the publication of Cobb's novel *J. Poindexter, Colored*, and the
same year that Davy and his friends critique the humanity of *Post* authors
Wiley and Cohen. It was also the year that Johnson—who almost certainly
traveled in some of the same circles as Edward Christopher Williams—
published his pioneering anthology *The Book of American Negro Poetry*.
In his preface to the collection, Johnson wrote, "The Negro in the United
States has achieved or been placed in a certain artistic niche. When he is
thought of artistically, it is as a happy-go-lucky, singing, shuffling, banjo-
picking being or as a more or less pathetic figure." Johnson's description is

applicable to any number of Black characters found in the *Saturday Evening Post*, including but certainly not limited to the Wildcat. Because of a culture that churns out caricatures like Wiley's, emphasized Johnson, "the status of the Negro in the United States is more a question of national mental attitude toward the race than of actual conditions." For Johnson, the best way to counter racism is to compel white Americans to recognize the achievements African Americans have been making all along: "No people that has produced great literature and art has ever been looked upon by the world as distinctly inferior." Williams, by writing his epistolary novel, further added to the body of literature initially anthologized by Johnson. And through the creation of a Black protagonist who is a working author and who cherishes a Black woman because of her literate self-possession, Williams demonstrated what Johnson called "the emotional endowment, the originality and artistic conception, and, what is more important, the power of creating that which has universal appeal and influence."[47] The *Saturday Evening Post* did its best to promote white supremacy and promulgate an anti-Black "national mental attitude," but as *When Washington Was in Vogue* demonstrates, the men and women of the Harlem Renaissance faced down "the menacing blue steel" of Jim Crow and wrote themselves into American literature and history.

Chapter Five

OCTAVUS ROY COHEN,
THE MIDNIGHT MOTION PICTURE COMPANY,
AND THE SHADOWS OF JIM CROW

On June 14, 1932, twenty young African Americans, including Langston Hughes, set sail for the Soviet Union to make a film about African Americans in Birmingham, Alabama, tentatively entitled *Black and White*. The film was never completed, but the undertaking enjoyed a fair amount of attention in the Black press as well as a few scant notices in mainstream newspapers. Six years earlier, in May 1926, another all-Black film troupe left Birmingham and sojourned in Europe and North Africa for nearly a year before returning to Alabama. While overseas, the Midnight Motion Picture Company made a considerable number of films that Black and white audiences in both Europe and the United States received warmly, with millions of readers regularly following the company's exploits. Both of these moments of early, international Black filmmaking are now mostly forgotten, and although Midnight Picture's transatlantic efforts achieved a larger following in the mid-1920s, we are more likely today to read about Hughes's near miss with Soviet film stardom. Of course, there's a good reason for this: whereas Hughes's moment with the Meschrapom film company actually happened, the Midnight Motion Picture Company, featured in the *Saturday Evening Post* from 1924 to 1930, was the entirely fictional creation of Octavus Roy Cohen, a white *Post* writer whose presence in African American literature of the 1920s is startlingly pervasive.[1]

The story of these two film companies highlights developments that inform every chapter of this book and were intrinsic to the United States in the first decades of the twentieth century—namely, the expansion and deepening of Jim Crow segregation and the concomitant rise of New Negro modernity and creativity. During this era, the nation experienced a robust print culture, new technologies of communication, expanding mass-market capitalism, and an increasingly global reach, *all* of which were predicated on white-supremacist ideology and practice. The *Post* was a well-known cog in this global machinery; although it "made no effort to encourage circulation outside North America . . . world travelers found it to be as ubiquitous as the Standard Oil can."[2] According to James Smethurst, post-*Plessy* segregation occurred "at almost exactly the same time as the United States becomes the predominant industrial power of the world and an international power with colonial possessions"; it was the "representations, re-creations, and reproductions of black voices, black bodies, and black culture [that] fueled the growth of . . . new mass culture industries."[3] The white *Post* authors I examine in this study sustained and profited from a vast machinery of racial exploitation, while twentieth century African American cultural producers such as Hughes strived—domestically and transnationally—to assert Black humanity and Black modernity. The film crews thus highlight two deeply entwined historical phenomena: on the one hand, the U.S. transition from Reconstruction to Redemption and toward global white supremacy and, on the other, the rise of New Negro artistry, critique, and resistance both at home and abroad.

Although it may be hyperbolic to suggest that Cohen loomed large during the Harlem Renaissance, it would be fair to claim that he cast his shadow everywhere and was a consistent, if unwanted, feature of the New Negro landscape. Along with Irvin S. Cobb and Hugh Wiley, Cohen was one of the *Post*'s primary writers of "humorous" Black dialect stories in the 1920s. By virtue of their widely circulated fiction, these authors were integral contributors to the soft power of Jim Crow ideology, which relied on the mechanical reproduction of predictable stereotyping to construct and maintain white racist fantasies, segregated spaces, and an alienated citizenry. Like Wiley and Cobb, Cohen was long ago relegated to the ash heap of literary history and is seldom discussed today, but he was mentioned regularly in the literature of the period, and he was clearly on the minds of many African

American writers of the era. This chapter focuses on one small element of Cohen's output—his movie company's foray abroad—but it is important at least to note that he fictionalized multiple aspects of Black modernity and was therefore a ubiquitous figure in the Jim Crow culture industry.

Before their transatlantic journey, Cohen's fictional moviemakers circulate primarily inside of America's segregated spaces. By sending his "Black" characters overseas and across international borders, Cohen exemplified Jim Crow's tendency toward ever-greater spatial expansion. As Smethurst notes, the steady rise of "separate but equal" politics and culture in the United States had the effect of making Blackness a sort of quasi-geographical space hemmed in by borders and hidden by shadows.[4] Grace Elizabeth Hale makes similar observations about the spatial and temporal dimensions of Jim Crow logic. Writing about southern historiography, for example, she notes, "History, a sense of the distance between the past and the present, became not only a time but a cultural space in which to craft a new southern border."[5] In fact, these motifs—borders and shadows—are a consistent feature of New Negro texts that grappled with the lived realities and representational strategies of segregation. In this chapter, I examine how Cohen's *Post* stories helped to construct and maintain the boundaries of Jim Crow America and to extend its reach both at home and abroad. I begin the chapter by considering how New Negro writers portrayed and challenged the spatialization of Jim Crow and conclude by examining how Cohen's fiction naturalized that segregation through short stories that simultaneously recognized and denied a developing African American modernity.

LINES, BORDERS, SHADOWS: EXPANDING JIM CROW

Segregation was, of course, experienced and practiced in actual spaces; on the page, Black writers recognized Jim Crow's "quasi-geography" and its expanding reach through references to lines, borders, and shadows, metaphors that recurred regularly during the long New Negro era and the more chronologically compact Harlem Renaissance. Just four years after the *Plessy v. Ferguson* decision in 1896 made segregation constitutionally acceptable, W. E. B. Du Bois described the American racial regime in spatial terms, declaring, "The problem of the Twentieth Century is the problem of the color-line."[6] This famous pronouncement, which he initially made at the first Pan-African Congress in London in 1900, succinctly described the policing and maintenance of racial borders in the United States, pointed toward the ways in which Black bodies were penned in and kept separate from white bodies, and gestured to the vast array of practices and policies that enabled white supremacy by shackling the social, economic, and political mobility of African Americans. Du Bois's spatial image of the color line resonated with his depiction of his own, post-Reconstruction childhood, when proliferating forms of legal racism were cohering into what would become the boundaries of Jim Crow. In Du Bois's telling, rising border walls cast their lengthening shadows across the terrain of Black experience: "The shades of the prison-house closed round about us all . . . relentlessly narrow, tall, and unscalable to sons of night who must plod darkly in resignation, or beat unavailing palms against the stone, or steadily, half hopelessly, watch the streak of blue above."[7] In addition to describing segregation spatially, Du Bois's moving passage also underscores the human-made nature of Jim Crow; the racial prison is a built structure that denies access to the fullness of the natural world.

Du Bois's anguished description of his confrontation with deepening racism and a rising tide of segregationist practices conveys the mental and spiritual pain inflicted by white supremacy, and his evocation of incarceration leads toward his perhaps even more famous statement about double-consciousness. Using the spatial metaphor of a measuring tape being drawn out, Du Bois described "this sense of always looking at one's self through the eyes of others, of measuring one's soul by the tape of a world that looks on in amused contempt and pity."[8] For Du Bois, being trapped inside the "shades of the prison-house" was bad enough; even worse, though, were the racist incursions from outside the self that crossed the color line at will by virtue of white racial privilege. In this sense, the term *double-consciousness* marks the unidirectional white colonization of Black self-regard. White people "made modern racial meaning not just by creating boundaries but also by crossing them," notes Hale,[9] and as Du Bois indicated, these hostile border crossings resonated both physically and psychically; collective Black spaces and individual Black minds were all subject to the depredations of Jim Crow.

By 1924, when Cohen's Midnight Motion Picture Company began its fictional journey to Europe, more than two decades had passed since Du Bois had exposed the color line at the Pan-African Congress. During those years, Jim Crow continued to push itself deeper and wider throughout American life, building ever higher walls and casting deeper shadows, and the *Saturday Evening Post* did its part to normalize this racist structure through its "humorous" fiction. As the Harlem Renaissance was gathering steam in the mid-1920s, Du Bois's observations about space and consciousness were just as germane as when he first made them. In Alain Locke's groundbreaking essay "The New Negro," which begins his anthology of the same title published in 1925, he amplified Du Bois's concern about the one-way borders built by white supremacy, and he pointed toward the culture industry filling this constructed space with demeaning caricature: "The Old Negro . . . has been a stock figure perpetuated as a historical fiction partly in innocent sentimentalism, partly in deliberate reactionism. . . . [F]or generations in the mind of America, the Negro has been more of a formula than a human being." According to Locke, because of the pervasiveness of stereotyping, the African American has internalized a distorted self-image; consequently, "his shadow . . . has been more real to him than his personality." Echoing Du Bois's idea of double-consciousness, Locke argued, "Little true social or self-understanding has come or could come from such a situation."[10] After twenty-five years of segregationist cultural work performed by hegemonic entities such as the *Post*, Locke saw how Jim Crow had populated the prison-house with characters of its own making.[11]

Both Locke and Du Bois also recognized that U.S. segregation and racial oppression were part of larger, transnational efforts to secure white supremacy, and this awareness was highlighted by Du Bois's very different contributions to, first, the *Survey Graphic* issue of March 1925 and, second, *The New Negro* anthology of December 1925, which was an expansion and revision of the *Survey Graphic* issue.[12] In the *Survey Graphic*, Locke published Du Bois's bitterly humorous story "The Black Man Brings His Gifts," which focuses on domestic white-supremacist behavior. Setting his story in Indiana, Du Bois exposed what might be called the "monoconsciousness" of the story's white subjects, people whose ignorance about history, religion, their world, and neighbors stands as testimony to the intellectual and ideological narrowness of Jim Crow.[13] By 1925, however, Du Bois was also firmly convinced that U.S. segregation was imbricated within a much broader "global color line." He had received part of his education in Berlin and was a key figure in the Pan-Africanist movement; from early in his career, he had cultivated a sense of transnational citizenship and had grappled with the interconnections between American and European formations of segregation, colonization, and imperialism.[14] Du Bois thus conceived of American racism as one aspect of a larger effort to exploit and subjugate nonwhite populations around the world. Taking aim at the erection of the global color line in his collection *Darkwater: Voices from Within the Veil* (1920), which was completed in the wake of World War I, Du Bois described whiteness as "a very modern thing" based on "the doctrine of the divine rights of white people to steal," and he claimed that the war was at root a contest among European nations and the United States for control over the nonwhite word. Further, rather than being a self-proclaimed engine of democracy and "a sort of natural peacemaker," the United States was in fact propelling what David Luis-Brown calls toxic "waves of whiteness" domestically and abroad. America "stands today shoulder to shoulder with Europe in Europe's worst sin against the civilization," Du Bois explained. "She aspires to sit among the great nations who arbitrate the fate of 'lesser breeds without the law' and she is at times heartily ashamed even of the large numbers of 'new' white peoples whom her democracy has admitted to place and power. . . . She trains her immigrants to this despising of 'niggers' from the day of their landing, and they carry and send the news back to the submerged classes in the fatherlands."[15] In his contribution to the revised and expanded *New Negro* collection, Du Bois also set his sights beyond the United States, moving from the national to the international, by writing about the global consequences of white imperialism.

Du Bois's title for his contribution, "The Negro Mind Reaches Out," dramatized the idea of a Black consciousness challenging and crossing the boundaries erected by white supremacy, and he began the essay with this recollection: "Once upon a time in my younger years and in the dawn of the century I wrote: 'The problem of the twentieth century is the problem of the color line.'" Du Bois concluded his essay by returning to this pronouncement, thereby asserting that Jim Crow and other forms of structural racism have persisted throughout the first decades of the new century and across the globe. In "The Negro Mind Reaches Out," Du Bois surveyed the European exploitation of Africa by returning to the trope of the shadow: "Here is a field of inquiry, of likening and contrasting each [imperial] land and its far-off shadow."[16] The shades of the American prison-house deepen to the shadows cast by global whiteness. The rest of "The Negro Mind Reaches Out" is divided into sections titled "The Shadow of Portugal," "The Shadow of Belgium," and so on. In other words, *The New Negro* anthology begins with Locke's domestic, U.S.-centered consideration of African American experience—a line of thought that echoes Du Bois's early writings—and concludes by considering Black lives and white supremacy in an international context, both across and within borders. Houston Baker describes Du Bois's contribution to *The New Negro* as "prophetic" because "Du Bois's critique of colonial terror, duplicity, and oppression was unequivocally a forerunner to our current expanded critique" of African American modernism and modernity in the global context.[17]

In December 1925, the same month and year as the publication of *The New Negro*, Rayford Logan (who coined the phrase "the nadir of American race relations" in 1954 to describe the post-Reconstruction rise of legal segregation), published the essay "Why We Should Study Negro History." Like Du Bois and Locke, Logan drew parallels between domestic racial practices and international borders, and his essay helps me to connect my initial observations about borders and shadows in New Negro writing to Cohen's contributions to the *Post*. Explaining the vital need for African Americans to study and control their own history, Logan began at the borders of the color line to warn about the expanding geographical and ideological terrain of Jim Crow:

> Madison Grant and Lothrop Stoddard succeeded so well in creating their "Nordic Myth" that one may truly say that our present immigration Law is founded on the precepts, dicta, sanctimonious homilies and pious platitudes that fill their books. These two men are no more industrious, however, in their way than Octavus Roy Cohen with his insulting, nonsensical stories in the *Saturday Evening Post*. Whether childish, sanctimonious, or humorous, a flood of literature from Southern pens is being disseminated throughout the [North]. Its effect is just beginning to be felt. Twenty years from now, the seed now sown will be a giant tree that we may not be able to fell. . . . Unless we write our own history . . . our place in American History will be a continuous stream of invective, disdain and ridicule. . . . Work of this nature must be begun at once. Otherwise Octavus Roy Cohen, . . . Stoddard and Grant will have such a hold on the public that it will be impossible to get a hearing.[18]

Logan's urgent call for a usable African American history[19] as a counter to white racism echoed and extended Arthur A. Schomburg's insistence in

"The Negro Digs Up His Past" (which Locke featured prominently in both the *Survey Graphic* and *The New Negro*) that the "American Negro must remake his past in order to make his future. . . . History must restore what slavery took away, for it is the social damage of slavery that the present generation must repair and offset."[20] Logan linked as examples of white-supremacist logic two immensely popular and well-respected promulgators of racial pseudoscience, Grant and Stoddard, with Cohen, one of the era's most famous white writers of Black dialect fiction. Grant's *The Passing of the Great Race* (1916) and Stoddard's *The Rising Tide of Color Against White World-Supremacy* (1920) had an enormous influence over American culture and are perhaps best remembered today for the nod they receive in *The Great Gatsby*, when Tom Buchanan declares, "Civilization's going to pieces," and cites as evidence " 'The Rise of the Colored Empires' by this man Goddard."[21] The name "Goddard" here is a winking conflation of Grant and Stoddard, who were also Fitzgerald's fellow Scribner authors.[22] These racial pseudoscientists' efforts to colonize both historical time and global space in the name of white supremacy led directly to the enactment of the border-closing Immigration Act of 1924, the law Logan also referred to in the passage quoted earlier. Stoddard was a regular contributor to the *Saturday Evening Post*, publishing fourteen essays in the magazine between 1923 and 1925, during which time Cohen was also a very active contributor. As Logan indicated, Stoddard and Grant's nativist, anti-immigrant racism was one side of the same coin shared by popular, "humorous" writers such as Cohen. The preference of George Horace Lorimer, editor of the *Saturday Evening Post*, for patronizing "darky" humor was matched—and perhaps even exceeded—by his penchant for anti-immigrant hysteria. Although Logan was writing specifically about the American context, his bundling together of Stoddard, Grant, and Cohen gestured toward the same globalized racial regime that Du Bois characterized metaphorically through the tropes of shadows and borders.[23]

OCTAVUS ROY COHEN: SEEN AND READ EVERYWHERE

Like most of the writers addressed in this book, Octavus Roy Cohen is no longer a household name, but he had a firm grip on American audiences of fiction, film, and radio for decades. Although his origin story includes well more than one hundred rejection letters before he was first published, including twenty-five from the *Post*,[24] Cohen fairly saturated American popular culture once his work found buyers. By 1916, he had coauthored *The Matrimaniac*, a novel that was adapted for the movies as a Douglas Fairbanks vehicle and helped launch Cohen's career as a screenwriter. Just three years later, the *Washington Herald* described Cohen as "only 27 years of age[, but] his work has appeared in nearly every magazine published in the United States."[25] Cohen got his real break when Lorimer convinced him to write fiction about African Americans. According to Tebbel, "It was [Lorimer's] suggestion . . . that turned Octavus Roy Cohen from the sports stories he had been trying to write, with indifferent success, to the hilarious pieces about the city Negro which brought him fame" (note Tebbel's description of them as "hilarious").[26] And these stories did indeed bring Cohen extraordinary success; by the end of his career, he had published fifty-six books and approximately two thousand stories. Of that number, nearly four hundred stories featured Black characters, and Cohen ultimately earned the distinction of selling "more stories to the *Saturday Evening Post* than any other writer." In addition to his printed work, Cohen's "credit appeared on thirty motion pictures" as well as on a number of *Amos 'n' Andy* radio scripts.[27] He enjoyed enormous popularity and was an essential contributing factor behind the *Post's* burgeoning circulation in the 1920s and beyond.[28] Cohen was the most frequently published author in the most widely read magazine in America; he might be largely forgotten now, but he was everywhere in the 1920s, and he cast the shadows and drew the borders that were intended to prevent any transition away from Jim Crow and toward full citizenship and acknowledged humanity for African Americans.

Because of Cohen's fame and notoriety as a white *Post* author of Black dialect stories, Harlem Renaissance writers referred to him frequently and in various print media. The African American press often noted the influence of his fiction and motion pictures, and the diminutive and dapper Florian Slappey—likely Cohen's most famous character—was a known quantity that required no explanation when his name appeared in Black newspapers. Most often, African Americans condemned Cohen for his stereotypical writing, but they also occasionally welcomed and praised him. In 1922, for example, he was invited to referee a football game between two historically Black colleges, and in 1933 the *Baltimore Afro-American* lauded Cohen's "talent as a writer of Negro humor."[29] In the main, however, Cohen was usually held up for scorn and disapprobation by African American writers, and as the following examples demonstrate, he must have been a regular topic of conversation in Black America more generally—from the polite parlors of Washington, DC, to the bohemian corners of Harlem and beyond. Early in Richard Bruce Nugent's novel *Gentleman Jigger* (written primarily between 1928 and 1933 but not published until 2008),[30] the protagonist, Stuartt, discusses the Negro Renaissance with a white character, "Bum" Borjolfsen (who is a clear analogue to Stephen Jorgenson in Wallace Thurman's novel *Infants of the Spring* [1932]), and Stuartt expands on how fictional representations shape racial perception: "First of all, Bum, I suppose you have never known a Negro before. That's the usual defense. And you expected to find us more or less uncivilized denizens of some great jungle city, believing in witch doctors and black magic and all that. Well, you're right. Or maybe you've read Harriet Beecher Stowe and feel sorry for us. Do. Or Octavus Roy Cohen and are amused, or Seabrook and are afraid. You know ... it really is too bad we aren't more different. What a disappointment we must be."[31] Stuartt scorns the white writers he names because they commit the artistic sin of creating flat Black characters that instigate only simple, predictable responses—pity, fear, and, in Cohen's case, patronizing humor—rather than developing any complexity or nuance. A similar discussion of the *Post* author occurs in Edward Christopher Williams's *When Washington Was in Vogue* (1925–1926), while the narrator and his friends enjoy a cup of tea at a far more respectable gathering and "read Octavus Roy Cohen and Hugh Wiley out of the human race altogether."[32] And in Du Bois's introduction to his landmark symposium in *The Crisis* magazine, "The Negro in Art: How Shall He Be Portrayed," in 1926, his opening paragraph also singled out Cohen as one of white America's worst offenders against Black humanity: "But the Negro has objected vehemently—first in general to the conventional Negro in American literature; then in specific cases: to the Negro portrayed in *Birth of a Nation* ... and in Stribling's *Birthright*; in Octavus Roy Cohen's monstrosities. In general they have contended that while the individual portrait may be true and artistic, the net result to American literature to date is to picture twelve million Americans as prostitutes, thieves and fools and that such 'freedom' in art is miserably unfair."[33]

Cohen's dominant position in American culture as a putative expert on African American life can further be gauged by H. L. Mencken's response to Du Bois's critique of Cohen, printed in the same symposium. The great iconoclast of Baltimore, it turns out, enjoyed chuckling along unreflexively with the *Post* writer's predictable caricatures and clichés: "It seems to me that in objecting to such things as the stories of Mr. Cohen the Negro shows a dreadful lack of humor."[34] Indeed, Cohen cast a large shadow across the writers, artists, and thinkers of the New Negro era, who labored to go beyond the ideological walls constructed by the literary arm of white supremacy. In other words, when "the Negro mind reache[d] out," when African Americans contested sentimental and reactionary stock figures, when they studied their history or dug up the past, they were trying to break the barriers and reverse the rising tide of Jim Crow that Lorimer, Cohen, and their ilk so assiduously—and profitably—erected.

THE MIDNIGHT MOTION PICTURE COMPANY
GOES TO EUROPE

Cohen began his tenure at the *Post* in 1918 with his story "The Missing Clink," and he then quickly developed an entire cast of characters whose lives revolved around Birmingham's "Darktown" (for more on "Darktown," see chapter 2). Writing about the Black community in Birmingham is consequential because Cohen's stories attest to an American modernity that requires additional critical attention in fields of study still dominated by the "Harlem" Renaissance. As Smethurst notes, Birmingham's Fourth Avenue was one of the many "black commercial centers" that developed in the South as segregation hardened in the years after the *Plessy* decision.[35] Indeed, the steady rise of Jim Crow not only produced segregated spaces increasingly marked by "For Colored" and "For White" signs but also led to the development of thriving Black business districts and social centers.[36] Cohen's "Bummin'ham" rivals other fictional, segregated localities— Faulkner's Yoknapatawpha County comes to mind—for its recurrent characters and their entangled relationships; as he continued contributing dialect stories to the *Post*, Cohen developed (in order to mock) locales such as the Penny Prudential Bank Building, Sally Crouch's Cozy Home for Colored, and Bud Pealgar's Barbecue Lunch Room and Billiards Parlor as well as organizations such as the Over the River Burying Society and the Sons and Daughters of I Will Arise. No Cohen story was complete without mention of at least some of these places and groups. In addition, Cohen imagined segregated Birmingham as being one node of a much larger web of both regional and national African American communities, drawn together by the extensive network of railroads that grew with extraordinary rapidity across the South after Reconstruction.[37] He developed this transregional focus especially through his stories about Epic Peters, a Pullman porter who makes frequent appearances in his work. Cohen's stories therefore register an important facet of African American history by demonstrating how the Great Migration was not only a movement out of the South to the North and West but also "a tremendous migration" *within* the South,[38] from rural areas to the evolving urban spaces that were arising because of the spread and deepening of both modernization and segregation.

After "The Missing Clink" and over the next six years alone, Cohen would publish more than fifty stories fictionalizing Black life in the *Post* (not to mention more fiction in other media platforms). Cohen's stories always have a punning title, including the painfully hurtful "Birth of a Notion," which makes sport of one of the most dangerous films ever made and reveals the violence that always lurks behind his comedy. Recurrent formulae—which Cohen deployed with sometimes mind-numbing frequency—include the making and breaking of legal contracts, romantic plots that hinge on manipulation and deceit, and physical harm meted out against unwitting victims. As often as not, the perpetrators of the violence are described as "bullet headed." And like Cohen's repeated invocation of certain locations and organizations in his fictional Darktown, his stories would seemingly not be complete without a syntax-twisting "fondest of" sentence. In all his Black dialect stories, Cohen maneuvers his dialogue to have at least one character make a statement that ends with an absurdly dangling preposition. For example, in one story Florian exclaims, "Oh golla! Tha's the fondest thing I'd be of," and in another a different character declares, "Bein' bawled out by a big ol' fat frog like you ain't the fondest thing I is of!"[39] Cohen's legions of readers knew they could count on these regular features for years on end.

Beginning with "Every Little Movie," published in August 1924, Cohen focused his stories in large part on the Midnight Motion Picture Corporation, an all-Black company producing slapstick two-reel comedies that play throughout the United States. Recurrent characters in the Midnight series include the company's owner and president, Orifice R. Latimer; directors

Caesar Clump and Eddie Fizz; male leads Opus Randall and Welford Potts (who bear a physical resemblance to Laurel and Hardy); female stars Sicily Clump and Glorious Fizz; and child actor Excelsior Nix. Lawyer Evans Chew appears regularly (to write and enforce all those contracts), and Florian Slappey—through trickery—attaches himself to Midnight as essentially the young Excelsior's agent. Cohen wrote at least thirty stories about Midnight, and in 1926 he sent the cast and crew to Europe and North Africa in a series of about a dozen stories. Exemplifying the white-supremacist practice of maintaining a color line that was permeable only from the outside, Cohen crammed his globetrotting characters—who remove themselves physically from Jim Crow America by sailing across the Atlantic—into the narrow, consciousness-crushing perimeters of minstrelsy. His stories abroad offer a fairly literal representation of Du Bois's trope of the shadows as his fiction casts its pall of racist fantasy over the sea to Europe and North Africa. In *Darkwater*, Du Bois described the psychosociological effects of white supremacy on all of humanity as "a world campaign . . . finally culminating in the evidence of modern profit which lies in degrading blacks,—all this has subconsciously trained millions of honest, modern men into the belief that black folk are sub-human."[40] And in his novel *Dark Princess: A Romance* (1928), he describes the global reach of white racism as "the white leviathan," "the same vast, remorseless machine in Berlin as in New York."[41] Cohen's fictional steamship, which departs from New York bearing his minstrel fantasies toward Europe, is most certainly the white whale of an all-consuming segregationist ideology as well as an example of the machinery of racism Du Bois condemned.

Cohen's movie stories offer useful examples of how *Post* dialect fiction registered and recontained Black modernity in the twentieth century. As Donald Bogle and Cedric J. Robinson note in their histories of African Americans in the film industry, several all-Black movie companies were formed in the 1920s and 1930s;[42] in addition to registering the shifting demographics of the Great Migration, therefore, Cohen's fiction also bore witness to a significant moment in expressive Black culture. Cohen drew on his own experiences in the industry by regularly portraying the technical, artistic, and business sides of filmmaking. Midnight Pictures stories thus include such elements as the sale of stock in the company, film sales and distribution, child actors and stunt doubles, the importance of daily rushes, the writing and production of genre pictures (and their slapstick burlesques), and the cultivation and development of new talent and larger audiences. And there is an eye to detail in the stories. For example, in "Endurance Vile" (December 5, 1925), the owner of the company, Orifice Latimer, travels to Chicago searching for a new screenwriter "who could impart to Midnight that ultimate touch of class . . . [someone] with whom he could intelligently talk plot, treatment, sequence and continuity." Latimer discovers Forcep Swain, who "entered literature through the back door" by working first as a reporter and then a fiction writer for a Black newspaper. Swain is almost certainly a spoof of recent New Negro authors, and, coincidentally, the *Post* published "Endurance Vile" in the very same month that Locke published his anthology. In all these stories, Cohen presented the nascent Black film industry while also portraying that rise within the images and language of minstrelsy:

> Mr. Swain had heard of Midnight; but, like many other successful artists, he held the unspoken drama in fine disdain.
> "It is not possessed of no soul," he informed Orifice. "Of course, artistically it has got some possibilities and it is a medium which reaches one and all, young and old; but so far it has not afforded a proper outlet for us literary inclined gentlemen of the pen."
> Mr. Latimer's eyes were distended.
> "Words what you utters, Brother Swain."[43]

This exchange typifies how Cohen, as a *Post* writer, registered and recontained Black modernity (and it also resonates with Rebecca Harding Davis's "silhouette" of Pearl Heminway twenty years earlier, as discussed in chapter 1). Latimer makes thoughtful efforts to improve the quality and commercial viability of his films, and he does so with both business acumen and an eye toward artistry; Swain is educated and has experience as a writer. At the same time, however, the narrator's formal, grammatically correct, and slightly supercilious voice contrasts with the two Black speakers' grammatically incorrect language, thus emphasizing their subordinate humanity.[44] In addition, Swain plays the dandy to Latimer's eye-popping buffoon, thereby reinforcing the stereotypes of minstrelsy.

Despite being used to further the racist comedy, Cohen's technical details also illustrate and memorialize work that must have been done by such pioneering Black film companies as the Lincoln Motion Picture Company, the Reol Motion Picture Corporation, and Oscar Micheaux's Book and Film Company. And when Cohen sent his characters abroad, he recognized the transnationalism and cosmopolitanism of the African diaspora by portraying such phenomena as French-speaking Black veterans of World War I, the experience of Black jazz musicians in Europe, Black expatriates living overseas, and Black Atlantic exchanges among Algerians, Moroccans, and Americans. In these ways, Cohen registered significant historical developments regionally, nationally, and internationally. But despite—or perhaps because of—these phenomena, which entailed wider horizons, a greater sense of capability, and a global perspective on the mechanisms of race and class, Cohen, like pretty much all his fellow white *Saturday Evening Post* authors, recontained these developments back into the formulations of caricature and the arrogance of white supremacy. His characters mangle every language they speak, steal from and scam each other regularly, and succeed through accident and foolishness more often than through intelligence and ability.

The European series—which would be republished as a collection in 1928 by Little, Brown and Company as *Florian Slappey Goes Abroad*—began in the May 8, 1926, issue of the *Post* with "Mercy, Monsieur!," which details Florian's successful efforts to trick his way into a free trip abroad. For the next nine stories, through March 5, 1927, the company takes up residence in various cities and produces two-reelers to send back home. As the penultimate story, set in Paris, summarizes, "They had sailed from New York on an Italian ship. They had sojourned in Naples, Rome, Florence, Venice, Milan. They had lived in Nice and Marseilles and Algiers."[45]

Cohen's story "Horns Aplenty" (September 4, 1926) illustrates the trends I am sketching out. Fifth in the European series, the story opens in the winter, on the train from Florence to Venice, where Florian Slappey takes advantage of his fellow Midnight employees by reselling food to his friends at an exorbitant profit. To take their minds off the cold, Professor Aleck Champagne, the troupe's bandleader, organizes a rehearsal under the official gaze of a "gentleman in a black shirt, acting as train inspector for the Fascisti." (As it happens, Lorimer was also enamored with Italy's transition to fascism under Benito Mussolini.) Champagne passes around sheet music for a new song, "The Gintown Blues," which lists his name as the composer, but two band members, the saxophonist Sam Gin and the cornet player Willy Trout, actually wrote the song, and they object to the bandleader stealing the credit for their work. The ensuing argument provides ample orthographic derision of the sort favored by the *Post*, with, for example, the bandleader describing his horn players as "muttonous," and their spoken language is consistently contrasted with the narrator's condescending voice. Fired for insubordination, Sam claims—in the sort of tortured syntax favored by dialect writers in the *Post*—"Aleck Champagne is the most man I hates."[46] By dismissing his horn players, the bandleader has exceeded the authority of his contract, and for much of the rest of Cohen's story Champagne juggles the competing desires to retain both his job and his ill-gained authorship of "The Gintown Blues." Meanwhile, Sam and Willy wander about the wintery canals of Venice with no money and no idea where the troupe is staying. They decide that the best way to reunite with the company is to play "The Gintown Blues" until someone hears it; before long, they have attracted the attention of a local jazz hall owner who is about to employ Champagne. He hires Sam and Willy instead, and by the end of the story the aggrieved musicians have not only retained control of their song but also connived an extra five hundred lire out of Champagne's pocket. Thus, the evolution of African American jazz in the European context— which is certainly one of the signal moments of twentieth-century transatlantic culture—is registered by a story that also simultaneously recontains this development within the stereotypical diction and formulaic plot structure of a predictable *Saturday Evening Post* story.[47] Cohen's film company might traverse the American color line by sailing east, but the shades of the Jim Crow prison-house follow them all the way across the Atlantic.

A subsequent story, "Low but Sure" (November 6, 1926), casts further shadows on the African American experience abroad. Set in Nice, where the "breath of Northern Africa ... wafted gently across the Mediterranean," the film company's owner, President Latimer, is beseeched by a character named Ethiope Wall for a job. Ethiope has been living in France for nearly nine years, which suggests he is probably a veteran of the Great War (and therefore another example of the *Post*'s fascination with Black doughboys), and he longs to return home. Despite Latimer's belief that France is "a heavumly place fo' cullud folks," Ethiope complains, essentially, that Europe is not segregated enough, and he shares the same fealty to Jim Crow articulated by other *Post* fantasies such as Blanche Goodman's Viney, Cobb's Poindexter, and Wiley's Wildcat: "Man, what I craves is to git me back to Georgia, where cullud folks is cullud folks and white is white." Through a series of typical twists and turns, Ethiope lands a job as the "stand-up man" (stand-in) for Malacca Jones, the company's overpaid, self-important, and temperamental male lead. When they are on set, one of Jones's star-struck fans, "Adorée Lafourche, a very colored lady who from birth until three years previous had been resident in Morocco," mistakes the stand-up man for the star and is immediately smitten. With the mechanical predictability of a Cohen story, Adorée is already engaged to the brutish Jean, "a very colored gentleman of pronounced physical prowess" who is "atrociously bad medicine, rather addicted to jealousy and an overplus of affection for the somewhat inconstant Adorée." Before long, the blissfully ignorant Ethiope is squiring Adorée around Nice, allowing her to believe that he is in fact Malacca Jones. When Jean discovers his fiancée's disloyalty, he becomes a stereotypical Black brute: "The hot unreasoning blood of African forebears coursed in his veins; he was a person of violent moods and more violent actions. The big, bulging muscles of his sinewy frame grew tense; his ham-like fists clenched, his bullet head was shoved forward and he splattered a stream of French profanity."[48] The plot continues on its unsurprising course as Jean hunts down the unwitting Malacca Jones and beats the star so badly that his victim immediately leaves Nice and abandons the film company. The story concludes exactly as one would expect: Ethiope Wall benefits from this spasm of violence and stumbles blindly into a movie career by finishing Jones's movie. In this story, as in most of Cohen's fiction—indeed, as in almost all *Saturday Evening Post* Black dialect stories—the "hero" succeeds only through a series of accidents and misrecognitions; Black success in this genre is never the consequence of skill, talent, intelligence, or artistry, and violence against Black bodies and Black psyches is relentlessly portrayed as a cause for laughter.

"Horns Aplenty" and "Low but Sure" are fairly representative of the *Post's* dialect fiction in general and of Cohen's in particular. Suffice it to say that you can read the first page of any Cohen story and predict the story's conclusion and that you will then plod through a written dialect that was never spoken by any actual human beings but contrarily lived for decades only in the pages of Lorimer's magazine and in popular culture more broadly. As Melville J. Herskovits noted in 1937, "One does not have to be a profound student of Negro life to understand that the stories of Octavus Roy Cohen are a travesty and a caricature of Negro life; and that while some persons of the type this writer portrays exist somewhere, they are found more often in the pages of the *Saturday Evening Post*, where these stories usually appear, than in the Negro communities of the United States."[49] Through stories that registered African American modernism and modernity but then recontained those experiences in the images and language of minstrelsy and post-Reconstruction fantasies of both Black insufficiency and excess, *Post* writers such as Cohen maintained the color line at home and—through his Midnight Motion Pictures misadventures—cast its shadows abroad.

Du Bois understood the problem Cohen in particular posed to African Americans from early in that writer's career at the *Post*. In a letter to Lorimer in 1922, Du Bois argued, "While it is possible that Cohen's caricatures may have some artistic merit, surely no editor can think that this is the whole truth. I am puzzled to know why it is, that only that type of Negro is allowed to put foot in your pages. . . . [It] seems to me that the larger duties and ideals of an editor in your influential place, ought to induce you to look for, or at least be willing to consider, other conceptions and portraits of Negroes, from those which you have persistently published." Lorimer responded with barely concealed disdain, calling Du Bois and other Black critics of his magazine "over sensitive. We do not remember having printed an ill-natured story of colored people. . . . We think that our critics really do not want equality of treatment but preferential treatment."[50] Like the narrow-minded white narrator in Du Bois's story "The Negro Brings His Gifts," Lorimer refused to recognize the real harm done to Black people by the "hilarious pieces about the city Negro" in his magazine. Nonetheless, Du Bois was clear-eyed about Cohen's potential to obscure, distort, and overshadow the lives, accomplishments, and needs of real Black people living in Jim Crow America. Four years after writing to Lorimer, he declared in "Criteria of Negro Art" in 1926 that "all art is propaganda," and he once again singled out Cohen as a chief propagandist in the slow-rolling race war that was Jim Crow. With cynical graciousness, Du Bois imagined Cohen as a hesitant collaborator of white supremacy who acceded to Lorimer's marching orders and cashed his royalty checks: "I should not be surprised if Octavus Roy Cohen had approached the *Saturday Evening Post* and asked permission to write about a different kind of colored folk than the monstrosities he has created; but if he has, the *Post* replied, 'No. You are getting paid to write about the kind of colored people you are writing about.' "[51]

"SOME HAM LIKE COHEN": HARLEM RENAISSANCE RESPONSES

The extraordinary success of the Harlem Renaissance can be measured in part by Octavus Roy Cohen's near-total disappearance from literary history and collective memory despite having been a major force in the U.S. media landscape for a very long time. It may have taken a while—and although white supremacy persists and is even resurgent in the MAGA era—but New Negro creativity effectively buried the purveyors of Old Negro fiction in American literary history. We are far more likely to read Wallace Thurman's roman à clef *Infants of the Spring* (1932) than anything Cohen published; but during the Harlem Renaissance, Thurman struggled against the cultural dominance of "the Octavus Roy Cohen school [of] modern 'cullid' folk," and he worried about the "dialect farce committed by an Octavus Roy Cohen to increase the gaiety of Babbits."[52] In a letter to Walter and Gladys White in 1932, Zora Neale Hurston explained that she wrote the stories that would be collected in *Mules and Men* (1935) in part because "it makes me furious when some ham like Cohen . . . gets off a nothing else but and calls it a high spot of Negro humor and imagery."[53] Cohen would probably never have dreamed of Hurston's current ubiquity in classrooms, bookstores, and the hearts of millions of readers, but his fiction certainly worked to deny the possibility of such success. And when we read Claude McKay's novel *Banjo* (1929) and peer out Latnah's "little shutter-window, the size of a *Saturday Evening Post*,"[54] we are more likely to imagine Hughes's Meschrapom film crew sailing into the port of Marseilles than the white leviathan bearing the Midnight Motion Picture Company.

Perhaps the most telling critique of Cohen's work and of his pernicious influence on American culture came not from a canonical literary figure of the Harlem Renaissance but from Swan Kendrick, an African American reader of the *Post* who wrote to the white author within the first year of his long tenure at the magazine. Kendrick served as secretary of the Washington, DC, branch of the NAACP, worked in the War Department, and "belonged to a correspondents club aimed at combatting aspersions against African Americans in public forums."[55] He opened his exceedingly polite and friendly letter of March 30, 1919, by explaining that he had been "a regular reader of the Post for the last eight or nine years" and had therefore "developed a sort of proprietary interest" in the magazine. Praising the excellence of Cohen's fiction and the author's "surprising knowledge of

colored folk," Kendrick noted his satisfaction that Cohen had "not introduced a single vicious [Black] character in [his] stories." But Kendrick also
asked Cohen to reconsider two elements of his writing. First, he faulted
Cohen's "constant use of the terms 'Nigger,' 'Darky,' 'Coon,' etc.," because
these words impeded the pleasure of both Black and white readers. "Try
running a blue pencil through the 'Niggers' and 'Coons' in your next story—
your publishers won't object, and I know of a few thousand readers who
will enjoy your stories much more." Kendrick's second objection was that
Cohen's stories misrepresented the attainments of African American
strivers:

> Your characters are introduced as being of the highest type of colored peo-
> ple in their towns, as graduates of the "cemetery," lawyers, etc. I am sure that
> you know well that cooks and chambermaids are not the highest type of col-
> ored people, and that colored lawyers and doctors don't use the dialect
> which you put into their mouths. This may not seem a very serious matter,
> but there is this aspect of it which you are probably not familiar with: Col-
> ored people are in an uphill struggle to show that they can assimilate the
> education the ideals and the other elements which go to make up the typi-
> cal American. Most Americans know very little of this struggle, or its "uphill-
> ness." When they read your stories, and find colored doctors and lawyers
> using dialect, find "cemetery" graduates doing cooking and house cleaning
> for a living, etc., it doesn't make that uphill climb of the average Negro any
> easier. Quite the contrary. Mind you, I don't object to the use of Negro dia-
> lect in stories. But I don't think it is quite fair to put it into the mouths of
> those whom the readers of the Saturday Evening Post would naturally con-
> clude should know better.[56]

Cohen responded promptly to Kendrick's letter on April 4, thanking him
for "the most valuable [criticism] I have yet received" and claiming that the
chief aim of his Darktown stories was "to provide amusement and, with it,
to be absolutely fair and honest. I want my readers not to laugh *at* the
negroes, but to laugh *with* them." Moving on to Kendrick's two complaints,
Cohen denied ever using the term *coon* and defended his use of *nigger* and
darkey; "I'm afraid I shall continue with [these terms], although never"—
Cohen claimed—"in an offensive sense." Then, without apparent irony or
self-awareness, he dismissed Kendrick's second critique about the spoken

language of Cohen's middle- and upper-class Black characters with this justification: "We have had no less than three servants in the past two years who hold diplomas from southern seminaries. Also, our janitor is a Tuskegee graduate and the prototype of my Lawyer Evans Chew is well known to me and inclined to dialect."[57] Like so many *Post* authors before him, Cohen claimed his employment of African American domestic workers made him an expert on Black people.

Kendrick's reply came a month later and appears to have garnered no response from Cohen. In this terser, more pointed letter, Kendrick noted that he had previously mailed Cohen a copy of the April 1919 issue of the bohemian leftist little magazine the *Liberator*. Kendrick urged Cohen to read Mary Burill's one-act play "Aftermath," which should be "of value in giving you an insight into the present trend of thought among colored people, and some of the circumstances which are producing that trend of thought."[58] Kendrick provided no summary of Burrill's play. If Cohen actually did read it, he would have encountered an antilynching piece populated by Black characters who speak entirely in dialect. Unlike the myriad japeries that characterize *Post* dialect stories such as Cohen's, Burrill's play is about a loving family torn apart by the extralegal killing of their husband and father. The only "deception" in the play is that the survivors have not told the son, John, who is a returning soldier from France, about his father's lynching. Most likely an allusion to Needham Roberts and Henry Johnson's example of heroism (discussed in chapter 3), John received the War Cross when he "fought off twenty Germuns all erlone an' saved his whole camp'ny an the gret French General come an' pinned de medal on him, *hisse'f!*" At the play's climax, John learns about the lynching, grabs his service revolvers, and declares, "You mean to tell me I mus' let them w'ite devuls send me miles erway to suffer an' be shot up fu' the freedom of people I ain't nevah seen, while they're burnin' and killin' my folks here at home! To Hell with 'em!"[59] The play ends as John and his younger brother head out for revenge—and almost certain death. Without saying it directly, Kendrick pointed toward the truth that Cohen failed to recognize—namely, that the violence of white supremacy was the inevitable outcome of Cohen's putatively innocuous "humor." If Cohen bothered to read "Aftermath," he might have also read Claude McKay's sonnet sequence "The Dominant White," which runs directly after Burrill's play in the *Liberator* and warns, "Oh

White Man! You have trifled with your trust! / And God shall humble you down to the dust."[60]

The only reason to remember *Post* writers such as Cohen is that they contextualize and underscore the achievements of the African American authors who challenged and subverted the images of Black life that dominated American print culture for much of the twentieth century. With these achievements in mind, I conclude with the words of an African American writer who did indeed travel the world, crossing borders and seeing beyond the shadows of American white supremacy. In 1926, while the *Post* was churning out the material that helped to prop up the Jim Crow regime and to wall in a people, and years before he tried his own hand at making a movie, Langston Hughes looked at the streak of blue that so tormented the young Du Bois and declared, "We build our temples for tomorrow, strong as we know how, and we stand on top of the mountain, free within ourselves."[61] We are far more likely to recall these words than anything written by Octavus Roy Cohen, notwithstanding his prominence and success— and this is a decidedly good thing.

Chapter Six

THE END OF THE LORIMER ERA

John Matheus's essay "Some Aspects of the Negro Interpreted in Contemporary American and European Literature," which Nancy Cunard included in her monumental collection *Negro: An Anthology* in 1934, took note of a recent trend in white-authored literature. A professor of romance languages, Matheus had previously won first prize from *Opportunity* magazine for his short story "Fog," which was later published in Locke's *New Negro* in 1925. In his essay, Matheus wrote approvingly about "the younger group of Southerners . . . Clement Wood, T. S. Stribling, Dubose Heyward, Julia Peterkin, Paul Green, Roark Bradford. . . . These writers have manifested a sympathetic interest in the Negro as a human being and within narrow circles have given artistic glimpses of his emotions and daily life."[1] Many of the authors in Matheus's appreciative list had already or would soon contribute their work to the *Saturday Evening Post*, which is perhaps surprising considering Lorimer's long history of publishing racist caricatures. But Matheus's appreciation came with qualifications in that he characterized these white writers' sympathy as bounded within "narrow circles" that provided just a few "artistic glimpses" of Black interiority. Matheus, in other words, suggested a perceptible, welcome evolution rather than a complete break with the white supremacism of so much American fiction. This observation about a noticeable change can be applied fruitfully to the

Saturday Evening Post in the final years of Lorimer's editorship, when a new slate of authors tested the limits of the *Post*'s long-established formula for representing African Americans.

In chapter 1, I charted the consolidation of Lorimer's approach to Black modernity in his first two decades as editor. In those early years, there was a significant change in the *Post*'s attitude toward African Americans, one that started with some interest in African American advancement but became increasingly hostile and dismissive and ultimately manifested *no* "sympathetic interest in the Negro as a human being." Early in Lorimer's tenure, he printed all manner of anti-Black material, but he was also amenable to Booker T. Washington's accommodationist racial politics, and he regularly published work by Paul Laurence Dunbar. This editorial practice was not a sign of Lorimer's enlightenment, but it did indicate, at the very least, some sort of openness—however qualified and perhaps disingenuous—to the project of racial uplift, if not necessarily racial equality. As the new century wore on, however, and as the logic and practices of Jim Crow deepened and spread, Lorimer eliminated all Black voices from his magazine and narrowed representations of African Americans until he published only the putatively humorous, white-authored dialect fiction that became a standard feature of the *Saturday Evening Post*. This representational strategy, I argue, registered and recontained Black modernity both to refute Black humanity and full citizenship as well as to deny white culpability for the violence and inequality of legal segregation. During the 1920s, which saw the rise of the Harlem Renaissance, this approach dominated the magazine's portrayal of African Americans and was further bolstered optically through the caricatures found in advertisements and story illustrations. But as the 1920s wore on, and as developments in Harlem enjoyed growing national interest, the magazine's approach to African Americans also evolved, albeit within "narrow circles." This chapter examines how Lorimer's long-standing preference for Black dialect humor lost its uniform quality in his final decade as the editor of the *Post*. Beginning as early as 1925 but then intensifying as the Great Depression and Franklin Delano Roosevelt's New Deal reshaped America in myriad ways, Lorimer published material that did not conform to the predictably limited range of characters and plot devices he so clearly favored for all his career.

In most ways, Lorimer's attitude toward representing African Americans remained consistent throughout his tenure. From 1899, when he became editor, through 1917, Black dialect stories and poems can be found in the *Post* on a regular basis, and they became an even more reliable feature of the magazine once Lorimer added Irvin S. Cobb and Harris Dickson to his roster of regulars. Between 1918, when the editor published Cobb's "Young Black Joe," and his retirement in 1936, he ran an average of eight dialect stories a year, but that number was often much higher in certain years. In 1924, for example, he published thirteen stories by Cohen and two by Wiley, which means that *Post* readers could expect a dose of Black dialect humor at least once a month; in addition, full-page advertisements for Cream of Wheat featuring Rastus, the grinning Black man often at the service of young white children, also ran prominently every four weeks, as did occasional ads with blackface characters for other products and entertainment. Lorimer relied on Cohen and the others for the bulk of this material. During the New Negro era, in other words, the stereotypical Old Negro was alive and well in Lorimer's *Post*.

Yet he also appears to have kept an eye out for new talent throughout his career and published some very different material in his last years as editor. This chapter begins by examining an essay that in 1925 introduced *Post* readers to the rise of Harlem as a promising Black "Mecca" and extolled the enclave as a locus of exciting possibilities rather than as a source of humor and derision. Next, I discuss some of the "younger group of Southerners" Matheus praised and show how their fiction challenged the conventions of *Post* dialect writers such as Wiley and Cohen. These newer approaches were amplified even further by the fiction of William Faulkner, who both pushed the envelope Lorimer had established through long practice and conformed to generic expectations, sometimes in surprising ways. Finally, I discuss how Lorimer's writers handled two phenomena of the sporting world that could not be ignored: the extraordinary Joe Louis and Jesse Owens. Leon Whipple described the *Post* in 1928 as a "magic mirror: it not only reflects, it creates us."[2] In the 1930s, the *Post* reflected, albeit faintly, an America that was taking some notice of the New Negro movement. But the magazine was, all the same, still trying to create a nation rooted firmly in segregation and white supremacy.

"THE WORLD'S LARGEST NEGRO CITY"

An early indication of the *Post*'s shift in representation is the growing attention it paid to Harlem as a burgeoning Black enclave. The magazine was relatively late coming to this bit of news; by and large, its fictional treatments of African Americans were rooted in such southern locations as Dickson's Vicksburg, Cobb's Paducah, Cohen's Birmingham, and Wiley's Memphis. Cobb produced the magazine's first extensive treatment of Harlem when he sent Jeff Poindexter to New York in 1922 for his adventures with Dallas Pulliam, and in 1936—to a certain amount of fanfare in the press—Cohen and his wife moved to New York, and the writer relocated Florian Slappey to Harlem for a few misadventures. "Colonel" Charles Givens, one of Lorimer's later acquisitions, also fictionalized Harlem, which I discuss later in this chapter.

The most extensive attention paid to Harlem in Lorimer's *Post* appeared in the August 8, 1925, issue, in an article by Chester T. Crowell entitled "The World's Largest Negro City." Crowell, a seasoned newspaperman with roots in Texas, started appearing in the *Post* in 1924 after his short story "Margaret Blake" took second place for the annual O. Henry Prize. He became a regular contributor to the magazine, publishing fiction and nonfiction more than fifty times during Lorimer's tenure. Crowell's article is surprising for two reasons. First, the relative objectivity of the essay, which was placed prominently toward the front of the issue, seems out of place compared to the usual fiction and advertisements in the magazine. The second reason is even more startling—namely, that Crowell's essay blatantly plagiarized from Alain Locke's special issue of the *Survey Graphic* magazine, "Harlem: Mecca of the New Negro," published in March of the same year. Considering the six- to eight-week production schedule of a *Saturday Evening Post* number, Crowell must have read through the *Survey Graphic* and then churned out his essay shortly after Locke's issue hit the newsstands. Nonetheless, "The World's Largest Negro City" marked the beginning of Lorimer's changing approach to representing African Americans in his magazine. For the first time in decades, a *Post* article reported at length on African American modernity without scorn, humor, or caricature. Crowell still resorted to stereotype, especially in his efforts to denature any possibility of Black political radicalism, but he also wrote with a level of respectful objectivity that had otherwise been missing in the *Post* since at least the publication of Thomas Dixon Jr.'s screed "Booker T. Washington and the Negro" in 1905.

My focus here is on how Crowell reshaped the material in Locke's "Harlem: Mecca of the New Negro" for consumption by the *Post*, but I also want to substantiate my charge of plagiarism. Crowell lifted material freely from across Locke's issue, but he leaned most heavily on James Weldon Johnson's historical overview, "The Making of Harlem." For example, Johnson wrote in his discussion of earlier concentrations of African Americans in Manhattan: "One of these hotels, The Marshall, became famous as the headquarters of Negro talent. . . . There one went to get a close-up of Williams and Walker, Cole and Johnson, Jim Europe, Aida Overton, Ernest Hogan, Will Marion Cook, and of others equally and less known. . . . [F]or seven or eight years the place was one of the sights of New York."[3]

In Crowell's hands, the passage became: "Fifty-third Street became famous because that was the golden age of negro entertainers. Williams and Walker, Dole [*sic*] and Johnson, Jim Europe, Aida Overton, Ernest Hogan, Will Marion Cook and numerous others were seen in that neighborhood. Jazz music, according to some authorities, was first heard in New York in a negro hotel that flourished under the name of the Marshall. . . . It was regarded as one of the sights of New York that visitors should not fail to see."[4]

When writing about employment and labor conditions, Crowell turned to the next essay in Locke's Harlem issue, lifting from Charles S. Johnson's "Black Workers and the City." Johnson wrote: "The distinctions are irrational. A Negro worker may not be a street or subway conductor because of the possibility of public objection to contact—but he may be a ticket chopper. He may not be a money changer in a subway station because honesty is required—yet he may be entrusted, as a messenger, with thousands of dollars daily."[5]

Crowell—implying that he conducted an actual interview—offered this revision: "From the colored man's point of view the restrictions imposed upon him are not very logical. For instance, one of them summarized the situation thus: 'A negro may not be a street railway or Subway conductor, but he may be a ticket chopper. He may not be a money changer in a Subway station, but he may be intrusted as a messenger with thousands of dollars daily'" (94). There are many more examples of Crowell's plagiarism throughout his essay; the quotes given here are just two samples of his love—but mostly theft—of Locke's work.

The more salient question, however, is not whether Crowell plagiarized Locke's special issue of the *Survey Graphic* but rather which elements he highlighted. Three broad topics attracted Crowell's attention: Black cosmopolitanism, developing political consciousness, and racial passing. After first taking his readers on an imaginary subway ride from a primarily white Times Square to a predominantly African American 135th Street, Crowell drew from the essay Locke contributed to the *Survey Graphic* "Harlem" issue as well as from the title of the issue by describing the area as "the negro's world capitol. Ambitious and talented colored youth on every continent looks forward to reaching Harlem. It is the Mecca for all those who seek Opportunity with a capital O" (8). Then, cribbing the statistics provided in Johnson's "Black Workers" essay, Crowell described Harlem's intermingling of native New Yorkers, migrants from the South, and Black immigrants, especially West Indians. "Borrowing" from Locke's "Enter the New Negro" essay, Crowell noted the development of a sophisticated, emergent Black worldview: "The effect produced upon former cotton pickers from the Southern states by this international community can scarcely be estimated. To most of them it is sensational news that a race problem of world-wide dimensions exists; that France, because of her African colonies, has it as well as our country. They discover that negroes have achieved at one time or another remarkable success in nearly every field of human endeavor, and the knowledge is stimulating" (8). Regular *Post* readers would have already encountered certain types of representations of Black cosmopolitanism and international experience in the work of Cobb, Cohen, and Wiley, but always and only as a cause for humor. Crowell's essay—for the first time in the magazine—portrayed the same dynamics with a minimum of condescension, and his characterization of Harlemites can be read as a clear divergence from the buffoonery of Cohen and his ilk: "As he learns more about his new community [Harlem], he begins to take vast pride in the achievements of his neighbors. Presently he feels a sincere pride in his race, a pride that makes him wish to go about his business with quiet dignity" (94). Before Crowell, there had not been a serious, relatively unbiased discussion of Black urban life in the *Post* since Lorimer published Dunbar's essay "Negro Society in Washington" in 1901.

Walter White's essay "Color Lines" in the *Survey Graphic* also caught Crowell's attention, perhaps because it would have appealed to Lorimer's sustained fears about white racial integrity. (The previous year, for example, Lorimer published a dozen articles by the notorious racist Lothrop Stoddard.) Crowell claimed to have personally interviewed White, which may be a questionable claim because he also plagiarized this source. But— another surprise—rather than raising the alarm about the possibilities of racial mixing provided by New York City, which teemed with "many hundreds of thousands of persons of swarthy complexion" (8), Crowell reassured *Post* readers that Harlem's success and the racial pride it instilled made passing less appealing to African Americans. Many *Post* readers, however, were probably not quite ready to understand this aspect of Crowell's argument (i.e., that a vibrant Harlem might actually maintain the integrity of the color line). For example, the editorial board at the *Newport News Daily Press* saw only peril in a rising Harlem: "Every negro who thus 'passes' from his own race into the white race is liable to mix negro blood with Anglo-Saxon blood, and that is the danger to which the Anglo-Saxon clubs are calling attention and seeking to guard against. The real menace is in the 'passing' to which Mr. Crowell refers."[6]

In fact, Crowell went to some lengths to assure *Post* readers that the developing cosmopolitanism and internationalism of Harlem posed little immediate threat to the established order. He took his cue from Locke's claim in the *Survey Graphic* that "fundamentally for the present the Negro is radical on race matters, conservative on others, in other words, a 'forced radical,' a social protestant rather than a genuine radical."[7] Echoing Locke—and even further minimizing the potential radicalism of the New Negro movement—Crowell wrote, "Harlem is not a center of agitation of any kind," adding further that "Harlem is utterly baffling to foreign radical propagandists in New York, as they themselves willingly admit. From their point of view, the American negro ought to be a radical convert at the first encounter. Hasn't he been segregated, barred from many fields of employment, and subjected to Jim Crow laws both by statute and common consent? Why then shouldn't he fall in with efforts to overthrow the present order, but he doesn't. He remains intensely patriotic" (93). What is interesting here in the context of the standard practices of the *Saturday Evening Post* is not that Crowell repeated Locke's sentiments about forced radicalism because ideas about foreign bodies and their indigestible ideas were commonplace in the *Post*.[8] What's new, even if it was stated sotto voce, was the recognition that legal segregation might not be as "naturally" welcome by African Americans as, for example, such ideological fantasies of innate subservience as Aunt Viney (chapter 2), Jeff Poindexter (chapter 3), and the Wildcat (chapter 4) might suggest. Despite his recognition of white culpability and Black resentment, however, Crowell ultimately did portray the Black Harlem population in language and imagery familiar to *Post* readers: "The negro has a marvelous capacity for forgetting what is unpleasant, cherishing the memories that give him pleasure, and above all else forgiving. . . . A people who sang its way to happiness while in slavery offers about as poor material for an organizer of discontent as the human species affords" (94).

The Black press welcomed Crowell's contribution to the *Post* and lauded its relative objectivity compared to the magazine's typical anti-Black material. *New York Age* praised the article as "an earnest endeavor to present the facts without bias or animus of any kind. . . . [The] article on the whole is eminently fair. It should have a healthy affect [*sic*] on public sentiment by its appearance in a medium of so widespread circulation as the Saturday Evening Post and prove a corrective to the burlesqueries of Roy Cohen and Hugh Wiley."[9] Floyd Calvin offered a similar observation in the *Pittsburgh Courier*, praising Crowell for his "very creditable and commendable article[;] . . . his effort at fairness and impartiality is really surprising."[10] For the most part, Crowell's wholesale plagiarism went unremarked in African American newspapers, but an unsigned press release (possibly written by J. W. Johnson) did make the wry note that Crowell "concurs with James Weldon Johnson, Secretary of the N.A.A.C.P." Nevertheless, because "the Saturday Evening Post has published many stories by Octavius [*sic*] Roy Cohen, appearance of this presentation of another side of Negro life is regarded as significant."[11] But the publication of Crowell's essay, which stood entirely alone in the *Post* as a straightforward treatment of Black modernity, did not herald a sea change for the magazine. In 1925 and until Lorimer's retirement, Cohen's stories continued to run on a reliable basis, Wiley and Dickson's by-lines also appeared, less frequently but with regularity, and Harlem continued to be a target of their mockery.

"THE YOUNGER GROUP OF SOUTHERNERS"

Starting in 1929, however, Lorimer started publishing a new set of authors, and consequently the uniformity of the register-and-recontain regime in the *Post* began to loosen. The first evidence of this change is the appearance of Roark Bradford in the magazine, which I discuss later in this chapter, but the more easily observable difference came on March 23, 1929, with the publication of "Racial Problems." This unsigned editorial (most *Post* editorials were unsigned) may or may not have been written by Lorimer,[12] but it would at the very least have required his approval and would have been subject to his blue pencil. The editorial began by welcoming the "multiplying signs of progress among the negro people," then detailed indications of improving public health and declining mortality rates in the Black population, and noted, "Tremendous progress economically, educationally, and culturally is taking place." It concluded with an assertion illustrating that, despite the magazine's earlier disavowal of Booker T. Washington twenty years earlier, the Tuskegean's brand of uplift still suited Lorimer's advocacy of up-from-the-bootstraps self-improvement: "They must rise upon the prosaic but solid basis of economic strength and adequate fitness to do their work."[13] As *New York Age* did with Crowell in 1925, it again took notice, echoing its previous characterization of the magazine. "As a rule," the editor wrote, the *Post* "has kept away from the subject of the Negro, except as a target for ridicule and burlesque by such writers as Octavus Roy Cohen and Hugh Wiley. These two have exploited the black ex-soldiers as devotees of Lady Luck and the adventures of a mythical company of moving picture actors from Birmingham at great length." But in the "Racial Problems" editorial, the *Age* noted, the *Post* had instead produced a treatment "of the Negro from a detached and dispassionate manner."[14] Crowell's Harlem article stood out, in part, because it stood alone; its relative objectivity was distinct from the otherwise incessant caricatures proffered by the *Post* at the time. The "Racial Problems" editorial, in contrast, was part of a small but significant cluster in the magazine that would culminate with fiction by William Faulkner and articles about Joe Louis and Jesse Owen. The first evidence of this shift is the publication of short stories by Roark Bradford, Colonel Givens, and Julia Peterkin in 1929. In their fiction, we find the "artistic glimpses" of "the Negro as a human being ... within narrow circles" that gave John Matheus some cause for optimism in 1934.

"River Negroes Are Wise": Roark Bradford's Tonal Shift

Roark Bradford was already on his way to becoming a nationally recognized and critically acclaimed white author of Black dialect fiction when Lorimer published his short story "The Final Run of Hopper Joe Wiley" in 1929. Two years earlier, one of Bradford's first published short stories, "Child of God," won the O. Henry Award, and in 1928 his first collection of stories, *Old Man Adam an' His Chillun* "was an immediate bestseller."[15] In 1930, Marc Connelly's stage play *The Green Pastures*—an adaptation of some of the stories in *Old Man Adam*—earned a Pulitzer Prize. Most of Bradford's magazine work appeared in *Collier's*, which published dozens of his stories before his early death in 1948. The *Post* ran only two short stories and two articles by Bradford, but their appearance nonetheless marked the beginning of the tonal shift in the material Lorimer would publish in the final years of his editorship.

In perhaps most ways, Bradford's contributions can be read as a continuation of the fiction and ideological project of white supremacy embodied by previous *Post* writers. Before his appearance in Lorimer's magazine, Bradford had already attracted the ire of Black readers with "Notes on the Negro," an essay published in *Forum* magazine in 1927 claiming that African Americans could be divided into three types: "nigger," "colored person," and "the Negro,—capital 'N.'" Bradford's first group is a primitivist idealization of Black folk as simultaneously savage and unwittingly sophisticated—and these types of characters populate much of his work. Bradford had nothing but contempt for his second type, the "colored person," who clearly served as a derogation of the New Negro movement: "He is ashamed of his color. Mentally, he is capable of sensing and feeling the injustices that befall his race, but he is incapable of arriving at an intelligent solution. . . . He is vicious in his heart, he hates the white man and loathes the black." The venom of this characterization recalls the viciousness behind much of Harris Dickson's work as well as Thomas Dixon Jr.'s screed against Booker T. Washington in 1905. Bradford's third type, the capital N Negro, is yet another example of the ideological construction of the contented former slave: "He knows that his government guarantees him civil equality and the right to pursue happiness, just the same as it grants the white man these rights. Usually, he only pursues civil equality and falls far short of obtaining it than does his white fellow citizen. But he can achieve happiness while the white man is pursuing it. He is sorry for the colored person but he knows that one must suffer through this stage of being before one can achieve the high estate of Negro."[16] The Black press was swift in its condemnation of Bradford's typology, and in 1933, when Sterling Brown wrote his inciteful critique "Negro Characters as Seen by White Authors," he chose Bradford's tripartite categorization as the starting point for his essay. Calling Bradford's views "obviously dangerous," Brown noted, "Mr. Bradford's stories remain highly amusing; his generalizations about *the* Negro remain a far better analysis of a white man than of *the* Negro."[17] Using italics to signal his ire and irony, Brown began his essay on white authors by holding up Bradford as a prime example of racist, reductive representations. Despite these accurate critical caveats, there is, nonetheless, some difference between Bradford's two *Post* stories, "The Final Run of Hopper Joe Wiley" (January 5, 1929) and "The Eagle Stirs the Nest" (August 15, 1931), and similar fiction in the magazine. At the level of plot and characterization, Bradford's stories do not hinge on the sort of selfishness, trickery, and comedic hijinks that dominate so much of the Black dialect fiction in the *Post*; also, the characters are more fully developed and embody a wider range of emotions and motivations, and the narrative voice is less condescending. At the same time, however, these stories once again normalize white demands for Black servility and submission. To demonstrate this line of criticism, I focus on Bradford's first *Post* story "The Final Run of Hopper Joe Wiley."

Bradford's protagonist is an elderly steamboat rouster who has been nearly crippled by a lifetime of lading freight. Impoverished and underemployed, Hopper Joe is hired for a good-paying river run by a white first mate who remembers the old man when he was young and reliably hardworking. Despite the sympathetic mate's attempts to give him lighter duties, Hopper Joe is driven by his pride until his physical labor kills him—and he is then reincarnated as a mule. Bradford portrays this transformation as a tribute to the old man's integrity and work ethic: "It is an established fact—among river negroes, at least—that when a good steamboating man dies he turns into a mule. River negroes are wise; they know things."[18] Hopper Joe's reincarnation, in other words, accords him a kind of nobility. The protagonist's purported elevation is qualified, however, in at least two ways. First, the suggestion that the highest form of African American humanity involves self-sacrifice to the demands of an exploitive labor system is merely an extension of Bradford's tripartite racial categorization, which places its highest value on "the Negro" who submits to white demands. Second, by honoring his character as a mule, Bradford merely reiterated the kind of demeaning animalism Cobb offered in "Young Black Joe" years earlier: "When you find a mule engaged in industry [you] find an American of African antecedents managing him."[19]

But Bradford's story also complicates, if only momentarily, his reification of fantasy and hierarchy. Reborn as an actual mule (Hopper Joe has, after all, been working like a mule his entire life), the story's protagonist finds himself harnessed in a brace along with the soul of his former white boss, Captain Dick, who had already come back to life as a mule. Being yoked together and doing the same work side by side seems to indicate some sort of parity between the Black laborer and his white employer. Parity, that is, but not equality, because in addition to changing into a mule, Hopper Joe returns to life as the kind of willing Black servitor fetishized in the *Post* for decades. As the story closes, the reincarnated steamboat captain speaks in the same sort of violent language that *Post* readers encountered elsewhere in the magazine. When Hopper Joe warmly greets the reincarnated captain, his boss exclaims, "Howdy, hell! I've been looking for you for years. . . . Don't argue with me boy. I've got things to do." Happy to return to a familiar level of subservience, Hopper Joe replies in the text's concluding line, "'Sho will,' he said—'me and you, Cap'm Dick.'"[20] Bradford mitigated the potential tragedy of his Black character's death by offering a happy ending that reifies the Jim Crow racial hierarchy, and Hopper Joe's status as a "boy" is the same as Jeff Poindexter's and the Wildcat's. In this way, Bradford's story is no different from similar *Post* fiction. The ideological continuity of "The Final Run of Hopper Joe Wiley" with previous *Post* stories is further reinforced by the story's accompanying illustrations by J. J. Gould, who had created almost all the caricatures for the *Post*'s dialect stories since 1919. Gould's illustrations would have been an unmistakable clue as to the type of story *Post* readers could expect. Nevertheless, despite all these caveats, Bradford did accord his protagonist a certain amount of dignity and did not impugn bad faith to Hopper Joe's actions. These qualities had been almost entirely absent in Black *Post* characters since the death of Paul Laurence Dunbar decades earlier.

Another significant difference in Bradford's stories is their narrative tone, which marked a new formal element in *Post* dialect fiction. In previous such material, the narrator's voice is consistently distant from and super-cilious toward the story's Black characters. Indeed, much of the "humor" in these stories derives from the wide gap between the narrator's gram-matical, ironic tone and the characters' ungrammatical, asyntactic lan-guage, which is meant to imply African American ignorance and subpar intelligence. This is not the case in Bradford's two *Post* stories. The first paragraph of "Hopper Joe Wiley" concludes with "River negroes are wise; they know things," and the story supports this claim through Hopper Joe's after-death transformation. He embodies folk wisdom rather than racial-ized ignorance. Similarly, in Bradford's other *Post* story, "The Eagle Stirs the Nest," which dramatizes an itinerant preacher's sermon in a bayou town, the preacher carries "himself with a certain majestic dignity." And a young female character who is having an affair with a married man is faulted for her youthful exuberance without being characterized as innately, racially hypersexual: "Fancy was just emerging from foolish childhood and was bringing into the adult state all the freshness of youth and much of her juvenile giddiness."[21]

However, although Bradford's more sympathetic narrative tone is evi-dent, I want to be careful in my claims about how different he really was from other *Post* writers, especially considering his often critical reception in the Black press and his lauded public status as a "famed . . . delineator of negro characters."[22] Perhaps most of Bradford's *Post* readers, in fact, noticed no difference between his work and that of other white writers for the mag-azine. For instance, at a meeting of the United Daughters of the Confed-eracy in early 1929 in Santa Ana, California, plans for the forthcoming annual Robert E. Lee dinner included readings from "a group of Octavus Roy Cohen's amusing tales of Birmingham's colored folk [and] selections from Roark Bradford."[23] Even though for the white women at this meeting there was little difference between Cohen's fiction and that of the newer *Post* author, I would still argue that the publication of Bradford's work marked an attitudinal shift for the magazine.

"He Is Human—Every Inch of Him": Colonel Givens's Blues

Five months after "The Final Run of Hopper Joe Wiley," Lorimer published Colonel Givens's story "Jig Time," which, despite its offensive title, also marked a change in the *Post*. Another long-forgotten *Post* author, Charles

Garland Givens seems to have made his biggest splash in November 1931, when he was discovered unconscious in a railway station after taking an overdose of sedatives. The authorities had to do a little sleuthing before they determined Givens's identity, and this very minor mystery was covered by newspapers across the country because of his stature as an author. Before and after his public embarrassment, Givens, who published as "Colonel Givens," was a newspaperman who worked for a variety of papers and often wrote sensational stories about crime, gangsters, the Scopes trial, and the backwoods characters of his native Tennessee. Between 1929 and 1933, Givens placed more than a dozen short stories with the *Post*, including three in 1929 that feature African American characters: "Jig Time" (May 25), "Pappy Blue Boy" (July 27), and "Mammy Ada" (December 7). These stories, like those by Bradford and Julia Peterkin (discussed later in this chapter), are not intended to be primarily humorous but are instead animated by a more sympathetic paternalism that relies on primitivism and essentialism rather than racial scorn. In "Mammy Ada," for example, Givens writes: "A laughing, happy, carefree people, the negro race, so most folks insist. And that perhaps is right. A negro shakes off trouble easily. But when tragedy does strike, it strikes quickly and goes deep. The negro is the most emotional, the most sentimental creature on this earth. His heart he wears outside his coat for all who care to see and touch. He loves harder, his hates are more bitter, he cries more easily and laughs quicker and more heartily than the white man. He is human—every inch of him."[24] There is nothing much new here in this fetishistic characterization except for its final insistence on Black humanity. Givens would go on to publish a handful of novels, and one, *The Devil Takes a Hill Town* (1939), was adapted for Broadway as *Mr. Peebles and Mr. Hooker* in 1946; it ran for just four performances in October 1946 before closing. Givens's story "Jig Time" is most pertinent to my argument here. It begins in Memphis, travels to Harlem, and then returns to Memphis, and it tells of the troubled marriage between "Mistuh Freddy," a barman and cocaine peddler, and his wife, Big Edna, a blues musician. Like Bradford's "Hopper Joe," Givens's story is narrated with a tone that was relatively novel in Lorimer's magazine.

The narrative structure and other formal elements of "Jig Time" are more ambitious than one finds in similar *Post* fiction. Although the first-person narrator is not involved in the action, he also has a more individuated voice and an implied background than do other narrators in the genre. Givens's speaker is fashioned as an amateur historian of the blues and a regional folklorist. He has "read a dozen books" on blues music and is familiar with a recent "article in a magazine by the Great Critic" but claims a more intimate knowledge of Black music through his personal experiences with riverboat captains, Beale Street, and the Mississippi River.[25] The poetic tone of the following passage is unlike anything that came before in *Post* dialect fiction:

> You don't believe the Big River cradled the blues? All right, you just go and sit on the edge of the bridge at Memphis some night and listen. Or anywhere South of Memphis. North of Memphis the Big River doesn't sing blue music. Up around St. Louis she seems to be too busy getting started on the long trip to the Gulf. She sings but it's a busy, bustling music. And she keeps up a fast tune until she gets nearly to Memphis. but nearing Memphis the music of the Big River gets slower; a lonesome blue note enters her song. And after she leaves Memphis her tune gets bluer and slower, slower and bluer, until by the time she passes New Orleans she's sobbing and crying as if her muddy heart would break.
>
> (26)

Nothing similar to this could be found in any *Post* dialect fiction since Dunbar's time. Unlike the overwhelming preponderance of similar stories, which jump almost immediately into plot, action, and dialogue, "Jig Time" begins with a meditative appreciation of "the sweetest and yet bluest tunes any man ever heard" (26). The effect of this opening is to establish the story as blues narrative rather than as a merely humorous tale. In addition, while the main characters are described with the sort of stereotyping familiar to *Post* readers—Mistuh Freddy is "a small negro, black as coal" (26), and his wife, Big Edna, is a "big yellow woman" (194) whose walk is invariably described as waddling—their troubled marriage succeeds because they love each other. They are not perfect, but they are also not merely a repetition of the simple caricatures churned out by the *Post*.

But "Jig Time," as its aggressively insulting title makes clear, is still a *Saturday Evening Post* story; this is most apparent in its middle section, which is set in Harlem. Here, Givens registers the rise of the New Negro movement but denies its authenticity or validity. After Freddy's arrival in Manhattan, he reinvents himself as a charlatan conjure man, calling

himself "Dr. Zelotes Jairus, mystic healer and master of juju" (193). Coun-
terfeit religious men are a staple in similar post *Post* fiction; the Black
Prophet Gabriel in *J. Poindexter, Colored* is one example, and Crowell's article in 1925 devoted several column inches to "Harlem's grafters" (97).
Edna follows Freddy to New York, renames herself "Madame Seely," and
soon becomes a protégé of a Jewish impresario who is also passing under
an anglicized name. Before long, Freddy is "stung by the intellectual bee"
and develops a racial consciousness mocked by the text: "We is folks, Madame
Seely . . . an' who but us kin uphold the dignity of the People?" (193). Freddy
insists that Edna stop singing blues and instead perform spirituals, a suggestion she resents. Edna reaches the limits of her patience at an event meant
to highlight Freddy's intellectual attainments:

> The break came in the Little Africa Cabaret, a black-and-tan in Harlem.
> Dr. Zelotes Jairus was giving a dinner party. He was proud of his guests;
> proud they were his guests. Big names—Laura Eason-Jones; Mrs. Freda
> Wyatt, who had written several books about the People; Pierre Antonin, the
> artist, with several of his friends from Greenwich Village; Samuel F. Lyon-
> Thommasson, a negro editor—why is it that the People love hyphenated
> names among their famous?; F. Floyd Bender, a music critic, who a few years
> before had been Baldy-Pie Bender, Louisville dice hustler; a mixture of whites
> who sought out the erotic and bizarre in Harlem, and blacks who led the list
> of big names in the negro world. These were Mistuh Freddy's guests. He was
> proud.
>
> (193)

Thus, by the middle of Givens's story, the poetic, folkloric tone of his opening frame has given way to standard *Post* jeering at African Americans'
achievements. There is no discernible difference between this passage, for
example, and the skepticism of Black intellectuals, artists, and strivers
embodied in Cohen's Midnight Picture stories.

"Jig Time" reaches its climax when Madame Seely takes the stage and
succumbs to the encouragement of the crowd to sing the blues once again
rather than supposedly more sophisticated spirituals because "Us craves jig
time!" (193). Edna brings the house down, but Freddy feels disgraced in front
of his highbrow guests. He returns to Memphis in a rage, and Edna follows
him, intending to throw herself off a bridge. But she pulls herself together,

and as the story concludes, the pair are reunited and have restored their marital status quo ante: Freddy has returned to his saloon, and Edna is once more the local queen of the blues, fueled by the cocaine her husband sells at the bar. Like Bradford's tale about the reincarnation of Hopper Joe into a mule, Givens's story incorporates several standard *Post* tropes and devices while also presenting a narrative tone that allows for at least a modicum of Black humanity. Within the thirty-year context of similar *Post* material, these shifts were small but appreciable.

Contesting "Primitive Buffoonery" in Julia Peterkin's "Heart Leaves"

The changing editorial practice I am tracing became even more apparent a few months later with the appearance of Julia Peterkin's story "Heart Leaves" on October 5, 1929. This was the only story Peterkin published in the magazine, but she came to the *Post* with a reputation as a critically acclaimed white author of Black subject matter. Earlier that year, her third book, *Scarlet Sister Mary*, became the first novel by a southerner to win the Pulitzer Prize for fiction, and she was generally held in high esteem by the Black press.[26] In 1927, for example, Sterling Brown wrote a glowing review of Peterkin's first novel, *Black April*, for *Opportunity* magazine:

> The Negroes in this writer's work are like none others we have had. Unlike Sherwood Anderson's, they are more than symbols, have further concerns than ejaculating deep-bellied laughter; unlike the Harlemites of Van Vechten these are primitive, far from *Nigger Heaven*, being of the earth earthy; unlike Walter White's, they have no problem with the "Nordics" tangling their days. They are more akin perhaps to Toomer's Karma and Karintha. If we leave literature and go to buncombe they differ from Dixon's in that they don't imitate Klansmen; and from Cohen's in that they are not jack-in-the-boxes. . . . The huge wonder is how this woman can write, and understand. Where does she get the uncanny insight into the ways of our folk.[27]

Despite this high praise, Peterkin still wrote within the "narrow circle" of white ideology. In 1926, she participated in Du Bois's *Crisis* symposium "The Negro in Art: How Shall He Be Portrayed," and her condescending claim that African Americans required the correct "racial pride" to admire and honor "the 'Black Negro Mammy'" does not age well at all: "It seems to me that a man who is not proud that he belongs to a race that produced the Negro Mammy is not and can never be either an educated man or a gentleman."[28] Also, in the summer of 1929, just months before the *Post* publication of "Heart Leaves," Peterkin sold the rights to *Scarlet Sister Mary* to Ethel Barrymore, who staged the play with an all-white cast in blackface, a decision that led to "unflattering reviews and raised questions about Peterkin's judgment."[29] Despite Peterkin's problematic acceptance of the dominant mammy stereotype and her endorsement of blackface, she understood her work—as did Sterling Brown—to be a significant departure from *Post* authors such as "Mr. Cohen[, whose characters are] "perpetual exponent[s] of primitive buffoonery."[30] According to Thomas Landess, Peterkin's "early reputation as a significant Southern writer rested largely on her ability to portray the blacks of her region as three-dimensional characters rather than as the pasteboard stereotypes found in the popular fiction of Old South apologists. When she won the Pulitzer Prize in 1929 for *Scarlet Sister Mary*, she was hailed by critics, both black and white, as a novelist whose works revealed a sympathetic and realistic stance toward the black community that was rare if not unique among Southern writers."[31] Peterkin was a prominent literary figure in 1929, and Lorimer recognized her stature by placing "Heart Leaves" toward the front of the October 5 issue, just after that week's initial story.

"Heart Leaves" limns the thoughts and memories of an elderly midwife named Maum Anaky, who—like so many other *Post* characters, white and Black—waxes nostalgic for premodernity. The story takes place on Maum Anaky's final day, at the end of which she is burned to death in her sleep by either the hearth fire, which she has tended and cooked on all her life, or by the pipe she always holds in her mouth when she sleeps. Because the story follows the protagonist's thoughts, the exact cause of the fire is purposely unclear. At the beginning of the story, Maum Anaky experiences heart problems as she worries over the changing times: "The old ways were tried and trusty; they had been handed down by experienced people from parents to children for many generations; they were known to be wise and right. How could sensible people agree to forsake them?" Most of the story charts the protagonist's inner critique of post-Emancipation changes in fashion, music, work habits, cooking practices, religion, education, burial practices, medicine, and so on, and much of her hostility is concentrated on a younger African American woman, Lena, who embodies everything modern. (In this detail, Maum Anaky closely resembles Blanche Goodman's Viney, who harbors similar feelings toward younger, modern Black women.) As the story proceeds, Peterkin introduces a second character, Daddy Cudjoe, "the best conjure doctor on the plantation."[32] Daddy Cudjoe is the recognizable old uncle to Maum Anaky's mammy, and together they illustrate the folk practices Peterkin intends to honor in her story.

Through Maum Anaky's death, Peterkin depicts a triumph of tradition over modernity. Upon dying, "Her heart stopped beating and her spirit leaped out free. Yes, thank God, she was free." After the fire is out, and Maum Anaky's house is just smoking rubble, Daddy Cudjoe searches through the ruins, hoping to find any trace of his friend's body—and he does. Buried in the ashes is the string Maum Anaky used to hold the heart-leaf tea on her chest as she slept, and next to the string he finds "a strange knot of old flesh. It was her heart—her strong old heart." At the story's climax, Lena sees the heart and falls on her knees to pray as she finally realizes the validity of Maum Anaky's traditionalism. "Lena knew the truth at last," and now "Maum Anaky was ready to go."[33]

Like the stories by Bradford and Givens, there are many ways in which "Heart Leaves" merely repeats the sort of stereotyping Lorimer preferred. Peterkin's mammy figure is yet another iteration of the type that Blanche Goodman, for example, exploited through her character Viney Harris, and Maum Anaky's freedom, which is acquired only through death, closely resembles the qualified dignity Hopper Joe acquires by dying and becoming a mule. Further, Daddy Cudjoe, who embodies the Old Negro, is pictured in the magazine with the same fringe of white curly hair that was used endlessly and ubiquitously by illustrators since at least the advent of Uncle Remus. There is little distance, if any, between Daddy Cudjoe and Dickson's Ole Reliable or Cobb's Jeff Poindexter—all being fantasies of the faithful servant who fed Lorimer's nostalgia for the ancien regime of American slavery.

But there are at least two striking differences between "Heart Leaves" and the fiction of previous *Post* authors. First, as in Bradford's and Givens's stories, Peterkin's narrator is more sympathetic toward her characters than the narrators featured by Cohen and Wiley. Maum Anaky and Daddy Cudjoe are illiterate and unsophisticated, but they are not morally bankrupt or intellectually inferior. There is no condescension or humorous scorn in the narrative tone. An even more striking difference in "Heart Leaves" is the story's very noticeable dearth of dialogue. For most *Post* dialect writers, orthographic derision, malapropisms, and bad grammar were driving engines of their fiction and were intended as a source of readerly pleasure. Peterkin, however, focuses almost exclusively on Maum Anaky's thoughts and feelings, and—even more uncharacteristically—no dialogue appears in the story until the second continuation page, toward the end of the story and the back of the issue. What's more, the language is not marked in any way as humorous but serves instead to enhance the realism of a local-color story. For example, Maum Anaky considers the usefulness of joining the local burial society, which is simply called the "Bury League." In other *Post* authors' work, African American civic organizations are inevitably mocked through grandiloquent names; the butt of many a Cohen joke is the Sons and Daughters of I Will Arise, and T. S. Stribling, a later addition to Lorimer's roster of dialect writers, featured the ill-fated Ludus Weems Mutual and Confidential Bur'al S'iety.[34]

When considered in light of his first thirty years as editor, Lorimer's choices in 1929 stand out as a departure from his previous practice. In addition to the "Racial Problems" editorial, he published a clutch of authors, all southern, who trafficked in familiar tropes and stereotypes but also expanded the possibilities of narrative tone and character development. To be sure, these writers' contributions were balanced out by fiction from Lorimer's usual lineup. In 1929 alone, he also published nine stories by Cohen, four by Wiley, and one by Dickson, so the magazine was still very heavily and very reliably providing readers with the same caricatures they could count on since Lorimer became editor in 1899. But it was only after 1929 that an ultimately more memorable author was able to place his work with the *Post*.

WILLIAM FAULKNER, *SATURDAY EVENING POST* AUTHOR

William Faulkner began making a concerted effort to become a *Saturday Evening Post* author almost immediately after the publication of Peterkin's "Heart Leaves" in October 1929. He had just published his fourth novel, *The Sound and the Fury*, that same year but was still working in relative obscurity. If Lorimer knew of Faulkner at all, it may well have been for a review of *The Sound and the Fury* that ran in a local Philadelphia paper, which concluded memorably: "The publisher does not state whether the entire

400 pages of the volume are intended as autobiography, but as an example of perfection in idiotic expressions it deserves to be ranked as such. After reading a few pages the reader feels tempted to apply for admission to the nearest insane asylum."[35] In 1929, Faulkner needed money, and this need only became greater in April 1930, when he purchased an old plantation house in need of much repair. Seeking financial security, he began deluging the *Post* with submissions; between 1930 and 1932, he managed to place five stories in the magazine, but he was also rejected twenty-seven times. This number alone indicates Faulkner's concerted effort to become a *Post* writer, and it was an ultimately profitable endeavor because he published more fiction there "than in any other magazine" over the course of his career. Faulkner's ability to place his work in the *Post*, according to James B. Meriwether, can be attributed to "his willingness to alter [his fiction] to suit the requirements of such a magazine."[36]

Before Lorimer's retirement at the end of 1936, he published ten Faulkner stories. (Faulkner would place eleven more with the magazine before it folded in 1969.) The editor appears to have valued Faulkner from the start; in a fairly unusual move, Lorimer placed Faulkner's name on the cover with the publication of his very first story in the magazine, "Thrift" (September 6, 1930), a humorous World War I aviation story. Faulkner's willingness to shape his work to the expectations of the remunerative *Post* resulted in fiction that managed both to conform to existing generic expectations and to explore more novel thematic and formal approaches that challenged the magazine's long-standing expectations about how to represent African Americans. This novelty is more apparent in some work than in others. Faulkner, for example, held in low regard the five *Post* stories that would later form the basis of his novel *The Unvanquished* in 1938 ("Ambuscade," "Retreat," "Raid," "The Unvanquished," and "Vendee"). In a letter in 1934, he did not conceal his disdain for what he considered to be merely commercial and generically unsophisticated writing: "As far as I am concerned, while I have to write trash, I don't care who buys it, as long as they pay the best price I can get; doubtless the Post feels the same way about it; anytime that I sacrifice a high price to a lower one it will not be to refrain from antagonizing the Post; it will be to write something better than a pulp series like this."[37] Literary scholarship has generally taken Faulkner's lead by characterizing *The Unvanquished* stories from the *Post* as dismissible magazine fiction. Susan V. Donaldson, who identifies generic subversion in Faulkner's subsequent revisions when he collected, revised, and expanded the stories into the book, sums up critical estimation of the originally published material: "The tales, reflecting the demands and expectations of *Post* readers, seem too slick and romanticized, too narrowly conceived and tightly unified, not to be damned as a 'readerly' text in the most derogatory sense ever meant by Roland Barthes."[38] Overall, these stories resemble similar *Post* adventure and romantic fiction about the Civil War, and the main Black character, Ringo, often speaks and acts like a character in a typical Cohen story. With the series that would end up in *The Unvanquished*, Faulkner produced *Post* stories for *Post* readers, and Lorimer paid him well for them.

Three of Faulkner's *Post* stories during the Lorimer years, however, both conformed to and challenged the expectations of previous, similar fiction in important and surprising ways. In "Red Leaves" (October 25, 1930), "A Mountain Victory" (December 3, 1932), and "A Bear Hunt" (February 10, 1934), we see how Faulkner tested the limits of *Post* fiction that includes African American characters by implicitly critiquing aspects of white-supremacist assumptions even while also ultimately reifying many of those assumptions.

"Red Leaves" and the Terror of Slavery

Beginning in media res and deploying flashbacks and shifting perspectives, "Red Leaves" presents a more challenging text than a standard *Post* story and therefore warrants a summary. Faulkner sets his tale in Mississippi in 1840 among a community of Chickasaws who own slaves. Their chief, Issetibbeha, died recently, and according to custom he must be buried with his horse, dog, and personal slave. By the end of the story, the unnamed slave, whom Faulkner identifies only as "the Negro," has been captured and is being led to his ritual murder, which readers infer but do not see. The story is divided into four sections; the first three are primarily comic in tone, while the fourth is tragic. The first section opens on two Native American characters named Three Basket and Louis Berry, who search the slave quarters of the Chickasaw clan's plantation for their intended victim. Their dialogue in this section begins to reveal a conflict between Issetibbeha and his son, Moketubbe, over a pair of slippers with red heels that symbolize leadership in their clan. The much longer second section of the story shifts abruptly to the chief's dwelling, the old "deck house of a steamboat" that Issetibbeha's father, Doom, had his slaves transport over land many years earlier. Faulkner then flashes back to Doom's story and his rise to power through the auspices of a shady Frenchman who called his protégé "*du homme*, and hence Doom."[39] Doom impregnates the daughter of a wealthy West Indian family, and she follows him back to Mississippi, where he has— perhaps by murdering his uncle—ascended to chief. Issetibbeha is soon born, and when his father dies nineteen years later, Issetibbeha becomes chief and inherits the "quintupled herd of blacks" Doom had accumulated during his reign. After selling forty slaves, Issetibbeha travels abroad, and in France he buys, among other things, the red-heeled slippers. After Issetibbeha's return to Mississippi, his young son, Moketubbe, begins his lifelong obsession with the shoes. Faulkner then shifts the narrative to Moketubbe, who is very short, grotesquely obese, and almost completely unwilling to move or to speak. The son's fetishization of the slippers, the text implies, indicates his desire to kill his father and become "the Man." Then, with an abrupt "that was yesterday" (56), the story leaps to its present-tense focus on Three Basket and Louis Berry, who worry that Issetibbeha's body is decomposing and will start to smell if they don't find their sacrificial victim soon enough. As this longer, second section concludes, they confront the completely silent Moketubbe, who has painfully squeezed his enormously fat feet into the tiny shoes, and they instruct him that he must lead the hunt for the escaped slave.

The abrupt changes in time and perspective continue in the story's third section. The narrative now introduces the Negro, Issetibbeha's "body servant" of twenty-three years, who is hiding in a barn and watching his master's death, and then jumps to the day before, when the Negro first became aware of his impending fate. In the barn, he hears the distant drumming of his fellow slaves, contemplates his extinction, and sees the arrival of scores of Chickasaws, who are preparing for the forthcoming funerary ritual. When he sees Issetibbeha's horse and dog tied to a tree in advance of their slaughter, the Negro leaves the barn and begins his attempted escape, which ultimately fails after he is poisoned by the bites of a cottonmouth moccasin. The third section, which again emphasizes the ineluctability of death, ends with the Negro's articulation that, despite his seeming surrender to the customs of his enslavers, "I do not wish to die" (62).

In the fourth and final section, Moketubbe "leads" the hunt while being borne on a litter and carrying the slippers. The search takes longer than the three days previously required to catch and sacrifice Doom's slave, and by the sixth day food for the assembled mourners has run out. Worse still, Issetibbeha's decomposing body is starting to reek. Finally, the exhausted, hopeless Negro is found and surrenders without a fight. "You ran well," his captors tell him. "Do not be ashamed" (64). As "Red Leaves" ends, the Indians offer the Negro food and water, but his terror prevents him from swallowing anything. Having concluded the ritualistic hunt for Issetibbeha's slave, the "patient, grave, decorous, implacable" Indians are on the verge of murder as Three Basket instructs the Negro, "Come" (64).

As this brief and incomplete summary indicates, "Red Leaves" is a more complex narrative than pretty much all the other fiction addressed in this book, and it is arguably more complicated even than many other stories in Faulkner's oeuvre. According to Hans Skei, "It is more problematic to follow the text of 'Red Leaves' than for most other Faulkner stories, since the reader must feel bewildered and disoriented for a long time."[40] This was certainly the case for *Post* readers, who raised loud objections to Lorimer's inclusion of the story in their magazine. According to Marjory Stoneman Douglas, who was a regular *Post* contributor in the 1920s and 1930s, Lorimer published Faulkner despite the negative responses elicited by "Red Leaves":

> I happened to say to Mr. Lorimer that I thought "Red Leaf" [*sic*] was big-time stuff, or words to that effect. And do you know that was the first kind word he had had on that story since it had been printed! On the contrary they had letters from all over the country, bushels of letters, protesting against that story. The great American public wanted love stories and happy ending [*sic*]. "Red Leaf" was too strong for its delicate nervous system, apparently. And Mr. Lorimer said, "There you are. It just goes to show. That story was great literature. And they don't want literature."[41]

Lorimer's continued publication of Faulkner after receiving so many negative responses to "Red Leaves" can be understood in several ways. At the most basic level, his subsequent promotion of Faulkner's work reinforced the notion that Lorimer had absolute say over the content of his magazine; he wanted to publish Faulkner, and so he did, whether his readers liked it or not. Further, Lorimer's belief in the literary quality of "Red Leaves," despite his paying customers' objections, demonstrated his foundational practice of "creating Americans" (as Jan Cohn puts it)[42] by striking a balance between what his readers wanted and what he thought they needed.

Douglas's exchange reveals that Lorimer understood "Red Leaves" as embodying something different for his subscribers, but Faulkner's story was not an entirely new departure for the magazine. The complexity of "Red Leaves" certainly offered a greater challenge to readers seeking light entertainment, but Faulkner's narrative voice and his nuanced exploration of his Black character's interiority followed in the wake of stories by Bradford, Peterkin, and Givens. Before "Red Leaves," in other words, Lorimer had already demonstrated a willingness to loosen the decades-long representational stranglehold exemplified by authors such as Cobb, Goodman, Cohen, and other writers like them. But "Red Leaves" also did something that was largely absent from the magazine, especially during the Harlem Renaissance—namely, Faulkner's story foregrounded slavery's inhumanity, and it highlighted the ever-present and often capricious violence undergirding the entire system. Uncharacteristically, "Red Leaves" offered no fantasy of a seemingly organic and mutually beneficial master–servant relationship (although this trope functions significantly in "A Mountain Victory," discussed later).

Coming after stories by Bradford, Givens, and Peterkin, Faulkner's depiction of African Americans constituted an evolution in characterization rather than a complete break, and "Red Leaves" both comports with and deviates from earlier *Post* fiction in multiple ways. First, the story thematizes the violence and terror of slavery, and it does so from the beginning. "Red Leaves" opens with a view of the slave quarters, which are initially pictured as a nostalgic image of the antebellum plantation: "Neat with whitewash. Of baked soft brick, the two rows of houses in which lived the slaves belonging to the clan faced one another across the mild shade of the lane" (6). But in the first lines of dialogue between Three Basket and Louis Berry, Faulkner quickly destabilizes the peaceful and almost nostalgic scene by having them complain about slavery, which is "not the good way," and through Three Basket's admission that he had previously engaged in the ritualistic cannibalization of a slave. Louis Berry responds to this information not with horror but with the observation that slaves have become "too valuable to eat [because] the white men will give horses for them" (6). With these details, Faulkner establishes slavery's violence and immorality in a marked deviation from the fetishized master–servant relationships that dominated similarly themed *Post* fiction. The rest of "Red Leaves" is dotted with reminders of slavery's cruelty rather than suggestions that it was mutually beneficial to all parties. The seemingly peaceful slave quarters, for example, are littered with the hastily dropped objects of its residents, who cower in fear at the impending murder, and in previous years Doom during his reign would entertain his guests by hunting slaves with dogs (54).

"Red Leaves" further critiques slavery through the Chickasaw characters' repeated observation that the system was imposed upon them by white settlers and that it is destroying their culture. "The world is going to the dogs," Three Basket complains. "It is being ruined by white men. We got along for years and years, before the white men foisted their Negroes upon us" (56). This cultural degradation is further symbolized by the ramshackle steamboat deckhouse that serves as the chief's home. A symbolic fish out of water, the ersatz palace is filled with objects of former grandeur that are now little more than trash. However, while Faulkner criticizes slavery through his Chickasaw characters, he also deflects that criticism away from white people by instead foregrounding a group of Indian slaveholders. Similarly, when he flashes back to a moment in the Negro's childhood when the recently enslaved boy eats a live rat (one assumes because of hunger), the author conjures up "the New England trader, the deacon in a church" (60), as more responsible than the boy's owners, who apparently do not feed him adequately. This deflection of moral blame away from the culpability of southerners and onto northerners (who were, to be sure, most certainly complicit with and profited from slavery) can be found in the *Post* throughout Lorimer's editorship. Despite this caveat, Faulkner's implicit condemnation of slavery's cruelty is an element that is not otherwise easy to find in Lorimer's magazine since his earliest years as its editor.

Faulkner's treatment of his African American characters, like the other elements of his story, is also complex. First, the unnamed Negro is a fully rounded character whose plight elicits readerly sympathy. He is not another iteration of such clownish *Post* figures as Florian Slappey and the Wildcat, the attempted escape is not a cause for humor, and his impending death is meant to symbolize the human condition rather than to afford an opportunity for readers to chuckle casually about a lynching. Asked many years later about the title of his story, Faulkner described the Negro's plight as symbolizing a universal experience: "Well, that was probably symbolism. The red leaves referred to the Indian. It was the deciduation of Nature which no one could stop that had suffocated, smothered, destroyed the Negro. That the red leaves had nothing against him when they suffocated him and destroyed him. They had nothing against him, they probably liked him, but it was normal deciduation which the red leaves, whether they regretted it or not, had nothing more to say in."[43]

However, despite gesturing toward a shared human experience, Faulkner also resorts to stereotypical images throughout the text, and he makes sport of the racial violence that he also critiques. On the story's first page, the Indian clan's slaves huddle fearfully in the dark, "out of which eyeballs rolled," and they are simply an unindividuated mass: "The Negroes said nothing. The smell of them, of their bodies, seemed to ebb and flux in the still hot air. They seemed to be musing as one upon something remote, inscrutable. They were like a single octopus. They were like the roots of a huge tree uncovered, the earth broken momentarily upon the writhen, thick, fetid tangle of its lightless and outraged life" (6). Faulkner repeats the minstrel image of eyeballs rolling throughout the story, and his depiction of African Americans' eyes in the dark calls to mind Cobb's very similar description in 1923 of Black prisoners awaiting the execution of a cellmate: "Plastered against the barred cell-doors beyond, like bats, hung ten or a dozen negroes, their eyeballs standing out from the shadowy background like so many pairs of shiny china marbles."[44] In "Red Leaves," Faulkner also describes the Black characters as having "faces like the death masks of apes" and the Black children as "pickaninnies" (58). The story's highest comedic moment comes when the clan debates what to do with their slaves. "We cannot eat them," they realize, because "there are too many of them. . . . Once we started, we should have to eat them all. And that much man flesh diet is not good for man" (54). Faulkner names this conversation a "conclave over the Negro question" (54), which is meant to elicit a laugh by deploying the same punning humor about Black uplift used everywhere in the magazine—for example, in the New York Vacuum Cleaner Company advertisement in 1909 with its tag line "Up from Slavery" (see chapter 1) and in the Cohen story title "Birth of a Notion" (see chapter 5).

Such stereotypical imagery and language would have been no surprise to *Post* readers, but what would undoubtedly have been a departure for them is Faulkner's presentation of Black dialogue. With the possible exception of Crowell's plagiarism of Locke's *Survey Graphic* issue, Black spoken language in Lorimer's *Post* was *always* written in white authors' version of Black dialect, and even the most sympathetic characters were inevitably portrayed with orthographic ridicule. If *Post* readers were flummoxed by Faulkner's convoluted narrative structure, they were probably also surprised that his Black characters speak in complete, grammatically correct sentences (as do his Chickasaw characters). In fact, the language of the Black characters is not only *not* a cause for laughter but also an indication of their dignity. During the Negro's flight, for example, he comes upon his fellow slaves in the swamp and has this exchange:

> "We have expected thee," the headman said. "Go, now."
> "Go?"
> "Eat, and go. The dead may not consort with the living; thou knowest that."
> (60)

Diction like this from Black characters was simply found nowhere else in the *Post*. Through this sort of dialogue alone, Faulkner accorded his characters more depth and humanity than could ever be found in the magazine Lorimer edited for thirty-seven years.

These differences in diction and tone extend to Faulkner's narrator. Like Bradford, Givens, and Peterkin did the previous year, Faulkner deviated from the standard, supercilious narrative tone that was essential to other white authors of Black dialect in the *Post*. In his analysis of "Red Leaves" published in 1975, the critic Edmond L. Volpe accurately explained the story's narrator, but at the same time he also inadvertently described the expectations a *Post* reader might reasonably have about fiction with a Black character in Lorimer's magazine. Volpe observed, "Faulkner tells the story in the third person with a minimum of authorial comment," which is entirely correct. Then he wrote, "Faulkner's style is highly sophisticated. He is writing about unsophisticated, primitive people from the viewpoint of a highly civilized white man. In presenting the Negro facing inevitable death, for instance, Faulkner enters the Black's consciousness and renders impressionistically his thoughts and feelings on a level far beyond the realistic capabilities of an untutored slave."[45] In an otherwise compelling analysis of "Red Leaves," Volpe's reading of the relationship between narrator and character reveals the sort of racialized, hierarchical, and largely unexamined thinking about racial difference that fueled *Saturday Evening Post* fiction for decades, and it also signals Faulkner's complicated engagement with the well-paying magazine. We can see the tension Faulkner creates between commercial stereotyping and a greater authorial sensitivity in his construction of some of the Negro's final thoughts before being killed. As the protagonist is being led toward his execution, he recalls "the peaceful hour when, Issetibbeha napping in the splint chair and waiting for the noon meal and the long afternoon to sleep in, the Negro would be free. He would sit in the kitchen door and talk with the women who prepared the food. Beyond the kitchen lane the quarters would be quiet, peaceful, with women talking to one another across the lane and the smoke of dinner fires blowing upon the pickaninnies, like ebony toys in the dust" (64). With this inner vision of shared community, Faulkner produces the thoughts of a fully rounded character, but then he undercuts the humanity of the passage by describing Black children as unindividuated "pickaninnies." In yet another shift, Faulkner also immediately problematizes the stereotype by comparing the children to "ebony toys in the dust," which both underscores their precarious circumstances as enslaved people and recalls the story's first paragraph, which describes the seemingly peaceful slave quarters as strewn "with a few homemade toys mute in the dust" (6). The toys are scattered about because the people in the quarters are rightly fearful about the violence that will soon descend upon their community. With this symbolic detail, Faulkner reminds his readers of the terror at the heart of American slavery, and in so doing he challenges the romanticization of the antebellum South that was otherwise a long-standing feature of the *Post*.

Suiting Lorimer's Requirements in "A Mountain Victory"

As Marjorie Stoneman Douglas's comments about "Red Leaves" indicate, Lorimer believed in Faulkner's quality as a literary author, but it would be well more than a year before he published another Faulkner story. In 1931, the associate editor Thomas B. Costain explained to Faulkner in a letter that the "business conditions" of the Great Depression were resulting in a shrinking number of pages per issue and the inability to run as many stories as before.[46] In February and March 1932, Lorimer ran the Faulkner Flem Snopes story "Lizards in Jamshyd's Courtyard" as well as "Turn About," a

World War I story set in England. For the purposes of this chapter, however, the next significant Faulkner contribution is "A Mountain Victory," which appeared in the December 3, 1932, issue, a contribution that warranted Faulkner's name on the cover and its placement as the first story in the issue. Like "Red Leaves," the very end of "A Mountain Victory" leaves the reader anticipating the inevitable death of the main Black character, but this is just about the only similarity between the two stories. "Red Leaves" is notable for its difficult plotting, relatively sympathetic narrator, and recognition of slavery's dehumanizing violence. "A Mountain Victory," by contrast, more closely resembles a standard *Saturday Evening Post* story by providing readers a straightforward tale that fits comfortably inside the magazine's long history of sentimentalizing the antebellum South and dehumanizing the people it enslaved. Whereas the earlier "Red Leaves" demonstrates Faulkner's interest in challenging the *Post*'s representational norms, "A Mountain Victory" reveals his willingness, as James Meriwether writes, to shape and revise his work "to suit the requirements" of Lorimer's magazine. In a letter to another associate editor, Merritt Hubbard, Faulkner wrote, "Here is 'A Mountain Victory' with the surgery which you suggested."[47] With this story, we see how Faulkner wrote a *Post* story that adhered more closely to Lorimer's expectations about depicting race.

Unlike the more convoluted "Red Leaves," the plot of "A Mountain Victory" is linear and easy to follow. Set after the defeat and surrender of the rebel forces, the story opens in Tennessee with a family looking out their cabin window as a Confederate officer and his now emancipated slave ride toward them. The two strangers ask for a night's lodging, which the family begrudgingly grants. The daughter is promptly smitten by the bedraggled and maimed but still dashing officer, while her older brother, who fought for the Union, is hostile and ready to kill the former enemy soldier immediately. The father just barely keeps the peace through a tense dinner, and he warns the visitor to leave immediately. However, the former slave gets blind drunk on the family's moonshine, and the officer feels compelled by honor to stay with him rather than go ahead alone. During the night, the family's younger son begs the officer to take him and his sister when he leaves, and the boy also offers to bring his sister to the officer so they can have sex. In the morning, the officer and his former slave depart, but they are soon ambushed by the father and his older son. By the end of the story,

the officer and the younger son have been shot dead, and the servant is staring at the barrel of the gun that is about to kill him. Unlike "Red Leaves,"
which develops characters and provides historical background through
unannounced, unexplained jump cuts and flashbacks, all previous details
about the characters in "A Mountain Victory" are delivered as dialogue and
in this way add to the story's relatively smooth reading experience. "A
Mountain Victory" is a tale of tragic inevitability, but the tensions Faulkner
creates through ambiguity and narrative complexity in "Red Leaves" are
largely absent in this later story.

In addition to the plot's linearity, "A Mountain Victory" is more like a
traditional *Post* story in its treatment of its African American character,
whom Faulkner only ever renders as an animal, a child, or a clown. When
first introduced, Jubal—who is only identified as "the negro" until after the
story continues toward the back of the magazine—is described as "a shape-
less something larger than a child" and then as "the creature." When the
door of the cabin opens, we meet "a creature little larger than a large monkey," and when he speaks (in dialect, unlike the Negro in "Red Leaves"), it
is with "a pompous, parrotlike tone." Acting as the stereotypical, grotesquely
dressed, self-important Black servant, Jubal behaves with "swaggering arrogance" toward the rustic family.[48] As the story continues, Faulkner
describes Jubal as "crouched like an ape" and his fur-wrapped legs as having "the appearance of two muddy animals the size of half-grown dogs" (39).
Faulkner also draws an implied comparison with yet another familiar *Post*
"animal": the Wildcat. Whenever Jubal takes a drink of moonshine, he
expostulates, "Whuf!" This is the same word the Wildcat had used regularly since 1919, and Wiley incorporated it into a story as contemporaneous
to "A Mountain Victory" as January 31, 1931; in "Microphony," the Wildcat
takes a swig of Prohibition-era lemon extract and exclaims, "Whuf! Dat's
mo' like it."[49] Ultimately, with the final sentence of the story, Faulkner leaves
Jubal on the verge of death: "Crouching, the negro's eyes rushed wild and
steady, like those of a cornered animal" (46). With his misplaced arrogance,
drunken lack of self-control, and internalized subservience, Jubal is a closer
replication of the sort of typical Black character, such as the Wildcat, that
is usually found in the pages of the *Post*. He is a far less complex character
than the unnamed Negro in "Red Leaves."

In addition to its straightforward plotting and more familiar presentation of a Black character, "A Mountain Victory" conforms more closely to

usual *Saturday Evening Post* stories through Faulkner's deeply sympathetic portrayal of its slave master, Major Saucier Weddel, whose gentlemanly demeanor and sense of obligation to his servant have antecedents in the *Post* stretching back to the very beginning of Lorimer's tenure, recalling such slave owners as Stuart Mordaunt in Dunbar's "Mr. Groby's Slippery Gift" and Colonel Spottiswoode in Dickson's Ole Reliable stories. From the opening image of "A Mountain Victory," Faulkner ennobles Weddel by contrasting him with Jubal's animalism, and as the story continues, he also develops the trope of ignoble Yankees who won the war but cannot lay claim to higher morality or more civilized behavior. As the family peer through the window, they watch "a man on foot, leading a horse. . . . The bridle was silver mounted, the horse a gaunt, mud-splashed Thoroughbred" (6). Walking his horse indicates Weddel's solicitude for those in his charge; the horse's breeding quality and its accoutrements suggest the major's elevated social status. This image is followed immediately by the comically brutish depiction of Jubal, who rides his horse (selfishly, by implication) and wears outlandish clothing. The story's illustrator also contrasts the implied differences between master and slave by portraying them both on horseback, but this time with a gallantly dressed Weddel posed heroically in the foreground, while Jubal appears obscured behind him.

As indicated by his story's concluding image of the crouching, fearful Black character, Faulkner maintains the contrast between Jubal's comical animality and Weddel's nobility throughout, and he intensifies this tension through the responsibility each character feels toward the other. Jubal is a loyal but childish retainer who tries to manage Weddel's behavior by threatening to tattle on him to his mother: "Even if I is forty, you twenty-eight. I ghy tell your maw. I ghy tell um" (39). Emphasizing Jubal's loyalty to his recent former enslavers even further, Faulkner adds the detail through Weddel that his mother died two years earlier, "though my boy refuses to believe she is dead. . . . But then, he is only a negro member of an oppressed race burdened with freedom" (39, 42). With its characterization of a forty-year-old man as a "boy" and the claim that freedom is a liability for African Americans, Faulkner's story announces its fidelity to the idea of naturalized racial hierarchy, subservience, and dominance that can be found in Lorimer's *Post* from its earliest days. Jubal's innate immaturity (according to the story's logic) drives him to the excessive drinking that delays the guests' departure and leads to fatal violence.

Weddel's death is a sacrifice to his sense of duty and honor because he
will not temporarily abandon his former slave, and it represents one of the
ironic victories in Faulkner's story. Throughout the story, Weddel embodies the ideals of dignity and honor that saturate romanticized mythologies
of the antebellum South. Ever the gentleman, Weddel always speaks politely
despite the older son's naked hostility; he makes sure his shoes are polished
before dinner; he declines an easy sexual encounter with the literal farm-
er's daughter; and—most importantly—he refuses to leave Jubal behind,
despite the obvious danger this act of loyalty entails. After Jubal becomes
incapacitated with drink, the father advises Weddel on multiple occasions
to ride ahead and leave his servant behind to sleep it off, but Weddel refuses:
"No. Not after four years. I've worried with him this far; I reckon I'll get
him on home" (39). Weddel's victory is not that he wins his final skirmish
but that he overcomes his fear of an increasingly inevitable death in order
to stand by his principles, thus symbolizing—and dying for—the mythology of the kindly master as the pinnacle of lost southern nobility. Faulkner's
final imagery makes this conclusion indisputable. After Weddel is shot
dead, his final possessions—his horse and his slave—demonstrate their loyalty to the end. The thoroughbred, "its eyes rolling" like many of Faulkner's
other Black characters, "went to where Weddel lay . . . and stood above Weddel's body, whinnying, watching." Jubal, rather than trying to run from
being shot, returns to his master to share his fate. Like the horse's eyes, Jubal's "irises [were] rushing and wild in the bloodshot whites. Then he
turned, and, still on hands and knees, he scuttled back to where Weddel
lay on his back" (46). Eyes rolling, scuttling like a crab, and crouching like
"a cornered animal," Jubal enacts a last act of fealty that is the ultimate proof
of Weddel's symbolic victory. The Confederate officer's noble sacrifice to
his subordinate also indicates his elevated status on the Great Chain of
Being, which Henry Louis Gates Jr. describes as "an eighteenth century metaphor that arranged all of creation on the vertical scale from animals and
plants and insects through man to the angels and God himself. By 1750, the
chain had become individualized; the human scale rose from 'the lowest
Hottentot' (black South Africans) to 'glorious Milton and Newton.'"[50]

The Confederate major is not the only ironic victor in Faulkner's tale.
His killers also achieve a sort of triumph by winning a last skirmish of the
Civil War, but their mountain victory comes with extraordinary loss and
symbolizes a nation that brutishly forced political union onto the putatively

greater nobility and civilization of a southern culture that, according to the story's logic, knew how to take proper care of its slaves and horses. Jubal's symbolic opposite is the family's older son, Vatch, who fought with the Union army and suffers from what we now call post-traumatic stress disorder. His professed cruelty during the war and current murderous inhospitality function, like the story's Black character, to ennoble the former slave owner by contrast. Vatch wants to shoot Weddel as soon as he sees him outside the cabin and accuses the newcomer of being "a nigra" when they first meet (7). At dinner, the father repeats Vatch's suggestion that their visitor is not fully white, which prompts Weddel to provide his family background. He is the son of a Choctaw chief and grandson of one of Napoleon's generals, and he comes from a large plantation called Contalmaison. Weddel tells Vatch he was a major, which provokes the Union soldier to describe his callous killing of a wounded Confederate major during a battle: "He was lying by a tree. We had to stop there and lie down, and he was lying by the tree, asking for water. 'Have you got any water, friend?' he said. 'Yes. I have water,' I said. 'I have plenty of water.' I had to crawl; I couldn't stand up. I crawled over to him and lifted him so that his head would be propped against the tree, turning his face a little with my hands" (42). Instead of giving the enemy water or even dispatching him quickly and humanely, Vatch crawled back a full hundred yards and used the wounded man for target practice, shooting him once in the throat before killing him with a second shot. Vatch is surly throughout the story, and his war story does nothing to mitigate the reader's perception of his brutality. This recounted incident from the war foreshadows the story's conclusion. When Weddel and Jubal continue their journey home, they are joined by the family's younger son, Hule, who is as enamored with Weddel as his sister is. Just after Hule jumps onto the thoroughbred with Jubal, he and Weddel are shot dead by Vatch and the father. Their mountain victory is even more terrible than Weddel's because their ambush succeeds, but they kill their own kin in the process. As Vatch did during the war, he again backs away from his intended victim, Jubal, and is about to pull the trigger as the story ends.

In both "A Mountain Victory" and "Red Leaves," Faulkner thematizes tragic violence against African Americans by white characters, which is a departure from similar *Post* fiction. There is plenty of physical violence in stories by Cohen, Wiley, and other standard *Post* writers, but it is always played for humor, always intraracial, and never attributed to the larger system of American white supremacy. Implicit in Faulkner's stories, by contrast, is a critique of slavery's inhumanity and the terror it produced. At the same time, however, all the violence in "Red Leaves" and "A Mountain Victory" is perpetrated by someone other than a white slave owner, thus deflecting responsibility away from the culture and economy that extracted so much misery from its victims.

"A Bear Hunt": Greater Complexity, Same Formula

The *Post* printed its next Faulkner story a little more than a year after "A Mountain Victory," and one way to read this new story is as a sly revision of the typical reversal-of-fortune tales familiar to the magazine's readers, especially those who relished the work of Cohen and Wiley. In "A Bear Hunt," the bully who once terrorized the local Black community becomes the victim of a prank that scares him nearly to death; this is exactly the sort of comeuppance one finds in the fiction of Wiley, Cohen, and other *Post* writers. The signal difference in "A Bear Hunt," though, is that the butt of the joke is a white man rather than a Black character. In 1933, Sterling Brown offered measured praise for this sort of difference. In the same essay castigating Roark Bradford for his tripartite classification of African Americans, Brown observed of Faulkner and other southern authors, including Erskine Caldwell and Thomas Wolfe, that "while their métier is the portraiture of poor whites, [they] help in undermining the stereotypes by showing that what have been considered Negro characteristics, such as dialect, illiteracy, superstitions, sexual looseness, violence, etc., are to be found among poor whites. When they do show Negro characters, they frequently show them to be burdened by economic pressure, the playthings of Southern justice, and the catspaws for sadistic superiors."[51] In Faulkner's hands, the Black character, who was once prey to a white character's sadism, finally gets his revenge. Being a *Post* story, however, "A Bear Hunt" also concludes by reaffirming the presuppositions of the existing racial order.

Faulkner frames his story, the bulk of which is told by a sewing machine salesman named Suratt, with an opening narration by an unnamed young white man who provides the contextualizing information for the comedy to come. In the story's first section, we are introduced to Suratt and to the story's ill-fated protagonist, Lucius Provine, a forty-year-old layabout and moonshiner who was a rowdy hooligan in his youth. Most notoriously, he

and his gang once terrorized an African American church picnic at gun-
point: "taking the Negro men one by one," they set fire "to the popular celluloid collars of the day, leaving each victim's neck ringed with an abrupt
and faint and painless ring of carbon."[52] The opening section also tells of
an ancient Indian burial mound located a few miles from Major de Spain's
hunting camp, where the bulk of the story takes place. According to the first
narrator, the local white residents consider the mound with a mixture of
fascination, superstition, and fear. In addition to these details about Provine
and the mound, the opening section also reveals the narrator's understanding of racial hierarchy, feelings that arguably extend to the white community as a whole. On the one hand, the narrator claims that the local Native
Americans are just regular people—"no wilder or more illiterate than the
white people" (8)—but, on the other, the narrator also minimizes the harm
done to Provine's victims by describing the marks left by the burned collars as "faint and harmless," thus minimizing the humiliation and fear the
Black picnickers experienced. Implicit in this opening section is the belief
that Native Americans occupy a higher rung on the Great Chain of Being
than do African Americans. Feeling greater solidarity with another white
character, regardless of his capricious violence, the narrator even harbors
some admiration for the "inarticulate zest for breathing" that prompted
Provine's act of racist terrorism (6).

Most of "A Bear Hunt" concerns the actions of its white characters, and
the telling of Provine's attack on the picnic, upon a first reading, might seem
more like a character detail than an essential plot point, especially since the
framing narrator pays greater attention to the community's feelings about
the Indian mound than to this incident. But the story's illustrator, George
Brehm, hints at the importance of the attack through his drawing on the
story's second page. In the center of the illustration, a widely smiling, mani-
acal looking Provine is about to burn a victim's collar with his cigar while
another white man, also smiling, holds the man. In contrast to the assail-
ants' glee, the fear on their intended victim's face is unmistakable, and it is
echoed by the other African Americans in the scene, including a woman
in the foreground with her arms raised in fearful anxiety. According to Jennifer Nolan, this paratextual clue is a reliable feature of the magazine:
"Opening illustrations for stories in the Post were universally proleptic, in
that they anticipated and thereby framed the textual events to follow. . . .
[The] second illustration generally depicted a culminating incident within

218

the story that did not occur until near the end of the text."[53] As Brehn's
second-page illustration implies, as we shall see, although the "culminating incident" happened well in the past, its effects persist into the present
moment of "A Bear Hunt."

Suratt, the sewing machine salesman, narrates the second, longer section and explains why he was suddenly assaulted by Provine at the hunting
camp. Men for miles around have assembled to eat, drink, and hunt, and
the improvident, boorish Provine gets the hiccups after overindulging. His
incessant hiccupping disturbs everyone else's sleep and threatens to impede
the hunt; finally, Suratt convinces him go to the mound and seek a cure
from the Native Americans. Unbeknownst to Provine, a Black character
named Old Man Bush races to the mound first, where he tells the Indians
to give Provine a good scare because, Bush prevaricates, Provine is a reve-
nuer coming for their moonshine. When the Indians pretend they are about
to burn Provine at the stake, he runs off in terror. Back at the hunting camp,
Suratt jokes about Provine's fear, which in turn prompts Provine to attack
him. We learn the details of Provine's capture and mock lynching in the
story's denouement, when Suratt forces Old Man Bush to tell him what happened, and it is at this point that "A Bear Hunt" most clearly resembles a
Cohen story. Bush was one of the church picnic goers twenty years earlier,
and he reveals the plot point George Brehm telegraphs with his second-page
illustration: that Bush is the African American character in Provine's grip,
and "Hit was him dat burnt mine [his celluloid collar]" (76). After twenty
years, Bush has finally taken his revenge.

Post readers would have been familiar with this type of conclusion and
would have expected a similar outcome in fiction by any other white *Post*
author writing in Black dialect. In the April 7, 1934, issue, for example,
Cohen ended a story with one character proudly explaining how he duped
another by expostulating, "Yeh! He'll find out all right. I kind of figured
on that when I sold him my contrack so cheap."[54] What makes Faulkner's
"A Bear Hunt" different from comparable fiction in the magazine is that a
Black character wreaks comic vengeance on a white character—and he does
so to satisfy his own feelings rather than to help or save a white character
(in particular a white employer or master). According to Brown, stereotypical contented servants "are used to solve the complications of their 'white-
folks.' They are in a long literary tradition—that of the faithful, clever
servant."[55] Jeff Poindexter's machinations in service of Dallas Pulliam in

J. Poindexter, Colored is a strong example of this device. Old Man Bush, by contrast, tricks the white characters for his own purposes. This upending of power dynamics is, on its face, highly unusual in Lorimer's *Post*, but it is also not the entire story because even though Faulkner's story challenges the expectations of a typical plot device, it also ultimately reestablishes the rigidity of the racial hierarchy and leaves intact the ideological fantasy of naturalized African American deference and moral inferiority.

As in "Red Leaves" and "A Mountain Victory," Faulkner's treatment of racial dynamics in "A Bear Hunt" is considerably more nuanced and textured than their treatment in the preponderance of material from the *Post* discussed in my book. This nuance can be discerned both formally and thematically. On the level of form, Faulkner develops a layered narrative structure, and by doing so he distinguishes the class differences between his first and second speakers. Although it is true that the unnamed narrator in the first section demonstrates an almost complete disregard for the Black characters terrorized by Provine, he also speaks in grammatically correct, standard English and refers to African Americans only with the respectful, capitalized term "Negro."[56] The first narrator in "A Bear Hunt," like those found in fiction from Harris Dickson onward, speaks from a higher social status than the characters he describes. Unlike the earlier fiction, however, and more akin to the recent contributions by Bradford, Givens, and Peterkin, this narrator is more sympathetic and less disdainful toward the story's Black characters. But "A Bear Hunt" is told primarily by Suratt, who speaks in essentially the same poor-white dialect as Provine, and he always uses the uncapitalized and often purposely harmful term *nigger* when he mentions any Black character. Taken together, Provine and Suratt embody much of the "dialect, illiteracy, superstitions, sexual looseness, violence, etc., to be found among poor whites" that Brown found notable in Faulkner's oeuvre. For most of the story, the socioeconomic and racial gap between speaker and subject is quite small, which allows readers the opportunity to interrogate their presuppositions; in more typical *Post* dialect fiction, the ironic distance is between narrator and characters rather than between narrator and reader.

Faulkner troubles a familiar formal structure by layering his narrative, but he also resolves the story by reasserting the same racial behaviors and expectations undergirding "Red Leaves," "A Mountain Victory," and *Post* fiction more generally. At the end of "A Bear Hunt," when Suratt wants to find out why Provine became angry enough to attack him, he locates Old Man Bush, who is oiling Major de Spain's boots, and Suratt describes him as "a durned old frizzle-headed ape" (76), a scene with details that recall Faulkner's depiction of the animalistic Jubal polishing Major Weddel's shoes in "A Mountain Victory." When Bush tries to keep mum about his involvement in the past night's events, Suratt threatens to tell on him to "Mr. Provine" and Major de Spain. Suratt uses "Mr." pointedly to remind the Black man of his place in the racial order, and we know this because Suratt says to his white auditors, "If I never told *Luke* [Provine], I could still tell Major" (76, emphasis added). In Jim Crow America—North, South, and the pages of the *Post*—first names are for white people only, and Suratt asserts his superior social position to get what he wants. With this interaction, Faulkner illustrates how the racial hierarchy is maintained in everyday life.

Faulkner's conclusion seems to suggest that Old Man Bush's deference and compliance are the consequence of white compulsion rather than innate African American servility, but then the author adds a final, complicating detail. Despite being an "Old Man," Bush is motivated by the same kind of childish vanity one finds in characters such as Florian Slappey rather than by any sense of self-worth or racial pride. Surrat asks, "And you waited all this time and went to all this trouble, just to get even with him?" Bush's answer comprises the story's final lines: "Hit warn't dat. . . . Hit wuz de collar. . . . Hit wuz blue, wid a red picture of de race betwixt de Natchez en de Robert E. Lee running around hit. He burnt it up. . . . En I jest wish I knowed where I could buy another collar like dat . . . I wish I did" (76).

With these words, Old Man Bush apparently accepts Provine's terrorism as natural but resents the loss of a bit of fancy apparel. What's more, he still wishes he had Robert E. Lee around his neck, a sentiment that resonates with Saucier Weddel's characterization of Jubal in "A Mountain Victory" as "a negro member of an oppressed race burdened with freedom"; Bush apparently longs to be symbolically yoked by the military leader of the slaveholding Confederacy. With the conclusion of "A Bear Hunt," therefore, Faulkner reproduces the same racial logic Lorimer's magazine had reproduced for decades, albeit with greater formal complexity. "A Bear Hunt," in other words, is an excellent *Saturday Evening Post* story, and we see once again how Lorimer's power as editor of America's largest-circulation magazine convinced yet another author to register and recontain African Americans within the confines of humor and stereotype.

TURNING AFRICAN AMERICAN ACHIEVEMENT INTO "BLACK GOLD": JOE LOUIS AND JESSE OWENS

As I have argued throughout this book, an essential and predictable component of Lorimer's editorial policy was his deployment of white-authored humor to refute African American humanity. Lorimer used the *Saturday Evening Post* to reinforce the ideology of white superiority and to discredit Black achievement whenever he could. In this chapter, I have argued that Lorimer's practice became a little less uniform after 1929 and that he allowed newer writers (although still always white) greater latitude to test the limits of his magazine's color line. Roark Bradford, "Colonel" Charles Givens, Julia Peterkin, and William Faulkner introduced some formal and/or thematic divergence from the decades of predictable *Post* fiction, but they also ultimately conformed to Lorimer's expectations. The limits of the magazine's color line would be tested even further in the final year of Lorimer's career, when, apparently, one aspect of African Americans' success became impossible to ignore or deny. In 1936, both Joe Louis and Jesse Owens exploded onto the American scene and into the American imagination. Professional and amateur sports had enjoyed significant attention in the *Post* for much of Lorimer's tenure, and it would have been inconceivable for the magazine to gloss over stories of such intense national interest. Nevertheless, more astute readers of the *Post* must have been at least a little surprised to find articles about Louis and Owens that featured flattering photographs of the two men and more-or-less straightforward analyses of their athletic prowess. I was certainly astonished when I first came across these articles. However, a closer look at the four articles—three concerning Louis, one on Owens—reveals more similarities to earlier *Post* material than divergences, and we see once again how the *Post* registered significant Black achievements only to recontain them inside the same color line Lorimer had maintained throughout his career.

Narrative perspective is again instructive. Both Louis and Owens's stories were told by white authors who established their elevated status over their subjects, while the Black athletes' voices were barely heard at all. The first Louis article, "Black Gold" (June 20, 1936), by the famed publicist Steve Hannagan, had more to say about the business arrangements surrounding Louis's first fight with Max Schmeling than about Louis. The article, which would have hit newsstands just days before the bout, began with the dollar amounts earned by Louis's previous fights, focused a great deal of attention on the Jewish promoters who arranged the fight, and concluded by again emphasizing the amount of money Louis was generating. Meanwhile, Hannagan quoted extensively from multiple sources, but Louis himself spoke nary a word. We hear the boxer only once, on the second continuation page after the initial jump from the front of the magazine. Asked how he would respond to a certain punch from an opponent, Louis gave his trainer an insufficient response:

> The boy answers. [The trainer] is not satisfied.
> "How?" he inquires.
> "This way," says Joe, and he demonstrates.
> "Right, boy . . . That'll get you out."[57]

In an article about Joe Louis, "the boy" spoke exactly two words. Unlike most *Post* material containing African American characters, Hannagan's article did not deliver copious dialogue intended for laughs. Louis was presented as a silent commodity, intended for sale and consumption, rather than as an intentional subject with independence and agency. All the same, "Black Gold" was mostly laudatory and concluded by portraying Louis and his promoter, Mike Jacobs, as model Americans in familiar *Post* terms. Jacobs, Hannagan wrote, got up early for work every morning, and Louis "doesn't drink, smoke or chew, and I've heard tell that he reads the Good Book. I guess they're just a combination to illustrate the efficacy of the old, homely virtues."[58] Despite this positive note, however, Hannagan also portrayed Louis as an almost accidental champion who, along with his Black handlers and backers, had seemingly stumbled his way into fame and fortune. With this detail, Louis was presented as yet another Black character who succeeds through no fault of his own.

Louis's almost complete voicelessness in "Black Gold" was rendered in even starker terms once the *Post* published a two-part series on his opponent, the Nazi darling Max Schmeling, who knocked Louis out in the twelfth round of their first match in 1936. (Louis managed the same feat in just one round when the pair met for a rematch in 1938.) "This Way I Beat Joe Louis" was published on August 29 and September 5, 1936. The installments are credited to Schmeling as the author, but "as told to Paul Gallico," a sportswriter. Most notably, then, the white Schmeling narrated his own story, and what he offered was a lengthy and almost scientific analysis of his study, preparation, and execution of the fight with Louis. Unlike the Black boxer's success, which Hannagan presented as seemingly inadvertent, the white Schmeling's ultimate win was depicted as the natural outcome of thoughtfulness and technique. In addition to the two-part, self-narration of the Schmeling articles, other paratextual clues indicate quite clearly where the *Post*'s sympathies lay. The Louis article appears on page fourteen, behind four multipage, highly illustrated stories, and it occupies just one page before continuing later in the issue. The photograph above the title features three of the white men involved in staging the fight. The first page also has a picture of Louis in the bottom-right corner, but that's it for illustrations.

The presentation of the Schmeling stories is far different. The first installment of "This Way I Beat Joe Louis" is the opener for the issue, its title and author are featured on the cover of the magazine, and it takes up three consecutive pages. Every one of the six photographs in the beginning pages includes Schmeling himself. There is even a picture of his wedding, in which Schmeling and his bride pass a phalanx of Hitler Youth. The second installment of "How I Beat Joe Louis" once again begins as a multipage spread toward the front of the issue. This time, photographs of Joe Louis dominate the pages, but they all emphasize the Black boxer's defeat. Further, the text on the first continuation page is flanked by ten smaller photos that illustrate Schmeling's precision. In contrast to the seemingly accidental rise of the nearly voiceless Louis, Gallico declared in his concluding "author's note" that Schmeling "[is] one of the brainiest pugilists ever."[59] As Kathryne V. Lindberg notes, the *Post* presented Schmeling—who was a poster child for Joseph Goebbels's Aryanism, after all—as a familiar example of the American Dream. Unlike Louis, the German embodied "good old American family values," and *Post* readers were "meant to appreciate [his] industry and upward mobility."[60] In other words, the three articles on the first Louis–Schmeling fight in 1936 presented Schmeling as a subject with agency but Louis as an object to be handled. Louis was, symbolically, "black gold" to be monetized.

Two months after the second Schmeling article, the *Post* ran "My Boy Jesse," written by Jesse Owens's coach, Larry Snyder.[61] Although there are some important differences between this article and "Black Gold," Owens was also presented as a kind of property requiring maintenance to produce the most value. Like the Louis article, "My Boy Jesse" follows four multi-page stories before appearing on page 14. However, Owens got a two-page spread, and the four photographs feature Owens at moments of triumph—except for the charming photograph of Owens with his mother. These images lionize the athletic champion and humanize a loving son, and they stand, therefore, in stark contrast to the images of Louis in defeat. This article was also dominated by its white narrator, and although Owens had more speaking lines than Louis, most of the quotations in the piece are either from white businessmen or primarily from Snyder himself. "My Boy Jesse"—beginning with a title that emphasizes a paternalistic relationship and infantilizes a man as a "boy"—is, like "Black Gold," the story of a white man handling his Black property. Accordingly, the article detailed how Snyder managed Owens, before, during, and after the Olympics in Munich in 1936.

Snyder concluded by trying to "explain the sudden rush of the colored race to the front in track-and-field athletics."[62] In addition to reasons rooted in perhaps questionable science, Snyder suggested that more and more African Americans were becoming successful in sports because they were inspired by the handful of Black athletes, such as Owens, who were already setting records and breaking barriers. And then, just as Chester T. Crowell did in his article on Harlem in 1925 when he advised that there was no need to fear a "people who sang its way to happiness while in slavery," Snyder comforted *Post* readers with a similar mollification: "There is a widespread belief that colored boys are constitutionally and temperamentally happy-go-lucky and are possessed of the bounce of a tennis ball. If it's true it's alright with me, for there is something mighty appealing about the simplicity of that kind of mentality. And I hope Jesse never loses it." But Snyder isn't worried because, he writes as his final sentence, "he's got his head screwed on right, and I like to think I helped screw it on for him."[63] These lines are almost but not quite the final word on African Americans in Lorimer's *Saturday Evening Post* before he retired at the end of 1936. (For his last Thanksgiving cover, Lorimer ran a J. C. Leyendecker illustration featuring a Black mammy figure preparing a turkey while a young child, presumably her son, looks on, wearing frayed clothing and worn-out shoes, and in the December 5 issue Lorimer published "Vendée," the last of Faulkner's *Unvanquished* stories.) With "My Boy Jesse," Lorimer provided his readers with a final example of Black achievement portrayed as the consequence of superior white agency and intelligence.

In 1942, six years after Lorimer retired, Norman Rockwell paid Ben Hibbs, the new editor of the *Post*, a visit in his Philadelphia office in the Curtis Building. Wesley Winans Stout had run the magazine for five years after Lorimer retired, and although he tried to maintain the Boss's standards, he was widely considered unsuccessful.[64] The first thing Rockwell noticed when he met Hibbs was that "the editor's office—Mr. Lorimer's office . . . hadn't changed. There were the same pictures and furniture, the same large windows behind the desk." Dead five years, Lorimer still exerted influence over the *Post* because "he had created an institution in his own image, out of himself, and of course he was one of the great magazine editors of all time. He was, in a sense, the *Post*, all of it. It was his magazine from the front cover to the back. And he had to assert himself in everything."[65] This assertion continued to be true for the magazine's treatment of African Americans. Although there were a few more examples of objective reporting and photography, most images of African Americans in the magazine were given in advertisements featuring domestic servants and Pullman porters, and Octavus Roy Cohen continued to place his stories until 1944.

Also in 1942, however, the same year as Rockwell's visit, Hibbs published Zora Neale Hurston's story "Lawrence of the River," the first piece of fiction by an African American author in the magazine since Dunbar's final story in 1903. In "Keeping Posted," which provided brief contributor bios at the front of the issue, Hibbs heralded Hurston's arrival and included a photograph of her. On page 18, her story features a large photograph of a smiling Black man on horseback that includes the tag line, "He's a dark brown, stockily built Negro of the cow lands of Central Florida—and his story is a symbol of the strength of our nation." These are heroic words, indeed, especially when considered in light of Lorimer's decades of caricatures and dehumanization. But paratext complicates this story and demonstrates one last time how the *Post*, even after Lorimer was gone, registered and recontained African Americans. On the recto page across from Hurston's story, Hibbs placed an article about German efforts to control the world's forests, and he named it "Nazis in the Woodpile." This title was an obvious play on the racist phrase "nigger in the woodpile," and it has the immediate effect of demeaning the man on horseback on the verso page—not to mention the author of the story he illustrated. George Horace Lorimer may have no longer occupied the office Rockwell visited, but for years after his retirement the *Saturday Evening Post* was still his magazine, front cover to back.

For practically the entire span of the New Negro era, the "dictator" of the *Saturday Evening Post* did his best to bolster the ideology of Jim Crow America and impede the rise of Black modernity. During the slow-rolling race war of post-*Plessy* legal segregation, Lorimer functioned in the upper echelons of the racial hierarchy that denied millions of Americans their rights and challenged their very humanity. Benjamin Stolberg aptly noted of Lorimer in 1930, "It was really the mentality of the American people that he has been editing."[66] George Horace Lorimer was, of course, not alone in his efforts to maintain the color line, but as the editor of the largest-circulation magazine in America during the rise and spread of anti-Black segregation, he used that platform to deny the full humanity of his fellow citizens rather than defend their rights and challenge inequality. "The tragedy of it," Lucius C. Harper wrote in response to Lorimer's whites-only last will and testament, "is that for over thirty years such a man as this dominated American culture and the literature it fed on."[67] Lorimer used the *Saturday Evening Post* to circulate Jim Crow in America, and no amount of Rockwellian nostalgia can remove the stain he left on the nation he professed to love.

EPILOGUE

I completed the first draft of this book on May 20, 2022, and I feel haunted by the following sentence, which I wrote in late April: "Through all sorts of legal trickery, including but not limited to disenfranchisement, through historical revisionism and cultural derogation, and through steadily increasing forms of segregation, white Americans *took back* the rights and property of the formerly enslaved, who had been making great strides during Reconstruction." Within days of my writing that sentence, *Politico* leaked a draft of Samuel Alito's Supreme Court majority decision to overturn *Roe v. Wade*, which would *take back* a long-established—if never adequately secure—right to privacy and bodily autonomy.[1] What else might be taken from us is yet to be determined, but it is not hard to imagine the same anti-abortion forces coalescing against other privacy issues, such as interracial marriage and marriage equality. The erosion of African Americans' rights and protections in post-Reconstruction America was ultimately deemed constitutional under *Plessy v. Ferguson* in 1896, but white supremacists required decades of cultural and political work before they could make that happen, and the *Saturday Evening Post* helped normalize the inequality and inhumanity of the Jim Crow era.

The dominance of print culture in the twentieth century has now been firmly supplanted by television and social media, and a similar combination of reactionary politics and homey nostalgia promoted through Lorimer's magazine can now be found in the digital realm, where the most popular cable "news" channel peddles conspiracies designed to undermine democracy and where the most widely watched personalities warn of being "replaced" in language that sounds no different than Thomas Dixon Jr.'s threat to kill African Americans if they dare to compete with white people. Dixon's threat, which embodies the same logic that now promotes the "Great Replacement Theory," resonates with a second recent event that is another tragic example of the white-supremacist effort to make America "great again." On May 14, just six days before I completed the first draft, a young white man radicalized by the same ideas that inform America's most viewed cable news network drove hundreds of miles to a supermarket in Buffalo, where he purposely slaughtered Black people who were simply going shopping. Margus D. Morrison, Andre Mackniel, Aaron Salter, Geraldine Talley, Celestine Chaney, Heyward Patterson, Katherine Massey, Pearl Young, and Ruth Whitfield were victims to the racist ideology espoused by the shooter, an ideology that flourishes in the dark corner of the internet but that gets normalized by the "mainstream" cable network that can be seen in homes, gyms, bars, and airports across the United States. In the first decades of the twentieth century, George Horace Lorimer promulgated white supremacy while disavowing the violence undergirding the Jim Crow regime. In the twenty-first century, prominent on-air personalities and politicians wring their hands and send their thoughts and prayers to the victims after every act of white-supremacist violence, all the while giving credence and intellectual cover to the concerted effort to *take back* the rights and safety of all Americans.

Writing in 1940, just before he fell victim to the Nazi regime, Walter Benjamin warned, "In every era the attempt must be made anew to wrest tradition away from a conformism that is about to overpower it. . . . Only that historian will have the gift of fanning the spark of hope in the past who is firmly convinced that even the dead will not be safe from the enemy if he wins. And this enemy has not ceased to be victorious."[2] Lorimer is long gone, but the racism and xenophobia he championed are still very much with us today, and as recent events at the Supreme Court and in Buffalo demonstrate, these forces may even be ascendant. As Charles W. Chesnutt wrote at the conclusion of *The Marrow of Tradition*, a novel that fictionalizes the Wilmington insurrection of 1898, "There's time enough, but none to spare."[3] In 1926, while the *Saturday Evening Post* dominated American print culture, Langston Hughes vowed to "build our temples for tomorrow, strong as we know how."[4] Nearly a century later, we are still building those temples, and this work must go on.

NOTES

INTRODUCTION

1. Quoted in "Lorimer Gave Art and Park to Public," *New York Times*, October 28, 1937.
2. Lucius C. Harper, "George Horace Lorimer (an Enemy)," *Chicago Defender*, November 20, 1937.
3. F. Scott Fitzgerald to Harold Ober, March 1925, in F. Scott Fitzgerald, *A Life in Letters*, ed. Matthew Bruccoli (New York: Simon & Schuster, 1994), 96; Robert S. Lynd and Helen Merrell Lynd, *Middletown: A Study in American Culture* (New York: Harcourt, Brace, 1929), 239; Joseph Freeman, *An American Testament: A Narrative of Rebels and Romantics* (New York: Farrar & Rinehart, 1936), 15; James Playstead Wood, *Magazines in the United States* (New York: Ronald Press, 1949), 150–51.
4. Leon Whipple, "'SatEvePost' Mirror of These States," *The Survey*, March 1, 1928, 699–701.
5. Benjamin Stolberg, "Merchant in Letters: Portrait of George Horace Lorimer," *Outlook and Independent*, May 21, 1930, 85, 115, 84, 117.
6. "George H. Lorimer, Noted Editor, Dies," *New York Times*, October 23, 1937.
7. Whipple, "'SatEvePost,'" 716.
8. Stolberg, "Merchant in Letters," 85, 86.
9. See in particular Frank Luther Mott, *A History of American Magazines*, vol. 4: *1885–1905* (Cambridge, MA: Harvard University Press, 1957).
10. James Playstead Wood, *The Curtis Magazines* (New York: Ronald Press, 1971), 104.
11. John Tebbel, *George Horace Lorimer and the* Saturday Evening Post (New York: Doubleday, 1948), 69, 100.
12. Jan Cohn, *Creating America: George Horace Lorimer and the* Saturday Evening Post (Pittsburgh, PA: University of Pittsburgh Press, 1989), 188.

13. Helen Damon-Moore, *Magazines for the Millions: Gender and Commerce in the Ladies' Home Journal and the Saturday Evening Post, 1890–1910* (Albany: State University of New York Press, 1994).

14. Henry Louis Gates Jr. and Gene Andrew Jarrett, introduction to *The New Negro: Readings on Race, Representation, and African American Culture, 1892–1938*, ed. Henry Louis Gates Jr. and Gene Andrew Jarrett (Princeton, NJ: Princeton University Press, 2007), 1, 3, emphasis in original. In the wake of more recent scholarship, Gates now extends the New Negro era back farther, to 1887. See Henry Louis Gates Jr., *Stony the Road: Reconstruction, White Supremacy, and the Rise of Jim Crow* (New York: Penguin, 2019), xvi.

15. Concerning the designation "Harlem Renaissance," Cherene Sherrard-Johnson asks, "Why are we still calling this moment the Harlem Renaissance? Given its fluid boundaries and the fact that the New Negro movement precedes the interwar period most often associated by historiographers with the Harlem Renaissance, how do we continue to argue for the specificity, the 'newness,' of this era without continuing to draw intellectual energy away from the literary 1890s and 1940s?" (Cherene Sherrard-Johnson, "Questionnaire Response," *Modernism/modernity* 20, no. 3 [2013]: 457). I share this concern about the consequences of nomenclature but still find the name useful. For a careful history of it, see Jak Peake, "'Watching the Waters': Tropical Flows in the Harlem Renaissance, Black Internationalism, and Other Currents," *Radical Americas* 3, no. 1 (2018): 1–52.

16. Some of the generic conventions found in white-authored Black dialect stories can be found more generally in *Post* fiction. In his guide for aspiring *Post* writers in 1930, Thomas H. Uzzel noted the magazine's preference for stories in which "the rogue whose cleverness thrills us ultimately gets his" (Thomas H. Uzzel, "'The Saturday Evening Post' Formula: Suggestions for Cutting the Corners in Arriving Safely at the Literary Department Store of America," in *The Writers 1930 Year Book & Market Guide*, ed. Aron M. Mathieu [Cincinnati: Writer's Digest, 1930], 21). My thanks to David Earle for this reference.

17. Robert Scholes, *Paradoxy of Modernism* (New Haven, CT: Yale University Press, 2006), 91, 35.

18. Robert Scholes and Clifford Wulfman, *Modernism in the Magazines: An Introduction* (New Haven, CT: Yale University Press, 2010), 27.

19. Darryl Dickson-Carr, *Spoofing the Modern: Satire in the Harlem Renaissance* (Columbia: University of South Carolina Press, 2015), 18.

20. Jeanette Eileen Jones, "'Brightest Africa' in the New Negro Imagination," in *Escape from New York: The New Negro Renaissance Beyond Harlem*, ed. Davarian L. Baldwin and Minkah Makalani (Minneapolis: University of Minnesota Press, 2013), 33.

21. Harris Dickson, "A Borgia of the Air," *Saturday Evening Post*, May 1, 1926, 192, 194.

22. Gates, *Stony the Road*, xvi, 4.

23. The formulation "register and recontain" bears a family resemblance to the New Historicist "subversion–containment debate," as articulated in Jonathan Dollimore, "Introduction: Shakespeare, Cultural Materialism, and the New Historicism," in *Political Shakespeare: Essays in Cultural Materialism*, 2nd ed., ed. Jonathan Dollimore and Alan Sinfield (Manchester: Manchester University Press, 1994), 12. My formulation adds to this area of cultural critique by emphasizing Lorimer's lifelong efforts to drag America back toward antebellum race relations; power would be

maintained and promulgated through gestures toward an imaginary, almost Edenic past. This is arguably the same political/emotional effort to "make America great *again.*"

24. David Earle, *All Man! Hemingway, 1950s Men's Magazines, and the Masculine Persona* (Kent, OH: Kent State University Press, 2009), 5.

25. Cohn, *Creating America*, 15.

26. Gates, *Stony the Road*, 126.

27. Walter White to E. R. Merrick, May 8, 1924, quoted in Charles Scruggs, "'All Dressed Up but No Place to Go': The Black Writer and His Audience During the Harlem Renaissance," *American Literature* 48, no. 4 (1977): 556.

28. Zora Neale Hurston to Walter and Gladys White, July–August 1932, in Zora Neale Hurston, *Zora: A Life in Letters*, ed. Carla Kaplan (New York: Anchor, 2002), 269.

29. Melville J. Herskovits, letter to the editor, *Folklore* 48, no. 2 (June 1937): 221.

30. Langston Hughes, statement mailed to various people, 1941, in *Remember Me to Harlem: The Letters of Langston Hughes and Carl Van Vechten*, ed. Emily Bernard (New York: Vintage, 2001), 179. For an extended analysis of Hughes in the *Post*, see Jennifer Nolan, "Langston Hughes: Refugee in the *Post*'s America," *American Periodicals: A Journal of History & Criticism* 29, no. 2 (2019): 163–77.

31. In *Jim Crow Networks: African American Periodical Cultures* (Amherst: University of Massachusetts Press, 2021), Eurie Dahn argues convincingly that we can conceptualize African American writers and Black periodical culture generally as a series of interlocking and overlapping networks of affiliation and influence. As my examples from White, Hurston, Herskovits, and Hughes indicate, the *Saturday Evening Post* was an influential and omnipresent "node within a sprawling network comprised of nodes that may include readers, advertisers, other periodicals, and literary texts" (12).

32. "The Flood of Immigration," editorial, *Saturday Evening Post*, February 6, 1904, 12; "Another White Man's Burden," editorial, *Saturday Evening Post*, February 6, 1904, 12.

33. "The Asylum Business," editorial, *Saturday Evening Post*, January 1, 1916, 22.

34. "Scum of the Melting Pot," editorial, *Saturday Evening Post*, May 4, 1918, 22. See also William T. Ellis, "The Overflowing Melting Pot: Why the Americanization of America Must Begin," *Saturday Evening Post*, March 2, 1918, 21–22, 37; Samuel Blythe, "Our Imported Troubles and Troublemakers," editorial, *Saturday Evening Post*, May 11, 1918, 3–4, 41–45; and David Lawrence, "America for Americans: Deleting the Hyphen—the Doctrine of 1918," editorial, *Saturday Evening Post*, June 15, 1918, 23, 42–50.

35. William Roscoe Thayer, "Despotism by the Dregs," *Saturday Evening Post*, May 4, 1918, 23.

36. Cohn, *Creating America*, 155; Tebbel, *George Horace Lorimer*, 90.

37. Tebbel *George Horace Lorimer*, 87.

38. *A Short History of the* Saturday Evening Post (Philadelphia: Curtis, 1936), 19.

39. "A Crime Against American School Children," *Ladies' Home Journal*, January 1909, 5.

40. "The Negro as an Artist," *Literary Digest*, September 19, 1925, 30.

41. Sean Latham and Robert Scholes, "The Rise of Periodical Studies," *PMLA* 121, no. 2 (2006): 529.

42. Pierre Bourdieu, "The Field of Cultural Production, or: The Economic World Reversed," in *The Field of Cultural Production: Essays on Art and Literature*, ed. and trans. Randal Johnson (New York: Columbia University Press, 1993), 30, emphasis in original; Kinohi Nishikawa, *Street Players: Black Pulp Fiction and the Making of a Literary Underground* (Chicago: University of Chicago Press, 2018), 7–8.

43. Dahn, *Jim Crow Networks*, 6–7, 12.

44. Richard Ohmann, "History and Literary History: The Case of Mass Culture," *Poetics Today* 9, no. 2 (1988): 362, 364–65, 373.

45. Cohn, *Creating America*, 162–63, emphasis in original.

46. Wood, *The Curtis Magazines*, 63, 66–67.

47. Cohn, *Creating America*, 3.

48. Cohn, *Creating America*, 3.

49. For general histories of the *Post*, see Frank Luther Mott, *A History of American Magazines*, vol. 4: *1885–1905* (Cambridge, MA: Harvard University Press, 1957), 671–716; Wood, *The Curtis Magazines*; and *A Short History of the* Saturday Evening Post.

50. Cohn, *Creating America*, 4.

51. Gavin Jones, *Strange Talk: The Politics of Dialect Literature in Gilded Age America* (Berkeley: University of California Press, 1999), 11. Lorimer, too, dabbled in dialect. Contained in the Lorimer Family Papers at the Hartgett Library of the University of Georgia is a handwritten copy of "Jim's Pup," which is written in, perhaps, a Yankee dialect. Lorimer wrote the poem in Brookline, Massachusetts, so most likely before he started at the *Post*.

52. Jones, *Strange Talk*, 10.

53. James Weldon Johnson, preface to *The Book of American Negro Poetry*, ed. James Weldon Johnson (New York: Harcourt, Brace, 1922), xli.

54. Miriam Thaggert, *Images of Black Modernism: Verbal and Visual Strategies of the Harlem Renaissance* (Amherst: University of Massachusetts Press, 2010), 40.

55. James Weldon Johnson, "Preface to the Revised Edition," in *The Book of American Negro Poetry*, rev. ed., ed. James Weldon Johnson (New York: Harcourt, Brace, 1931), 4.

56. Michael North, *The Dialect of Modernism: Race, Language, and Twentieth-Century Literature* (New York: Oxford University Press, 1994).

57. Edward Christopher Williams, *When Washington Was in Vogue* (1925–1926) (New York: Amistad, 2004), 176.

58. Before my sabbatical, my undergraduate assistant Chad Infante (now Professor Infante at the University of Maryland) did some initial work looking through microfilm reels of the *Post*, and I am grateful for his initial observations and discoveries.

59. James Baldwin, *Notes of a Native Son* (Boston: Beacon Press, 1955), 6.

60. Anonymous source quoted in Sylvie McNamara, "Clarence Thomas's Billionaire Benefactor Collects Hitler Artifacts," *Washingtonian*, April 7, 2023, https://www.washingtonian.com/2023/04/07/clarence-thomass-billionaire-benefactor-collects-hitler-artifacts/. Sharif Tarabay's webpage can be found at https://brewstercreative.com/illustration-artist/sharif-tarabay/.

61. Clarence Thomas, concurring opinion, *Dobbs v. Jackson Women's Health Organization*, 594 U.S.___ (2023).

1. GEORGE HORACE LORIMER AND RISING JIM CROW

1. For more extensive discussions of the origins of the *Post* and Lorimer's early years, see Tebbel, *George Horace Lorimer*, 15–20; Wood, *The Curtis Magazines*, 33–45; and Cohn, *Creating America*, 21–27.
2. Cohn, *Creating America*, 27–28.
3. Tebbel, *George Horace Lorimer*, 40.
4. *A Short History of the* Saturday Evening Post, 19.
5. Cohn, *Creating America*, 192.
6. C. Vann Woodward, *The Strange Career of Jim Crow* (New York: Oxford University Press, 1957), 56.
7. W. E. B. Du Bois, "Of the Faith of the Fathers," *Atlantic Monthly*, August 1897, reprinted in *The Souls of Black Folk: Essays and Sketches* (Chicago: A. C. McClurg, 1903), 194.
8. "'Uncle Booker' and His People," *Saturday Evening Post*, February 24, 1900, 763.
9. Lindsay Swift, "A Remarkable Autobiography," *Saturday Evening Post*, June 1, 1901, 17; Paul Laurence Dunbar, "The Leader of His Race," *Saturday Evening Post*, November 9, 1901, 15.
10. Charles W. Chesnutt, "On the Future of His People," *Saturday Evening Post*, January 20, 1900, 646.
11. Robert J. Norrell, *Up from History: The Life of Booker T. Washington* (Cambridge, MA: Harvard University Press, 2009), 200.
12. William H. Holtzclaw, "The Black Man's Burden: A Battle with Ignorance and Poverty, and How One Negro Won It," *Saturday Evening Post*, April 22, 1905, 4.
13. Deborah Davis, *Guest of Honor: Booker T. Washington, Theodore Roosevelt, and the White House Dinner That Shocked a Nation* (New York: Atria, 2012), 206–7.
14. *Memphis Scimitar*, October 18, 1901, quoted in Davis, *Guest of Honor*, 207.
15. "Niggers in the White House," *Windsor (Missouri) Review*, October 31, 1901, 2.
16. Clarence Lusane, *The Black History of the White House* (San Francisco: City Lights, 2011), 225.
17. *Collier's Weekly*, for example, praised Roosevelt because "he remains unshaken by reproof, and his repose is strengthened by the manifest indifference of Northern people to the color of his guests" (editorial, *Collier's Weekly*, November 9, 1901, 1). *Frank Leslie's Popular Monthly* claimed that most Americans were "astonished" at the backlash engendered by the "old prejudice" of the "color line" ("Men, Women, and Books," *Frank Leslie's Popular Monthly*, January 1902, 381).
18. "Mr. Roosevelt and the Bad Men," editorial, *Saturday Evening Post*, December 14, 1901, 12.
19. Paul Laurence Dunbar, "Negro Society in Washington," *Saturday Evening Post*, December 14, 1901, 9.
20. "The Record of a Notable Year," editorial, *Saturday Evening Post*, January 11, 1902, 10.
21. Reynolds J. Scott-Childress, "Paul Laurence Dunbar and the Project of Cultural Reconstruction," *African American Review* 41, no. 2 (Summer 2007): 373.
22. Norrell, *Up from History*, 118–20.
23. Dunbar, "Negro Society in Washington," 9.
24. Dunbar, "Negro Society in Washington," 9.

25. "Paul Dunbar's Gifted Wife," *Saturday Evening Post*, May 5, 1900, 984; Paul Laurence Dunbar, *In Old Plantation Days* (New York: Dodd, Mead, 1903).
26. George Horace Lorimer to W. E. B. Du Bois, December 29, 1922, in W. E. B. Du Bois, *The Correspondence of W. E. B. Du Bois*, vol. 1: *Selections, 1877–1934*, ed. Herbert Aptheker (Amherst: University of Massachusetts Press, 1973), 259–60.
27. Lillian S. Robinson and Greg Robinson, "Paul Laurence Dunbar: A Credit to His Race?," *African American Review* 41, no. 2 (Summer 2007): 215–25.
28. Peter Revell, *Paul Laurence Dunbar* (Boston: Twayne, 1979), 49.
29. Gene Andrew Jarrett and Thomas Lewis Morgan, introduction to Paul Laurence Dunbar, *The Complete Stories of Paul Laurence Dunbar*, ed. Gene Andrew Jarrett and Thomas Lewis Morgan (Athens: Ohio University Press, 1998), xviii.
30. John Timberman Newcomb, *Would Poetry Disappear? American Verse and the Crisis of Modernity* (Athens: Ohio University Press, 2004), 82.
31. Paul Laurence Dunbar, "Mr. Groby's Slippery Gift," *Saturday Evening Post*, June 24, 1899, 830.
32. Dunbar, "Mr. Groby's Slippery Gift," 830.
33. Paul Laurence Dunbar, "When Sam'l Sings," *Saturday Evening Post*, August 10, 1899, 123.
34. Dunbar, "When Sam'l Sings," 123.
35. Paul Laurence Dunbar, "Two Little Boots," *Saturday Evening Post*, April 12, 1902, 3.
36. Jay Martin and Gossie H. Hudson, "General Introduction," in Paul Laurence Dunbar, *The Paul Laurence Dunbar Reader*, ed. Jay Martin and Gossie H. Hudson (New York: Dodd, Mead, 1975), 24.
37. Jones, *Strange Talk*, 184.
38. "The Man—Not the Money," editorial, *Saturday Evening Post*, January 24, 1903, 12.
39. North, *The Dialect of Modernism*, 21.
40. Grace Elizabeth Hale, *Making Whiteness: The Culture of Segregation in the South, 1890–1940* (New York: Vintage, 1998), 54–55.
41. Gates, *Stony the Road*, 92.
42. Joel Chandler Harris, "The Negro as the South Sees Him," *Saturday Evening Post*, January 2, 1904, 1, 23.
43. Hale, *Making Whiteness*, 53.
44. Hale, *Making Whiteness*, 53.
45. Joel Chandler Harris, "The Negro of To-Day: His Prospects and Discouragements," *Saturday Evening Post*, January 30, 1904, 2. The African American railroad porter is a recurrent figure in the *Post*. He can be found in scores of advertisements and illustrations and in the fiction of Irvin S. Cobb, Hugh Wiley, and Octavus Roy Cohen (Cohen's porter, Epic Peters, is the protagonist of his own series). In 1915, Lorimer published an appreciation of "Your Porter" by Edward Hungerford.
46. Harris, "The Negro of To-Day," 3.
47. Harris, "The Negro of To-Day," 3.
48. Harris, "The Negro of To-Day," 3.
49. William Faulkner, "A Mountain Victory," *Saturday Evening Post*, December 3, 1932, 42.
50. Harris, "The Negro of To-Day," 4.
51. Harris, "The Negro of To-Day," 4, 5.

52. Booker T. Washington to George Horace Lorimer, February 9, 1904, George Horace Lorimer Family Papers, Hargett Rare Book and Manuscript Library, Athens, GA.
53. Joel Chandler Harris, "The Negro Problem: Can the South Solve It—and How?," *Saturday Evening Post*, February 27, 1904, 6, 7.
54. Harris, "The Negro Problem," 7.
55. Harris, "The Negro Problem," 7, emphasis added.
56. Rebecca Harding Davis, "Has the Free Negro Failed? What Forty Years of Independence Have Brought Him," *Saturday Evening Post*, July 2, 1904, 13.
57. Davis, "Has the Free Negro Failed?," 13.
58. Davis, "Has the Free Negro Failed?," 13.
59. Rebecca Harding Davis, "Half a Dozen Silhouettes," *Saturday Evening Post*, August 12, 1905, 6, 7.
60. Davis, "Half a Dozen Silhouettes," 7.
61. Michele K. Gillespie and Randall L. Hall, introduction to *Thomas Dixon Jr. and the Birth of Modern America*, ed. Michele K. Gillespie and Randall L. Hall (Baton Rouge: Louisiana State University Press, 2006), 7.
62. Samuel K. Roberts, "Kelly Miller and Thomas Dixon, Jr. on Blacks in American Civilization," *Phylon* 41, no. 2 (1980): 204.
63. "The Curse of Caste vs. 'The Leopard's Spots,'" *Baltimore Afro-American*, August 15, 1903.
64. Thomas Dixon Jr., "Booker T. Washington and the Negro," *Saturday Evening Post*, August 19, 1905, 1.
65. Roberts, "Kelly Miller and Thomas Dixon, Jr.," 205.
66. Dixon, "Booker T. Washington," 2.
67. Dixon, "Booker T. Washington," 2.
68. Kelly Miller, *As to the Leopard's Spots: Open Letter to Thomas Dixon, Jr.* (Washington, DC: Hayworth, 1905), 3, 16, 18, 20.
69. Albert Bushnell Hart, "The African Riddle: Another Side of Mr. Dixon's Negro Question," *Saturday Evening Post*, October 28, 1905, 14, 15.
70. Bernard A. Drew, *Black Stereotypes in Popular Series Fiction, 1851–1955: Jim Crow Authors and Their Characters* (Jefferson, NC: McFarland, 2015), 82–83.
71. Harris Dickson, "The Way of the Reformer," *Saturday Evening Post*, January 12, 1907, 6, 22.
72. Harris Dickson, "Please Y'Onner: The Testimony and Facts in Certain Cote-House Scrapes," *Saturday Evening Post*, February 16, 1907, 12, 13.
73. Harris Dickson, "The Vardaman Idea: How the Governor of Mississippi Would Solve the Race Question," *Saturday Evening Post*, April 27, 1907, 3, emphasis in original.
74. Dickson, "The Vardaman Idea," 4–5.
75. "'Ole Reliable' and 'Hambone,'" *Commercial Appeal* (Memphis), January 21, 1923.
76. "Parsons's Theater," *Hartford Daily Courant*, January 30, 1917.
77. Strickland Gillilan, "Washington Wash," *Los Angeles Times*, October 5, 1931.
78. Harris Dickson, "The Job Hunter," *Saturday Evening Post*, January 8, 1910, 12, 13.
79. Harris Dickson, "That Mule, Old Bluffer," *Saturday Evening Post*, February 13, 1909, 10.
80. Gates, *Stony the Road*, 130.

2. LITERARY ASPIRATION AND INTIMATE MINSTRELSY

1. Stanley J. Lemons, "Black Stereotypes as Reflected in Popular Culture, 1880–1920," *American Quarterly* 29, no. 1 (1997): 102, 104.
2. Rhae Lynn Barnes, "Darkology: The Hidden History of Blackface Minstrelsy and the Making of Modern America, 1860–1970," PhD diss., Harvard University, 2016, 4, 186, emphasis in original.
3. Barnes, "Darkology," 5.
4. "The Crescent Club," *Downs (Kansas) News and the Downs Times*, May 13, 1920.
5. See also Blanche Goodman, "A Change of Heart," *Saturday Evening Post*, August 28, 1909, 50.
6. "Mrs. Eisendrath, Liberal Thinker and Writer, Example of Feminine Leadership," *Chattanooga News*, January 9, 1936.
7. "Miss Blanche Goodman Will Wed Mr. Oscar Eisendrath This Evening," *Chattanooga News*, January 4, 1910.
8. Blanche Goodman, "A Toast," *Clarksville (Tennessee) Daily Leaf-Chronicle*, February 15, 1905; Blanche Goodman, "A Bachelor's Den," *Chattanooga Daily Times*, May 15, 1904; Blanche Goodman, "Johnny on the Weather," *Chattanooga Daily Times*, June 5, 1904.
9. "Drawing-Room Chat," *Chattanooga Daily Times*, March 16, 1904.
10. Barnes, "Darkology," 35, 38, 41.
11. Barnes, "Darkology," 2.
12. "'Darktown' Easter Egg Hunt," *Chattanooga Daily Times*, April 4, 1904.
13. Barnes, "Darkology," 107.
14. Barnes, "Darkology," 143.
15. Crest Trading Company advertisement, *Saturday Evening Post*, December 16, 1905, 27.
16. Barnes, "Darkology," 24.
17. "Miss Blanche Goodman," *Nashville Banner*, July 6, 1907.
18. "Leaves Public Schools for Literary Work," *Chattanooga Star*, July 10, 1907.
19. "Women Writers of Tennessee," *Chattanooga Daily Times*, May 11, 1908.
20. "Chattanooga Day by Day: Social and Personal," *Chattanooga Daily Times*, December 16, 1908.
21. Harris, "The Negro as the South Sees Him," 1.
22. Blanche Goodman, "Helping Rosabel," *Saturday Evening Post*, December 5, 1908, 56; all ellipses in quotations from fiction are my insertions to indicate omission of text.
23. Dickson, "The Way of the Reformer," 22.
24. Blanche Goodman, "Out on Bail," *Saturday Evening Post*, March 4, 1911, 30, 31.
25. Dixon, "Booker T. Washington and the Negro," 2.
26. "Literary Club Members Receive New Year Books," *Wausau (Wisconsin) Daily Record-Herald*, August 8, 1929.
27. Blanche Goodman, "Educating Sally Ann," *Saturday Evening Post*, April 9, 1910, 37, 38, 39.
28. Goodman, "Educating Sally Ann," 39.
29. Cohn, *Creating America*, 74.
30. "Why Women Go to Seed," editorial, *Saturday Evening Post*, December 10, 1904, 12.

31. Cohn, *Creating America*, 74.
32. Cohn, *Creating America*, 77.
33. Blanche Goodman, "The Equalizing Bug," *Saturday Evening Post*, April 8, 1911, 37.
34. Blanche Goodman, "White Folks' Rights," *Saturday Evening Post*, December 2, 1911, 16.
35. Blanche Goodman, "Checkmating Miss Fanny," *Saturday Evening Post*, October 11, 1913, 8, 62.
36. Alain Locke, "The New Negro" (1925), in *The New Negro: Voices of the Harlem Renaissance* (1925), ed. Alain Locke, with a new introduction by Arnold Rampersad (New York: Atheneum, 1992), 3.
37. Goodman, "Out on Bail," 30.
38. "Why Chattanoogans Can Claim High Rank in Literary World; Numerous Books Written Here," *Chattanooga News*, October 30, 1911.
39. "Wide-Awake [?] Meeting of Local Suffragists," *Chattanooga News*, December 21, 1918.
40. Barnes, "Darkology," 52.
41. "Real Grand Daughters of Revolutionary Heroes Honored," *Tampa Tribune*, November 26, 1919; "Arbor Day Observed by Fannin School Parent-Teachers' Association and School Children," *El Paso Times*, March 10, 1923.
42. Barnes, "Darkology," 19.
43. "Old-Time Minstrel Men, by an Old-Timer," *Saturday Evening Post*, September 29, 1900, 22.
44. Uzzel, "'The Saturday Evening Post' Formula," 21.
45. F. Scott Fitzgerald, "The Ice Palace," *Saturday Evening Post*, May 22, 1920, 18, 19, 167. Fitzgerald appears to have one-upped Lorimer's racism. When Fitzgerald collected "The Ice Palace" in his first short story volume, *Flappers and Philosophers*, he revised the phrase "firefly evenings and noisy street fairs" to "firefly evenings and noisy *niggery* street fairs" (F. Scott Fitzgerald, "The Ice Palace," in *Flappers and Philosophers* [New York: Scribner's, 1920], 51, emphasis added).
46. Matthew J. Bruccoli, *Some Sort of Epic Grandeur: The Life of F. Scott Fitzgerald*, 2nd rev. ed. (Columbia: University of South Carolina Press, 2002), 107.
47. F. Scott Fitzgerald, "The Offshore Pirate," *Saturday Evening Post*, May 29, 1920, 99.
48. Hugh Wiley, "Mister Lady Luck," *Saturday Evening Post*, January 17, 1920, 14.
49. Jade Broughton Adams, *F. Scott Fitzgerald's Short Fiction: From Ragtime to Swing Time* (Edinburgh: Edinburgh University Press, 2019), 19.
50. Fitzgerald, "The Offshore Pirate," 99.
51. Michael Nowlin, "F. Scott Fitzgerald's Elite Syncopations: The Racial Make-up of the Entertainer in the Early Fiction," *ESC: English Studies in Canada* 26, no. 4 (December 2000): 418.
52. Nowlin, "F. Scott Fitzgerald's Elite Syncopations," 420.
53. Fitzgerald, "The Offshore Pirate," 11, 99, 109.
54. Nowlin, "F. Scott Fitzgerald's Elite Syncopations," 419.
55. F. Scott Fitzgerald, "Myra Meets His Family," *Saturday Evening Post*, March 20, 1920, 49.
56. F. Scott Fitzgerald, "The Camel's Back," *Saturday Evening Post*, April 24, 1920, 16–17, 157–65.
57. Charles W. Chesnutt, *The Marrow of Tradition* (New York: Houghton Mifflin, 1901), 115, 117, 118, 120, 223.

58. Chesnutt, *The Marrow of Tradition*, 233.
59. Ann Petry, *The Narrows* (1953), with a new introduction by Keith Clark (Evanston, IL: Northwestern University Press, 2017), 133.
60. Barnes, "Darkology," passim, 143.
61. Petry, *The Narrows*, 134, 135.
62. Sonnet H. Retman, "*Black No More*: George Schuyler and Racial Capitalism," *PMLA* 123, no. 5 (2008): 1458.
63. F. Scott Fitzgerald, *The Great Gatsby* (1925; reprint, New York: Scribner's, 2003), 22, 73.
64. Cedric J. Robinson, *Forgeries of Memory and Meaning: Blacks and the Regimes of Race in American Theater and Film Before World War II* (Chapel Hill: University of North Carolina Press, 2007), 141.

3. IRVIN S. COBB: MAKING THE NEW NEGRO OLD AGAIN

1. Alain Locke, "Enter the New Negro," *Survey Graphic* 53, no. 11 (March 1, 1925): 631.
2. Martha Jane Nadell, *Enter the New Negroes: Images of Race in American Culture* (Cambridge, MA: Harvard University Press, 2004), 51.
3. David Levering Lewis, *When Harlem Was in Vogue* (New York: Oxford University Press, 1989), 115.
4. Martha Madison, "Smiles and Minor Chords Are Found in *Black Cameos*," *Brooklyn Daily Eagle*, January 24, 1925; "A Book About the Colored Man," *Emporia Gazette*, January 29, 1925.
5. Karl K. Kitchen, "Up and Down Broadway," *Owensboro (Kentucky) Messenger*, March 16, 1925.
6. Alain Locke, ed., *The New Negro: An Interpretation* (New York: Albert and Charles Boni, 1925).
7. Drew, *Black Stereotypes in Popular Series Fiction*, 90.
8. Tebbel, *George Horace Lorimer*, 46.
9. Tebbel, *George Horace Lorimer*, 64.
10. Debbie Lelekis, *American Literature, Lynching, and the Spectator in the Crow: Spectacular Violence* (Lanham, MD: Lexington Books, 2015), 65.
11. Sandra Lieb, "Irvin S. Cobb," in *American Humorists, 1800–1950*, ed. Stanley Trachtenberg, Dictionary of Literary Biography, vol. 11 (Detroit, MI: Gale, 1982), Gale Literature Resource Center, https://link-gale-com.ez.lib.jjay.cuny.edu/apps/doc/H1200000940/GLS?u=cuny_johnjay&sid=bookmark-GLS&xid=0596240c.
12. Drew, *Black Stereotypes in Popular Series Fiction*, 90.
13. Irvin S. Cobb to George Horace Lorimer, May 22, 1908, George Horace Lorimer Family Papers, Hargrett Rare Book and Manuscript Library, Athens, GA.
14. Lieb, "Irvin S. Cobb," 2.
15. William E. Ellis, *Irvin S. Cobb: The Rise and Fall of an American Humorist* (Lexington: University Press of Kentucky, 2017), 6.
16. Hale, *Making Whiteness*, 59.
17. "Fiction Characters, Irvin Cobb's Week-End Guests," *San Antonio Express*, February 24, 1924.

18. Toni Morrison, *Playing in the Dark: Whiteness and the Literary Imagination* (Cambridge, MA: Harvard University Press, 1992), 6.
19. Wayne Chatterton, *Irvin S. Cobb* (New York: Twayne, 1986), 103.
20. Samuel Blythe, "The Senator's Secretary," *Saturday Evening Post*, January 5, 1907, 19.
21. Dixon, "Booker T. Washington and the Negro," 2.
22. "Did You Ever Hear This?," *Cosmopolitan*, September 1909, 550.
23. Irvin S. Cobb, "Praise God from Whom All Blessings Flow, for the Ku Klux Has Failed in Paducah!," *Paducah News-Democrat*, December 30, 1922.
24. Irvin S. Cobb, *Stickfuls (Myself to Date)* (New York: George H. Doran, 1923), 43–44, 45, 50.
25. Richmond B. Adams, "All Code Is Local: Irvin Cobb's 'The Mob from Massac' and the Edging Shifts in Post-bellum American Culture," *Ethos: A Digital Review of Arts, Humanities, and Public Ethics* 2, no. 1 (2015): 50.
26. Irvin S. Cobb, "The Mob from Massac," *Saturday Evening Post*, February 10, 1912, 5, 6, 31; all ellipses in quotations from fiction are my insertions to indicate omission of text.
27. Cobb, "The Mob from Massac," 33.
28. Cohn, *Creating America*, 103.
29. George Horace Lorimer to Irvin S. Cobb, April 23, 1918, and Cobb to Lorimer, undated, Lorimer Family Papers.
30. George Horace Lorimer to Irvin S. Cobb, August 25, 1918, Lorimer Family Papers.
31. Irvin S. Cobb, "Young Black Joe," *Saturday Evening Post*, August 24, 1918, 7. On the Harlem Hellfighters, see Lewis, *When Harlem Was in Vogue*, 3–24; Mark Whalan, *The Great War and the Culture of the New Negro* (Jacksonville: University Press of Florida, 2008), passim; and Chad L. Williams, *Torchbearers of Democracy: African American Soldiers in the World War I Era* (Chapel Hill: University of North Carolina Press, 2010), passim.
32. Cobb, "Young Black Joe," 8.
33. On the U.S. Army's efforts to export Jim Crow ideology overseas, see David A. Davis, introduction to Victor Daly, *Not Only War: A Story of Two Great Conflicts* (Charlottesville: University of Virginia Press, 2010), xv–xvi.
34. Cobb, "Young Black Joe," 78.
35. Cobb, "Young Black Joe," 78.
36. "Ball Game at Wearn Field," *Charlotte News*, August 23, 1918. The *Post* was officially published on Saturdays but delivered on Thursdays, so this article was published after the August 22 delivery of the August 24 issue.
37. "Young Black Joe," *Louisville Courier-Journal*, August 28, 1918.
38. "The Looking-Glass," *The Crisis* 16, no. 6 (October 1918): 277; "High Tribute to Negro Soldiers," *Nashville Globe*, December 13, 1918.
39. James Weldon Johnson, "Irvin Cobb on the Negro Soldiers," *New York Age*, August 31, 1918, 4.
40. Handbill quoted in Robert Kimball and William Bolcomb, *Reminiscing with Sissle and Blake* (New York: Viking, 1973), 74–75.
41. Pace & Handy Music Company advertisement, *The Crisis* 12, no. 2 (December 1918): 98.

42. David Chinitz, *Which Sin to Bear? Authenticity and Compromise in Langston Hughes* (New York: Oxford University Press, 2013), 96.

43. Williams, *Torchbearers of Democracy*, 100.

44. Irvin S. Cobb to George Horace Lorimer, July 9, 1913, Lorimer Family Papers.

45. Sloane Gordon, "The Story of Irvin S. Cobb," *Pearson's Magazine*, March 1915, 278.

46. Irvin S. Cobb to George Horace Lorimer, January 5, 1917, Lorimer Family Papers.

47. Irvin S. Cobb, "The Ravelin' Wolf," *Saturday Evening Post*, February 21, 1920, 12; subsequent page citations to this story are given parenthetically in the text.

48. Cobb, "Young Black Joe," 8.

49. Shane Vogel, *The Scene of the Harlem Cabaret: Race, Sexuality, Performance* (Chicago: University of Chicago Press, 2009), 2.

50. Irvin S. Cobb, *J. Poindexter, Colored* (New York: George H. Doran, 1922), 16–17, 18; subsequent page citations to this novel are given parenthetically in the text. To avoid confusion, I cite the book publication rather than the magazine version of Cobb's novel.

51. Saidiya V. Hartman, *Scenes of Subjection: Terror, Slavery, and Self-Making in Nineteenth-Century America* (New York: Oxford University Press, 1997), 135.

52. Hale, *Making Whiteness*, 60.

53. Rudolph Fisher, "The City of Refuge" (1925), in *The New Negro: Voices* (1992), ed. Locke, 59.

54. Hale, *Making Whiteness*, 262.

55. North, *The Dialect of Modernism*, 11.

56. Michelle Alexander, *The New Jim Crow: Mass Incarceration in the Age of Colorblindness*, rev. ed. (New York: New Press, 2012), 14.

57. George Horace Lorimer to Irvin S. Cobb, November 14, 1921; Cobb to Lorimer, December 16, 1921; Lorimer to Cobb, December 19, 1921, all in Lorimer Family Papers.

58. Hartman, *Scenes of Subjection*, 5.

59. Hartman, *Scenes of Subjection*, 134.

60. On Garvey and the Black Star Line, see Lewis, *When Harlem Was in Vogue*, 37–39.

61. In this passage, Cobb alludes to Lorimer's other racist preoccupation: the immigration of non-Nordic people from southern and eastern Europe. Between 1923 and 1925, for example, Lorimer ran fourteen items by Lothrop Stoddard, whose book *Rising Tide of Color* was often considered the unofficial bible of the Ku Klux Klan.

62. George Wood, "*J. Poindexter, Colored*," book review, *New York Herald*, July 30, 1922.

63. Cora Annette Harris, "Review of the Latest Books," *Charlotte Observer*, January 21, 1923.

64. Eric Lott, *Love and Theft: Blackface Minstrelsy and the American Working Class* (New York: Oxford University Press, 1993), 6.

65. Hale, *Making Whiteness*, 21.

66. Locke, "The New Negro," 6.

67. Benjamin Brawley, "The Negro in American Literature," *The Bookman: A Review of Books and Life*, October 1922, 59.

68. Benjamin Brawley, "The Negro in Contemporary Literature," *English Journal* 18, no. 3 (March 1929): 195.

4. HUGH WILEY, EDWARD CHRISTOPHER WILLIAMS, AND BLACK DOUGHBOYS

1. Cobb, "Young Black Joe," 7.
2. Dunbar, "Negro Society in Washington," 9.
3. Williams, *When Washington Was in Vogue*, 121, 119; subsequent page citations to the novel are given parenthetically in the text, and all ellipses in quotes from fiction are my insertions to indicate omission of text. In fact, it would take an entire century before Congress finally passed the Emmett Till Antilynching Act in 2022.
4. Davy's "of course" calls to mind Pierre Bourdieu's claim that "one of the major difficulties of the social history of philosophy, art, or literature is that it has to reconstruct these spaces of original possible which, because they were part of the self-evident givens of the situation, remained unremarked and are therefore unlikely to be mentioned in contemporary accounts, chronicles or memoirs" ("The Field of Cultural Production," 31).
5. Davis, introduction to Victor Daly, *Not Only War*, xxix.
6. I had the good fortune of rediscovering Williams's serialized novel and shepherding it through its republication in book form. For a discussion of the novel's initial publication in the *Messenger* and its reception in 1925–1926 as well as for bio-bibliographical information about Williams, see my introduction to *When Washington Was in Vogue*, xiii–xxxiv. For a discussion of the retitling of the novel, see Adam McKible, "Editing Edward Christopher Williams: From 'The Letters of Davy Carr' to *When Washington Was in Vogue*," in *Editing the Harlem Renaissance*, ed. Joshua Murray and Ross Tangedal (Clemson, SC: Clemson University Press, 2021), 207–22.
7. Neval H. Thomas, "The District of Columbia—a Paradox of Paradises," *Messenger*, October 1923, 839.
8. Thomas, "The District of Columbia," 839.
9. For an excellent analysis of the "Black bourgeoisie" and class making in Washington, DC, see Pamela L. Caughie, "'The Best People': The Making of the Black Bourgeoisie in Writings of the Negro Renaissance," *Modernism/modernity* 20, no. 3 (2013): 519–37.
10. Drew, *Black Stereotypes in Popular Series Fiction*, 188–89.
11. Williams, *Torchbearers of Democracy*, 26, 283–84.
12. Columbia Records advertisement, *Saturday Evening Post*, January 25, 1919, 64.
13. Drew, *Black Stereotypes in Popular Series Fiction*, 184.
14. Tebbel, *George Horace Lorimer*, 100.
15. Hugh Wiley, "The Four-Leaved Wildcat," *Saturday Evening Post*, March 8, 1919, 10.
16. Hugh Wiley, "Memphis Bound," *Saturday Evening Post*, March 13, 1920, 173.
17. Hugh Wiley, "Boom-a-Loom Boom," *Saturday Evening Post*, July 19, 1919, 10.
18. Wiley, "Boom-a-Loom Boom," 117.
19. Adding a layer of psychological complexity that resonates with Eric Lott's observation of the white "sympathetic identification" with minstrel characters (*Love and Theft*, 8), Wiley's friends—including Lorimer—regularly called him "Wildcat."

20. My thanks to David Earle for his discussions of the rapidity of literary production in periodicals, "City of Print: New York and the Periodical Press," at the National Endowment for the Humanities Summer Institute in 2015.

21. Hugh Wiley, "Prowling Prodigal," *Saturday Evening Post*, November 22, 1919, 178.

22. Wiley, "Mister Lady Luck," 91.

23. Hugh Wiley, "The Pluvitor," *Saturday Evening Post*, June 5, 1926, 24–25; Hugh Wiley, "C.O.D.," *Saturday Evening Post*, January 8, 1921, 18.

24. "Two Writers Use Same Character," *Charlotte News*, January 11, 1921.

25. W. W. M., "Don't Worry," *Oklahoma City Times*, April 14, 1920; Franklin P. Adams, "The Conning Tower," *New-York Tribune*, August 13, 1920; "Short Story Writer Talks," *Lincoln Journal Star*, October 4, 1920; Alexander Woollcott, "Second Thoughts on First Nights," *New York Times*, April 9, 1922.

26. "Bert Williams: A Film," *Los Angeles Times*, January 29, 1920.

27. "Al Jolson Will Enter Moving Picture Field as Leading Man in Wiley's 'The Wildcat,'" *Salt Lake Tribune*, July 4, 1922.

28. "Around the Lobbies," *San Francisco Examiner*, July 4, 1922.

29. "Short Story Writer Talks."

30. Peter C. Rollins and Harry W. Menig, "Regional Literature and Will Rogers: Film Redeems a Literary Form," *Literature/Film Quarterly* 3, no. 1 (1975): 73.

31. "Wildcat, Lily, and Lady Luck Invited to City of Salinas," *The Californian* (Salinas), April 17, 1923, 1.

32. "Hugh Wiley to Give Wildcat, Lily, Lady Luck Trip to Salinas," *The Californian* (Salinas), April 30, 1923, 4.

33. Hugh Wiley, "Pop," *Saturday Evening Post*, November 7, 1925, 191.

34. Hugh Wiley, *The Wildcat* (New York: George H. Doran, 1920).

35. "Tribute of One Humorist to Another," *Winston-Salem Journal*, January 30, 1921.

36. "Golf Is the Curse of American Literature, Hugh Wiley Asserts; Has Given It Up, Except the African Brand," *Minneapolis Star Tribune*, December 18, 1921.

37. Hugh Wiley, "Sick Per Cent," *Saturday Evening Post*, November 21, 1925, 20–21, 134–40.

38. "What Comes Down Our Creek," Fidelity Trust Company advertisement, *Knoxville Journal*, December 17, 1925, emphasis in original.

39. "NEGRO LYNCHED FOR INSULTS—Riddled Body Is Answer to Remarks to White Woman," *Knoxville Journal*, December 17, 1925.

40. On this training camp for Black officers, see Whalan, *The Great War*, 124.

41. Mary White Ovington, "The Wild Cat," *Baltimore Afro-American*, June 2, 1922.

42. On the significance of speaking French for African American soldiers, see Whalan, *The Great War*, 10. In the story "Mercy, Monsieur!" (1926), Cohen mocks this aspect of African American modernity when Florian Slappey fakes speaking French (Octavus Roy Cohen, "Mercy, Monsieur!," *Saturday Evening Post*, May 8, 1926, 28–29, 46–51).

43. Christina Moore, "Traditional Rebirth: The Epistolary Genre in *When Washington Was in Vogue*," *African American Review* 46, no. 2 (2013): 414.

44. My understanding of the notion of the "thingness" of African American caricatures draws inspiration from Barbara Green's illuminating essay "Feminist Things,"

in *Transatlantic Print Culture, 1880–1940: Emerging Media, Emerging Modernisms*, ed. Ann Ardis and Patrick Collier (New York: Palgrave MacMillan, 2008), 66–79.

45. According to Cheryl Knott Malone, Williams enjoyed a thirty-year career as a librarian, during which he "built collections at Western Reserve and Howard Universities, contributed to library science education, helped establish a state library association, and encouraged other African Americans to pursue the profession of librarianship" (Cheryl Knott Malone, "Toward a Multicultural American Public Library History," *Libraries and Culture* 35, no. 1 [2000]: 79). On the development of a Black readership during the Harlem Renaissance, see Shawn Anthony Christian, *The Harlem Renaissance and the Idea of a New Negro Reader* (Amherst: University of Massachusetts Press, 2016).

46. W. E. B. Du Bois, "Returning Soldiers," *The Crisis* 18, no. 1 (May 1919): 14, emphasis in the original.

47. Johnson, preface to *The Book of American Negro Poetry* (1922), ed. Johnson, xli, vii, viii.

5. OCTAVUS ROY COHEN, THE MIDNIGHT MOTION PICTURE COMPANY, AND THE SHADOWS OF JIM CROW

1. For discussions of the Meschrapom *Black and White* venture, see Langston Hughes, *I Wonder as I Wander*, 2nd ed. (New York: Hill and Wang, 1993), 65–99; Lewis, *When Harlem Was in Vogue*, 288–93; Vera Kutzinski, *The Worlds of Langston Hughes: Modernism and Translation in the Americas* (Ithaca, NY: Cornell University Press, 2012), 15–30; Robert Jackson, *Fade in Crossroads: A History of the Southern Cinema* (New York: Oxford University Press, 2017), 133–36; Steven S. Lee, *The Ethnic Avant-Garde: Minority Cultures and World Revolution* (New York: Columbia University Press, 2015), 119–48. There is virtually no scholarship on Cohen's fictional film company.

2. Tebbel, *George Horace Lorimer*, 120.

3. James Smethurst, *The African American Roots of American Modernism: From Reconstruction to the Harlem Renaissance* (Chapel Hill: University of North Carolina Press, 2011), 6.

4. Smethurst, *The African American Roots of American Modernism*, 96.

5. Hale, *Making Whiteness*, 50.

6. Du Bois, *Souls of Black Folk*, vii.

7. Du Bois, *Souls of Black Folk*, 3.

8. Du Bois, *Souls of Black Folk*, 3.

9. Hale, *Making Whiteness*, 8.

10. Locke, "The New Negro," 3–4.

11. Spatial representations of the construction of segregation can be found throughout and beyond the Jim Crow era. In Ann Petry's novel *The Street* (1946; reprint, Boston: Houghton Mifflin, 1974), her protagonist thinks, "From the time she was born, she had been hemmed into an ever-narrowing space, and now she was very nearly walled in and the wall had been built up brick by brick by eager white hands" (323–24). In his introduction to *Shadow and Act* (New York: Vintage, 1964), Ralph

Ellison describes "the palings of almost every fence which those who controlled social and political power had erected to restrict our roles in the life of the country" (xiv).

12. On the transformation of the *Survey Graphic* issue into the collected volume *The New Negro* later in 1925, see Anne Elizabeth Carroll, *Word, Image, and the New Negro* (Bloomington: Indiana University Press, 2005), 159–77; Nadell, *Enter the New Negroes*, 35–36, 53–54; George Hutchinson, *The Harlem Renaissance in Black and White* (Cambridge, MA: Harvard University Press, 1995), 392–400; Peake, "'Watching the Waters,'" 10–18.

13. W. E. B. Du Bois, "The Black Man Brings His Gifts," *Survey Graphic* 53, no. 11 (March 1, 1925): 655–57, 710.

14. David Luis-Brown, *Waves of Decolonization: Discourses of Race and Hemispheric Citizenship in Cuba, Mexico, and the United States* (Durham, NC: Duke University Press, 2008), 2, 22.

15. W. E. B. Du Bois, *Darkwater: Voices from Within the Veil* (1920; reprint, Garden City, NY: Dover, 1999), 17, 27, 28, 29; Luis-Brown, *Waves of Decolonization*, 9.

16. W. E. B. Du Bois, "The Negro Mind Reaches Out" (1925), in *The New Negro: Voices* (1992), ed. Locke, 385, 386.

17. Houston Baker, "Questionnaire Response," *Modernism/modernity* 23, no. 3 (2013): 434.

18. Rayford Logan, "Why We Should Study Negro History," *New Journal and Guide*, December 12, 1925, 16.

19. On African American historiography and the search for a "usable past," see Clare Corbould, *Becoming African Americans: Black Public Life in Harlem, 1919–1939* (Cambridge, MA: Harvard University Press, 2009), 57–87.

20. Arthur A. Schomburg, "The Negro Digs Up His Past" (1925), in *The New Negro: Voices* (1992), ed. Locke, 231.

21. Fitzgerald, *The Great Gatsby*, 17.

22. For an extended discussion of the connections among F. Scott Fitzgerald, Madison Grant, and Lothrop Stoddard, see Adam McKible, *The Space and Place of Modernism: The Russian Revolution, Little Magazines, and New York* (New York: Routledge, 2002), 133–56.

23. Logan was writing about domestic racism, but his twenty-year timeline was ominously prescient for the international scene. As James Q. Whitman notes, Stoddard and Grant were essential to the rise of Nazi ideology. "During the interwar period the United States was not just a global leader in assembly-line manufacturing and Hollywood popular culture. It was a global leader in [the] 'scientific' eugenics" promoted by Stoddard and Grant. "Their teachings filtered into immigration law not only in the United States but also in other Anglophone countries[;] . . . in Nazi Germany . . . the works of Grant, Stoddard, and other American eugenicists were standard citations" (James Q. Whitman, *Hitler's American Model: The United States and the Making of Nazi Race Law* [Princeton, NJ: Princeton University Press, 2018], 8).

24. Wood, *The Curtis Magazines*, 104.

25. "Octavus Roy Cohen Writes Hard, Plays Hard, in Southland," *Washington Herald*, February 16, 1919.

26. Tebbel, *George Horace Lorimer*, 69.

27. Drew, *Black Stereotypes in Popular Series Fiction*, 132, 141. The number of Cohen's screen credits is probably higher than Drew claims. According to IMDb, Cohen was screenwriter for thirty-three films and ten television episodes. He also wrote five plays and appeared in at least three films ("Octavus Roy Cohen (1891–1959)," IMDb, n.d., https://www.imdb.com/name/nm0169665/).

28. Because Florian Slappey was such a well-known character, Lorimer featured him in one of a series of advertisements that linked popular *Post* characters with seemingly unrelated products—in this case, Alemite lubricants. See "Millions of Friends for Florian Slappey," advertisement, *Saturday Evening Post*, March 24, 1934, 90.

29. "Octavus Roy Cohen Watches Football Game," *Chicago Defender*, November 25, 1922; "'Porgy' Star in Radio Mystery," *Baltimore Afro-American*, February 11, 1933.

30. Information on the publication of *Gentleman Jigger* comes from Thomas H. Wirth, introduction to Richard Bruce Nugent, *Gentleman Jigger*, ed. Thomas H. Wirth (Boston: Da Capo, 2008), x–xviii, dates given on xi.

31. Nugent, *Gentleman Jigger*, 37.

32. Williams, *When Washington Was in Vogue*, 176.

33. W. E. B. Du Bois, introduction to *The Crisis* Symposium, "The Negro in Art: How Shall He Be Portrayed" (1926), in *The New Negro*, ed. Gates and Jarrett, 190.

34. H. L. Mencken, response in *The Crisis* Symposium, "The Negro in Art: How Shall He Be Portrayed"(1926), in *The New Negro*, ed. Gates and Jarrett, 191.

35. Smethurst, *The African American Roots of American Modernism*, 8.

36. Hale, *Making Whiteness*, 193–200.

37. Hale, *Making Whiteness*, 123.

38. Smethurst, *The African American Roots of American Modernism*, 97.

39. Octavus Roy Cohen, "The Pay of Naples," *Saturday Evening Post*, July 17, 1926, 18; Octavus Roy Cohen, "Neapolitan Scream," *Saturday Evening Post*, August 14, 1926, 22.

40. Du Bois, *Darkwater*, 41.

41. W. E. B. Du Bois, *Dark Princess: A Romance* (1928), ed. Henry Louis Gates Jr. (New York: Oxford University Press, 2007), 6.

42. Donald Bogle, *Toms, Coons, Mulattoes, Mammies, and Bucks: An Interpretive History of Blacks in American Films*, 3rd ed. (New York: Continuum, 1999); Robinson, *Forgeries of Memory and Meaning*.

43. Octavus Roy Cohen, "Endurance Vile," *Saturday Evening Post*, December 5, 1925, 32.

44. Brooks Hefner notes that dialect emphasizes the "difference between the reader and the speaker; by nature, dialect is the language of an outsider, a subaltern" (Brooks E. Hefner, *The Word on the Street: The American Language of American Modernism* [Charlottesville: University of Virginia Press, 2017], 11).

45. Octavus Roy Cohen, "Mercy, Monsieur!" *Saturday Evening Post*, May 8, 1926, 28–29, 46–51; Octavus Roy Cohen, "Stew's Company," *Saturday Evening Post*, February 5, 1927, 137.

46. Octavus Roy Cohen, "Horns Aplenty," *Saturday Evening Post*, September 4, 1926, 34, 36.

47. The rise of jazz as a musical form and as a broader cultural phenomenon was a regular feature of Cohen's stories in particular and in the *Saturday Evening Post* in general. A telling example of Lorimer's devotion to Jim Crowing American history

and culture can be found in his publication of the band leader Paul Whiteman's memoir *Jazz* (1926). In the book publication, Whiteman gave at least scant credit to the African and African American roots of jazz, but in the book's simultaneous serialization in the *Post* Lorimer excised nearly all such references.

48. Octavus Roy Cohen, "Low but Sure," *Saturday Evening Post*, November 6, 1926, 46, 56, 58, 60.

49. Herskovits, letter to the editor, *Folklore*, 221.

50. W. E. B. Du Bois to George Horace Lorimer, December 22, 1922, and Lorimer to Du Bois, December 29, 1922, in Du Bois, *The Correspondence of W. E. B. Du Bois*, 1:259–60.

51. W. E. B. Du Bois, "Criteria of Negro Art" (1926), in *The New Negro*, ed. Gates and Jarrett, 259.

52. Wallace Thurman, "Negro Artists and the Negro," in *The Collected Writings of Wallace Thurman: A Harlem Renaissance Reader*, ed. Amritjit Singh and Daniel M. Scott III (New Brunswick, NJ: Rutgers University Press, 2003), 195, 197–98.

53. Zora Neale Hurston to Walter and Gladys White, July–August 1932, in Hurston, *Zora*, 269.

54. Claude McKay, *Banjo: A Story Without a Plot* (1929; reprint, New York: Harcourt Brace, 1957), 17.

55. "Scope and Content Note," 6, for Kendrick-Brooks Family Papers, Library of Congress, Washington, DC, https://lccn.loc.gov/mm00084736.

56. Swan Kendrick to Octavus Roy Cohen, March 30, 1919, Kendrick-Brooks Family Papers.

57. Octavus Roy Cohen to Swan Kendrick, April 4, 1919, Kendrick-Brooks Family Papers, emphasis of *at* and *them* in original.

58. Kendrick Swan to Octavus Roy Cohen, May 4, 1919, Kendrick-Brooks Family Papers.

59. Mary Burrill, "Aftermath: A One-Act Play of Negro Life," *Liberator*, April 1919, 11, emphasis in original.

60. Claude McKay, "The Dominant White," *Liberator*, April 1919, 14.

61. Langston Hughes, "The Negro Artist and the Racial Mountain," *The Nation*, June 23, 1926, 694.

6. THE END OF THE LORIMER ERA

1. John Matheus, "Some Aspects of the Negro Interpreted in Contemporary American and European Literature," in *Negro: An Anthology* (1934), ed. Nancy Cunard, ed. and abridged by Hugh Ford (New York: Continuum, 2002), 84.

2. Whipple, "'SatEvePost' Mirror of These States," 699.

3. James Weldon Johnson, "The Making of Harlem," *Survey Graphic* 53, no. 11 (March 1, 1925): 635.

4. Chester T. Crowell, "The World's Largest Negro City," *Saturday Evening Post*, August 8, 1925, 9; subsequent page citations are given parenthetically in the text.

5. Charles S. Johnson, "Black Workers and the City," *Survey Graphic* 53, no. 11 (March 1, 1925): 643.

6. "'Passing' of Negroes," *Newport News (Virginia) Daily Press*, August 8, 1925.

7. Locke, "Enter the New Negro," 633.

8. My thanks to Johannes Burgers for pointing out the connection in the *Post* between indigestibility and immigrants.

9. "Harlem Viewed from Without," *New York Age*, August 15, 1925, 4.

10. Floyd Calvin, "The Digest," *Pittsburgh Courier*, August 15, 1925.

11. "Saturday Evening Post Publishes Article on Harlem," NAACP Press Service release, *Mobile Weekly Standard*, August 22, 1925.

12. The editorial may have been written by Albert Atwood, but it would have required Lorimer's approval before publication; see Cohn, *Creating America*, 175.

13. "Racial Problems," editorial, *Saturday Evening Post*, March 23, 1929, 28.

14. "Where the Race Is Gaining," *New York Age*, April 20, 1929, 4.

15. Wade Hall, "Roark (Whitney Wickliffe) Bradford," in *American Short-Story Writers, 1910–1945: First Series*, ed. Bobby Ellen Kimbel, Dictionary of Literary Biography, vol. 86 (Detroit, MI: Gale, 1989), Gale Literature Resource Center, https://link.gale.com/apps/doc/H1200000052/GLS?u=cuny_johnjay&sid=bookmark-GLS&xid=5bdcdcdd.

16. Roark Bradford, "Notes on the Negro," *Forum* 78, no. 5 (November 1927): 790–91.

17. Sterling Brown, "Negro Characters as Seen by White Authors," *Journal of Negro Education* 2, no. 2 (April 1933): 179, emphasis in original.

18. Roark Bradford, "The Final Run of Hopper Joe Wiley," *Saturday Evening Post*, January 5, 1929, 48.

19. Cobb, "Young Black Joe," 7.

20. Bradford, "The Final Run of Hopper Joe Wiley," 79; all ellipses in quotations from fiction are my insertions to indicate omission of text.

21. Roark Bradford, "The Eagle Stirs the Nest," *Saturday Evening Post*, August 15, 1931, 17.

22. "Roark Bradford Pictures Recent Outachita Journey in Magazine Article," *Commercial Appeal* (Memphis), January 7, 1929.

23. "Confederate Daughters Enjoy Meeting in Mayfield Home," *Santa Ana (California) Register*, January 11, 1929.

24. "Colonel" Charles Garland Givens, "Mammy Ada," *Saturday Evening Post*, December 7, 1929, 71.

25. "Colonel" Charles Garland Givens, "Jig Time," *Saturday Evening Post*, May 25, 1929, 26; subsequent page citations are given parenthetically in the text.

26. Elizabeth Robeson, "The Ambiguity of Julia Peterkin," *Journal of Southern History* 61, no. 4 (1995): 762, 764.

27. Sterling Brown, "The New Secession," *Opportunity*, May 1927, 148.

28. Julia Peterkin, response in *The Crisis* Symposium, "The Negro in Art: How Shall He Be Portrayed" (1926), in *The New Negro*, ed. Gates and Jarrett, 201.

29. Robeson, "The Ambiguity of Julia Peterkin," 777.

30. Peterkin, response in *The Crisis* Symposium, "The Negro in Art," 201.

31. Thomas Landess, "Julia Mood Peterkin," in *American Novelists, 1910–1945*, ed. James J. Martine, Dictionary of Literary Biography, vol. 9 (Detroit, MI: Gale, 1981), Gale Literature Resource Center, https://link.gale.com/apps/doc/H1200000432/GLS?u=cuny_johnjay&sid=bookmark-GLS&xid=d2bb6e60.

32. Julia Peterkin, "Heart Leaves," *Saturday Evening Post*, October 5, 1929, 5, 153.

33. Peterkin, "Heart Leaves," 156.

34. T. S. Stribling, "N. Ah. A," *Saturday Evening Post*, January 26, 1935, 12.

35. Howard Rockey, "Fiction Largely European and Very Good in the Average," *Philadelphia Inquirer*, November 30, 1929.

36. James B. Meriwether, "Faulkner's Correspondence with the *Saturday Evening Post*," *Mississippi Quarterly* 30, no. 3 (Summer 1977): 461, 464.

37. William Faulkner to Morton Goldman, August 1934, in William Faulkner, *Selected Letters of William Faulkner*, ed. Joseph Blotner (New York: Random House, 1977), 84.

38. Susan V. Donaldson, "Dismantling the *Saturday Evening Post* Reader: *The Unvanquished* and Changing 'Horizons of Expectations,'" in *Faulkner and Popular Culture*, ed. Doreen Fowler and Ann J. Abadie (Jackson: University Press of Mississippi, 1990), 179.

39. William Faulkner, "Red Leaves," *Saturday Evening Post*, October 25, 1930, 7; subsequent page citations are given parenthetically in the text.

40. Hans Skei, *Reading Faulkner's Best Short Stories* (Columbia: University of South Carolina Press, 1999), 140.

41. Marjory Stoneman Douglas, quoted in Grace Norman Tuttle, "Echoes of Miami," *Miami Herald*, May 4, 1931.

42. See Cohn, *Creating America*.

43. William Faulkner, "Session Six, March 9, 1957," in William Faulkner, *Faulkner in the University*, ed. Frederick L. Gwynne and Joseph Blotner (Charlottesville: University Press of Virginia, 1995), 39.

44. Cobb, *Stickfuls*, 45.

45. Edmond L. Volpe, "Faulkner's 'Red Leaves': The Deciduation of Nature," *Studies in American Fiction* 3, no. 2 (Autumn 1975): 125.

46. Thomas B. Costain to William Faulkner, January 21, 1931, in Meriwether, "Faulkner's Correspondence," 475.

47. William Faulkner to Meritt Hubbard, October 4 (?), 1932, in Meriwether, "Faulkner's Correspondence," 464, 468.

48. Faulkner, "A Mountain Victory," 6; subsequent page citations are given parenthetically in the text.

49. Hugh Wiley, "Microphony," *Saturday Evening Post*, January 31, 1931, 41.

50. Henry Louis Gates, Jr., *The Signifying Monkey: A Theory of African-American Literary Criticism* (New York: Oxford University Press, 1988), 130.

51. Brown, "Negro Characters as Seen by White Authors," 202.

52. William Faulkner, "A Bear Hunt," *Saturday Evening Post*, February 10, 1934, 6; subsequent page citations are given parenthetically in the text.

53. Nolan, "Langston Hughes," 169.

54. Octavus Roy Cohen, "The Muchright Man," *Saturday Evening Post*, April 7, 1934, 85.

55. Brown, "Negro Characters as Seen by White Authors," 185.

56. The capitalization of "Negro," despite Roark's castigation, was welcomed by Black activists as a social advancement. On April 5, 1930, for example, the *Baltimore Afro-American* welcomed the news with the headline "114 Daily Papers Now Capitalize the Word 'Negro.'"

57. Steve Hannagan, "Black Gold," *Saturday Evening Post*, June 20, 1936, 76.

58. Hannagan, "Black Gold," 78.

59. Paul Gallico, "This Way I Beat Joe Louis," *Saturday Evening Post*, September 5, 1936, 34.

60. Kathryne V. Lindberg, "Mass Circulation Versus the Masses: Covering the Modern Magazine Scene," *Boundary 2* 20, no. 2 (1993): 69.

61. Larry Snyder, "My Boy Jesse," *Saturday Evening Post*, November 7, 1936, 14–15, 97–101.

62. Snyder, "My Boy Jesse," 100.

63. Snyder, "My Boy Jesse," 100–101.

64. Wood, *The Curtis Magazines*, 150.

65. Norman Rockwell, *My Adventures as an Illustrator* (New York: Harry N. Abrams, 1994), 307, 311.

66. Stolberg, "Merchant in Letters," 85.

67. Harper, "George Horace Lorimer (an Enemy)."

EPILOGUE

1. Josh Gerstein and Alexander Ward, "Supreme Court Has Voted to Overturn Abortion Rights, Draft Opinion Shows," *Politico*, May 2, 2022, https://www.politico.com/news/2022/05/02/supreme-court-abortion-draft-opinion-00029473.

2. Walter Benjamin, "Theses on the Philosophy of History," in *Illuminations: Essays and Reflections*, ed. Hannah Arendt, trans. Harry Zohn (New York: Schocken, 1968), 255.

3. Chesnutt, *The Marrow of Tradition*, 239.

4. Hughes, "The Negro Artist and the Racial Mountain," 694.

BIBLIOGRAPHY

ARCHIVAL SOURCES

Hargrett Rare Book and Manuscript Library, Athens, GA.
Lorimer, George Horace, Family Papers.
Library of Congress, Washington, DC.
Kendrick-Brooks Family Papers. https://lccn.loc.gov/mm00084736.

SECONDARY SOURCES

"114 Daily Papers Now Capitalize the Word 'Negro.'" *Baltimore Afro-American*, April 5,
  1930.
Adams, Jade Broughton. *F. Scott Fitzgerald's Short Fiction: From Ragtime to Swing Time.*
  Edinburgh: Edinburgh University Press, 2019.
Adams, Franklin P. "The Conning Tower." *New-York Tribune*, August 13, 1920.
Adams, Richmond B. "All Code Is Local: Irvin Cobb's 'The Mob from Massac' and the
  Edging Shifts in Post-bellum American Culture." *Ethos: A Digital Review of Arts,
  Humanities, and Public Ethics* 2, no. 1 (2015): 48–66.
Alexander, Michelle. *The New Jim Crow: Mass Incarceration in the Age of Colorblind-
  ness.* Rev. ed. New York: New Press, 2012.
"Al Jolson Will Enter Moving Picture Field as Leading Man in Wiley's 'The Wildcat.'"
  Salt Lake Tribune, July 4, 1922.
"Another White Man's Burden." Editorial. *Saturday Evening Post*, February 6, 1904, 12.
"Arbor Day Observed by Fannin School Parent-Teachers' Association and School Chil-
  dren." *El Paso Times*, March 10, 1923.
"Around the Lobbies." *San Francisco Examiner*, July 4, 1922.
"The Asylum Business." Editorial. *Saturday Evening Post*, January 1, 1916, 22.

Baker, Houston. "Questionnaire Response." *Modernism/modernity* 23, no. 3 (2013): 433–35.

Baldwin, James. *Notes of a Native Son*. Boston: Beacon Press, 1955.

"Ball Game at Wearn Field." *Charlotte News*, August 23, 1918.

Barnes, Rhae Lynn. "Darkology: The Hidden History of Blackface Minstrelsy and the Making of Modern America, 1860–1970." PhD diss., Harvard University, 2016.

Benjamin, Walter. "Theses on the Philosophy of History." In *Illuminations: Essays and Reflections*, ed. Hannah Arendt, trans. Harry Zohn, 253–64. New York: Schocken, 1968.

Bernard, Emily, ed. *Remember Me to Harlem: The Letters of Langston Hughes and Carl Van Vechten*. New York: Vintage, 2001.

"Bert Williams: A Film." *Los Angeles Times*, January 29, 1920.

"Black Cameos." Advertisement. *Survey Graphic* 53, no. 11 (March 1, 1925): back cover.

Blythe, Samuel. "Our Imported Troubles and Troublemakers." Editorial. *Saturday Evening Post*, May 11, 1918, 3–4, 41–45.

——. "The Senator's Secretary." *Saturday Evening Post*, January 5, 1907, 19.

Bogle, Donald. *Toms, Coons, Mulattoes, Mammies, and Bucks: An Interpretive History of Blacks in American Films*. 3rd ed. New York: Continuum, 1999.

"A Book About the Colored Man." *Emporia Gazette*, January 29, 1925.

Bourdieu, Pierre. "The Field of Cultural Production, or: The Economic World Reversed." In *The Field of Cultural Production: Essays on Art and Literature*, ed. and trans. Randal Johnson, 29–73. New York: Columbia University Press, 1993.

Bradford, Roark. "The Eagle Stirs the Nest." *Saturday Evening Post*, August 15, 1931, 16–17, 67–69

——. "The Final Run of Hopper Joe Wiley." *Saturday Evening Post*, January 5, 1929, 48–50, 74–79.

——. "Notes on the Negro." *Forum* 78, no. 5 (November 1927): 790–91.

Brawley, Benjamin. "The Negro in American Literature." *The Bookman: A Review of Books and Life*, October 1922, 56–60.

——. "The Negro in Contemporary Literature." *English Journal* 18, no. 3 (March 1929): 194–202.

Brown, Sterling. "Negro Characters as Seen by White Authors." *Journal of Negro Education* 2, no. 2 (April 1933): 179–203.

——. "The New Secession." *Opportunity*, May 1927, 147–48.

Bruccoli, Matthew J. *Some Sort of Epic Grandeur: The Life of F. Scott Fitzgerald*. 2nd rev. ed. Columbia: University of South Carolina Press, 2002.

Burrill, Mary. "Aftermath: A One-Act Play of Negro Life." *Liberator*, April 1919, 10–14.

Calvin, Floyd. "The Digest." *Pittsburgh Courier*, August 15, 1925.

Carroll, Anne Elizabeth. *Word, Image, and the New Negro*. Bloomington: Indiana University Press, 2005.

Caughie, Pamela L. "'The Best People': The Making of the Black Bourgeoisie in Writings of the Negro Renaissance." *Modernism/modernity* 20, no. 3 (2013): 519–37.

"Chattanooga Day by Day: Social and Personal." *Chattanooga Daily Times*, December 16, 1908.

Chatterton, Wayne. *Irvin S. Cobb*. New York: Twayne, 1986.

Chesnutt, Charles W. *The Marrow of Tradition*. New York: Houghton Mifflin, 1901.

——. "On the Future of His People." *Saturday Evening Post*, January 20, 1900, 646.

Chinitz, David. *Which Sin to Bear? Authenticity and Compromise in Langston Hughes.* New York: Oxford University Press, 2013.

Christian, Shawn Anthony. *The Harlem Renaissance and the Idea of a New Negro Reader.* Amherst: University of Massachusetts Press, 2016.

Cobb, Irvin S. *J. Poindexter, Colored.* New York: George H. Doran, 1922.

——. "The Mob from Massac." *Saturday Evening Post*, February 10, 1912, 5–7, 32–33.

——. "Praise God from Whom All Blessings Flow, for the Ku Klux Has Failed in Paducah!" *Paducah News-Democrat*, December 30, 1922.

——. "The Ravelin' Wolf." *Saturday Evening Post*, February 21, 1920, 12–13, 66–69.

——. *Stickfuls (Myself to Date).* New York: George H. Doran, 1923.

——. "Young Black Joe." *Saturday Evening Post*, August 24, 1918, 7–8, 77–78.

Cohen, Octavus Roy. "Endurance Vile." *Saturday Evening Post*, December 5, 1925, 32–33, 53–54.

——. "Horns Aplenty." *Saturday Evening Post*, September 4, 1926, 34–46.

——. "Low but Sure." *Saturday Evening Post*, November 6, 1926, 46–48, 56–60.

——. "Mercy, Monsieur!" *Saturday Evening Post*, May 8, 1926, 28–29, 46–51.

——. "The Muchright Man." *Saturday Evening Post*, April 7, 1934, 18–19, 80–85.

——. "Neapolitan Scream." *Saturday Evening Post*, August 14, 1926, 22–23, 120–26.

——. "The Pay of Naples." *Saturday Evening Post*, July 17, 1926, 18–19, 121–31.

——. "Stew's Company." *Saturday Evening Post*, February 5, 1927, 22–23, 173–78.

Cohn, Jan. *Creating America: George Horace Lorimer and the* Saturday Evening Post. Pittsburgh, PA: University of Pittsburgh Press, 1989.

Columbia Records advertisement. *Saturday Evening Post*, January 25, 1919, 64.

"Confederate Daughters Enjoy Meeting in Mayfield Home." *Santa Ana (California) Register*, January 11, 1929.

Corbould, Clare. *Becoming African Americans: Black Public Life in Harlem, 1919–1939.* Cambridge, MA: Harvard University Press, 2009.

"The Crescent Club." *Downs (Kansas) News and the Downs Times*, May 13, 1920.

Crest Trading Company advertisement. *Saturday Evening Post*, December 16, 1905, 27.

"A Crime Against American School Children." *Ladies' Home Journal*, January 1909, 5.

Crowell, Chester T. "The World's Largest Negro City." *Saturday Evening Post*, August 8, 1925, 8–9, 93–97.

"The Curse of Caste vs. 'The Leopard's Spots.'" *Baltimore Afro-American*, August 15, 1903.

Dahn, Eurie. *Jim Crow Networks: African American Periodical Cultures.* Amherst: University of Massachusetts Press, 2021.

Damon-Moore, Helen. *Magazines for the Millions: Gender and Commerce in the Ladies' Home Journal and the* Saturday Evening Post, *1890–1910.* Albany: State University of New York Press, 1994.

"'Darktown' Easter Egg Hunt." *Chattanooga Daily Times*, April 4, 1904.

Davis, David A. Introduction to Victor Daly, *Not Only War: A Story of Two Great Conflicts*, vii–xxxiii. Charlottesville: University of Virginia Press, 2010.

Davis, Deborah. *Guest of Honor: Booker T. Washington, Theodore Roosevelt, and the White House Dinner That Shocked a Nation.* New York: Atria, 2012.

Davis, Rebecca Harding. "Half a Dozen Silhouettes." *Saturday Evening Post*, August 12, 1905, 6–7.

———. "Has the Free Negro Failed? What Forty Years of Independence Have Brought Him." *Saturday Evening Post*, July 2, 1904, 13.

Dickson, Harris. "A Borgia of the Air." *Saturday Evening Post*, May 1, 1926, 26, 193–94.

———. "The Job Hunter." *Saturday Evening Post*, January 8, 1910, 12–13, 38–39.

———. "Please Y'Onner: The Testimony and Facts in Certain Cote-House Scrapes." *Saturday Evening Post*, February 16, 1907, 12–14, 29.

———. "That Mule, Old Bluffer." *Saturday Evening Post*, February 13, 1909, 10–11, 40–42.

———. "The Vardaman Idea: How the Governor of Mississippi Would Solve the Race Question." *Saturday Evening Post*, April 27, 1907, 3–5.

———. "The Way of the Reformer." *Saturday Evening Post*, January 12, 1907, 6–7, 22.

Dickson-Carr, Darryl. *Spoofing the Modern: Satire in the Harlem Renaissance.* Columbia: University of South Carolina Press, 2015.

"Did You Ever Hear This?" *Cosmopolitan*, September 1909, 550.

Dixon, Thomas, Jr. "Booker T. Washington and the Negro." *Saturday Evening Post*, August 19, 1905, 1–2.

Dollimore, Jonathan. "Introduction: Shakespeare, Cultural Materialism, and the New Historicism," In *Political Shakespeare: Essays in Cultural Materialism*, 2nd ed., ed. Jonathan Dollimore and Alan Sinfield, 2–17. Manchester: Manchester University Press, 1994.

Donaldson, Susan V. "Dismantling the *Saturday Evening Post* Reader: *The Unvanquished* and Changing 'Horizons of Expectations.'" In *Faulkner and Popular Culture*, ed. Doreen Fowler and Ann J. Abadie, 179–95. Jackson: University Press of Mississippi, 1990.

"Drawing-Room Chat." *Chattanooga Daily Times*, March 16, 1904.

Drew, Bernard A. *Black Stereotypes in Popular Series Fiction, 1851–1955: Jim Crow Authors and Their Characters.* Jefferson, NC: McFarland, 2015.

Du Bois, W. E. B. "The Black Man Brings His Gifts." *Survey Graphic* 53, no. 11 (March 1, 1925): 655–57, 710.

———. *The Correspondence of W. E. B. Du Bois.* Vol. 1: *Selections, 1877–1934.* Ed. Herbert Aptheker. Amherst: University of Massachusetts Press, 1973.

———. "Criteria of Negro Art" (1926). In *The New Negro: Readings on Race, Representation, and African American Culture, 1892–1938*, ed. Henry Louis Gates Jr. and Jean Andrew Jarrett, 257–60. Princeton, NJ: Princeton University Press, 2007.

———. *Dark Princess: A Romance* (1928). Ed. Henry Louis Gates Jr. New York: Oxford University Press, 2007.

———. *Darkwater: Voices from Within the Veil.* 1920. Reprint. Garden City, NY: Dover, 1999.

———. Introduction to *The Crisis* Symposium, "The Negro in Art: How Shall He Be Portrayed" (1926). In *The New Negro: Readings on Race, Representation, and African American Culture, 1892–1938*, ed. Henry Louis Gates Jr. and Jean Andrew Jarrett, 190. Princeton, NJ: Princeton University Press, 2007.

———. "The Negro Mind Reaches Out" (1925). In *The New Negro: Voices of the Harlem Renaissance* (1925), ed. Alain Locke, with a new introduction by Arnold Rampersad, 385–414. New York: Atheneum, 1992.

———. "Of the Faith of the Fathers." *Atlantic Monthly*, August 1897. Reprinted in *The Souls of Black Folk: Essays and Sketches*, 189–206. Chicago: A. C. McClurg, 1903.

——. "Returning Soldiers." *The Crisis* 18, no. 1 (May 1919): 13–14.

——. *The Souls of Black Folk: Essays and Sketches.* Chicago: A. C. McClurg, 1903.

——. "Strivings of the Negro People." *Atlantic Monthly*, August 1897, 194–98.

Dunbar, Paul Laurence. *The Complete Stories of Paul Laurence Dunbar.* Ed. Gene Andrew Jarrett and Thomas Lewis Morgan. Athens: Ohio University Press, 1998.

——. *In Old Plantation Days.* New York: Dodd, Mead, 1903.

——. "The Leader of His Race." *Saturday Evening Post*, November 9, 1901, 15.

——. "Mr. Groby's Slippery Gift." *Saturday Evening Post*, June 24, 1899, 830.

——. "Negro Society in Washington." *Saturday Evening Post*, December 14, 1901, 9–10.

——. "Two Little Boots." *Saturday Evening Post*, April 12, 1902, 3.

——. "When Sam'l Sings." *Saturday Evening Post*, August 10, 1899, 123.

Editorial. *Collier's Weekly*, November 9, 1901, 1.

Earle, David. *All Man! Hemingway, 1950s Men's Magazines, and the Masculine Persona.* Kent, OH: Kent State University Press, 2009.

Ellis, William E. *Irvin S. Cobb: The Rise and Fall of an American Humorist.* Lexington: University Press of Kentucky, 2017.

Ellis, William T. "The Overflowing Melting Pot: Why the Americanization of America Must Begin." Editorial. *Saturday Evening Post*, March 2, 1918, 21–22, 37.

Ellison, Ralph. *Shadow and Act.* New York: Vintage, 1964.

Faulkner, William. "A Bear Hunt." *Saturday Evening Post*, February 10, 1934, 8–9, 74–76.

——. *Faulkner in the University.* Ed. Frederick L. Gwynne and Joseph Blotner. Charlottesville: University Press of Virginia, 1995.

——. "A Mountain Victory." *Saturday Evening Post*, December 3, 1932, 6–7, 39–46.

——. "Red Leaves." *Saturday Evening Post*, October 25, 1930, 6–7, 54–64.

——. *Selected Letters of William Faulkner.* Ed. Joseph Blotner. New York: Random House, 1977.

"Fiction Characters, Irvin Cobb's Week-End Guests." *San Antonio Express*, February 24, 1924.

Fisher, Rudolph. "The City of Refuge" (1925). In *The New Negro: Voices of the Harlem Renaissance* (1925), ed. Alain Locke, with a new introduction by Arnold Rampersad, 57–74. New York: Atheneum, 1992.

Fitzgerald, F. Scott. "The Camel's Back." *Saturday Evening Post*, April 24, 1920, 16–17, 157–65.

——. *The Great Gatsby.* 1925. Reprint. New York: Scribner's, 2003.

——. "The Ice Palace." In *Flappers and Philosophers*, 49–86. New York: Scribner's, 1920.

——. "The Ice Palace." *Saturday Evening Post*, May 22, 1920, 18–19, 163–70.

——. *A Life in Letters.* Ed. Matthew J. Bruccoli. New York: Simon & Schuster, 1994.

——. "Myra Meets His Family." *Saturday Evening Post*, March 20, 1920, 40–53.

——. "The Offshore Pirate." *Saturday Evening Post*, May 29, 1920, 10–11, 99–109.

"The Flood of Immigration." Editorial. *Saturday Evening Post*, February 6, 1904, 12.

Freeman, Joseph. *An American Testament: A Narrative of Rebels and Romantics.* New York: Farrar & Rinehart, 1936.

Gallico, Paul. "This Way I Beat Joe Louis." *Saturday Evening Post*, August 29, 1936, 5–7, 40–41; September 5, 1936, 10–11, 32–34.

Gates, Henry Louis, Jr. *The Signifying Monkey: A Theory of African-American Literary Criticism*. New York: Oxford University Press, 1988.

——. *Stony the Road: Reconstruction, White Supremacy, and the Rise of Jim Crow*. New York: Penguin, 2019.

Gates, Henry Louis, Jr., and Gene Andrew Jarrett. Introduction to *The New Negro: Readings on Race, Representation, and African American Culture, 1892–1938*, ed. Henry Louis Gates Jr. and Gene Andrew Jarrett, 1–20. Princeton, NJ: Princeton University Press, 2007.

——, eds. *The New Negro: Readings on Race, Representation, and African American Culture, 1892–1938*. Princeton, NJ: Princeton University Press, 2007.

"George H. Lorimer, Noted Editor, Dies." *New York Times*, October 23, 1937.

Gerstein, Josh, and Alexander Ward. "Supreme Court Has Voted to Overturn Abortion Rights, Draft Opinion Shows." *Politico*, May 2, 2022. https://www.politico.com /news/2022/05/02/supreme-court-abortion-draft-opinion-00029473.

Gillespie, Michele K., and Randall L. Hall. Introduction to *Thomas Dixon Jr. and the Birth of Modern America*, ed. Michele K. Gillespie and Randall L. Hall, 1–22. Baton Rouge: Louisiana State University Press, 2006.

Gillilan, Strickland. "Washington Wash." *Los Angeles Times*, October 5, 1931.

Givens, "Colonel" Charles Garland. "Jig Time." *Saturday Evening Post*, May 25, 1929, 26–27, 193–94.

——. "Mammy Ada." *Saturday Evening Post*, December 7, 1929, 32–33, 91–94.

"Golf Is the Curse of American Literature, Hugh Wiley Asserts; Has Given It Up, Except the African Brand." *Minneapolis Star Tribune*, December 18, 1921.

Goodman, Blanche. "A Bachelor's Den." *Chattanooga Daily Times*, May 15, 1904.

——. "A Change of Heart." *Saturday Evening Post*, August 28, 1909, 50.

——. "Checkmating Miss Fanny." *Saturday Evening Post*, October 11, 1913, 8, 61–62.

——. "Educating Sally Ann." *Saturday Evening Post*, April 9, 1910, 37–39.

——. "The Equalizing Bug." *Saturday Evening Post*, April 8, 1911, 36–37.

——. "Helping Rosabel." *Saturday Evening Post*, December 5, 1908, 56.

——. "Johnny on the Weather." *Chattanooga Daily Times*, June 5, 1904.

——. "Out on Bail." *Saturday Evening Post*, March 4, 1911, 30–31.

——. "A Toast." *Clarksville (Tennessee) Daily Leaf-Chronicle*, February 15, 1905.

——. "White Folks' Rights." *Saturday Evening Post*, December 2, 1911, 16.

Gordon, Sloane. "The Story of Irvin S. Cobb." *Pearson's Magazine*, March 1915, 278–84.

Green, Barbara. "Feminist Things." In *Transatlantic Print Culture, 1880–1940: Emerging Media, Emerging Modernisms*, ed. Ann Ardis and Patrick Collier, 66–79. New York: Palgrave MacMillan, 2008.

Hale, Grace Elizabeth. *Making Whiteness: The Culture of Segregation in the South, 1890–1940*. New York: Vintage, 1998.

Hall, Wade. "Roark (Whitney Wickliffe) Bradford." In *American Short-Story Writers, 1910–1945: First Series*, ed. Bobby Ellen Kimbel. Dictionary of Literary Biography, vol. 86. Detroit, MI: Gale, 1989. Gale Literature Resource Center, https://link.gale .com/apps/doc/H1200000052/GLS?u=cuny_johnjay&sid=bookmark-GLS&xid =5bdcdcdd.

Hannagan, Steve. "Black Gold." *Saturday Evening Post*, June 20, 1936, 14, 74–78.

"Harlem Viewed from Without." *New York Age*, August 15, 1925, 4.

Harper, Lucius C. "George Horace Lorimer (an Enemy)." *Chicago Defender*, November 20, 1937.
Harris, Cora Annette. "Review of the Latest Books." *Charlotte Observer*, January 21, 1923.
Harris, Joel Chandler. "The Negro as the South Sees Him." *Saturday Evening Post*, January 2, 1904, 1–2, 23.
——. "The Negro of To-Day: His Prospects and Discouragements." *Saturday Evening Post*, January 30, 1904, 2–5.
——. "The Negro Problem: Can the South Solve It—and How?" *Saturday Evening Post*, February 27, 1904, 6–7.
Hart, Albert Bushnell. "The African Riddle: Another Side of Mr. Dixon's Negro Question." *Saturday Evening Post*, October 28, 1905, 13–16.
Hartman, Saidiya V. *Scenes of Subjection: Terror, Slavery, and Self-Making in Nineteenth-Century America*. New York: Oxford University Press, 1997.
Hefner, Brooks E. *The Word on the Street: The American Language of American Modernism*. Charlottesville: University of Virginia Press, 2017.
Herskovits, Melville J. Letter to the editor. *Folklore* 48, no. 2 (June 1937): 220–21.
"High Tribute to Negro Soldiers." *Nashville Globe*, December 13, 1918.
Holtzclaw, William H. "The Black Man's Burden: A Battle with Ignorance and Poverty, and How One Negro Won It." *Saturday Evening Post*, April 22, 1905, 4–5.
"The Housekeepers' Directory." *Good Housekeeping* 49, no. 6 (December 1909): n.p.
"Hugh Wiley to Give Wildcat, Lily, Lady Luck Trip to Salinas." *The Californian* (Salinas), April 30, 1923, 4.
Hughes, Langston. *I Wonder as I Wander*. 2nd ed. New York: Hill and Wang, 1993.
——. "The Negro Artist and the Racial Mountain." *The Nation*, June 23, 1926, 692–94.
Hurston, Zora Neale. *Zora: A Life in Letters*. Ed. Carla Kaplan. New York: Anchor, 2002.
Hutchinson, George. *The Harlem Renaissance in Black and White*. Cambridge, MA: Harvard University Press, 1995.
Jackson, Robert. *Fade in Crossroads: A History of the Southern Cinema*. New York: Oxford University Press, 2017.
Jarrett, Gene Andrew, and Thomas Lewis Morgan. Introduction to Paul Laurence Dunbar, *The Complete Stories of Paul Laurence Dunbar*, ed. Gene Andrew Jarrett and Thomas Lewis Morgan, xv–xliii. Athens: Ohio University Press, 1998.
Johnson, Charles S. "Black Workers and the City." *Survey Graphic* 53, no. 11 (March 1, 1925): 641–43, 718–21.
Johnson, James Weldon. "Irvin Cobb on the Negro Soldiers." *New York Age*, August 31, 1918, 4.
——. "The Making of Harlem." *Survey Graphic* 53, no. 11 (March 1, 1925): 635–39.
——. Preface to *The Book of American Negro Poetry*, ed. James Weldon Johnson, vi–xlviii. New York: Harcourt, Brace, 1922.
——. "Preface to the Revised Edition." In *The Book of American Negro Poetry*, rev. ed., ed. James Weldon Johnson, 3–8. New York: Harcourt, Brace, 1931.
Jones, Gavin. *Strange Talk: The Politics of Dialect Literature in Gilded Age America*. Berkeley: University of California Press, 1999.
Jones, Jeanette Eileen. "'Brightest Africa' in the New Negro Imagination." In *Escape from New York: The New Negro Renaissance Beyond Harlem*, ed. Davarian L.

Baldwin and Minkah Makalani, 31–51. Minneapolis: University of Minnesota Press, 2013.

Kimball, Robert, and William Bolcomb. *Reminiscing with Sissle and Blake*. New York: Viking, 1973.

Kitchen, Karl K. "Up and Down Broadway." *Owensboro (Kentucky) Messenger*, March 16, 1925.

Kutzinski, Vera. *The Worlds of Langston Hughes: Modernism and Translation in the Americas*. Ithaca, NY: Cornell University Press, 2012.

Landess, Thomas. "Julia Mood Peterkin." In *American Novelists, 1910–1945*, ed. James J. Martine. Dictionary of Literary Biography, vol. 9. Detroit, MI: Gale, 1981. Gale Literature Resource Center, https://link.gale.com/apps/doc/H1200000432/GLS?u=cuny_johnjay&sid=bookmark-GLS&xid=d2bb6e60.

Latham, Sean, and Robert Scholes. "The Rise of Periodical Studies." *PMLA* 121, no. 2 (2006): 517–31.

Lawrence, David. "America for Americans: Deleting the Hyphen—the Doctrine of 1918." *Saturday Evening Post*, June 15, 1918, 23, 42–50.

"Leaves Public Schools for Literary Work." *Chattanooga Star*, July 10, 1907.

Lee, Steven S. *The Ethnic Avant-Garde: Minority Cultures and World Revolution*. New York: Columbia University Press, 2015.

Lelekis, Debbie. *American Literature, Lynching, and the Spectator in the Crow: Spectacular Violence*. Lanham, MD: Lexington Books, 2015.

Lemons, Stanley J. "Black Stereotypes as Reflected in Popular Culture, 1880–1920." *American Quarterly* 29, no. 1 (1997): 102–16.

Lewis, David Levering. *When Harlem Was in Vogue*. New York: Oxford University Press, 1989.

Lieb, Sandra. "Irvin S. Cobb." In *American Humorists, 1800–1950*, ed. Stanley Trachtenberg. Dictionary of Literary Biography, vol. 11. Detroit, MI: Gale, 1982. Gale Literature Resource Center, https://link-gale-com.ez.lib.jjay.cuny.edu/apps/doc/H1200000940/GLS?u=cuny_johnjay&sid=bookmark-GLS&xid=0596240c.

Lindberg, Kathryne V. "Mass Circulation Versus the Masses: Covering the Modern Magazine Scene." *Boundary* 2 20, no. 2 (1993): 51–83.

"Literary Club Members Receive New Year Books." *Wausau (Wisconsin) Daily Record-Herald*, August 8, 1929.

Locke, Alain. "Enter the New Negro." *Survey Graphic* 53, no. 11 (March 1, 1925): 631–34.

——. "The New Negro" (1925). In *The New Negro: Voices of the Harlem Renaissance* (1925), ed. Alain Locke, with a new introduction by Arnold Rampersad, 3–16. New York: Atheneum, 1992.

——, ed. *The New Negro: An Interpretation*. New York: Albert and Charles Boni, 1925.

Logan, Rayford. "Why We Should Study Negro History." *New Journal and Guide*, December 12, 1925, 16.

"The Looking-Glass." *The Crisis* 16, no. 6 (October 1918): 277.

"Lorimer Gave Art and Park to Public." *New York Times*, October 28, 1937.

Lott, Eric. *Love and Theft: Blackface Minstrelsy and the American Working Class*. New York: Oxford University Press, 1993.

Luis-Brown, David. *Waves of Decolonization: Discourses of Race and Hemispheric Citizenship in Cuba, Mexico, and the United States*. Durham, NC: Duke University Press, 2008.

Lusane, Clarence. *The Black History of the White House*. San Francisco: City Lights, 2011.

Lynd, Robert S., and Helen Merrell Lynd. *Middletown: A Study in Contemporary American Culture*. New York: Harcourt, Brace, 1929.

Madison, Martha. "Smiles and Minor Chords Are Found in *Black Cameos*." *Brooklyn Daily Eagle*, January 24, 1925.

Malone, Cheryl Knott. "Toward a Multicultural American Public Library History." *Libraries and Culture* 35, no. 1 (2000): 77–87.

"The Man—Not the Money." Editorial. *Saturday Evening Post*, January 24, 1903, 12.

Martin, Jay, and Gossie H. Hudson. "General Introduction." In Paul Laurence Dunbar, *The Paul Laurence Dunbar Reader*, ed. Jay Martin and Gossie H. Hudson, 15–24. New York: Dodd, Mead, 1975.

Matheus, John. "Some Aspects of the Negro Interpreted in Contemporary American and European Literature." In *Negro: An Anthology* (1934), ed. Nancy Cunard, ed. and abridged by Hugh Ford, 83–88. New York: Continuum, 2002.

McKay, Claude. *Banjo: A Story Without a Plot*. 1929. Reprint. New York: Harcourt Brace, 1957.

——. "The Dominant White." *Liberator*, April 1919, 14.

McKible, Adam. "Editing Edward Christopher Williams: From 'The Letters of Davy Carr' to *When Washington Was in Vogue*." In *Editing the Harlem Renaissance*, ed. Joshua Murray and Ross Tangedal, 207–22. Clemson, SC: Clemson University Press, 2021.

——. Introduction to Edward Christopher Williams, *When Washington Was in Vogue*, xiii–xxxiv. New York: Amistad, 2004.

——. *The Space and Place of Modernism: The Russian Revolution, Little Magazines, and New York*. New York: Routledge, 2002.

McNamara, Sylvie. "Clarence Thomas's Billionaire Benefactor Collects Hitler Artifacts." *Washingtonian*, April 7, 2023. https://www.washingtonian.com/2023/04/07/clarence-thomass-billionaire-benefactor-collects-hitler-artifacts/.

Mencken, H. L. Response in *The Crisis* Symposium, "The Negro in Art: How Shall He Be Portrayed" (1926). In *The New Negro: Readings on Race, Representation, and African American Culture, 1892–1938*, ed. Henry Louis Gates Jr. and Jean Andrew Jarrett, 191. Princeton, NJ: Princeton University Press, 2007.

"Men, Women, and Books." *Frank Leslie's Popular Monthly*, January 1902, 381.

Meriwether, James B. "Faulkner's Correspondence with the *Saturday Evening Post*." *Mississippi Quarterly* 30, no. 3 (Summer 1977): 461–75.

Miller, Kelly. *As to the Leopard's Spots: Open Letter to Thomas Dixon, Jr.* Washington, DC: Hayworth, 1905.

"Millions of Friends for Florian Slappey." Advertisement. *Saturday Evening Post*, March 24, 1934, 90.

"Miss Blanche Goodman." *Nashville Banner*, July 6, 1907.

"Miss Blanche Goodman Will Wed Mr. Oscar Eisendrath This Evening." *Chattanooga News*, January 4, 1910.

Moore, Christina. "Traditional Rebirth: The Epistolary Genre in *When Washington Was in Vogue*." *African American Review* 46, no. 2 (2013): 413–24.

Morrison, Toni. *Playing in the Dark: Whiteness and the Literary Imagination*. Cambridge, MA: Harvard University Press, 1992.

Mott, Frank Luther. *A History of American Magazines*. Vol. 4: *1885–1905*. Cambridge, MA: Harvard University Press, 1957.

"Mr. Roosevelt and the Bad Men." Editorial. *Saturday Evening Post*, December 14, 1901, 12.

"Mrs. Eisendrath, Liberal Thinker and Writer, Example of Feminine Leadership." *Chattanooga News*, January 9, 1936.

Nadell, Martha Jane. *Enter the New Negroes: Images of Race in American Culture*. Cambridge, MA: Harvard University Press, 2004.

"The Negro as an Artist." *Literary Digest*, September 19, 1925, 29–30.

"NEGRO LYNCHED FOR INSULTS—Riddled Body Is Answer to Remarks to White Woman." *Knoxville Journal*, December 17, 1925.

Newcomb, John Timberman. *Would Poetry Disappear? American Verse and the Crisis of Modernity*. Athens: Ohio State University Press, 2004.

"New Servant in the House." Advertisement. *Saturday Evening Post*, November 6, 1909, 62.

"Niggers in the White House." *Windsor (Missouri) Review*, October 31, 1901.

Nishikawa, Kinohi. *Street Players: Black Pulp Fiction and the Making of a Literary Underground*. Chicago: University of Chicago Press, 2018.

Nolan, Jennifer. "Langston Hughes: Refugee in the *Post*'s America." *American Periodicals: A Journal of History & Criticism* 29, no. 2 (2019): 163–77.

Norrell, Robert J. *Up from History: The Life of Booker T. Washington*. Cambridge, MA: Harvard University Press, 2009.

North, Michael. *The Dialect of Modernism: Race, Language, and Twentieth-Century Literature*. New York: Oxford University Press, 1994.

Nowlin, Michael. "F. Scott Fitzgerald's Elite Syncopations: The Racial Make-up of the Entertainer in the Early Fiction." *ESC: English Studies in Canada* 26, no. 4 (December 2000): 409–43.

Nugent, Richard Bruce. *Gentleman Jigger: A Novel of the Harlem Renaissance*. Edited and with an introduction by Thomas H. Wirth. Boston: Da Capo, 2008.

"Octavus Roy Cohen (1891–1959)." IMDb, n.d. https://www.imdb.com/name/nm0169665/.

"Octavus Roy Cohen Watches Football Game." *Chicago Defender*, November 25, 1922.

"Octavus Roy Cohen Writes Hard, Plays Hard, in Southland." *Washington Herald*, February 16, 1919.

Ohmann, Richard. "History and Literary History: The Case of Mass Culture." *Poetics Today* 9, no. 2 (1988): 357–75.

"Old-Time Minstrel Men, by an Old-Timer." *Saturday Evening Post*, September 29, 1900, 22–23.

"'Ole Reliable' and 'Hambone.'" *Commercial Appeal* (Memphis), January 21, 1923.

Ovington, Mary White. "The Wild Cat." *Baltimore Afro-American*, June 2, 1922.

Pace & Handy Music Company. Advertisement. *The Crisis* 12, no. 2 (December 1918): 98.

"Parsons's Theater." *Hartford Daily Courant*, January 30, 1917.

"'Passing' of Negroes." *Newport News (Virginia) Daily Press*, August 8, 1925.

"Paul Dunbar's Gifted Wife." *Saturday Evening Post*, May 5, 1900, 984.

Peake, Jak. "'Watching the Waters': Tropical Flows in the Harlem Renaissance, Black Internationalism, and Other Currents." *Radical Americas* 3, no. 1 (2018): 1–52.

Peterkin, Julia. "Heart Leaves." *Saturday Evening Post*, October 5, 1929, 5, 153–56.

——. Response in *The Crisis* Symposium, "The Negro in Art: How Shall He Be Portrayed" (1926). In *The New Negro: Readings on Race, Representation, and African American Culture, 1892–1938*, ed. Henry Louis Gates Jr. and Jean Andrew Jarrett, 201–2. Princeton, NJ: Princeton University Press, 2007.

Petry, Ann. *The Narrows* (1953). With an introduction by Keith Clark. Evanston, IL: Northwestern University Press, 2017.

——. *The Street.* 1946. Reprint. Boston: Houghton Mifflin, 1974.

"'Porgy' Star in Radio Mystery." *Baltimore Afro-American*, February 11, 1933.

"Racial Problems." Editorial. *Saturday Evening Post*, March 23, 1929, 28.

"Real Grand Daughters of Revolutionary Heroes Honored." *Tampa Tribune*, November 26, 1919.

"The Record of a Notable Year." Editorial. *Saturday Evening Post*, January 11, 1902, 10.

Retman, Sonnet H. "*Black No More*: George Schuyler and Racial Capitalism." *PMLA* 123, no. 5 (2008): 1448–64.

Revell, Peter. *Paul Laurence Dunbar*. Boston: Twayne, 1979.

"Roark Bradford Pictures Recent Outachita Journey in Magazine Article." *Commercial Appeal* (Memphis), January 7, 1929.

Roberts, Samuel K. "Kelly Miller and Thomas Dixon, Jr. on Blacks in American Civilization." *Phylon* 41, no. 2 (1980): 202–9.

Robeson, Elizabeth. "The Ambiguity of Julia Peterkin." *Journal of Southern History* 61, no. 4 (1995): 761–86.

Robinson, Cedric J. *Forgeries of Memory and Meaning: Blacks and the Regimes of Race in American Theater and Film Before World War II*. Chapel Hill: University of North Carolina Press, 2007.

Robinson, Lillian S., and Greg Robinson. "Paul Laurence Dunbar: A Credit to His Race?" *African American Review* 41, no. 2 (Summer 2007): 215–25.

Rockey, Howard. "Fiction Largely European and Very Good in the Average." *Philadelphia Inquirer*, November 30, 1929.

Rockwell, Norman. *My Adventures as an Illustrator*. New York: Harry N. Abrams, 1994.

Rollins, Peter C., and Harry W. Menig. "Regional Literature and Will Rogers: Film Redeems a Literary Form." *Literature/Film Quarterly* 3, no. 1 (1975): 70–82.

"Saturday Evening Post Publishes Article on Harlem." NAACP Press Service release. *Mobile Weekly Standard*, August 22, 1925.

Scholes, Robert. *Paradoxy of Modernism*. New Haven, CT: Yale University Press, 2006.

Scholes, Robert, and Clifford Wulfman. *Modernism in the Magazines: An Introduction*. New Haven, CT: Yale University Press, 2010.

Schomburg, Arthur A. "The Negro Digs Up His Past" (1925). In *The New Negro: Voices of the Harlem Renaissance* (1925), ed. Alain Locke, with a new introduction by Arnold Rampersad, 231–37. New York: Atheneum, 1992.

Scott-Childress, Reynolds J. "Paul Laurence Dunbar and the Project of Cultural Reconstruction." *African American Review* 41, no. 2 (Summer 2007): 367–75.

"Scum of the Melting Pot." Editorial. *Saturday Evening Post*, May 4, 1918, 22.

Scruggs, Charles. "'All Dressed Up but No Place to Go': The Black Writer and His Audience During the Harlem Renaissance." *American Literature* 48, no. 4 (1977): 543–63.

Sherrard-Johnson, Cherene. "Questionnaire Response." *Modernism/modernity* 20, no. 3 (2013): 454–57.

A Short History of the Saturday Evening Post. Philadelphia: Curtis, 1936.

"Short Story Writer Talks." *Lincoln Journal Star,* October 4, 1920.

Skei, Hans. *Reading Faulkner's Best Short Stories.* Columbia: University of South Carolina Press, 1999.

Smethurst, James. *The African American Roots of American Modernism: From Reconstruction to the Harlem Renaissance.* Chapel Hill: University of North Carolina Press, 2011.

Snyder, Larry. "My Boy Jesse." *Saturday Evening Post,* November 7, 1936, 14–15, 97–101.

Stolberg, Benjamin. "Merchant in Letters: Portrait of George Horace Lorimer." *Outlook and Independent,* May 21, 1930, 83–86, 115–17.

"The Story of My Life and Work." Advertisement. *Saturday Evening Post,* December 14, 1901, 15.

Stribling, T. S. "N. Ah. A." *Saturday Evening Post,* January 26, 1935, 10–12, 36–38.

Swift, Lindsay. "A Remarkable Autobiography." *Saturday Evening Post,* June 1, 1901, 17.

Tebbel, John. *George Horace Lorimer and the* Saturday Evening Post. New York: Doubleday, 1948.

Thaggert, Miriam. *Images of Black Modernism: Verbal and Visual Strategies of the Harlem Renaissance.* Amherst: University of Massachusetts Press, 2010.

Thayer, William Roscoe. "Despotism by the Dregs." *Saturday Evening Post,* May 4, 1918, 23–24, 126–29.

Thomas, Neval H. "The District of Columbia—a Paradox of Paradises." *Messenger,* October 1923, 837–41.

Thurman, Wallace. "Negro Artists and the Negro." In *The Collected Writings of Wallace Thurman: A Harlem Renaissance Reader,* ed. Amritjit Singh and Daniel M. Scott III, 195–99. New Brunswick, NJ: Rutgers University Press, 2003.

"Tribute of One Humorist to Another." *Winston-Salem Journal,* January 30, 1921.

Tuttle, Grace Norman. "Echoes of Miami." *Miami Herald,* May 4, 1931.

"Two Writers Use Same Character." *Charlotte News,* January 11, 1921.

"'Uncle Booker' and His People." *Saturday Evening Post,* February 24, 1900, 763.

Uzzel, Thomas H. "'The Saturday Evening Post' Formula: Suggestions for Cutting the Corners in Arriving Safely at the Literary Department Store of America." In *The Writers 1930 Year Book & Market Guide,* ed. Aron M. Mathieu, 21–23. Cincinnati: Writer's Digest, 1930.

Vogel, Shane. *The Scene of the Harlem Cabaret: Race, Sexuality, Performance.* Chicago: University of Chicago Press, 2009.

Volpe, Edmond L. "Faulkner's 'Red Leaves': The Decidation of Nature." *Studies in American Fiction* 3, no. 2 (Autumn 1975): 121–31.

Whalan, Mark. *The Great War and the Culture of the New Negro.* Jacksonville: University Press of Florida, 2008.

"What Comes Down Our Creek." Fidelity Trust Company advertisement. *Knoxville Journal,* December 17, 1925.

"Where the Race Is Gaining." *New York Age,* April 20, 1929, 4.

Whipple, Leon. "'SatEvePost' Mirror of These States." *The Survey,* March 1, 1928, 699–703, 714–20.

Whitman, James Q. *Hitler's American Model: The United States and the Making of Nazi Race Law*. Princeton, NJ: Princeton University Press, 2018.

"Why Chattanoogans Can Claim High Rank in Literary World; Numerous Books Written Here." *Chattanooga News*, October 30, 1911.

"Why Women Go to Seed." Editorial. *Saturday Evening Post*, December 10, 1904, 12.

"Wide-Awake [?] Meeting of Local Suffragists." *Chattanooga News*, December 21, 1918.

"Wildcat, Lily, and Lady Luck Invited to City of Salinas." *The Californian* (Salinas), April 17, 1923, 1.

Wiley, Hugh. "Boom-a-Loom Boom." *Saturday Evening Post*, July 19, 1919, 10–11, 117–25.

———. "C.O.D." *Saturday Evening Post*, January 8, 1921, 18–19, 146–49.

———. "The Four-Leaved Wildcat." *Saturday Evening Post*, March 8, 1919, 9–11, 45–49.

———. "Memphis Bound." *Saturday Evening Post*, March 13, 1920, 16–17, 170–78.

———. "Microphony." *Saturday Evening Post*, January 31, 1931, 16–17, 41–47.

———. "Mister Lady Luck." *Saturday Evening Post*, January 17, 1920, 14–15, 86–91.

———. "The Pluvitor." *Saturday Evening Post*, June 5, 1926, 24–25, 213–18.

———. "Pop." *Saturday Evening Post*, November 7, 1925, 26–27, 191–97.

———. "Prowling Prodigal." *Saturday Evening Post*, November 22, 1919, 10.

———. "Sick Per Cent." *Saturday Evening Post*, November 21, 1925, 20–21, 134–40.

———. *The Wildcat*. New York: George H. Doran, 1920.

Williams, Chad L. *Torchbearers of Democracy: African American Soldiers in the World War I Era*. Chapel Hill: University of North Carolina Press, 2010.

Williams, Edward Christopher. *When Washington Was in Vogue* (1925–1926). New York: Amistad, 2004.

Wirth, Thomas H. Introduction to Richard Bruce Nugent, *Gentleman Jigger: A Novel of the Harlem Renaissance*, ed. Thomas H. Wirth, x–xviii. Boston: Da Capo, 2008.

"Women Writers of Tennessee." *Chattanooga Daily Times*, May 11, 1908.

Wood, George. "*J. Poindexter, Colored*." Book review. *New York Herald*, July 30, 1922.

Wood, James Playstead. *The Curtis Magazines*. New York: Ronald Press, 1971.

———. *Magazines in the United States*. New York: Ronald Press, 1949.

Woodward, C. Vann. *The Strange Career of Jim Crow*. New York: Oxford University Press, 1957.

Woollcott, Alexander. "Second Thoughts on First Nights." *New York Times*, April 9, 1922.

W. W. M. "Don't Worry." *Oklahoma City Times*, April 14, 1920.

"Young Black Joe." *Louisville Courier-Journal*, August 28, 1918.

INDEX

Adams, Franklin P., 149
Adams, Jade Broughton, 97
Adams, Richmond, 114
African American/Black modernity, 6,
    8–11, 18, 126, 161–162, 189; global, 166;
    Locke's aspirational image of, 105;
    Lorimer's parameters for
    representing, 27, 183; represented by
    Harlem, 28, 108, 127, 185; *Saturday
    Evening Post* recontainment, 15, 19,
    22, 24, 34, 36, 66, 70, 73, 107–108, 124,
    136, 172–173, 183
Alexander, Michelle, 132
Alito, Samuel, 227
Anderson, Sherwood, 198
Armour, P. D., 34
Atlantic Monthly, 36, 42
Atwood, Albert, 249n12

Baker, Houston, 166
Baldwin, James, 31
Baltimore Afro-American, 60, 168
Banneker, Benjamin, 76
Barnes, Rhae Lynn, 74, 79, 91, 101–102
Barrymore, Ethel, 199
Barthes, Roland, 203

Benét, William Rose, 18
Benjamin, Walter, 228
Beveridge, Albert, 36
Biggers, Earl Der, 15
Black cosmopolitanism, 174, 187
Black dialect fiction, 5, 7, 10, 18–19, 28,
    44, 69–70, 81, 93, 95, 104, 117, 123–124,
    140, 155, 171, 184, 196, 219; African
    American–authored, 17, 24; anti-
    Black "humor," 34, 76, 99, 107, 161,
    176, 179; caricature, 96–97, 107, 183,
    193; encoding racist beliefs, 22;
    familiar tropes, 147; formulaic, 7, 77,
    176; poetry, 37, 47, 75, 184; public
    circulation/performance, 25, 74, 83,
    93–94, 99; reactionary, 7; recontained
    Black modernity, 15, 24, 84, 107, 172,
    183; romanticized master-slave
    relationship, 37, 148; stereotypical,
    142; white-authored, 4, 11, 13, 15, 17, 21,
    27, 36, 51, 66, 74–75, 84, 87, 131, 138,
    149, 152, 167–168, 191, 209, 218, 232n16
Black interiority, 28, 48, 130, 182, 206
Blount, Alfred, 81
Blythe, Samuel, 111–112, 151
Bogle, Donald, 172

Johnson, James Weldon, 23, 119, 140,
    158–159, 186, 189
Jones, Gavin, 22, 49
Jones, Jeanette Eileen, 9

Karloff, Boris, 145
Kendrick, Swan, 178–180
Kennedy, R. Emmet, 104–107, 138
King, Martin Luther, Jr., 51

Ladies' Home Journal, 6, 16–18, 21,
    35, 88
Landess, Thomas, 199
Larsen, Nella, 141
Latham, Sean, 19
Lemons, Stanley J., 73–74
Lewis, David Levering, 104
Leyendecker, J. C., 91–92, 224
Liberator, 142, 180
Lindberg, Kathryne V., 223
Literary Digest, 16–18
Locke, Alain, 6, 16, 18, 27–28, 91,
    104–107, 137–138, 152, 164, 166–167,
    173, 182, 185; plagiarized by Crowell,
    185–188, 209
Logan, Rayford, 166–167, 246n23
Lorimer, George Claude, 34
Lorimer, George Horace, 6–7, 9–11,
    20–24, 26, 28–30, 33, 37–42, 45–51,
    53–56, 59–60, 63–65, 69, 72, 75, 82,
    87–89, 91, 94–95, 99–100, 103, 108, 111,
    116–117, 119–120, 124, 126–127, 129,
    131–132, 136, 138, 142, 145, 148–149, 155,
    168, 174, 183–185, 187–191, 195,
    199–200, 202–203, 206–207, 209–211,
    213, 219–221, 224–228; abridging J.
    Poindexter, Colored, 127, 134–135;
    absolute control over Saturday
    Evening Post, 3–4, 21, 34–35, 205;
    anti-Black racism, 5, 13–14, 16, 19, 31,
    36, 44, 71, 73; an anti-Black racist
    even in death, 1–2, 31; anti-
    immigration, 13–14, 125, 167;
    anti-suffrage, 90, 92; appetite for
    Black dialect, 25; appetite for racist
    caricature, 16, 44, 109; devotion to
    Jim Crowing American history,

247n47; endorsement of Thomas
    Dixon, 61; erasing Black personhood,
    137; ethnic white nationalism, 13–14;
    publishing racist caricatures, 6, 10,
    12, 16–18, 27, 31, 44, 66, 70, 73–74,
    76–77, 83–84, 96–97, 107, 110, 143, 170,
    176–177, 182, 201; tonal shift, 73, 191,
    194; xenophobia, 15
Lott, Eric, 136, 243n19
Louis, Joe, 19, 29, 184, 190, 221, 223;
    "Black Gold," 222; silent commodity,
    222–223
Luis-Brown, David, 165
Lusane, Clarence, 41
Lynd, Helen Merrell and Robert S. Lynd, 2

Mackniel, Andre, 228
Malone, Cheryl Knott, 245n45
Marquand, John P., 15
Martin, Jay, 49
mass culture, 4, 21, 161
Massey, Katherine, 228
Matheus, John, 182, 184, 190
McConnell, Emlen, 50, 61, 64
McKay, Claude, 141, 178, 181
Mencken, H. L., 96, 169
Menig, Harry, 150
Meriwether, James, 202, 211
Messenger, 16, 106, 141–143, 154
Miller, Kelly, 63
minstrelsy, 18, 43, 70, 77, 80, 94, 96, 98,
    100, 118, 126, 137, 143, 147, 172–173, 177;
    active consumers of, 25, 77, 81–82, 94,
    99; amateur, 74, 77, 99–103; and racial
    appropriation, 136; and white
    supremacy, 80, 103
Moore, Christina, 156
Moore, Susan Teackle, 75
Morgan, Thomas Lewis, 45
Morrison, Margus D., 228
Morrison, Toni, 111
Mott, Frank Luther, 5
Mussolini, Benito, 174

Nadell, Martha Jane, 104
Nathan, George Jean, 96
New Deal, 4, 76, 148, 183

209, 216, 218–219; and idealized images of white womanhood, 91; and national identity, 3; as "Niagara of print," 3, 29; racist caricatures in, 5, 11, 25, 73, 83, 91, 96, 107, 139, 159, 176–177, 182, 201; racist ideology of, 30–31, 226; and romanticized antebellum slavery, 11, 36, 51 148, 206, 211, 232n23; and white terrorism, 7, 110–111, 114, 152, 220

Schmeling, Max, 222–224

Scholes, Robert, 8, 19

Schomburg, Arthur A., 166

SerVaas, Joan, 30

Sherrard-Johnson, Cherene, 232n15

Sims, Marian, 75

Singmaster, Elsie, 18, 75

Sissle, Noble, 120

Skei, Hans, 205

Smethurst, James, 161–162, 170

Snyder, Larry, 224

Spitzer, Marian, 18

Stabler, Harry Snowden, 69

Stanton, Frank L., 37

Stoddard, Lothrop, 13, 15, 125, 166–167, 188, 242n61, 246n23

Stolberg, Benjamin, 3–5, 226

Stout, Wesley Winans, 12, 225

Stowe, Harriet Beecher, 51, 169

Stribling, T. S., 19, 140, 169, 182, 201

Supreme Court, 32, 227–228

Survey Graphic, 2, 18, 28, 104–107, 138, 164, 167, 185, 187–188, 209

Swift, Lindsay, 39

Talley, Geraldine, 228

Tarabay, Sharif, 32

Tebbel, John, 5, 35, 145, 168

Thaggert, Miriam, 23

Thayer, William Roscoe, 14–15, 22

Thomas, Clarence, 32

Thomas, Neval H., 142

Thurman, Wallace, 169, 178

Tuskegee, 40, 56, 61–62

Twain, Mark, 109, 150

Uzzell, Thomas H., 95

Van Loan, Charles E., 90

Vardaman, James K., 68–69

Vassar College, 29–30

Vogel, Shane, 127

Volpe, Edmund L., 209

Washington, Booker T., 6, 24, 33–34, 37–42, 49–50, 52, 54–59, 61, 64, 66, 71, 73, 87, 191, 237n52; acceptability of, 37; accommodationism of, 39–40, 42, 51, 68, 111, 183; endorsement of segregation, 122; evolving status in *The Saturday Evening Post*, 38, 60, 87. 190; reputation, 37, 50; threat to white hegemony, 62; *Up from Slavery*, 39, 41; and uplift, 50–51, 60–61, 70, 190; Washington-Roosevelt dinner, 40–42, 44, 50

Whalan, Mark, 244n40, 244n42

Whipple, Leon, 3–5, 29, 36, 184

White, Walter, 12, 141, 178, 188, 198

Whiteman, Paul, 248n47

white supremacy, 11, 16, 19, 26–27, 30, 37, 39, 42, 50, 60, 103, 113, 115, 134, 161, 181, 184, 191; arrogance of, 174; critique of, 28, 64; denial of inherent violence, 108, 114–115, 177; global, 36, 161, 164, 166–167; intellectual life of, 74; and intimate performance, 95; normalization of, through "humor," 5, 80, 93, 112, 115, 177, 180, 216; patriarchal, 90; profitability of, 127, 132; resistance to, 22, 37, 39–40, 55, 158–159, 163–165, 170, 172, 178; terrorism undergirding, 7, 54, 114, 228

Whitfield, Ruth, 228

Whitman, James Q., 246n23

Wiley, Hugh, 5, 12, 15, 18, 26, 28, 66, 97–98, 107, 140–142, 146, 151–153, 156, 158, 161, 169, 184–185, 187, 200–201, 215–216; Black dialect stories, 15; burlesque, 189–190; dismissive of Black veterans, 148; Lily the goat, 97, 145, 149–150; praise from white America, 150, Wildcat stories, 15, 142–151, 154–155, 158–159, 175, 212; ubiquity during the Harlem Renaissance, 27